INTRODUCING THE OLD TESTAMENT

INTRODUCING THE ✤ OLD TESTAMENT

COMPLETELY REVISED AND UPDATED

JOHN DRANE

FORTRESS PRESS
MINNEAPOLIS

A Lion Book
an imprint of
Lion Hudson plc
Wilkinson House, Jordan Hill Road,
Oxford OX2 8DR, England
www.lionhudson.com
ISBN 978-0-7459-4290-2 (hb)
ISBN 978-0-7459-5016-7 (pb)

First edition 1987
Revised edition 2000
10 9 8 7

A catalogue record for this book is available
from the British Library

Typeset in 9.5/12 Poppl Pontifex
and 9.5/11 Humanist 777 Light Condensed

Printed and bound in China

Picture acknowledgments

AKG London: 318, 356

ASAP/Richard Nowitz: 116, 201

British Museum: 32, 59, 127, 154, 188, 258, 261, 262, 271, 274, 280, 296

Capitoline Museum, Rome/The Art Archive: 232

Dinu Mendrea: 112

Hanan Isachar: 208, 322–23

J. Catling Allen Picture Library: 83

Jon Arnold: 14, 52, 92, 124, 150, 198, 270, 316

Julie Baines: 33, 40, 57, 60, 64–65, 72–73, 74, 81, 109, 140, 142, 154–55, 166–67, 187, 209, 213, 219, 220, 231, 235, 239, 251, 268–69, 273, 280, 284, 290, 295, 299, 308, 312, 324, 330, 333, 334, 340–41

Lion Hudson: 19, 43, 128, 152, 174, 346/Alan Millard 82/Cairo Museum 63/David Alexander 15, 24, 129, 133, 153, 264, 359/David Townsend 240/Frank Dabba Smith 287

Mary Evans Picture Library: 342, 343

Reproduced by courtesy of the Trustees of the National Gallery, London: 20

PhotoRMN/H. Lewandowski: 279

Preußischer Kulturbesitz/Agyptisches Museum: 205

Sonia Halliday Photographs: 34, 48, 50, 138, 181, 254, 337/James Wellard 195, 218/Jane Taylor 223, 348

Stockmarket: 302, 331

Werner Braun: 329

Zev Radovan: 98, 164, 165, 313, 350, 357

COVER: *Abraham and Isaac* by Johann Heinrich Ferdinand Olivier (1817) (NG6541). Reproduced by courtesy of the Trustees of the National Gallery, London

All maps and charts: Joshua Smith

Contents

Special Articles

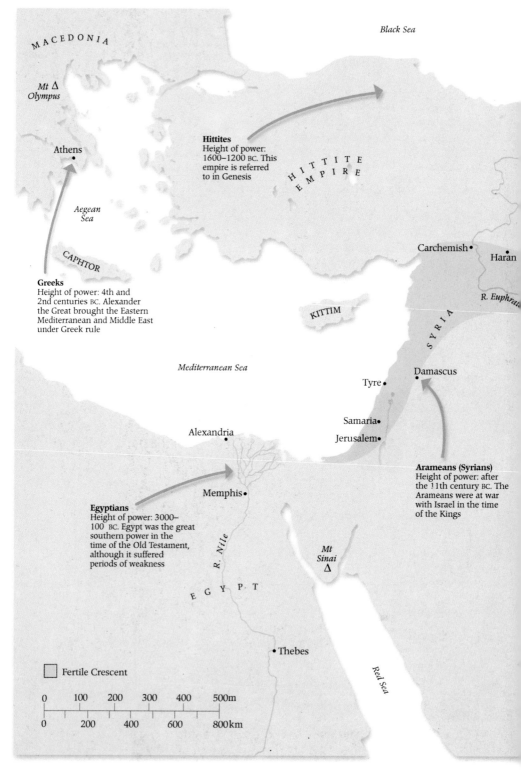

Black Sea

MACEDONIA

Mt Δ
Olympus

Athens •

*Aegean
Sea*

Hittites
Height of power:
1600–1200 BC. This
empire is referred
to in Genesis

HITTITE
EMPIRE

Carchemish •

Haran •

R. Euphrat

SYRIA

CAPHTOR

KITTIM

Greeks
Height of power: 4th and
2nd centuries BC. Alexander
the Great brought the Eastern
Mediterranean and Middle East
under Greek rule

Mediterranean Sea

Tyre •

Damascus •

Samaria •
Jerusalem •

Alexandria
•

Arameans (Syrians)
Height of power: after
the 11th century BC. The
Arameans were at war
with Israel in the time
of the Kings

Memphis •

Egyptians
Height of power: 3000–
100 BC. Egypt was the great
southern power in the
time of the Old Testament,
although it suffered
periods of weakness

R. Nile

*Mt
Sinai*
Δ

E G Y P T

• Thebes

Red Sea

☐ Fertile Crescent

0	100	200	300	400	500m
0	200	400	600	800km	

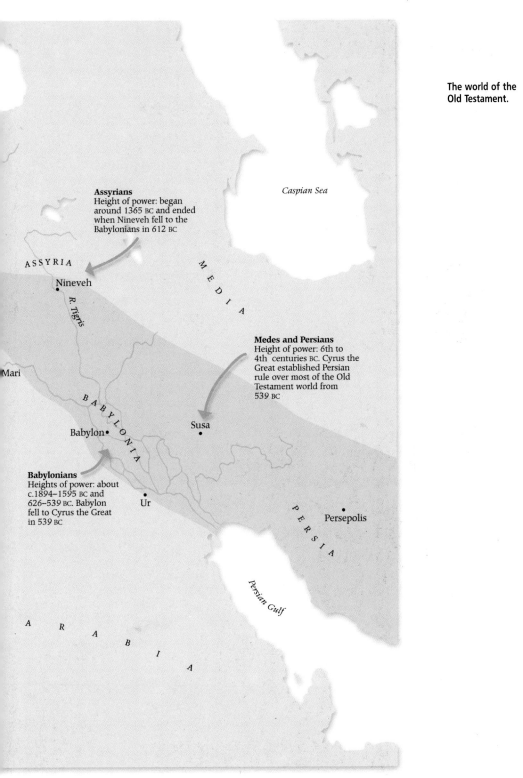

The world of the Old Testament.

Assyrians
Height of power: began around 1365 BC and ended when Nineveh fell to the Babylonians in 612 BC

Caspian Sea

ASSYRIA

Nineveh

R. Tigris

M E D I A

Mari

B A B Y L O N I A

Medes and Persians
Height of power: 6th to 4th centuries BC. Cyrus the Great established Persian rule over most of the Old Testament world from 539 BC

Susa

Babylon

Babylonians
Heights of power: about c.1894–1595 BC and 626–539 BC. Babylon fell to Cyrus the Great in 539 BC

Ur

P E R S I A

Persepolis

A R A B I A

Persian Gulf

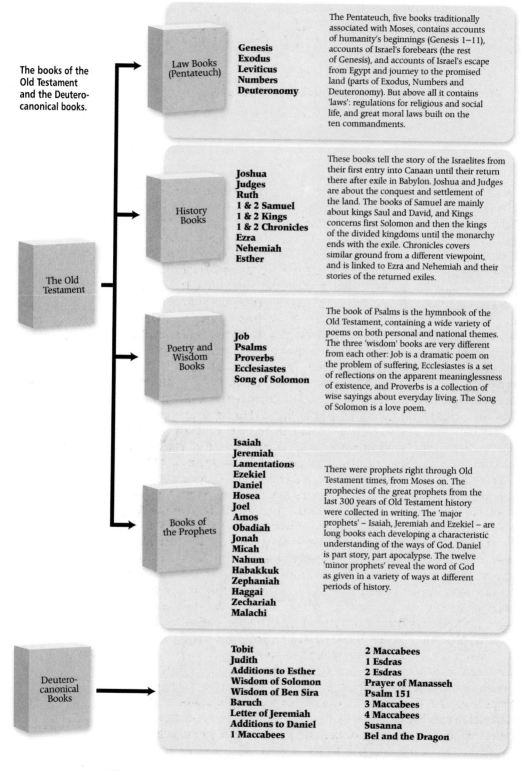

The books of the Old Testament and the Deutero-canonical books.

The Old Testament

Law Books (Pentateuch)

Genesis
Exodus
Leviticus
Numbers
Deuteronomy

The Pentateuch, five books traditionally associated with Moses, contains accounts of humanity's beginnings (Genesis 1–11), accounts of Israel's forebears (the rest of Genesis), and accounts of Israel's escape from Egypt and journey to the promised land (parts of Exodus, Numbers and Deuteronomy). But above all it contains 'laws': regulations for religious and social life, and great moral laws built on the ten commandments.

History Books

Joshua
Judges
Ruth
1 & 2 Samuel
1 & 2 Kings
1 & 2 Chronicles
Ezra
Nehemiah
Esther

These books tell the story of the Israelites from their first entry into Canaan until their return there after exile in Babylon. Joshua and Judges are about the conquest and settlement of the land. The books of Samuel are mainly about kings Saul and David, and Kings concerns first Solomon and then the kings of the divided kingdoms until the monarchy ends with the exile. Chronicles covers similar ground from a different viewpoint, and is linked to Ezra and Nehemiah and their stories of the returned exiles.

Poetry and Wisdom Books

Job
Psalms
Proverbs
Ecclesiastes
Song of Solomon

The book of Psalms is the hymnbook of the Old Testament, containing a wide variety of poems on both personal and national themes. The three 'wisdom' books are very different from each other: Job is a dramatic poem on the problem of suffering, Ecclesiastes is a set of reflections on the apparent meaninglessness of existence, and Proverbs is a collection of wise sayings about everyday living. The Song of Solomon is a love poem.

Books of the Prophets

Isaiah
Jeremiah
Lamentations
Ezekiel
Daniel
Hosea
Joel
Amos
Obadiah
Jonah
Micah
Nahum
Habakkuk
Zephaniah
Haggai
Zechariah
Malachi

There were prophets right through Old Testament times, from Moses on. The prophecies of the great prophets from the last 300 years of Old Testament history were collected in writing. The 'major prophets' – Isaiah, Jeremiah and Ezekiel – are long books each developing a characteristic understanding of the ways of God. Daniel is part story, part apocalypse. The twelve 'minor prophets' reveal the word of God as given in a variety of ways at different periods of history.

Deutero-canonical Books

Tobit
Judith
Additions to Esther
Wisdom of Solomon
Wisdom of Ben Sira
Baruch
Letter of Jeremiah
Additions to Daniel
1 Maccabees

2 Maccabees
1 Esdras
2 Esdras
Prayer of Manasseh
Psalm 151
3 Maccabees
4 Maccabees
Susanna
Bel and the Dragon

1 Introducing the Old Testament

Of all the literature that has been handed down from the world's ancient civilizations, none is as compelling – or as provocative – as the Hebrew Bible. It is one of the great classics, highly esteemed as sacred scripture by three of the world's major faiths – Islam, Judaism and Christianity. That alone has ensured not only its survival, but also its widespread dissemination and continuing appeal to people far removed from either the cultural or the religious context in which it originated. Though its stories happened long ago and in unfamiliar places, they have an ongoing fascination for today's readers. Furthermore, in a postmodern society with a growing scepticism about what is modern and scientific, many of today's spiritual searchers are powerfully attracted by the possibility of discovering new directions for the future through uncovering spiritual truths that have been locked away for centuries in ancient and esoteric texts, which reflect other worlds and different ways of being. Whatever else may be said, the Hebrew Bible – or Old Testament – has plenty of mystery about it. Its pages contain the rich literary treasures of a whole nation – the ancient people of Israel – and its story embraces the formative period of world civilization as we know it today, beginning in the Stone Age and ending in the world of the Roman empire. That makes even the most recent parts more than 2,000 years old, while the origins of its earliest works are likely to remain for ever hidden in the mists of antiquity. Moreover, it is not a dull book, and its unique combination of epic stories, history, reflective philosophy, poetry and political commentary is woven together with all the elements of adventure, excitement and suspense that we might expect to find in a Hollywood thriller. Indeed, its traditional stories have themselves become the raw material for many movies on the grand scale, while at the same time they continue to provide personal inspiration for the millions of people all over the world who still read it regularly.

Even a quick glance through its pages soon shows that the Old Testament is, of course, not just one single book. In reality, it is a whole library of books, and it is the sheer diversity of its contents that partly helps to explain its perennial appeal. From the great epic stories of national heroes like Moses, Deborah, David or Esther, to the more reflective books such as Job or Ecclesiastes, there is something here for everyone's taste and for many different moods and emotions. Enchanting – and sometimes disturbing – stories of personal intrigue and passion stand side by side with philosophical enquiries into the meaning of human life. Trying to make sense of these apparently disparate books is, however, not a straightforward matter, and in the course of the last 200 years many theories have been put forward as scholars have sought to understand and explain their origins and relevance to the world in which their many authors lived and worked. Most hypotheses have not survived for long, and the last twenty years of the twentieth century saw the collapse of many opinions that previous generations would have regarded as the assured results of scholarship. But one conviction has survived: if we are to understand the books of the Hebrew Bible most fully, we must delve into the reality of the world in which they were written. Intepreting this literature is a complex and multi-layered enterprise, but a key element in this has always been the quest to uncover what these books meant when they were originally written. How did they relate to the needs and aspirations of their authors and their original readers? And what can an understanding of other cultures of the time tell us about the ancient nation of Israel? In order to address such questions, many different specialist disciplines need to be employed, including archaeology, sociological analysis, literary theory and historical investigation as well as more obviously religious and spiritual methodologies.

For much of the nineteenth and twentieth centuries, scholarship often emphasized the diversity of the materials contained within this collection, but for the community within which they originated the one thing that held them all together was the simple fact that they are part of a common story. Moreover, the heart of that common story focused on a set of spiritual perceptions, and without taking account of that it is virtually impossible to understand what the Old Testament writers were trying to articulate. Notwithstanding their diverse concerns and interests – and the centuries that separated them – they were all convinced that their books, and the experience of the nation which they reflected, came into being not just through social, economic or political pressures, but because of the activity of God running through it all. Beyond the obvious human interest of its individual stories, the Hebrew Bible is a deeply spiritual book, affirming that this world and all its affairs are not merely a haphazard sequence of coincidences, but are somehow the work of a divine being who is God of both creation and history. More-over, this God is not depicted in terms of a remote, unknowable divine force, but is understood in essentially personal terms as one with whom human beings can – and do – have personal dealings. This message is set out in the opening pages of the first book (Genesis), and it is explained and emphasized many times in what follows. Today's readers will no doubt have many different reactions to such overtly religious claims, some of which will be examined in more detail in later chapters

here. But whatever response all this may evoke, any understanding
of the Old Testament which does not take serious account of its world-
view is likely to provide only a very partial insight into its meaning and
significance.

The story

One of the difficulties often encountered by the reader approaching
the Old Testament for the first time is trying to distinguish the main
storyline from the many individual stories which help to make it up.
This is partly related to the way in which these books evolved over
many centuries, and the fact that the collection as a whole went
through several different editing processes before reaching its present
form. As a consequence, it is not difficult to identify what look like
conflicting opinions within its pages. For example, the framework of the
entire collection clearly affirms that the God of whom it speaks has
universal jurisdiction over the whole world, whereas much of the story
seems to imply almost the opposite, for in the early stories God mostly
appears as a living reality only in the life of a particular ethnic group.
These apparent tensions within the narratives will receive a good deal of
attention in later chapters. But it will be worthwhile here surveying the
story as it stands. Scholars have often forgotten that, whatever else may
be said about their literary origins, the way these books were combined
to form the final edition of the Hebrew Bible was intended to present a
coherent message that would both sum up and take forward the stories
told by the individual writers. While it is certainly not illegitimate to
speculate on the various stages of development through which the
various books passed, the meaning of the collection as a whole is to be
judged on the basis of the end product. Just as the impact of a well-
cooked meal is more than the sum of its individual ingredients, so the
significance of the Old Testament transcends the insights contained
within its various components.

The stage is set on a grand, international scale in the opening pages,
and though the main focus is on the life of a specific group of people, the
earliest episodes span most of the ancient world. Before long, though, the
main interest centres on a childless couple – Abraham and Sarah – living
in the Mesopotamian city of Ur (Genesis 11:31 – 12:5). This unlikely
couple then become parents to a great nation who, by the end of the
introductory stories, have settled in a land so idyllic that it can be
described as 'flowing with milk and honey' (Deuteronomy 6:3). In
between these two points, the books from Genesis to Deuteronomy
recount many memorable stories about the children who were eventually born into this family, and of how their descendants unwittingly
ended up as slaves in Egypt. In the telling of the story of Israel's earliest
days, this time of enforced slavery became one of the pivotal points of
their experience, but under Moses, a dynamic leader trained in the royal

courts of Egypt, it was to become a central element in Israel's national consciousness. Generations of later writers had no doubt that even this was a part of God's plan for the people, and with great insight and sensitivity the eighth-century BC prophet Hosea pictured God at this time as a loving parent (probably a mother, given the form of the imagery) and Israel as God's child: 'When Israel was a child, I loved him and called him out of Egypt as my son... I was the one who taught Israel to walk. I took my people up in my arms... I drew them to me with affection and love. I picked them up and held them to my cheek; I bent down to them and fed them' (Hosea 11:1, 3–4). Almost 200 years later again, and after many more calamities, this conviction was still of central importance, as highlighted by Ezekiel's assurance to the people that 'When I chose Israel, I made them a promise. I revealed myself to them in Egypt and told them: I am Yahweh your God. It was then that I promised to take them out of Egypt and... lead them to a land I had chosen for them, a rich and fertile land, the finest land of all' (Ezekiel 20:5–6).

Escape from Egypt

With their dramatic escape from slavery in Egypt – the event subsequently referred to as the 'exodus' – Israel's destiny began to take shape. But between the exodus and their entry to the 'land flowing with milk and honey' (Canaan), there is the story of God's Law given to Moses at Mount Sinai. As the Old Testament writers reflected on the meaning of their nation's experience of God, they always gave this Law (Torah) a central place. The occasion when the Law was given is depicted as a

The ancient and impressive civilization of Egypt must have intimidated the Hebrew slaves. This is the Temple of Karnak at Luxor.

fearful and serious moment: 'The whole of Mount Sinai was covered with smoke, because Yahweh had come down on it in fire. The smoke went up like the smoke of a furnace, and all the people trembled violently... Moses spoke, and God answered him with thunder' (Exodus 19:18–19). To people nurtured on the values of Western democracy, the laws of the Hebrew Bible (contained mostly in the books of Exodus, Leviticus and Numbers) can seem harsh and unreasonable.

Surprisingly, perhaps, the people of Israel never regarded them in that way, and though God was to be honoured and respected, observing the requirements of the Law was never regarded as a heavy burden. On the contrary, it was something to be kept with great joy, for the people looked back beyond the smoke and fire of Sinai to the events that went before it – and in that context they could see that God's Law was very firmly based on God's love, and that their continued obedience was the free and loving devotion of those who are grateful for unexpected and undeserved benefits. It is no coinci-

dence that the ten commandments begin not with an instruction, but with a reminder of God's love and goodness: 'I am Yahweh your God who brought you out of Egypt, where you were slaves' (Exodus 20:2).

God promised the Israelites that they would settle in a fertile land. The cultivation of olive trees became part of their agricultural life.

In due course, the nomadic way of life that could be traced right back to Abraham and Sarah gave way to a settled farming life in a new land. Here, Israel began to ask new questions about their faith in God. So far, they had known the God Yahweh whom Moses served as a God of the desert. But new questions began to bother them. Did this God know how to grow crops – or have any experience in rearing sheep to have many lambs? In a technological age, these can seem to be rather naïve questions, but for these people they were the most important questions of all. Life itself depended on the answers, and in one way or another the struggle to find those answers dominates the rest of the Old Testament story. For when Israel settled in their new land, other gods and goddesses were already well established there – and they had long and apparently successful experience in agricultural matters. So there began a long battle of loyalties between Yahweh, the God of the desert, and the gods and goddesses of the land of Canaan: Baal, Asherah, Anat and other members of their pantheon. The people of Israel were tempted to forsake their own God in preference for these others. The unfolding epic of the nation describes how, from the earliest times, there were local heroes like the so-called 'judges' who were prepared to resist such spiritual treason. But as time passed, things went from bad to worse, and the great prophets found themselves protesting over many generations that the people of Israel had left their own true God for the worship of false deities.

National decline

The story describes Israel's national fortunes reaching their high point in the days of David and Solomon (dated by some to about 1010–930 BC). But following them, it fell into serious decline as the great kingdom was partitioned, to be followed by the collapse first of the northern part (Israel), and then in due course by the southern part (Judah). Prophets, from the radical and outspoken Elijah to the introspective Jeremiah, spoke out in both north and south against the social and political corruption which they believed had led to the inevitable disintegration of the entire nation. Though the many prophets spoke in different circumstances, to the people of their own time, they were all united in their belief that the nation of Israel had come to ruination because of its neglect of the Law given at Mount Sinai, and an increasing fondness for the gods and goddesses of Palestine.

This figure is a Cannanite Baal, or storm god. The struggle against idolatry recurs throughout the Old Testament. Was Israel's Lord just one god among many, or was this the only true God?

By 586 BC, the entire nation was finished. In that year the city of Jerusalem was captured by the Babylonian king Nebuchadnezzar II, and its Temple and most of the other significant buildings were destroyed. This was a disaster of immense proportions, whose impact on the national consciousness lasted for many centuries. But once more, out of the ashes of defeat new life was kindled by new leaders who, if anything, had an even more expansive vision than their predecessors. The sheer scale of the calamity forced a thoroughgoing reappraisal not only of national strategy, but more especially of the national faith, and as those who survived this dark time reflected on its meaning, they concluded that even this new disaster was all a part of God's plan for their people. As they set out to review the lessons of the past, they were quite sure that God would not forget the earlier promises. There would be a new creation and a new exodus on an even greater scale than before, for the whole world would now be the scene of God's renewed activity, and Israel's role in this new world would be to function as 'a light to the nations – so that all the world may be saved' (Isaiah 49:6).

With this, the story had come full circle. It began with Abraham and Sarah and the promise that through their family God would bless many nations (Genesis 12:1–3). In the intervening centuries, this promise had been repeatedly challenged from many different directions. Politically and economically, it was always under threat – whether from the Egyptians, the Canaanites, the Assyrians or the Babylonians. Religiously, it was undermined from within as the people of Israel were tempted to forget Yahweh, the God of their forebears, and turn instead to other forms of worship in religions which, the prophets complained, allowed their moral and spiritual responsibility to be left behind in the shrine instead of forming the basis of everyday life in home and market place.

But God's intention for this world never deviated: 'the holy God of Israel remains faithful to the promises... I, Yahweh, was there at the beginning, and I, Yahweh, will be there at the end' (Isaiah 49:7; 41:4).

Understanding the story

It is not too difficult to gain a general impression of the Old Testament story. But once we begin to dig beneath the surface, this most fascinating of books also presents many puzzles. In later chapters, we will be looking at its complexities from different perspectives, but at the outset it is worth making just a few general comments on some of the most distinctive features of the Old Testament and its contents, which will identify some broad principles of interpretation that can then be applied to the exploration of specific questions.

■ Most readers today probably encounter the Old Testament as the first half of the Christian Bible. The fact that it is commonly called 'the Old Testament' only serves to emphasize this position, for in this context it is 'old' not because it is ancient, but by contrast to the records of the early church which are conventionally designated 'the New Testament'. Given that the Christian faith emerged from within Judaism, it is hardly surprising that Christians should have taken it for granted that these two quite separate collections of writings properly belong together. Within the Christian tradition, it has always been assumed that the events surrounding the origins of the Christian faith were yet a further stage in God's dealings with men and women that began through the ancient nation of Israel, recorded in the Old Testament. This of course is a particular interpretation of these books, for the Old Testament was not written by Christians, nor is its message intrinsically and necessarily a Christian message. Long before the emergence of Christianity, these books were the sacred writings of the Jewish faith (Judaism), and that is obviously their primary reference point. To understand them fully, they need to be read in their own original context, and in the light of their underlying spiritual orientation. Though Christians may legitimately feel that the Old Testament is incomplete without its Christian sequel, it can never be fully understood if it is viewed only through exclusively Christian spectacles. This is why many contemporary writers prefer not to speak of 'the Old Testament' at all, but rather of 'the Hebrew scriptures' or 'the Hebrew Bible'. Here, we have used both sets of terminology more or less interchangeably.

■ It is also important to remember that the Old Testament is quite different in character from a modern book. It is even different from the books that make up the New Testament, all of which had their origin in the same social and religious context as one another. Moreover, whereas we can, on the whole, be tolerably sure of the identity of the New Testament authors, and of the reasons why they wrote, the same cannot be said in the case of the Old Testament, and here there are very few books for which it is possible to give a positive identification of either a particular author or a specific date. The Old Testament is essentially an edited anthology – a collection of writings by different people, and from different ages. Nobody ever sat down to gather the New Testament into one unified collection: it just arose spontaneously from the reading habits of the early church. But somebody *did* set out to edit and organize the books of the Old Testament, to form a coherent account of the life of the nation of Israel. In fact, more than one person or group of people did so. The earliest editions of Old Testament materials were probably gathered together during the reigns of David and Solomon, who provided the stability and economic prosperity necessary for the flourishing of such an enterprise. It was natural that the people of Israel should begin at this time to take a keen interest in their past, revisiting the stories of their forebears as a way of identifying and celebrating their emerging national consciousness. Before this time, they no doubt had their own tribal histories which had been preserved and handed on by word of mouth from one generation to another, but they had not been written down. People whose life was a daily struggle for survival had neither time nor appetite for creating literary masterpieces: that was left to scribes working in the more leisurely atmosphere of the later royal courts of Israel.

Naturally, such researchers could only bring the story up to their own time, and the task of preserving and interpreting Israel's history was an ongoing and never-ending one, lasting through many generations. Much of the Old Testament is associated with the names of the prophets, and many of its books contain their words and actions dealing with various aspects of national life and policy. Parts of the history books were doubtless written by those whose outlook was deeply influenced by these prophets, though the final stage in the Old Testament story was reached only after the destruction of the state by Nebuchadnezzar of Babylon, which the prophets had so clearly foreseen and warned about. As new leaders emerged after that tragedy and began to reconstruct the broken pieces of a great heritage, they consciously set out to apply the lessons of the past to their own hopes for the future. To help do that, they began to collect the whole of Israel's national literature, as well as writing their own assessment of the nation's achievements, and it was out of this post-exilic reappraisal that the Hebrew Bible finally emerged in the form it has today.

■ A further distinguishing mark of the Old Testament is the enormous time span that it covers. Whereas the whole of the New Testament was written in the space of something like sixty or seventy years, the Old Testament story covers many centuries. There is a good deal of debate about where historical narrative in the proper sense begins, but even if (as many think) that was only in the time of David or Solomon, it still takes us back 1,000 years before the Christian era. In addition, though, the Old Testament contains accounts of things that appear to pre-date that, by a long way. The very earliest parts of its literature are located in a world where civilization itself was a relatively recent arrival. Its story begins in the region of what is now Iraq, in what the ancients called 'the Fertile Crescent', a part of the world that had witnessed many remarkable developments long before the story of Israel's history began. Great empires had come and gone, and as early as 3000 BC the Sumerian people of ancient Mesopotamia had written down their traditional stories and beliefs for the generations that would follow them. One of their most noteworthy successors was the Babylonian king Hammurabi, whose law code written on clay tablets some 1,700 years BC still survives as a lasting monument to the culture of those ancient times. Many other texts from this ancient world have come to light – from Nuzi in Iraq, from Ebla in northern Syria and from Ugarit further to the south. In addition, there are the many records and monuments of that other great and ancient civilization centred on the River Nile in Egypt.

By comparison with these empires, the people who wrote the Old Testament were undoubtedly latecomers on the world stage. The shape of their culture was already formed by other nations, and to understand their story fully it is necessary to know something of the story of these other peoples too. The fortunes of Israel were always inextricably bound up with the manoeuverings of the two superpowers of the day: the one based on the Nile, and the other based on the rivers Tigris and Euphrates. But then the Old Testament takes us beyond even the last of these great empires, for Israel survived longer than them all, and the latest books of their national literature reflect the concerns of the period that saw the rise and fall of Alexander the Great, and which was eventually to herald the arrival of the next great superpower of world history, the Roman empire.

The Old Testament is the Bible of the Jew as well as the Christian. It describes a grand vision for the transformation of the world. The difference lies in the two understandings of how these promises are being fulfilled.

It is hardly surprising if today's readers find the Old Testament slightly confusing at times, for its pages cover almost half the history of civilization as it has been documented in the West. In addition, the circumstances of the early parts of the story are quite different from the situation encountered in the later parts, while none of it bears much resemblance to the world as it is today.

■ Something of the Old Testament's distinctive character can also be observed when its books are viewed purely as literature. As has already been observed, it is above all a book infused with spiritual values. It does not set out to give what might be regarded as an impartial, independent account of the events it describes. The Old Testament story has been written for a purpose, and its different parts were used by men and women living at different times to speak to the people of their own

When Renaissance painters illustrated scenes from the life of Jesus, they portrayed people in the dress of their own day, rather than attempting to show them in biblical clothing. Similarly, the writers of the Old Testament were recording and reviewing life as they understood it from their perspective.

generation. Some have taken this to imply that the story it contains must be essentially fictional – a kind of moralizing tale, which is valuable for whatever lessons it teaches, but out of touch with what actually happened. In reality, things are much more complicated than this. For example, many events and people mentioned in the Old Testament also appear in the records of other nations of the time, which at least means that we need to explore the relationship between these various accounts. The truth is that there is probably no such thing as the 'bare facts' of history, whether biblical or otherwise – and if there was, they would be much less useful than people often imagine. To understand the past – or, for that matter, the present – events need to be interpreted, placed in a context and set alongside other aspects of human experience in order that their full significance might be discerned. A historian who merely reported past events in a disinterested way would not be a good historian. It is the judgments made by others on what things mean that actually enable us to form our own opinions

and understandings. In everyday life, we take all this for granted, and we know that when, for instance, we watch a television documentary, the overall perspective is going to reflect the world-view and opinions of the programme-maker, but we would not normally regard this as a barrier to understanding. We may wish to make a different judgment ourselves on this or that matter, but we simply take it for granted that to understand any situation fully we need to take account not only of the facts, but also of the outlook of our sources of information. It is the same with the Old Testament. The more clearly we can understand the intentions of those who wrote and handed on these books, the more likely we are to arrive at a useful appreciation of their significance and meaning.

In addition, we should remember that these writings are not just one person's assessment of the history of a nation: they are a national archive. The people who wrote and edited these books were themselves a part of that nation and its history. It is not easy for the detached observer to grasp exactly what this means. But we can find a useful analogy in the pictures that medieval artists painted of the life and times of Jesus. The crucifixion was a favourite theme, and there are many great works showing Jesus hanging on a cross between two thieves. But, on closer inspection, the people around the crosses often seem some-what out of place, and instead of Roman soldiers, there are soldiers of sixteenth-century Europe. The people too belong to that age – and the city where the scene takes place is not Jerusalem in AD 33, but Venice or Rome in AD 1500. When today's art critics look at such pictures they do not usually feel that they cast doubt on the reality of the crucifixion of Jesus. Indeed, some may unconsciously follow the artist's example, and pencil in an image of themselves and today's social context. In a way, this is what the writers of the Old Testament story were doing as they depicted their national past. From generation to generation, they knew that the story of their national heroes and heroines was their own story. They were a part of it, because they saw in it the continuing story of God's dealings with their nation. It was this conviction that enabled them to recognize in the failures and triumphs of the past the realities and the potential of their own age, and gave them the freedom to reinterpret the traditional stories so as to equip new generations to address the challenges of the present.

The story and the faith

What of the distinctively religious aspects of the Old Testament books? It is, of course, possible to read the Old Testament and never discover its faith. Certainly, if definitions of spirituality or faith are restricted to collections of carefully articulated systematic beliefs or doctrines, then there is little in the Old Testament that would fit that description. The truth is that the story and the faith are so inextricably interwoven that it is both impossible and pointless to try to disentangle them from one another. But even accepting that and adopting a more open-ended approach, it is not easy to identify something that can plausibly be labelled 'the faith of the Old Testament', for several reasons:

■ It has already been observed that the Old Testament is not a single, unified book. It contains many different types of literature, and together they cover the greater part of 1,000 years in the history of ancient Israel. For this reason alone it is a good deal easier to identify the faith of various Old Testament authors than it is to discover a comprehensive system that might be described as 'Old Testament faith' in some definitive sense. Indeed, many scholars would argue that the best we can hope for is to find ways of speaking of 'the faith of the prophets', or 'the faith of the psalmists', and so on.

■ Was the Old Testament ever intended to be a guide to what people should believe, or is it rather a record of what people in ancient Israel did as a matter of fact believe? As a book of history, it contains elements of both these things, but depending on which one of the two is labelled 'Old Testament faith', quite different conclusions can be reached. For example, the prophets declared that true worship of God had to include the way a person behaved in everyday life, and could not just be restricted to ritual actions carried out at a shrine – but both prophets and historians make it perfectly clear that this understanding of worship was never shared by the majority of people in ancient Israel. Similar diversity of opinion can be found on many other issues, which means that from the outset we need to clarify what we are looking for when we talk of the Old Testament faith. Is it the sort

How many books are in the Old Testament?

There were thirty-nine books in the original Hebrew Bible. All Christian Bibles include these thirty-nine books as part of the Old Testament, but some contain additional works, which are variously referred to as the Apocrypha or deuterocanonical books. These were mostly written in Greek in the centuries immediately preceding the Christian era, and never formed a part of the Hebrew Bible. Different selections of them are contained in different versions of the Old Testament, though they typically include the following: Tobit, Judith, Wisdom of Solomon, Wisdom of Ben Sira, Baruch, 1–2 Esdras, The Letter of Jeremiah, 1–4 Maccabees, the Prayer of Manasseh, Psalm 151, and various additions to the books of Esther and Daniel.

After the time of the Persian empire, the world changed very rapidly, and it was not long before the ancient language of Hebrew was forgotten by all but a few, and Jewish people (the descendants of ancient Israel) were living in many different countries. In the time of Jesus, for example, there were more Jewish people in Alexandria in Egypt than there were in Jerusalem. The language most of these expatriates (or members of the Jewish Diaspora) spoke was Greek. By the time of the New Testament, the Hebrew scriptures were widely read in Greek translation, in a version known as the Septuagint (LXX). It was through this Greek version that these 'extra' books found their way into the Christian canon of the Old Testament, and their inclusion is related to the way the Septuagint evolved.

It is customary today to speak of 'the Septuagint' as if it were simply a Greek Old Testament. But the facts are not so simple.

of religious beliefs that were generally held in Israel, or are we trying to extract some system of normative beliefs out of the Old Testament records?

■ Just to complicate things a little more, we know for certain that both actual practice and the ideals of people such as the prophets did not remain static from one period of Israel's history to another, but were continually evolving to match new circumstances. The question of marriage and family provides a good example of this. By the time of Ezra (towards the end of the Old Testament period), it was assumed that one man would marry one woman, and both of them would be ethnically Israelite. In earlier times, though, it was the common practice for a man to have several wives, and not only is this practice never explicitly forbidden, but also almost all the leading male characters in the Old Testament stories had multiple regular sexual partners, who were not necessarily their wives. Nor were they all Israelites: the list of Solomon's wives and partners reads like a roll-call of all the nations of the ancient world! The same diversity can be found in the laws governing things such as food, keeping the sabbath day or circumcision, all of which were applied in a much more relaxed way before the time of exile in Babylon than they ever were after it.

In view of such complex problems, some doubt whether it will ever be possible to articulate anything remotely like a comprehensive account of the spiritual and religious teachings of the Hebrew Bible. On this

---

Modern translators would begin with a complete Bible in Hebrew and Greek, and produce its equivalent in their own language. But what is now called the Septuagint was never a complete Bible until the early centuries of the Christian era. Before that, no one knew the techniques necessary to bind such a large collection of literature into one single volume. Writing materials were painstakingly made by hand and individual sheets would then be glued or stitched together to make a strip long enough to contain a single book. This would then be rolled up for storage, and to possess a complete Hebrew Bible required a large number of different rolls. In addition to this, different people were busy making their own translations of the Old Testament books into Greek – and when the Christians eventually produced a single-volume Greek Old Testament, they simply made a selection from the translations that were available to them.

In the days before the Old Testament could literally become one book, bound together inside a single cover, the various rolls in which its writings were contained needed to be stored safely and were often kept in small boxes. These boxes were all of the same size, and were used as a classification system. If a particular box had unused space in it, it would be natural to fill it up by storing similar kinds of writings in the same boxes. This was probably how the deuterocanonical books came to be associated with the original writings of the Hebrew Bible. In content and style, they were not all that different from the books that had been translated from Hebrew, and it made good sense to keep them all together. In time, they came to be automatically accepted as constituent elements of the literature that collectively

The scrolls of the Law in a Jewish synagogue remind us of the high place the Old Testament writings have always held in Judaism. For Jews and Christians see these books as the record of how God's will was revealed to humanity.

How many books are in the Old Testament?
continued

made up the Greek version of the Old Testament, and so when the early Christians came to bind them all into one volume, it was natural to include them, even though they had never been part of the Hebrew scriptures that evolved throughout the life of ancient Israel.

Like the original thirty-nine books, they represent different types of literature. Some are clearly history books (1 – 2 Maccabees), while others are books of philosophy and religious poetry (Wisdom of Solomon, Wisdom of Ben Sira), and yet others are moralistic novels (Tobit, Judith, and the additions to Esther and Daniel), or apocalyptic writings claiming to give a clairvoyant view of the future (2 Esdras). Though these books are known primarily from early Christian copies of the Greek Septuagint, it is highly unlikely that they all came from the same sources. Fragments of some of them have been discovered written

in Hebrew, while others were certainly first composed in Greek, and yet others were probably first written in Hebrew, but have only survived in their Greek or Latin versions. It is unclear how the Jewish community in Egypt, among whom the Greek version was produced, regarded these books, though there is no evidence to suggest that it was a matter of great importance until after the emergence of Christianity, when Judaism found it necessary to define which books were to be considered authoritative – partly in response to the way Christians were then using sections of the Hebrew scriptures. The New Testament contains references to the deuterocanonical literature (compare, for instance, Hebrews 1:3 with Wisdom of Solomon 7:25; Hebrews 11:37 with 2 Maccabees 5–7; John 10:22 with 1 Maccabees 4:59 and 2 Maccabees 10:1–8), and second-century Christian

view, the best that might be achieved would be a carefully researched description of the history of Israelite religion, tracing the ways it developed and changed over many generations. This kind of historical understanding is certainly a vital part of any assessment of the message of the Old Testament, and much of this book is taken up with the discussion of questions that will help to identify how the Old Testament faith related to the world in which it developed. In the process of doing this, it needs to be compared with the religious beliefs and aspirations of other nations of the time, in order to highlight whatever it was that made its message distinctive. Many of the features that seem especially strange and unfamiliar to today's readers were just a natural part of everyday life in the ancient Middle East. Things like animal sacrifices, and much of the structure of Israelite worship, were common to many different cultural contexts in Old Testament times, so by understanding this context it is often possible to gain invaluable insights into religious themes in the Old Testament itself. Even the language used of Yahweh is at times very similar, if not identical, to terms used in other religions of the day, and this, too, can help to illustrate the full meaning of apparently obscure Old Testament passages.

But, of course, the Old Testament has another context than just the world of ancient Israel, and that is determined by the circumstances of the contemporary interpreter. A Jewish person will see something different in the Hebrew Bible from what a Christian sees, and a Muslim

---

writers regularly quote from or refer to these books. However, following the increasing circulation of all kinds of documents purporting to be Christian 'gospels', it became necessary for Christians to define exactly which books they could accept as authoritative – and that inevitably meant that some kind of decision had to be made about the shape of the Old Testament, as well as the New. Jerome (AD c. 345–419) regarded the books of the Hebrew Bible as specially authoritative, though he felt that the others could be useful for more general edification, and he accordingly included them all in his Latin version of the Bible (the Vulgate). However, at the same period Augustine (AD 354–430), one of the early church's greatest theologians, regarded the deuterocanonical books as fully authoritative. Subsequent generations of Christians perpetuated this ambivalence. The Protestant Reformer Martin Luther, for example, adopted Jerome's policy of commending the deuterocanonical literature as valuable but not authoritative, though the Westminster Confession of Faith in 1646 denounced them as completely unbiblical. A century earlier, though, the Roman Catholic Council of Trent had insisted that (with the exception of 1–2 Esdras and the Prayer of Manasseh) they were an integral part of the canon. The Orthodox Church, for its part, has always accepted an even larger collection of literature as an authentic part of the Christian Old Testament scriptures.

will discern its message differently again, while a secular atheist will have another perspective, and a New Ager will perceive it from yet another angle. While seeking to be aware of the various insights that can be gained from different standpoints and personal perspectives, it is not the intention of this book to present a comprehensive account of all the possibilities. As with the companion volume, *Introducing the New Testament*, this one is written from a self-consciously Christian position. When the Old Testament is approached from a Christian standpoint, it is not adequate to regard it solely as part of the religious history of the ancient world. Purely historical and literary matters are not unimportant, but they are not the whole story, and theological questions also need to be addressed. These include such matters as how the religious ideas of the Old Testament might be related to the Christian faith as it is explained in the teaching of Jesus and the rest of the New Testament, and whether it is possible to square the Old Testament's ideas with Christian beliefs. Even many Christians find it hard to think that what they understand of the descriptions of God in the Old Testament can be reconciled with the message of the New, while in some quarters it is taken for granted that there is an unbridgeable chasm between the ethical perspectives of the two parts of the Christian Bible. And what about things like sacrificial worship? To most Western Christians this has always been frankly offensive. But is it saying something fundamental about God's nature and about true religious belief and practice, or is it a peripheral part of the culture of the day that can easily be discarded?

These are all big questions, perhaps too big to be properly addressed in the scope of a book like this. But they are key questions for every Christian reader of the Old Testament, which is why it seems worth making the effort. Matters of faith are examined especially towards the end of the book, and the way they are dealt with there reflects the kind of questions that contemporary readers may wish to ask. But before coming to that, some considerable attention needs to be applied to setting the Old Testament faith in its proper social and historical context. Once we have understood it in its own world, we have a better chance of interpreting it sensibly in ours.

Ordering the books

Types of literature

The Old Testament is a complete library of literature, containing books of many different types. If they were taken separately to a modern library, it is certain that they would not all be placed on the same shelf, for they represent many different literary genres, each with its own distinctive style and requiring different methods of interpretation to appreciate their individual contributions to the overall picture.

HISTORY

Some books are easily recognizable as a kind of history: Genesis, Joshua, Judges, 1 and 2 Samuel, 1 and 2 Kings, 1 and 2 Chronicles, Ezra and Nehemiah. These tell the story of the nation's life, which is then continued in the deuterocanonical books of 1 and 2 Maccabees. But none of them merely records past events. They all report some things and not others, and always interpret what they include, explaining its significance in the light of the distinctive religious faith of their various writers. The nearest we come to historical archives in the generally accepted sense would be some sections of Chronicles.

LAW

Other books (Exodus, Leviticus, Numbers and Deuteronomy) are obviously law codes, though they are hardly the kind that today's Western lawyers might use, for they contain a mixture of civil and religious laws, as well as some stories that could just as readily be classified as a kind of history.

POETRY

There is a lot of poetry in the Old Testament, and some books consist of nothing else: religious poetry in Psalms and Lamentations, and love poems in the Song of Solomon. But many other books also contain poetry, including Job, Proverbs, and (from the deuterocanonical books) the Wisdom of Solomon and Wisdom of Ben Sira. The prophets also seem to have expressed many of their messages in poetic form, no doubt making it easier to remember and repeat.

STORIES

People have always loved good stories, and the Hebrews were no exception. Stories that were obviously carefully crafted, maybe by professional storytellers, include Job, Jonah and Esther, along with parts of Daniel and the stories about Joseph contained in Genesis. Among the deuterocanonical books, Tobit, Judith and the various additions to the stories of Daniel and Esther all fall into this category. They are all narratives that have obviously been skilfully designed, like a good novel, to engage the reader's attention and to get a message across at the same time. Some scholars believe they are novels, presenting a distinctive message by means of a fictional story, while others would rather classify them as history – though, nevertheless, history with a meaning. The stories of Job and Jonah have features which suggest they may originally have been meant to be performed as drama.

VISIONS

Visions are found scattered throughout the Hebrew Bible, but Daniel in particular is full of them, as also is the deuterocanonical 2 Esdras. These books were written in a distinctive apocalyptic style, and at a time when their writers and readers were suffering persecution and injustice. By looking at what was going on from God's angle in some other world, they were able to put such suffering in a wider perspective and assure their readers that it was only a temporary thing. They use symbolic images in a very precise way, which means they require quite specific interpretative skills.

LITURGICAL MATERIALS

The book of Psalms is, in effect, the liturgical handbook of the Jerusalem Temple. It is a specialized form of poetry, and includes prayers, litanies and songs, often with instructions for the musicians, and detailed directions for dancers and other worship leaders.

PHILOSOPHY AND ETHICS

Many books contain advice about how to live. Much of it, such as that found in Proverbs, is simple homespun wisdom of the sort found in every society across the world. Other books, however, wrestle with the great issues of life and death and the ultimate meaning of things – the existence of God, or the problem of undeserved suffering and the presence of evil in the world. These include Job and Ecclesiastes and (from the deuterocanonical collection) the Wisdom of Solomon and Wisdom of Ben Sira.

FAITH STORIES

Books of philosophy tend to address big questions in abstract ways, but people of all cultures have usually preferred to tell stories to one another, to explain things that just could not be explored in any other way. Many different terms have been used to describe such stories, 'myth' being one of the most popular – though in common speech, that can suggest they are somehow untrue or unreliable, which is why I have preferred the term 'faith stories' here because, far from being untrue, these stories express the most profound truths imaginable about some of life's most complex questions. The Old Testament begins with stories of this kind in the book of Genesis and, in doing so, sets the scene for all that then follows.

Sections of the Hebrew Bible

The order of the books in the Christian Old Testament is derived not from the manuscripts of the Hebrew Bible, but from a Greek version (the Septuagint) that seems to have originated in Egypt sometime before the beginning of the Christian era. The Hebrew Bible arranged its contents in a totally different way, with three separate sections: the Law, the Prophets and the Writings.

THE LAW

This consists of the first five books (Genesis, Exodus, Leviticus, Numbers and Deuteronomy), believed to be of special importance as they were traditionally regarded as the work of Moses himself. Genesis, of course, contains nothing at all that would nowadays be recognized as 'law'. It is a collection of stories, and at first sight it might more naturally be regarded as some sort of historical narrative. That reflects current understandings of 'law' as being a set of rules and regulations, a legal code that can be interpreted by lawyers and applied in a court by a judge. It would certainly be hard to imagine a modern person agreeing with one of the poets of ancient Israel who wrote that 'the law is my delight' (Psalm 119:77). But the biblical notion of 'law' was significantly more comprehensive and far-ranging than ours. The fundamental meaning of the Hebrew word conventionally translated 'law' (Torah) was 'guidance' or 'instruction', and the 'law' of the Hebrew Bible was the place where people could discover what to believe about God, and how they should live in order to reflect God's will. This is why the Torah and its development is so closely bound up with the stories of Israel's history. It is a basic assumption in the Old Testament that knowing and obeying God is not just a matter of blind obedience to a few religious and moral rules, but is rather a question of experiencing God's concern and love in a personal and social context. Though the Law might include principles of justice, it also needed to incorporate stories which could serve as everyday illustrations and case studies of how people were intended to live – and the likely consequences if they chose to follow other practices.

THE PROPHETS

This is the largest section of the Hebrew Bible, and takes its name from a number of religious and political activists who sought to influence the life of the nation over a period of several centuries. This collection of books itself falls into two distinct sections, 'the former prophets' and 'the latter prophets'. Since 'the latter prophets' are more obviously connected with the individuals whose names they bear, it will be most useful here to look at them first.

■ **The latter prophets** Prophets are mentioned throughout the history of the Israelite people. They were not primarily writers, but speakers and political activists. One of the central planks of the Old Testament faith in its final form was the conviction that spirituality is not so much concerned with the kind of rituals that go on in shrines and temples, but relates to everyday styles of life. As the people looked back to the traditional stories of how their forebears had lived, they came to the conclusion that God's values were essentially concerned with justice and freedom. Since their own ancestors had been enslaved in Egypt, and God had stood by them in their distress, before finally orchestrating their freedom through Moses, it was natural to conclude that God must be on the side of the poor and the oppressed – and this belief came to be enshrined in many of the nation's laws, particularly the book of Deuteronomy.

It is easy to hold such beliefs, but much more difficult to put them into practice. The prophets functioned as the conscience of the nation, always reminding the people of how much they themselves owed to God's generosity and love – and encouraging them to demonstrate these same values in their dealings with one another and with other nations. It was an uphill struggle, and many of the prophets were persecuted, imprisoned or even killed. But this message was at the heart of authentic Hebrew faith, and plays a large part in the books of the Old Testament.

Not all the prophets had books named after them. Of those who did, Isaiah, Jeremiah and Ezekiel (the so-called 'major prophets') have the longest, while twelve others (the 'minor prophets') are credited with much shorter books: Hosea, Joel, Amos, Obadiah, Jonah, Micah, Nahum, Habakkuk, Zephaniah, Haggai, Zechariah and Malachi. From what we know of them, it seems that the prophets themselves rarely made long speeches. They usually delivered short messages that could be easily remembered – many of them in poetry, though prophets were also on occasion mime artists and dramatists, acting out their messages in the market places and on street corners.

■ **The former prophets** These are the books of Joshua, Judges, 1–2 Samuel and 1–2 Kings, and in the Hebrew Bible they appear before 'the latter prophets'. At first sight, they look to be so different that it is not obvious why they too should have been included as part of the Prophets. They read more like history books, telling the story of the nation from the time when their ancestors escaped from slavery, through to the time in the sixth century BC when their national capital was destroyed by the Babylonian empire and its people were deported. In between, we read of how, under kings David and Solomon, Israel briefly enjoyed a period of political stability and influence. But most of the remainder of the story describes how their grand kingdom split into two parts (Israel and Judah), both of which struggled to maintain their independence in the face of growing pressures from larger states, notably Egypt, Assyria, Babylon and Syria.

The thing that makes these books also 'prophets' is that they do not merely relate the stories but – like all good history books – interpret them, informing their readers what the stories mean and showing how they were to be understood in relation to the sweep of wider world history of the time. In doing that, their writers looked at things from the perspectives they had learned from the prophets. As they reviewed their nation's history, they could see that whenever the people had commit-fted themselves to God's values and ways of doing things, they prospered – but when God's demands for justice and love were forgotten, then the nation suffered. As we have already observed, Israelite faith was not focused on philosophical abstractions, but began with the way God had dealt with people in the experiences of everyday life. History was therefore very important, and was one of the key places where God's activity could be seen. By a proper appreciation of its meaning and significance, as explained by the prophets, the people

could discover how they were meant to live. All the prophetic works –
former and latter – were regarded as accounts of how God had spoken
to the people, sometimes through the events of history and at other
times through the words of people. But in each case it was the same
God, and the same message.

THE WRITINGS

This section includes all the remaining books of the Hebrew Bible. They
are not all the same kind of works. Psalms, Proverbs and Job are very
different from one another in content, for example, but they are all
poetry. Then there are those books known as the 'Megilloth', or 'five
scrolls': Ruth, Song of Solomon, Ecclesiastes, Lamentations and Esther.
Again, these five are all different styles and genres, but they were
grouped together because each of them had a particular association
with significant religious festivals: Ruth was used at Pentecost, Song
of Solomon at Passover, Ecclesiastes at Tabernacles, Lamentations to
commemorate the destruction of Jerusalem and Esther at Purim. There
are also the books of Ezra, Nehemiah and 1–2 Chronicles, all of which
relate to the situation in which the remnants of the people of Judah
found themselves after they were allowed to return to their homeland in
the years following 538 BC, when the Persian emperor Cyrus the Great
managed to overthrow the Babylonian empire. Last of all, there is the
book of Daniel, containing visions and some stories, and relating to a
later period still.

The reason for this unusual arrangement of the books was probably
historical, and the three sections roughly represent the three stages in
which the Old Testament was put together. The first part of it to be
permanently recorded was the Law, followed by the Prophets, and then
much later by the Writings. This is why the books of Ezra, Nehemiah
and Chronicles were included in the final section, rather than being
placed alongside the other history books in 'the former prophets', for
they were written much later and from the perspective of the age that
survived the destruction of Jerusalem in the sixth century BC. The books
of Chronicles contain many of the same stories as the books of Samuel
and Kings, but they are an analysis of the meaning of those stories and
an application of their lessons to the people of a later generation. By
then, both the Law and the Prophets were widely accepted as sacred and
important collections of books, and it would not have been possible to
make any further additions to their contents.

Archaeology and the Old Testament

Comparing books on the Old Testament written a century or more ago with one written today, the thing that is most obvious is the radical change that has taken place in our knowledge of the world of the Bible. In the nineteenth century, study of the Old Testament was largely a literary affair: the text itself was studied in minute detail, and dissected in much the same way as a pathologist might deal with a corpse. But today, Old Testament study is vibrant and living, and is dominated by social and cultural considerations that would have been quite foreign to earlier generations of scholars. One of the major concerns of contemporary scholarship is to understand how the Old Testament fits into the world of its day, and to analyse its contents not just ideologically, but historically

The Rosetta Stone, found by scholars who accompanied Napoleon's army when he occupied Egypt, is in Greek, in demotic and in ancient Egyptian hieroglyphs. It provided the first clues for understanding ancient Egyptian; the first hieroglyphs were deciphered through distinguishing the name 'Ptolemy' in all three scripts.

and sociologically. This has all been made possible through an enormous expansion of knowledge of the ancient world, and thanks to the consistent efforts of archaeologists we now have a better idea than ever before of what it was actually like to live in the world of ancient Israel. It is possible to appreciate the social and political realities of life in a new way that has shed untold light on many difficult passages of the Old Testament.

Explorers have always had an interest in the materials left over from earlier civilizations. In the seventeenth century many ancient objects of interest and beauty were randomly seized and taken by such people to their wealthy patrons all over Europe, but it was not until the eighteenth century that anyone took a systematic interest in the subject. The archaeological exploration of Bible lands began when Napoleon's armies invaded Egypt in 1798, taking with them a team of scholars to study the ancient monuments. They made many significant discoveries, one of the most useful being the Rosetta Stone which had an inscription in both Greek and Egyptian hieroglyphs, and enabled scholars to decipher ancient Egyptian for the first time. However, it was only at the end of the nineteenth century that rigorous procedures began to be applied to sites in the Bible lands on a widespread scale.

A typical site in Palestine will take the form of a large mound, or *tell*. Many of these sites look just like large hills, perhaps as high as thirty or forty metres, and covered with trees or grass, but under the surface is to be found the remains of an ancient city. Sometimes cities were built on a natural hill, for that was an easy site to defend. But many of these tells began at ground level, and have been raised to their present height by the normal processes of building over many years. In the ancient world most buildings were made of mud and wood, and when a settlement was either destroyed by an enemy or just fell into decay, the inhabitants would gather

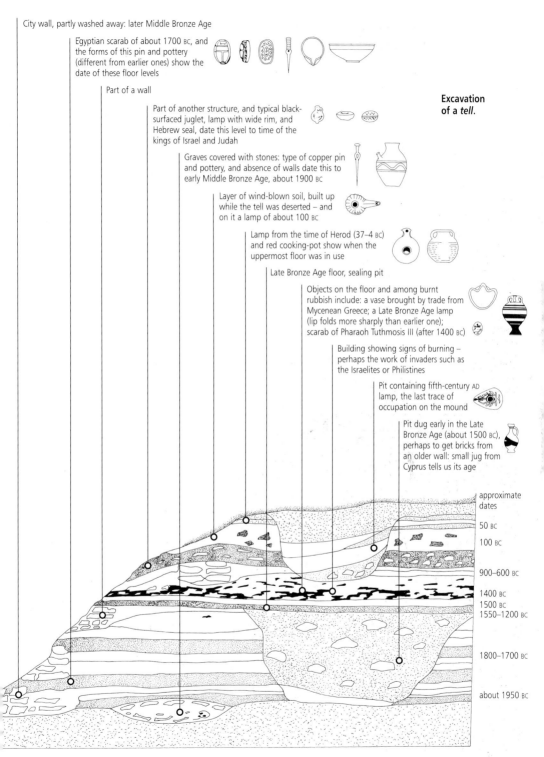

City wall, partly washed away: later Middle Bronze Age

Egyptian scarab of about 1700 BC, and the forms of this pin and pottery (different from earlier ones) show the date of these floor levels

Part of a wall

Excavation of a *tell*.

Part of another structure, and typical black-surfaced juglet, lamp with wide rim, and Hebrew seal, date this level to time of the kings of Israel and Judah

Graves covered with stones: type of copper pin and pottery, and absence of walls date this to early Middle Bronze Age, about 1900 BC

Layer of wind-blown soil, built up while the tell was deserted – and on it a lamp of about 100 BC

Lamp from the time of Herod (37–4 BC) and red cooking-pot show when the uppermost floor was in use

Late Bronze Age floor, sealing pit

Objects on the floor and among burnt rubbish include: a vase brought by trade from Mycenean Greece; a Late Bronze Age lamp (lip folds more sharply than earlier one); scarab of Pharaoh Tuthmosis III (after 1400 BC)

Building showing signs of burning – perhaps the work of invaders such as the Israelites or Philistines

Pit containing fifth-century AD lamp, the last trace of occupation on the mound

Pit dug early in the Late Bronze Age (about 1500 BC), perhaps to get bricks from an older wall: small jug from Cyprus tells us its age

approximate dates

50 BC

100 BC

900–600 BC

1400 BC
1500 BC
1550–1200 BC

1800–1700 BC

about 1950 BC

Archaeology and the
Old Testament
continued

together any available materials that could be reused, and set to work to build their own new town on the ruins of the old. The new level could be as much as two or three metres higher than the one that preceded it, which meant that over time the ground level was gradually raised, and the whole mound took on the structure of a giant gateau with many different layers superimposed one on top of the other.

Archaeologists have developed a number of basic procedures to guide their investigations at sites like this:

Great care is required as an archaeological dig progresses. Each fragment of pottery or other artefact has to be catalogued and the level at which it is found must be carefully noted.

● Digging is done in such a way as to keep separate and distinct the successive strata, or layers, of occupation. The ideal way to do this, of course, would be to start at the top and slice off each layer in turn. But this would be impractical, taking up too much time and for that reason being impossibly expensive. Instead, the archaeologist usually cuts into the mound in much the same way as a slice might be cut from a cake. This technique can provide access to a cross-section of the mound's contents in a process known as 'stratigraphic excavation'. The one disadvantage is that the archaeologist can easily cut a slice at the wrong place in the mound and miss significant remains as a result. For instance, the site of the city of

Hazor in northern Israel was excavated in 1928 by archaeologist John Garstang, who concluded that the city was deserted between 1400 and 1200 BC. But thirty years later, the Israeli archaeologist Yigael Yadin dug a trench at a different point on the same mound, and found extensive evidence of people living there at just that period!

● If objects were to be removed and taken away indiscriminately, it would be impossible to assess their significance. To understand what they mean, they need to be studied in relation to the precise spot where they are uncovered and with respect to other items that are found alongside them. Making an accurate record of every level that is excavated and of every object that is found is therefore an essential part of the process. Plans must be drawn and photographs taken, because once a layer of a mound is removed, no one can put it back together again.

● Archaeologists must also compare what they find with what others have found in other places. Pottery provides a good example of the importance of this. For every basket of significant objects recovered, dozens of baskets of pottery are unearthed. This is because pottery was always in common use, and it was very easily broken – but it was virtually impossible to destroy completely. Fashions in pottery changed from time to time, and though some styles were in use for a long period, distinctive aspects of size, shape, texture and decoration were generally limited to a specific period. So when the same types are discovered at several different locations, it is reasonable to conclude that the layers in which they are found were occupied at about the same time. In fact, pottery is one of the most important clues to the dating of a particular find. Early in the twentieth century, English archaeologist Sir Flinders Petrie realized this, and by comparing pottery from different sites and noting the various distinctive styles, he developed what he called a 'Ceramic Index' – a catalogue of typical pottery types which could be accurately dated, and which has proved to be an invaluable aid to the work of all subsequent excavators.

In trying to apply information discovered in this way to the study of the Old Testament, there are some basic principles that should always be borne in mind:

● Though the records of the Assyrian and Babylonian kings contain a good number of accounts of events that are also mentioned and described in the Old Testament, this kind of direct correlation is unusual. It is only rarely that archaeologists have discovered things with a direct and specific reference to events and people mentioned in the Bible.

● More often, archaeology helps to place the Old Testament story in its true context. It is, for example, highly unlikely that any archaeologist will ever find a reference to the story of Abraham, but investigations have shown that migrations like those described in the Genesis stories were taking place all over the Fertile Crescent during the second millennium BC, and that some of the customs mentioned in Genesis were practised at the time.

● Occasionally, the findings of archaeo- logists can illuminate specific passages in the Old Testament. In 1 Samuel 4 there is the story of how the Philistines captured the ark of the covenant from Israel in a fierce battle near the town of Shiloh, where the ark was kept. Readers of the Bible had often surmised that Shiloh itself must have been destroyed at the same time, for when Israel recovered the ark it was not returned there. Excavation at the site has confirmed that Shiloh was indeed destroyed at the time of this incident in the eleventh century BC.

● Archaeology is also often a help in interpreting difficult parts of the Old Testament. For example, Ezekiel 14:14 mentions three people as examples of great goodness: Daniel, Noah and Job. But it is curious that the prophet should place Daniel, believed to be one of his own

contemporaries, in the same class as two ancient figures. Archaeology has shown that he was probably not talking of the hero of the Old Testament book of Daniel at all, but of an ancient king of similar name renowned for his religion and justice, who is mentioned in religious poems from Assyria to Canaan, some of which are nearly 1,000 years older than Ezekiel.

● Sometimes the findings of archaeology seem as if they cannot be reconciled with what is found in the Old Testament. For example, according to Joshua 7:1 – 8:29 a great battle was fought at a place called Ai during the conquest of Canaan, whereas archaeological evidence shows the town was destroyed about 2400 BC and was not rebuilt, which means there cannot have been a town there in the days of Joshua. Of course, there could be many reasons for this apparent discrepancy. It may be that archaeologists have wrongly identified the site: it would certainly not be the first time such a mistake had been made, though it seems unlikely in this instance. It is also possible that other discoveries could be made in the future which would resolve the problem. Or it could be, as many think, that we should look for the meaning of the Old Testament story elsewhere – perhaps in the fact that the word *Ai* in Hebrew means simply 'the ruin'. Whatever the full explanation may be, it is important to take seriously both the Old Testament picture and the evidence that can be provided by archaeological investigation.

2 The Founding of the Nation

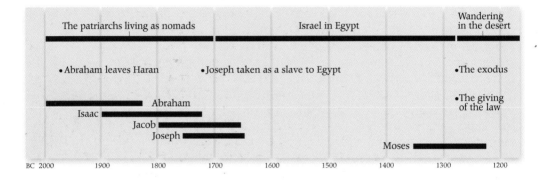

The patriarchs living as nomads			Israel in Egypt				Wandering in the desert	

•Abraham leaves Haran   •Joseph taken as a slave to Egypt   •The exodus

Abraham
Isaac
Jacob
Joseph   •The giving of the law

Moses

BC 2000   1900   1800   1700   1600   1500   1400   1300   1200

Where does Old Testament history begin? At one time, it was taken for granted that there was a very simple answer to that question: 'real' history began on the very first page of Genesis, with an account of the origins of all things, and the remainder of the story just unfolded consecutively from there. That was the basis on which Archbishop James Ussher (1581–1656) was able to claim confidently that the creation of the world took place in 4004 BC, for by adding up all the chronological indications contained in the early books of the Old Testament, and working backwards from dates that seemed to be assured, that was the mathematical result that would inevitably be arrived at. No one would now expect to be able to make such a calculation in any sort of convincing way, for a variety of very good reasons.

■ As has already been indicated in the last chapter, it is obvious from the literary genre of the writings contained in the opening books of the Old Testament that they were not all intended to be historical writing. Nineteenth-century Bible students allowed themselves to be caught up in lengthy debates about how the creation stories of Genesis could be harmonized with the emerging scientific consensus about the origins of the world, and in the process not only found themselves unable to reach a conclusion, but also frequently brought biblical faith as a whole into disrepute, and allowed religious believers to be portrayed as cranks who were more interested in halting progress than in discovering the truth. With greater detachment from the heat of that particular battle, scholars of all persuasions can now see that, whatever the original purpose of these stories was intended to be, they were certainly not attempting to provide an account of human history that would satisfy the rationalistic science inspired by the European Enlightenment. They are immediately distanced from that by the fact that God is actually their central character, and while there can be different opinions of their claims about God, the methodology of scientific rationalism is not going to be the way to evaluate them. That is why discussion of these matters is left aside here until much later in the book, when we come to consider the spiritual dimensions of the Old Testament and its message.

■ While the stories found in Genesis 1–11 clearly belong to a different genre from that of history writing, there are others found in the remainder of Genesis, and extending forward through Joshua and Judges, that do have an appearance of perhaps being 'real' history, in the sense of being intended to document the actual events surrounding the origins of the Israelite nation. Notwithstanding the fact that several key sections of these narratives have clearly been carefully crafted so as to read like a good story, they do more obviously tell stories that appear to integrate with events in the real world, and while once again the appearance of God as a major player marks them out as distinctive, much of what they report is not at all hard to envisage actually taking place. For example, the stories of Abraham and Sarah, and the later members of their family, contain incidents that are true to family life, and could easily be paralleled in many families, even today in the twenty-first century. Indeed, the abuse and violence that is perpetuated from one generation to another in Bible families is all too familiar to modern people. But therein lies just the problem, when we try to discern where Old Testament history in the narrow sense actually starts. For all these stories are domestic episodes, a feature which at once renders them more interesting (for everyone likes to explore the dynamic of human relationships), as well as making it more complicated to try to estimate how – if at all – they might be intended to provide some definitive account of Israel's actual historical origins. As we shall see, many of their details are certainly historically plausible within the context of the kind of ancient nomadic lifestyle they depict. But that is not the same thing as being able to establish their literal accuracy, for a novel can be historically plausible without being an actual account of the experience of real people.

■ A historical novel, of course, finds its plausibility precisely in the fact that, while it may not be the actual story of particular individuals, it nevertheless reflects the kind of challenges and opportunities that most people continually face, and they recognize their own struggles within it. In that sense, it is absolutely 'true' despite not being a historical narrative – and certainly more relevant to the lives of later generations than a mere chronicle of events would be likely to be. In the case of these early Old Testament stories, we know for certain that they have been shaped over time so as to address such questions of life and its ultimate meaning with relevance to the experiences not of one, but of several generations of readers. The central conviction of the narratives remained unchanged – that God can be trusted to make, and keep, great promises – but in articulating that message in new ways, the goal of the community of faith was not to preserve its own history as some kind of antiquarian exercise, but rather to ensure that each new generation would receive adequate teaching about the ways of God.

Questions of this sort are a major concern in relation to all the early Old Testament stories – not only the accounts of Israel's earliest ancestors, but also the stories of the exodus and the subsequent settlement of the tribes in the land of Canaan. In different ways, we shall need to keep returning to them throughout our discussion of these narratives. For the moment, it will be sufficient to observe that they are among the most complex of all the questions we need to deal with, and there are no simple answers. Indeed, in the context of an introductory book like this perhaps the most we can aim for is a clear understanding of the nature of the questions, with some indication of possible ways of addressing them. In terms of procedure, I have decided to follow the course of events as they are outlined in the Old Testament narratives, while recognizing that different sections may be of different literary genres and therefore require us to adopt a variety of interpretative approaches. At the same time, I have aimed to keep a clear focus on the underlying spiritual concerns of the final editors of these stories, so as not to lose sight of the message that was the ultimate purpose for which the books were written in the first place.

National identity

The one thing that can be said without any fear of contradiction is that the people of ancient Israel had a well-developed sense of their own national identity. They were especially conscious of the fact that their own values and way of life were different from that of many of their neighbours. The main concern of the average Palestinian farmer was with agriculture, and much of the prevailing religious worship was designed to ensure that nothing would interrupt the cycle of the seasons from one year to another. By contrast, Israel believed that the key to understanding life's mysteries was not to be found primarily in the world of nature, but in the unique and unrepeatable facts of history, and God's hand could therefore be traced in the stories passed down from their forebears, for as far back as it was possible to go.

By the time these stories had been gathered together and written down, the people of ancient Israel were themselves farmers, and they too

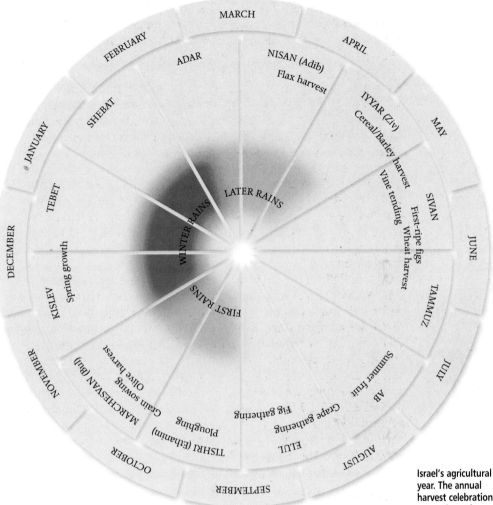

The diagram shows Israel's agricultural year with the following labels arranged in a circle:

MARCH, APRIL, MAY, JUNE, JULY, AUGUST, SEPTEMBER, OCTOBER, NOVEMBER, DECEMBER, JANUARY, FEBRUARY (outer ring months)

ADAR, NISAN (Adib), IYYAR (Ziv), SIVAN, TAMMUZ, AB, ELUL, TISHRI (Ethanim), MARCHESVAN (Bul), KISLEV, TEBET, SHEBAT (Hebrew months)

LATER RAINS, WINTER RAINS, FIRST RAINS

Flax harvest
Cereal/Barley harvest
Vine tending
First-ripe figs Wheat harvest
Summer fruit
Grape gathering
Fig gathering
Ploughing
Grain sowing Olive harvest
Spring growth

Israel's agricultural year. The annual harvest celebration was a time when the Israelites remembered their indebtedness to God. They gave the 'firstfruits' of the harvest as an offering to maintain the worship of Yahweh.

celebrated the annual gathering of the harvest in a religious ceremony. But as they did so, their thoughts centred not on the operations of ploughing, sowing and reaping, but on the past experience of their nation, in partnership with God. As they presented a part of the harvest to God in a religious ceremony, they affirmed their deepest convictions about life in words that have been central to the faith of Jewish people throughout the centuries:

> *My ancestor was a wandering Aramean, who took his family to Egypt to live. They were few in number when they went there, but they became a large and powerful nation. The Egyptians treated us harshly and forced us to work as slaves. Then we cried out for help to Yahweh, the God of our ancestors, who heard us and saw our*

suffering, hardship, and misery. By God's great power and strength we were rescued from Egypt, amidst miracles and wonders, and all kinds of terrifying events. God brought us here and gave us this rich and fertile land. So now I bring to Yahweh the first part of the harvest (Deuteronomy 26:5–10).

No other statement sums up so eloquently what the Old Testament is all about. In just a few words, this ancient creed recalls the most important elements in the remembered story. It tells how God had rescued a disorganized group of slaves from Egypt and made them a nation in their own right; and how in response to this undeserved goodness, the people had given to this God, Yahweh, their worship and obedience.

The founders

The 'wandering Aramean' is occasionally given the name 'Israel', someone who is more often referred to in the Old Testament as Jacob (Genesis 32:28). It is not clear why he should have been referred to as an 'Aramean'. The Arameans became prominent only after about the eleventh century BC, when they established a small empire based in Syria. But like the Israelites, who also emerged as a nation at about the same time, their origins must go further back than that. Throughout the third millennium BC (3000–2000 BC) large numbers of wandering nomads were constantly moving from the deserts of Arabia into the territories controlled by the great civilization centred on Mesopotamia. The reasons for these movements are complex and uncertain. In about 2000 BC, groups of people whom the Babylonians called 'Ammuru' ('westerners'), and who are perhaps to be associated with the Amorites of the Old Testament, moved in and established their own culture in Babylon itself, at Mari, and elsewhere. Many scholars believe that some of these people were the ancestors not only of the Arameans and the Canaanites, but also of Israel. The Old Testament certainly suggests there was some close ethnic connection between all these groups, and this is the context in which its earliest stories of Jacob's ancestors are placed.

This figure of a goat was excavated from the Royal Graves at the site of Ur. It has been dated to approximately 2500BC. The site of this ancient city, associated with Abraham, gives evidence of a civilization that reached back to the fifth millennium BC.

The story proper begins with Abraham and Sarah – or, rather, with Abraham's father Terah – in the city of Ur, at the very heart of the ancient Mesopotamian civilization (Genesis 11:27–30). For some undisclosed reason, they left their home city and the whole family moved some 560 miles (900 km) north-west to the city of Haran. Both these towns had important shrines for the worship of the moon god Sin, and if they were devoted to this deity the move could have been part of a journey of pilgrimage to different centres of worship. There is certainly plenty of evidence to show that Abraham and his family were not originally worshippers of Yahweh: in another account of the same events, a much later leader of Israel began his story of the nation's history with the words, 'Long ago your ancestors lived on the other side of the River Euphrates and worshipped other gods' (Joshua 24:2). Some have discerned traces of religious arguments which involved Abraham's family in physical danger, for in a rather obscure passage he is said to have been 'rescued' from Ur (Genesis 15:7; Isaiah 29:22) in just the same way as the escaping slaves were later 'rescued' (the same Hebrew word) from Egypt (Exodus 20:2; Deuteronomy 5:6).

On the other hand, it is only in the Hebrew manuscripts of Genesis 11 that the city of Ur is mentioned at all. The Greek (Septuagint) version places Abraham and Sarah's original home 'in the land of the Chaldeans', and this could have been a place much nearer to Haran in northern Syria than to Ur, which is on the Persian Gulf. Other stories certainly suggest that their roots were much stronger in Haran than in Ur, for when messengers were later sent to find a wife for their son Isaac, they were told to go to the country of Abraham's birth, a location which turns out to be not Ur, but the area around Haran (Genesis 24:4).

Haran, in modern Syria. From here Abraham, the 'wandering Aramean', with Sarah his wife, moved south into Canaan.

Despite this close connection with the town of Haran and its surrounding countryside, Abraham and Sarah did not make a permanent home there. Instead, they moved on to a different part of the Fertile Crescent – this time travelling another 450 miles (720 km) south-west, into the land of Palestine. There they lived a wandering life, moving about from place to place to find enough grazing for flocks and food for the family. This was the only way newcomers could settle, for the best parts of the land were already occupied by both farmers and city dwellers. This no doubt explains why their movements seem to have been mostly in the south of the country, just to the north and west of the Dead Sea. This was not the best land, but it had many areas suitable for grazing, and only a small resident population. When the grass was exhausted there, nomadic tribes could move either to an oasis like Beersheba or into the fields adjoining towns like Shechem and Hebron. No doubt this land was farmed by the Canaanites, but they probably allowed nomadic groups to put their animals onto it after the crops had been gathered. Even this source of supply was uncertain, though, and like many others of the period, Abraham and Sarah were forced to move as far afield as Egypt at times of particular hardship (Genesis 12:10–20).

Early expressions of faith

Though matters of historical accuracy have become of great concern to modern readers of the Old Testament, this is not where the central interest of the book of Genesis is to be located. In a very specific way, all its books are about God – in particular, about Israel's God, Yahweh – and the entire collection has been formulated in the light of what came to be recognized as the normative spirituality described by the later prophets. God is actually the central character of all these early stories. Abraham and Sarah's move from Haran was not determined by political and social issues, but by their experience of God. Nor was this

Were Abraham and Sarah and their family real people?

One of the major preoccupations of Old Testament scholars for the greater part of the twentieth century concerned the question of how these stories about Israel's ancestors might be understood in the light of what is known of wider events taking place at this time in the lands of which they speak. By the end of the nineteenth century, the stories had come to be commonly regarded either as fiction, or as the vaguely remembered exploits of tribes – even at times of ancient deities – personified to become the story of just a few individuals. On this view, people like the families of Abraham, Isaac and Jacob (conventionally referred to by scholars as 'the patriarchs', though of course many women were among them) could not be regarded as real people, but as representations of various social and religious movements in the millennium before Israel became a nation in the true sense.

As the twentieth century progressed, however, it became obvious that the matter was not quite as simple as that. Expanding knowledge of life in the region during the Middle Bronze Age (2000–1500 BC) has highlighted the fact that, whatever may be said of the details of the stories, the way of life attributed to these people and the kind of activities they are said to have been engaged in do seem to reflect an authentic perception of what was happening in these lands at this time. Ancient documents found at the sites of places like Mari and Nuzi have alerted us to the fact that this was a period of creative cultural innovation initiated by people with a long history of

civilization behind them. By the middle of the twentieth century, increasing numbers of scholars were concluding that these 'patriarchal' stories actually described the existence of real people. One of the leading Old Testament scholars of the day (John Bright) claimed: 'We can assert with full confidence that Abraham, Isaac, and Jacob were actual historical individuals... a part of that migration of seminomadic clans which brought a new population to Palestine in the early centuries of the second millennium BC.' In the light of further study, few people would now wish to express an opinion with quite the same degree of confidence, not least because we can now appreciate that the actual questions to be addressed are more complex than was once imagined. But the various pieces of evidence which were claimed to prove that the patriarchs were 'real people' still stand, and are worth reviewing here, even if they do need to be placed in a somewhat wider context.

Names

Names with linguistic forms similar to Abraham, Isaac, Jacob and others have been found in many ancient documents. This kind of name seems to have been especially popular among the Amorite peoples living in various parts of northern Mesopotamia about 2000 BC. Other names familiar from Genesis – Terah, Nahor, Serug, Benjamin, Levi, Ishmael – were also widely used, though not always as the names of people. Sometimes they appear as place names. Of course none of the occurrences of these names outside the Bible actually refers to the specific people mentioned in the Old Testament as the

something unique to them, for it was also the common experience of all their descendants, most notably their son Isaac and grandson Jacob.

The central thread of the Old Testament story shows how personal experience of God was to be a vital element in the very survival of the whole nation of Israel, over many generations. Yet there is a clear demarcation made here between 'Yahweh', the God on whom Israel's later

---

ancestors of Israel. But these coincidences do show that names of this type were commonly used during the second millennium BC.

Lifestyle

The Tale of Sinuhe describes a nomadic chief in about 1900 BC living in much the same way as is portrayed in the stories of Abraham's family. Like Abraham (Genesis 14:1–16), this clan leader also took part in a war with an alliance of kings. Here again, the names of the kings mentioned in the Old Testament story are typical of the kind of names people had at the time – though there is no way of connecting those with whom Abraham fought to actual named people in other sources. There is, however, plenty of evidence to show that the wandering style of existence portrayed in Genesis reflects many aspects of what is otherwise known of life in the early part of the second millennium BC. Evidence from Mari in particular shows that many tribes were moving about freely at this time, adopting both nomadic and sedentary lifestyles at different times depending on particular circumstances. Those who were wandering lived in a generally stable relationship with those who based themselves in towns and villages. Indeed, they each needed the other to provide goods and services, and the one thing that they both resisted was the attempt of larger city states to exercise a centralized political control over them. All these features are found in the Genesis narratives. The forebears of Israel generally camp near to smallish settlements (Genesis 12:6–9; 13:12–18; 33:18–20),

sometimes staying for long enough to become farmers (26:12), and at times of particular stringency they even become town-dwellers for a while (12:10–20; 20:1–18; 26:6–11). According to some, these narratives depict them operating in locations which would not have been places where wandering nomads could have found a temporary home in later times, a feature of the narratives which has therefore been claimed as further circumstantial support for the overall plausibility of the Genesis narratives.

Customs

The social and legal customs attributed to this period are often different from those which were advocated in later Israel. For example, the law of Leviticus 18:18 forbids a man to be married to two sisters at once, though Jacob certainly was (Genesis 29:15–30). Abraham himself married his half-sister Sarah (Genesis 20:12), though this was also

The nomadic existence described in Genesis fits in well with the picture built up by archaeologists of life in the region in the early part of the second millennium BC.

faith focused, and the religion of the ancestors. One later passage makes it quite clear that these people did not know 'Yahweh', but worshipped a deity they referred to as 'El Shaddai' (Exodus 6:2–3). This phrase has often been translated into English as 'God Almighty', which rather obscures the fact that El was actually a personal divine name, just like Yahweh. 'El Shaddai' meant 'El, the God of the mountain', and in addition the stories of Israel's forebears also mention 'El Elyon' ('El, the Exalted

---

Were Abraham and Sarah and their family real people?
continued

prohibited later (Leviticus 18:9, 11; 20:17; Deuteronomy 27:22). The fact that these anomalies have been preserved in the early stories seems to suggest that the people who wrote them down did not try to assimilate them to the practices of their own day, but handed on authentic traditions in the form they had received them.

This general impression may be confirmed by certain legal documents discovered at Nuzi, for some of the customs described there seem to explain and illuminate otherwise obscure parts of the Old Testament stories. For instance, there is the story of how Abraham's childless wife Sarah presented him with a slave girl by whom to have a child (Genesis 16:1–14). A text from Nuzi explains how in certain marriage contracts a childless wife could be required to provide her husband with just such a substitute. Furthermore, if a child was subsequently born to such a slave, Nuzi law prohibited the expulsion of the slave – a custom that could provide a cultural context to explain why Abraham was so reluctant to send away Hagar and Ishmael (Genesis 21:9–13). Another way in which childless couples at Nuzi could ensure the continuation of their family line was by adopting a slave who would take the place of a son. Such a slave would then inherit their property – though if a natural son was eventually born, the slave-son would lose his rights. When Abraham expressed a fear that his slave Eliezer would succeed him (Genesis 15:1–4), some such custom could be implied. Other social conventions that appear in the stories of Jacob have also been documented at Nuzi.

Considerations of this kind may seem to provide compelling reasons for thinking that these stories of Abraham and Sarah and their descendants make most sense when understood as straightforward narratives of people living in the early part of the second millennium BC. But there are some arguments on the other side.

Anachronisms
Some elements of the stories certainly do not fit into the historical circumstances of the Middle Bronze Age. For example, we know for certain that neither Philistines (Genesis 21:34; 26:6–22) nor Chaldeans (Genesis 11:31; 15:7) were around at that period. It is also the case that camels (Genesis 12:16; 24:35; 30:43; 32:7, 15) were not in widespread use before the twelfth century BC. It is of course not difficult to explain such features as incidental anachronisms that were introduced unconsciously when the stories were first written down, reflecting the knowledge and experience of those who preserved and edited the stories at a much later date. They could even have been introduced deliberately, as a way of hinting at how the old traditions might still be relevant to the concerns of a changing world. Whatever the explanation, they do highlight the fact that these stories have been passed on and reformulated over several generations, and the form in which we now have them is the end product of a fairly extensive process of reinterpretation. By definition, therefore, the reinterpretation needs to be taken into account when seeking to understand them. At the same time, we should remember that the fact that a story has come through a long

One', Genesis 14:18–20), 'El Olam' ('El, the eternal one', Genesis 21:33), as well as 'El-Elohe-Israel' ('El, the God of Israel', Genesis 33:20). El was the chief deity of the Canaanite pantheon, documented most extensively in the religion of ancient Ugarit (which we consider in more detail in a later chapter). By the time of the final editing of the Old Testament books, it tended to be taken for granted that, though they had apparently not realized it, the God who actually was working in the lives of these

period of transmission does not of itself determine its literary genre. A narrative about events that allegedly took place sometime between 2000 and 1200 BC could easily have been written down much later without intrinsically being worthless as history. This is especially the case with stories that have been handed on by word of mouth for many generations before being committed to writing, and there are many examples of this in world literature, particularly accounts preserved in a non-Western context. The existence of anachronisms does not undermine this general consideration.

Interpreting cultural parallels

The way that some scholars have used the evidence from Nuzi and Mari to argue in favour of the essentially historical character of these stories has come under critical scrutiny, particularly from a methodological point of view:

● For such parallels to be really relevant and illuminating, they need to come from a time and place with which the Hebrew ancestors could reasonably be associated. In this case, the place is no problem, for both Mari and Nuzi are located in areas that feature prominently in the Genesis stories. But the date is another question. It has usually been claimed that these parallels date the patriarchs somewhere between 2000 and 1800 BC. The Nuzi texts, however, only go back to about 1500–1400 BC. Against this, it can be argued that customs of the sort described do not come from nowhere. They most typically evolve over a long period of time, and must therefore have existed long before they were written down. That is

probably true, but it proves less than some interpreters imagine, for they also continued long after the date of the written evidence, and most of the practices to which attention has been drawn were probably carried on throughout the whole period from 2000 to 1200 BC.

● The Nuzi materials have sometimes been used quite selectively. For example, the childless wife who gave her husband a slave girl was not at all typical of Nuzi practice in general. The more normal practice would have been for the man to be allowed to find another wife. There are in excess of 300 known texts from Nuzi that deal with family affairs, but less than half a dozen of them have been used to reconstruct a possible cultural background for the Genesis stories.

● In the past, some Nuzi texts have been misinterpreted in the enthusiastic rush to find parallels to the Old Testament. It was at one time claimed that a Nuzi text could explain Rachel's theft of Laban's household gods (Genesis 31:17–21). It was supposed that the possession of them would give her certain rights of inheritance. But it is now clear that the text believed to provide a 'parallel' does not suggest this at all. Of course, one mistaken parallel does not discount the others, but it should alert us to the difficulties involved in making such comparisons accurately so many centuries later. Part of the difficulty is that the Nuzi texts are legal documents, whereas in Genesis social and legal practices are described only incidentally. In such circumstances, it is all too easy to try to fill in what we perceive as gaps by stretching the external evidence to fit – even when it could be quite irrelevant.

ancient figures was the God Yahweh, whose full character was only apparent from the time of Moses onwards. But the stories themselves clearly preserve reminiscences of a belief that Israel's ancestors had been fully a part of the religious culture of Canaan, and when the nation's allegiances were later transferred to Yahweh, that was the starting point for the emergence of a different outlook on life.

Another feature common to these narratives is the way in which

---

Were Abraham and Sarah and their family real people? *continued*

It is clear from all this that some scholars have in the past tried to claim too much, in particular on the question of precise dates for the patriarchs. But it is equally clear that the way of life depicted in these stories in Genesis is quite different from the practices of later Israel, and has some significant similarities to what can otherwise be known of life in the second millennium BC. Any understanding of the historical setting of the family stories of Abraham, Isaac and Jacob must account for these features, which is why many scholars continue to believe that, whatever questions remain unsolved, the way to understand them is by starting from the

assumption that they preserve a broadly accurate account of the activities of those characters whom they describe. Perhaps in reality, though, the most that can be claimed with certainty is that the experiences these stories describe correspond to what is known of population movements that were taking place in the Fertile Crescent throughout the Middle and Late Bronze Ages (roughly 2000–1200 BC). Desert tribes were constantly moving into the Fertile Crescent from outside, and within this rich area individual tribes were always moving from one place to another in search of food and water for themselves and their flocks.

Abraham and Sarah's journeys.

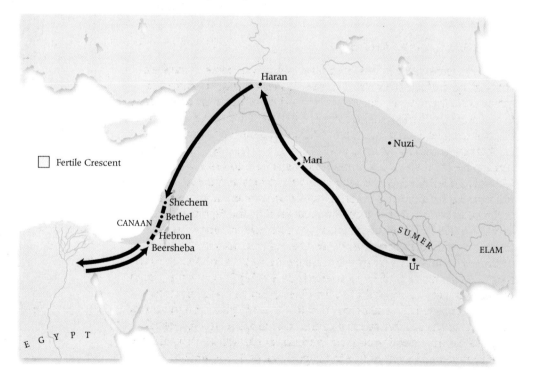

46

God is depicted not as a remote, impersonal force, but as a personal presence deeply connected to the concerns of everyday life. God helped them to find spouses and to have children, as well as meeting their deepest personal and emotional needs. This close involvement of God with the life of the family is repeatedly highlighted by the description of God as 'the God of my father' (Genesis 26:24; 31:5, 29, 42, 53; 32:9; 46:1, 3; 48:15; 49:25; 50:17). God was as close to them as their own family – indeed, in one sense could be thought of as a part of their family. God was the tribal leader. Though from today's perspective, we can no doubt appreciate the potential dangers in this way of thinking of God – for it was easily utilized in the establishment of a patriarchal culture in which men (tribal leaders) were placed in a unique relationship to God, ahead of that available to women and children – that should not prevent us from appreciating this insight into the personal nature of God as one of the most valuable spiritual legacies of this early generation not only to later Israel, but through them to Western culture more widely. There is a deep commitment here to the belief that faith can never be fully satisfied within the rituals of sacred spaces and times, but must be relevant and meaningful in the context of everyday life. Though Abraham's behaviour is frequently less than worthy, it is this aspect of the stories that caused later generations to bestow upon him the accolade of being a 'man of faith' (Hebrews 11:17–19), for he and Sarah found their new destiny through a wholehearted and open-ended commitment to what they knew of the God whom they worshipped.

The birth of the nation

A similar theme underlies the narrative that was to become the foundational story of the nation's self-consciousness: the deliverance of a group of their ancestors from slavery in Egypt in the event which came to be known as the exodus. We have now moved well beyond the story of Abraham and Sarah's first visit to Egypt, and into the family life of Jacob, their grandson. As a result of feuding and jealousy among Jacob's family, one of his sons found himself being sold into Egypt as a slave (Genesis 37:2–28). However, after many hardships and misadventures the unfortunate Joseph was unexpectedly elevated to an important position in Egyptian society. In the face of a great famine, the Egyptian king appointed this foreigner to supervise the rationing of food, and especially to control its distribution to those wandering pastoralists who would inevitably make their way over the Sinai peninsula from Canaan to the more prosperous land of Egypt (Genesis 41:14–57). It was while Joseph was engaged in this work that his brothers (who had sold him into slavery years before) came before him to ask for food, although he was unknown to them. After much suspense and heart-searching, Joseph revealed his true identity, and the brothers, along with their aged father, were reunited and went to live in Egypt (Genesis 42:1 – 45:28).

An Egyptian frieze depicts the harvesting of cereals. The Israelites were leaving the cultivated regions round the Nile for a wilderness where water was scarce and crops non-existent.

Their new-found prosperity was, however, only temporary. Jacob, Joseph, and the rest all died in old age, but their descendants were not to have a happy life. A new Egyptian ruler came to power, and he did not like what he saw: 'These Israelites are so numerous and strong that they are a threat to us' (Exodus 1:9). So the family of Jacob was gradually reduced to slavery, poverty and despair. It is tempting to set the story of Joseph in the times of the Hyksos empire in Egypt. These rulers were themselves non-Egyptians, and for that reason may have been more likely to appoint an outsider like Joseph to a position of some authority. Much of the detail of the Old Testament story seems to reflect what we know of the life of Egypt at this time – and the 'new king, who knew nothing about Joseph' (Exodus 1:8) would perhaps be an appropriate way to describe a native Egyptian king who came to power after the Hyksos had been removed from office.

Here again, this narrative displays the same tantalizing features as the earlier ancestral stories. While preserving just enough historical details to imply that all this could plausibly be related to what is otherwise known of Egyptian culture, the Old Testament takes no interest in such matters, preferring to concentrate on more intimate personal stories. For though this period of slavery was a real evil, it was also ultimately the source of great triumph, and this knowledge is what has determined the way in which the story was told to later generations. As the oppression of the slaves grew worse, so the need for deliverance grew stronger – deliverance that at first was an impossible dream, but which finally became a reality through the dynamic leadership of a man called Moses. Though he had an Egyptian name, and was brought up as an Egyptian, Moses had been born into an Israelite family (Exodus 2:1–10). Moses is depicted as a person with close familiarity with Egyptian

life and culture. Indeed, some have suggested there is enough evidence in the narrative to conclude that he was deeply influenced by the religion of Egypt, especially the worship of the sun god Aten. Akhen-aten, pharaoh of Egypt from 1369 to 1353 BC, had been a fanatical worshipper of this one god, and Moses also turned out to be devoted to the service of just one God, though not the same one. There are certainly some resemblances between Atenism and the worship of Yahweh introduced by Moses. Like Moses' God, Aten was described as 'the god beside whom there is none other'. The worshippers of Aten also laid heavy emphasis on teaching, just as the Torah later came to be associated with Moses. Parts of Psalm 104 praise the wonders of Yahweh's creation in language similar to an Egyptian hymn to the sun that was attributed to Akhen-aten. None of this proves anything specific about Moses and Egypt, for this use of similar language and imagery in worship was common throughout the ancient world. In any case many scholars think that the hymn of Akhen-aten was itself based on another piece of religious poetry that originated in Canaan.

What Moses taught the slaves from Egypt actually had many distinctive features that are not found in Egyptian religion. Like the early ancestors, Moses knew a God who was not just a manifestation of the world of nature, but the God who controlled the world and who could be known in a personal way. The origin of Moses' faith was found not in Egypt, but in the deserts of the Sinai Peninsula. After dropping out of Egyptian society, Moses had come to this region where he met Jethro, the leader of a nomadic tribe. He married Jethro's daughter, and looked after his flocks. It was while doing so that he met God, and standing by a bush that was on fire, yet seemed as if it would not burn away, Moses was commissioned by 'the God of Abraham, Isaac, and Jacob' to rescue the slaves from Egypt (Exodus 3:1–10). At that time, Moses had no interest in seeing either the Egyptians or the slaves, but he finally agreed to return to Egypt to try to persuade the king to release them. But he also had a message for the slaves themselves. In their affliction, they had not always remembered God. But now they would experience God for themselves in a new and dynamic way. For Moses took with him a fresh and deeper understanding of the nature of God: he was to tell the slaves in Egypt, 'The one who is called Yahweh has sent me to you' (Exodus 3:14). There are many unresolved questions about the precise meaning of this personal name of God, which are discussed more fully in a later chapter. It is not absolutely certain that the Hebrew letters YHWH should even be spelled or pronounced as 'Yahweh'. But in spite of that, the general significance of this personal name of God is clear. The meaning given in Exodus is 'I am who I am', that is, a declaration that Yahweh is the creator and sustainer of the whole world and its history. God's work began in the past, continues in the present, and will reach into the future.

The exodus

As with most of the earliest stories in the Hebrew Bible, there continues to be vigorous debate about the nature of the account of the exodus. But there has never been any doubt about its significance either for ancient Israelite faith, or for the Jewish religious tradition more widely. It is a central part of modern Judaism, celebrated in the annual Passover festival. At this, the Jewish child asks about its meaning, and is given the answer in the following traditional terminology:

> *We were Pharaoh's slaves in Egypt, and the Lord our God brought us forth with a mighty hand and an outstretched arm. And if the Holy One, Blessed be He, had not brought our forefathers forth from Egypt, then we, our children, and our children's children would still be slaves in Egypt. So, even though all of us were wise, all of us full of understanding... we should still be under the commandment to tell the story of the departure from Egypt. And the more one tells the story of the departure from Egypt, the more praiseworthy He is.*

Brick-making in Egypt has not changed all that much from the days of Israel's slavery. But they were reduced to making bricks without straw.

As far back as we can probe within the developing Old Testament library, it is impossible to find a single strand of the tradition which does

not, in some shape or form, have a place for the deeply held conviction that in these events God had been directly at work on the people's behalf. The conviction that in this event Israel had their true beginning is deeply embedded in the very oldest parts of the literature. As we shall see, there is much debate about the historical significance of it all, though it is hardly the sort of story that a proud nation would invent to explain its origin, if it had absolutely no basis in fact. Other Old Testament passages contain indications that suggest what later became the nation of Israel consisted of an amalgam of people drawn from various racial and cultural backgrounds, but it was to this event of the exodus, and to this particular group of ancestors, that Israel traced their unique relationship with God. They had not escaped by their own effort, for they had so internalized their oppression that the prospect of overcoming it had never occurred to them. Nor did they have a specially deserving cause, for the world of their day was full of dispossessed ethnic groups suffering at the hands of those who were more powerful.

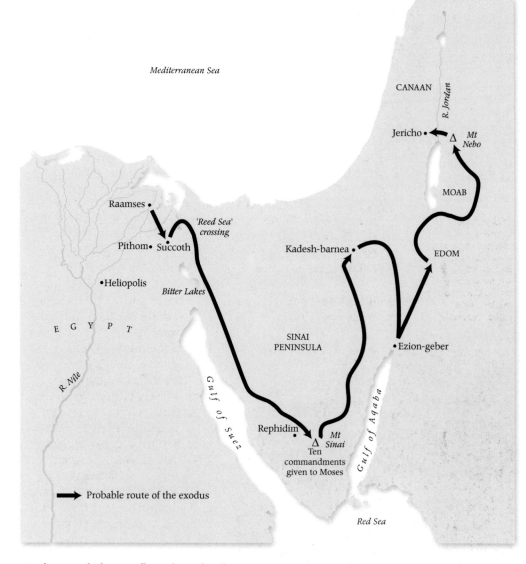

The probable route of the exodus.

As the people later reflected on this formative experience of their nation, they could only conclude that it happened to them only because the God of whom Moses spoke had, for some inexplicable reason, chosen to deliver them.

The account of that momentous deliverance contains all the characteristic ingredients of a great epic story. The slaves leave secretly in the middle of the night, only to be pursued by the Egyptian armies. Then, just as they are about to be caught, trapped by a stretch of water, a way miraculously opens before them and the slaves get to the other side, while the pursuing army perishes beneath the waves (Exodus 12:1–51; 13:17–22; 14:1 – 15:27). Guided by Moses, they head out into the Sinai desert, and to their first and most important destination: Mount Sinai (Exodus 16:1 – 18:27). Much energy has been expended in trying to pinpoint an actual location for all these events. For example, the crossing of the water was traditionally located at some point on the Red Sea, though the Old Testament itself does not make this identification. The Hebrew text speaks of a 'sea of reeds', which would be an unlikely name for the Red Sea. In any case, the area of Goshen where the slaves had lived was much further north than the Red Sea, probably near the city of Avaris. It is therefore likely that, insofar as the writers of the story intended to point to a particular geographical location, the water that divided to allow the escaping slaves to cross was most probably somewhere in the region of what is now the Suez Canal.

The location of Mount Sinai is also a matter of some dispute. Traditionally, it has been located in the south of the Sinai Peninsula, at the site now called Jebel Musa. But since Moses' father-in-law Jethro, who was a Midianite, is clearly associated with this mountain, some have suggested that it should be located much further east, across the Gulf of Aqaba, which was the land of the Midianites (Exodus 3:1; 18:1–12). Others have suggested that Sinai should be located at Jebel Hilal, just to

The mountains of Sinai, where Israel's covenant relationship with Yahweh was formed.

the south of Palestine itself, since the escaping slaves had an encounter with Amalekites, who also lived much further north than the traditional site (Exodus 17:8–16). But it is difficult to locate the mountain by such considerations, for both these other ethnic groups were pastoral nomads themselves, and at any given moment could have been found almost anywhere in the region. It is certainly not unlikely that a group such as the Old Testament describes would have headed south on their escape from Egypt, rather than going directly east, for the main roads between Egypt and Canaan were patrolled by many Egyptian garrisons, whereas the only activity in the south centred around a number of isolated copper mines.

The covenant

The exodus itself was just the beginning of the story, and it was not until the escaping slaves reached Mount Sinai that the full impact and meaning of all this became clear to them. Just as the escape from Egypt formed the core of later Israel's national consciousness, so the events at Mount Sinai became the crucial factor in their religious outlook. For here in a solemn convocation, prompted by Moses, the escaping slaves recognized their debt to Yahweh

and pledged themselves to serve and worship this God alone (Exodus 19:1 – 24:18). Though the narrative contains both dramatic and terrifying descriptions of the presence of God on the holy mountain, the central feature of this awesome occasion was actually the commitment that God made to Israel, and the obligations that Israel accepted in return. God's care and concern for these enslaved people had been active even before they were aware of it. The escape from Egypt was the culmination of God's purposes for them, and the memory of that momentous event and the people's response to it came to dominate the national life of Israel. This is what the Old Testament means by 'the covenant': an agreement in which the freed slaves were reminded of what God had done for them, and they were called in return to promise to be loyal to the laws Moses now gave them in God's name. Somewhat surprisingly, these commands were essentially moral require-ments rather than being narrowly concerned with the observance of more obviously religious duties, such as worship. The tension between these two ways of understanding true spirituality was to extend throughout the subsequent history of the nation, but the central theme of the Old Testament is that honesty, truth and justice were far more important to Yahweh than the perfunctory performance of religious rites. These values are summarized in the ten commandments (Exodus 20:1–17) and, in important ways, can be said to have formed the basic foundation for the whole of later Israelite society.

At one time it was imagined that the high moral ideals recorded in the book of Exodus and elsewhere are too sophisticated to have originated in the primitive age of Moses, and therefore must have been read back into Israelite history at a relatively late stage in the editing of the stories, after the age of the great prophets. In the nineteenth century, there was much support for an evolutionary view of history, which imagined that the moral development of the human race must have

---

The ark of the covenant

The Old Testament depicts the spiritual realities of the covenant relationship being expressed in Israel's worship of God right from the very start, even in the desert. Worship there is described in a special tent-shrine, often called the 'tabernacle', at the centre of which was a wooden box called 'the ark of the covenant'. Like similar 'holy boxes' in Egypt, it was decorated with religious symbols, and overlaid with gold. Naturally, it needed to be portable, and was equipped with rings so it could be carried shoulder-high on poles. According to one of the most ancient pieces of poetry in the Old Testament, this portable ark represented in symbol the fact that God was with the escaping slaves (Numbers 10:35–36). Yahweh was not a God who could be depicted in a visual way, through a statue or some other artifact, but the ark served as a visible throne for the invisible Yahweh. It was a symbolic reminder of the central events of Mount Sinai, declaring that God was always with the people, and was to be their only guide. Indeed, the connection with the covenant-making events may have been quite a literal one, for at least one passage suggests that the ark itself contained the actual tablets on which the covenant agreement had been set out (1 Kings 8:9).

As time passed, the ark assumed even greater importance in the life of the people. The fates of Israel's earliest kings, Saul and David, hinged on their treatment of the ark. Saul despised it, and was rejected; David respected it, and was politically successful. It also came to play an important part in the worship of the Temple at Jerusalem. The liturgy contained within Psalm 132 suggests that in a covenant renewal ceremony the ark would be paraded through the streets of Jerusalem, before returning to the Temple as a sign of God's renewed and lasting presence with the nation. Other psalms also reflect its important position in the ritual of worship at the Temple, though they do not always mention it by name. Many scholars believe that when the Old Testament uses the title 'the Lord of hosts', this is a cryptic reference to God's presence as symbolized in the ark. Other terms, such as 'glory', also seem to be used regularly in reference to it (e.g. 1 Samuel 4:21–22). The Old Testament gives no hint of the ark's ultimate fate, though it is reasonable to suppose that it would be one of the religious objects that later kings of Judah moved in and out of the Temple as they changed their religious allegiances in the desperate effort to preserve political independence. Certainly, all trace of it disappears after the invasion of Nebuchadnezzar in 586 BC.

followed the principles of biological evolution, moving from primitive to more sophisticated moral attitudes. Since the prophets clearly had a highly developed moral sensitivity, then by definition previous generations must have operated with much cruder assumptions and expectations. Philosophically, this way of understanding human development was killed off early in the twentieth century by the manifest brutality of the First World War, and then later the Nazi holocaust, which showed that highly sophisticated people could easily behave in barbaric ways. In any case, growing knowledge of life in the ancient civilizations of the Akkadians, the Sumerians, the Egyptians and others has shown that their standards of morality were very highly developed, and much of the civil (case) law of the Old Testament bears a close resemblance to concepts of justice going back at least as far as the law code of King Hammurabi of Babylon (c. 1700 BC). Some scholars have argued that the distinctively religious and moral requirements of the Old Testament law (the apodictic law) can also be traced to a very early period. It seems that an important aspect of the religious life of Israel was a festival held every autumn, in which the covenant between God and the people was both celebrated and renewed. On this occasion, the people were reminded of what God had done for them, and of the responsibilities placed on them in return – to which they in turn would then reaffirm their allegiance. It is assumed

---

The form of the covenant

The general idea of a 'covenant' was not unique to ancient Israel. Covenants regulated all sorts of behaviour in the ancient world, notably international relations. Close scrutiny of the legal framework of the covenant drawn up between Israel and God at Mount Sinai reveals a number of similarities to other legal documents from the Late Bronze Age period (1550–1200 BC). One of the clearest examples of this legal form is to be found in a series of treaties relating to the Hittite empire, spelling out the duties of smaller states which had been annexed by the more powerful Hittites. Similar legal formulations were also used by other nations, and naturally their subject matter was generally of a political nature. But they are of interest to Old Testament scholars because of a number of formal elements that they have in common with the way the covenant made at Mount Sinai was expressed. The following similarities can be traced:

● **Introduction of the speaker** In a political treaty, the king would introduce himself by name, just as God does in the introduction to the ten commandments (Exodus 20:2).

● **Historical background** The king then reminded the other party of what he had done on their behalf – usually military intervention of some kind. In the Old Testament, God reminds the people of their unexpected deliverance from Egypt (Exodus 20:2).

● **Requirements** Then follow the obligations which are placed by the king on the other party. In a political treaty these would normally be military obligations, while in the Old Testament they consist of the requirements of the Law.

● **The document** Arrangements were then made for the treaty to be written down, and deposited in a suitable place to be read at specified times. There is no such provision directly linked to the ten commandments in the book of Exodus, but similar instructions are given in Deuteronomy 27:1–8.

that the ten commandments, and other laws associated with them in the book of Exodus, would be recited on these occasions. Since evidence for such a covenant renewal ceremony appears quite early in the narratives of Israel's story, there is every reason to suppose that the high ideals found there, and the covenant basis on which they exist, go back to the earliest period of Israel's experience of God.

To the promised land

Most of the material in the books of Exodus, Leviticus, Numbers and Deuteronomy is set in the context of an extended journey by the liberated slaves, as they crossed the desert from Egypt to the land of Canaan, where they would eventually settle. Like other aspects of the earliest stories of the nation, all this was eventually edited into its present form from the perspective of a quite different political and spiritual situation many centuries after the events it describes. Embedded within the narratives, however, are glimpses of the kind of challenges that people would have encountered at that historical period. Like many emerging nations, they began as a motley collection of refugees, who were joined by other people as they left the land of Egypt, and the events at Mount Sinai then became the first stage in the process by which this disparate bunch of people began to be moulded into the nucleus of a

---

The form of the covenant *continued*

● **Witnesses** were called to seal the covenant – usually the deities of both states. The Old Testament contains several examples of witnesses to the covenant. In Exodus 24, twelve pillars were set up, probably for this purpose, while a central part of the covenant ceremony recorded in Joshua 24 consisted of a large stone being put in a public place to serve as a witness to the promises that had been made (Joshua 24:25–28).

● **Curses and blessings** were then invoked, depending on whether the treaty was observed or disregarded. In the Old Testament, there is a long series of such curses and blessings in the book of Deuteronomy (Deuteronomy 27:11 – 28:68).

It is not suggested that a legal document of this kind was self-consciously used to form a basis for the way in which the covenant between Yahweh and Israel was set out. Indeed, it is not possible to make an exact correlation between the covenant made at Mount Sinai and these covenant forms used in the political sphere. For example, while it is not at all

difficult to locate all the elements of the secular treaty form somewhere in the Old Testament, there is no one single context which contains them all. In addition, since the Israelites perceived themselves as being in covenant with God, rather than with a military ruler, that must presumably have added a distinctive element to how the covenant would be understood and expressed. However, there are indications that Israel was familiar with this form of political covenant, for they made one themselves with the Gibeonites (Joshua 9). In addition, the fact that the events at Mount Sinai were articulated and preserved in a form of words that had such a widespread use in the Late Bronze Age – which was certainly the time of Israel's emergence as a nation – can be taken to imply that, whatever other questions may remain outstanding, the origin of Israel's distinctive faith may quite plausibly be traced back to the earliest period of national consciousness.

Flocks of migrating quails would appear in the wilderness, and they became a source of food for the Israelites as they journeyed through the desert. Quails were also eaten by the Egyptians, as depicted in this wall painting of men using nets to catch the birds.

single nation. As they pressed on towards their ultimate goal, the journey through the desert was to prove hazardous. Not only were the refugees forced to work out the full implications of their embryonic faith in terms of their everyday living, but they also found themselves in conflict with other groups of wandering nomads who, like them, were wanting to establish a permanent homeland for themselves. But these isolated political and military skirmishes are not the central concern of the story. The one thread that holds everything else together is Moses' faith and determination. Though he himself did not live to set foot in the land that was to become his people's national home, he had no doubt of the final outcome of their quest for self-determination. Like the members of Abraham and Sarah's family before him, he was convinced that the direction of his own life, and the future of the escaped slaves and their descendants, was not at the mercy of impersonal social and political forces, but would always be under the care and protection of a loving and all-powerful God: 'People of Israel, no god is like your God... There is no one like you, a nation saved by Yahweh [who is] your shield and your sword, to defend you and give you victory' (Deuteronomy 33:26, 29).

Dating the exodus and conquest of Canaan

The question of Israel's emergence as a nation is one of the most hotly debated aspects of Old Testament scholarship today. There are many diverse and mutually exclusive views on the matter. Some have complete confidence in using the Bible stories of exodus and conquest as a basis for historical investigation, while others dismiss these narratives entirely as the creation of later generations, specifically the attempts of the royal house of David to establish a long historical pedigree for itself. In between, it is possible to find every imaginable shade of opinion on the matter. So asking how we might date these events is not a simple matter, and many scholars would say it is a waste of time to try to do so anyway. There are certainly many complex issues involved, and there is much confusion over basic issues, such as the nature of the 'conquest' itself. This debate is discussed in relation to the emergence of Israel as an identifiable nation in Canaan in the next chapter. Here we shall confine ourselves to a review of some of the evidence that has been deemed to relate to a possible date for the exodus.

Attempts to set a date for the exodus have ranged from the third millennium to the eleventh century BC, though three possibilities have received more support than others:

● Some place the exodus in the middle of the sixteenth century BC, at the time when the Hyksos were expelled from Egypt. This view goes back at least as far as the first-century AD Jewish historian Josephus, who equated the two events (*Against Apion* 1.16). This is certainly the only known large-scale population movement of ethnically Asiatic peoples from Egypt in roughly the direction of Canaan. In spite of its attractions, this view is hard to justify, if only because it would imply that a further 400 years elapsed before the formation of anything that can be identified as an Israelite state, under Saul and David.

● Others, beginning from what seems to be the chronology of the Bible itself, have placed the exodus in about 1440 BC. But this is problematical for a variety of reasons, especially the difficulty of correlating it with any possible interpretation of the archaeological evidence relating to early Israel, and again the excessively long time span that would need to be covered by the period of the Judges.

● The most widely accepted date would place the exodus somewhere between about 1280 and 1240 BC. This seems to accord with some of the archaeological evidence, and also matches what is otherwise known about population movements and the emergence of new settlements not only in Canaan itself, but in the region to the east of the River Jordan as well.

The chronological evidence which has been used to try to establish some plausible date for the exodus falls into three main categories: the biblical material, various textual remains and the discoveries of archaeologists in Canaan. They do not always all point in the same direction as one another, hence the diversity of opinions on the matter.

Old Testament dates

According to 1 Kings 6:1, Solomon began to build the Temple in Jerusalem in the fourth year of his reign, which is said to be 'Four hundred and eighty years after the people of Israel left Egypt'. Working back from Solomon's time, this would imply that the editor of Kings believed the exodus took place in about 1440 BC. However, even the evidence of the Old Testament itself does not consistently support that:

● The book of Judges contains a good many chronological indications, and adding together the successive periods of rule of the various judges gives a minimum time between the exodus and Solomon of 554 years. Of course, we do not know for certain that the judges followed one another in chronological succession. Since they were mainly local leaders, there was probably a good deal of overlap between them, in which case the total time span indicated in Judges could in reality be much less than it first seems to be. In addition, the period of forty years often figures in these stories, and that was a conventional way of referring to the time from one generation to the next – so perhaps it was never intended to be a very precise measurement of time.

● At the end of the book of Ruth, the genealogy of Solomon separates him from Nahshon, his ancestor who lived at the time of the exodus (Numbers 1:7), by only six generations. That would normally be about 200 years – though here, as in other biblical ancestor lists, some generations may have been left out.

● According to Exodus 12:40, the Israelite tribes left Egypt after they had lived there for 430 years. That would seem to imply a possible date for the exodus in about 1250 BC, which in turn would mean that Joseph went to Egypt in the time of the Hyksos rulers, something that at least sounds plausible because as non-Egyptians themselves they would have been more likely than native rulers to favour a person like Joseph. This timescale would also appear to rule out the traditional view that the exodus took place around 1440 BC, because adding 430 years to that would arrive at a date for Joseph much earlier than any plausible dating of the generation represented by the stories of Abraham. Here again, though, even the biblical evidence is not straightforward for the Septuagint makes the 430 years include both the time the Israelites were in Egypt, and the time they were in Canaan prior to that.

The only reasonable conclusion is that the dates in the Old Testament are inconsistent, and in particular the indication contained in 1 Kings 6:1 is problematic. Of course, it may well be that it was never intended to be taken as a strictly chronological statement, for 480 years is twelve times forty, which could be

a way of indicating a dozen generations, or simply a very long time. Insofar as the other biblical dates can be harmonized with one another, they appear to imply a thirteenth-century date for the exodus.

Evidence from other texts

The Amarna Letters are one particular source of information used by scholars to elucidate aspects of this period. They consist of a series of pillar-shaped tablets written in cuneiform script, mostly in a form of Akkadian, which was the diplomatic language of the time. They date from the early fourteenth century, and were written by various rulers in Canaan

The Amarna Letters, tablets written in cuneiform script, give evidence of a period of instability in their relationships between Egypt and its neighbours in the years before Israel settled in Canaan.

and Syria to Pharaoh Akhen-aten (1369–1353 BC) and his predecessor Amenhotep III (1398–1361 BC). In particular, they complain of the activities of groups of people called 'apiru' (also

Dating the exodus and conquest of Canaan *continued*

variously spelled 'hapiru', 'habiru' and 'aperu'), whose warlike activities were creating tensions and disturbance throughout the area. The names 'apiru' and 'Hebrew' probably have some linguistic connection, though it is not possible to make a simple identification between these groups and the stories of Israel's early life in Canaan. At least one letter refers to them as former slaves, while the general picture is of a significant underclass on the fringes of Canaanite society who, if they succeeded in their aims, were regarded as likely to provide a rallying-point around which other disadvantaged people might gather and instigate some sort of social revolution. As we will see when we move on to the stories of Joshua and Judges, this seems to have been one aspect of the upheavals that took place as Israelite culture came to birth.

The 'shasu' are another group of nomadic people mentioned in various Egyptian texts compiled between about 1500 and 1150 BC. Their lifestyle is also

described in terms reminiscent of the Old Testament depictions of early Israel, wandering in and out of Egyptian settlements, sometimes living peaceably, at other times engaged in military skirmishes, and again occasionally being captured as slaves.

While various scholars have claimed that either or both of the apiru and shasu peoples are to be identified with groups that later became part of Israel, the main value of these records is to show that the kind of population movements described in the accounts of the exodus do seem to reflect what was happening on the borders of Egypt and Canaan during the Late Bronze Age. Insofar as they may be relevant, these texts therefore seem to support a date for the exodus in the thirteenth century BC.

Archaeological evidence

Exodus 1:11 names two Egyptian cities and claims that 'The Israelites built the cities of Pithom and Rameses to serve as supply centres for the king [of Egypt].'

This relief, from the temple of Rameses II, depicts prisoners of different nationalities, and gives some indication of the extent of Egyptian military activity. From the left, a Libyan, a Syrian, a Hittite, a Philistine and another Syrian.

Pithom was actually an old town, but the finest structure in it was a temple built by Rameses II (1290–1224 BC), and there is no evidence for any earlier pharaoh building there. Rameses is certainly to be identified with the capital city of Rameses II, built by him on the site of the ancient capital Tanis. This may have been the capital of the Hyksos kings in the century preceding their expulsion in 1540 BC, but the pharaohs of the succeeding dynasty had their capital at Thebes (except for Akhen-aten, who moved even further from Tanis). All this would appear to support the notion that the exodus took place sometime after 1290 BC. Evidence from the reign of a later pharaoh, Merneptah, suggests that it could not have been later than about 1240 BC, for in 1220 BC he recorded an attack on various peoples in Canaan, in the course of which he mentions 'Israel' as a recognizable component of the Canaanite population.

The archaeological evidence from Canaan itself, however, is more uncertain and its interpretation continues to be the subject of changing fads and fashions among scholars. There is a more extensive account of this debate in the next chapter, but a number of points should be noted in relation to its possible relevance to dating the exodus:

● At one time, the strongest argument for dating the exodus towards the end of the fifteenth century BC was the conclusion of archaeologist John Garstang that Jericho had been taken by Joshua not later than 1400 BC. Indeed, he excavated the remains of walls and other buildings which he believed proved the literal truth of the Old Testament story even down to its details. However, it is now known for certain that his interpretation of the evidence does not square with the facts.

● Much the same is true for most other sites that have been excavated. For while there is much evidence of destruction throughout Canaan in the thirteenth century BC, there is nothing much that can positively be connected with the Old Testament story. Many sites do provide evidence of a destruction in which the sophisticated culture of the Canaanite city states was replaced by a much more primitive lifestyle, and some scholars have taken this as evidence of the Israelite invasion. But in reality, it is not quite so simple, for there is no real knowledge about the nature of a typically Israelite culture at this period, other than what might be deduced from the self-validating assumption that this less sophisticated style must have been Israelite. In any case, with only a few exceptions, the cities that have yielded most evidence for such a thirteenth-century destruction are not those that feature most prominently in the Old Testament record.

There are so many different possible conclusions to be drawn from all this conflicting data that almost the only safe thing to say is that we cannot certainly date the exodus, though a majority of scholars who engage with this discussion would tend to place it in the thirteenth century. However, there are so many uncertainties in this entire enterprise that a growing number of scholars are wondering whether this is the right kind of question to be asking. Should it be that, instead of searching for evidence of a once-for-all conquest of Canaan by the Israelite tribes, their arrival in the land ought rather to be understood from a completely different perspective – either by supposing that only one particular group of what later came to be Israel was involved in the exodus events, or by seeing the emergence of Israel as a nation more in terms of the internal development and change of Canaanite society itself? These possibilities cannot be considered in relation to the exodus without also taking account of the stories of the Israelite conquest of Canaan contained in the books of Joshua and Judges.

3 A Land Flowing with Milk and Honey

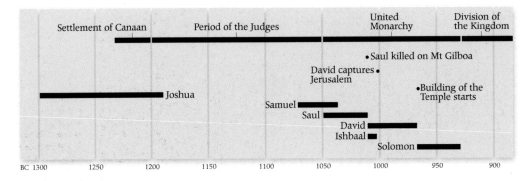

Settlement of Canaan | Period of the Judges | United Monarchy | Division of the Kingdom

Saul killed on Mt Gilboa

David captures Jerusalem

Joshua

Building of the Temple starts

Samuel

Saul

David

Ishbaal

Solomon

BC 1300   1250   1200   1150   1100   1050   1000   950   900

Canaan and its history

The land of Canaan had a long and illustrious history. Documents discovered at Ebla in north Syria testify to the existence of many important towns there as early as 2300 BC, and the city of Jericho is believed to be the oldest inhabited settlement in the world, going back perhaps as far as 9000 BC. Throughout most of the second millennium BC this land was controlled by the Egyptians, who generally governed it through local rulers, of whom there were a great many. Both Egyptian records of the time and archaeological findings from different sites reveal a complex system of intensely populated city states, especially in the central, most fertile parts of the country. Each city was independent and self-sufficient, with its own land and its own rulers. The next city might be as little as 3 miles (5 km) away, but every local king was considered to be directly responsible to Egypt, rather than to other neighbouring rulers. This was an important part of Egyptian policy, and helped to minimize the possibility of local alliances emerging to challenge Egyptian rule. Throughout ancient times, the land of Canaan was always of strategic importance to whatever major power was dominant in the region. The great trade routes linking Egypt with Mesopotamia ran through this land, and the greatest concentration of small city states was to be found alongside the road from Egypt to Syria, ensuring that strategic sites were controlled by vassal rulers who could be trusted to maintain Egypt's own security. In the hill country, things

This stone monument (or 'stele') was erected by King Merneptah of Egypt after a military expedition into Canaan. Its text includes the earliest reference to 'Israel' outside the Bible.

were never quite so well organized. Fewer people wanted to live there anyway, and in addition, a city in the hills needed much more land to be self-sufficient. For this reason, it had always been easier for pastoralist nomads to move about in these more remote areas of the country.

By the end of the Late Bronze Age, however, Egypt's power was diminishing, and towards the end of the thirteenth century BC we find the first reference outside the Bible to 'Israel' as the name of a nation. After a military expedition into Canaan, Pharaoh Merneptah of Egypt (1213–1203 BC) constructed a stone monument as a record of his exploits. In its inscription, he gives an account of various Canaanite people whom he had defeated: 'Ashkelon has been overcome; Gezer has been captured; Yanoam is made non-existent; Israel is laid waste and his seed is not.' The actual terminology used in this inscription is significant in understanding the nature of 'Israel' at this period. The fact that Israel is listed alongside other significant powers within Canaan suggests that it was a force to be reckoned with, and in military terms was their equal, if not an actual partner in some anti-Egyptian coalition. However, the phraseology of the inscription draws a subtle distinction between Ashkelon, Gezer and Yanoam as fortified city states, and Israel as a more loosely organized people group, which may not have had fixed territorial boundaries.

This inscription is complemented by a series of four battle reliefs in the temple at Karnak, which were once believed to have been commissioned by Rameses II, but are now considered to be the work of Merneptah, depicting the same three city states and the 'people' of Israel. This is the earliest-known visual representation of Israelites, and the

For centuries before the time of Israel's entry into Canaan, Egypt had raided other lands and taken captives. This relief from a temple at Abusir shows an Egyptian ocean-going vessel laden with Syrian prisoners. The masts of the boat have been lashed down, and the three rudders lifted out of the water.

interesting thing about it is that it shows them dressed in exactly the same way as the other Canaanites, and not like nomadic 'shasu', implying that these particular Israelites, at least, were not nomadic migrants, but indigenous Canaanites.

In the event, Merneptah's optimism about his military achievements turned out to be unjustified, for Egypt's power in the area soon collapsed, and the strong alliance of Egyptian-backed Canaanite city states began to lose its grip. Within a short time, the whole land had fallen into the hands of only four or five separate rulers, all of whom were newcomers. Israel was certainly one such group, while the Philistines were another. Egyptian records mention the arrival of at least two separate waves of 'Sea Peoples' during the thirteenth and twelfth centuries BC. They consisted of several groups of migrants, all of whom threatened Egyptian dominance of the region. Prominent in the second wave were the Philistines, though they were not the only group among these 'Sea Peoples', which also included the Tjeker, Shekelesh, Denyen and Weshnesh – none of whom feature in the narratives of the Old Testament. These related groups appear to have originated from Crete and the area around the Aegean Sea, to the east of Greece, and had been recruited as mercenaries to help fortify and defend the Canaanite city states. A temple inscription of Rameses III (1198–1167 BC) depicts these people, and shows not only soldiers, but also women and children, suggesting that they were not just armies, but entire populations, searching for a new place in which to live. The Philistines later appear in the Bible narratives as Israel's major competitors, struggling to gain control of the same land. They eventually settled mainly along the sea coast, adopting the same kind of political structure that the Egyptians had imposed, and establishing five city states of their own: Gaza, Ashkelon, Ashdod, Ekron and Gath. They also eventually gave their name to the whole country (Palestine). But at this earlier period, they were just one of several ethnic groups – Israel included – who were struggling to establish a foothold in Canaan, and given that what became Israel seems to have incorporated people of different origins, it is even conceivable that some of those who were originally the 'Sea Peoples' were included in what later became 'Israel'.

The one distinguishing feature of the state that eventually emerged as 'Israel' seems to have been its concept of statehood. Under the old regime in Canaan, political power had always gone hand in hand with the possession of a city, which in turn meant that real power always resided in the hands of just a few privileged people. But the kind of state that developed under the influence of the covenant from Mount Sinai was underwritten by a different understanding of human society, in which class structure had no part to play. For a nation whose corporate identity was forged out of the story of a group of people who had been slaves, it was difficult to justify any one individual claiming a position of personal superiority, for in the beginning they had all been nobodies, and the only thing that made them a nation was the undeserved generosity of God. Israelite national identity was always firmly based on their understanding of the nature of God, and this was to have far-reaching consequences not only during the formative period of their history, but also throughout their entire existence as a nation. It meant that all elements of their population were of equal importance, and their ultimate responsibility was not to some centralized power structure, but to God alone.

The emergence of Israel

These changes in Canaanite political life are all well documented from Egyptian records, as well as by archaeological evidence from various sites throughout the land itself. Between about 1400 and 1200 BC, there was radical transformation of many aspects of life in Canaan. The power of Egypt declined, and the relatively advanced culture of the Canaanite city states was mostly replaced by a different way of life, and shortly after the end of this period, Israel had emerged as a recognizable national entity of some kind. So much is clear. But beyond that there is no generally agreed understanding of the course of Israel's development at this period, and in trying to integrate all the many different strands of information relating to the changing culture of Late Bronze Age Canaan, perhaps the only certain conclusion is that the story of how the nation of Israel first took shape within this context is going to be very complex. Great political and social movements leading to the formation of a new nation can hardly be simple and straightforward, though there is always a strong temptation to search for neat solutions to questions about such matters. It is intrinsically probable that the people of Israel became a nation in their own land by adopting different tactics at different times and places. The Bible story itself describes a 'mixed multitude' of various ethnic origins attaching themselves to the Israelite slaves who left Egypt (Exodus 12:38), and other hints throughout the narratives of Joshua and Judges imply that the emergence of Israel did not happen in a simple linear fashion. The Old Testament itself incorporates diverse strands in its stories, and during the course of the twentieth century different scholars formed their own theories in the effort to explain exactly how these strands related to one another and how they can be understood in the light of known facts about changes taking place in Canaan during the Late Bronze Age and on into the beginning of the Iron Age. All of them can claim some support in the Old Testament itself, but none is entirely free from problems. Over the years, at least three main models have been used to try to give the best explanation of how the nation of Israel emerged from the changing social and political circumstances of Canaan at this period.

Armed struggle

A quick reading of the stories in the Old Testament book of Joshua can give the impression that the land of Canaan became the land of Israel almost overnight, as a result of a series of spectacular battles and conquests. In fact, the account in Joshua records the capture of only a few Canaanite city states, and makes it clear that even at the end of Joshua's successful military exploits much of the land remained unconquered (Joshua 13:1–7). Nevertheless, the successes of Joshua's armies form the core of the Old Testament story, and many scholars believe that the successful establishment of the Israelite tribes in Canaan owed more to this than to any other cause.

The evidence of archaeology has often been claimed to support this belief. In the 1930s, John Garstang carried out extensive excavations at the site of Jericho, and discovered what he took to be incontrovertible evidence of Joshua's capture of the city: walls that had literally fallen flat, and much evidence of destruction by fire (Joshua 6). On his calculations, this destruction had happened not long after 1400 BC, and since he gave a fifteenth-century date to the exodus, this therefore coincided almost exactly with the time when he believed the Israelite armies were invading the land. Investigations by later archaeologists, however, have shown this conclusion to be totally false. Following the usual procedure, Garstang dated his finds by reference to the layer of the mound at Jericho in which he found them, but what he did not know was that over the centuries much of the top of the mound had

Although the book of Joshua suggests that the Canaanites were easily defeated by Israel, this may only have been because the separate city states failed to unite. Their weaponry, from war chariots down to swords and daggers such as these, was fairly sophisticated.

been worn away at this point – and for that reason, the remains he found were actually from a much lower level than they appeared to be. In fact, they were from a city that had existed on the site a full 1,000 years earlier than the time of Joshua. Unless other finds come to light (and archaeologists have not yet worked over the whole mound of Jericho), it seems that nothing substantial is left of the city that stood there at the end of the Late Bronze Age.

Evidence from other sites is more specific, and shows signs of widespread violence and disruption in many cities during the thirteenth century BC. The fact that this destruction was apparently followed by the emergence of a more primitive culture than the one it replaced has been taken to prove that it was the work of the Israelite tribes, on the assumption that nomads coming in from the desert would have a less sophisticated way of life than that of the Canaanite city states. None of this can prove by itself that the destruction uncovered by archaeologists was the work of Israel's armies, or indeed that it happened as a result of any kind of invasion from outside: it is at least as plausible that this evident collapse of Canaanite culture came about because of internal feuding among the city states, which in turn was encouraged by the decline of the Egyptian power that had so successfully united the land. In addition, since the people who later emerged as 'Israel' were not the only ones trying to establish themselves at this time, much of this disruption could as easily be attributed to Philistines, Ammonites or others.

Facing page: the division of Canaan between the tribes of Israel.

While it is natural to speculate, the truth is that archaeology really has little useful information to offer on a possible Israelite conquest of the land. This has led some to doubt whether there ever was a 'conquest' in any significant sense. They point out that the military strength of the Canaanite city states would easily have repelled wandering tribes with no previous experience of warfare, especially since the Canaanites possessed relatively sophisticated equipment, such as chariots. This argument, however, can be turned on its head in light of the fact that the existing Canaanite culture was already declining at this time – not to mention the fact that, throughout history, minority groups inspired by a vision of what they believe to be right have often been able to overthrow highly organized and well-equipped armies that in theory should have quelled their opposition effortlessly. The whole picture of Israel's early history is so dominated by the stories of military success that it is hard to ignore it completely without dismissing the Old Testament account altogether. Equally, however, it is not the only element in the Old Testament story, even if it is the most prominent. The book of Joshua itself claims only that military campaigns secured a foothold in the central hill country which was to be the heart of Israelite territory, while the flatter and more fertile areas like the Plain of Jezreel were not taken over at this time – and in addition, many fortified towns such as Jerusalem and Gezer also stayed firmly in Canaanite hands.

Peaceful infiltration

The apparently incomplete nature of the initial conquest of the country has led other scholars to suggest that much – or even all – of the land was taken over in a different way as the Israelite tribes gradually infiltrated Canaanite society until eventually they became the dominant group. This understanding of the situation has been especially articulated by the German scholar Albrecht Alt. He began by analysing the social structure of the land both before and after the period when Israel was emerging as a nation, noting that the organization of Israelite society was quite different from the closely controlled hierarchies that had been established under the Canaanite city states. But he also drew attention to the fact that those invaders like the Philistines, who settled where the city states had been strongest, were forced by social and economic pressures to take over this form of government themselves. Since this did not happen in Israel, he argued that the Israelites must have established their rule first in those parts of the land where the power of the city states was minimal, that is in the hill country. Instead of a violent conquest, Alt believed that the Israelite tribes had settled in a gradual way. As pastoral nomads they had originally wandered about with their flocks from season to season, but as they began to stay for longer periods in particular places they were able to penetrate the structure of the few power centres that were to be found in the hill country, and eventually became the most significant element of the settled population.

This view clearly has some considerations in its favour:

■ It is consistent with the fact that the new settlements were in the poorer hill country rather than the central plains. Nomadic people attempting to settle permanently would be more likely to inhabit remote villages first, rather than taking on the military might of the strong city states.

■ It also fits with the archaeological evidence, which bears witness to occasional battles and destruction of cities rather than to a coherent and extensive military invasion.

■ The way of life of the 'shasu' described in Egyptian documents corresponds closely to Alt's hypothesis, and according to some interpreters, texts referring to them can be understood to imply that they worshipped a god with a name similar to Yahweh.

■ The Old Testament itself provides evidence that some cities came into Israelite hands by other means than conquest. Shechem is a good example, for there is no record of a military conquest there by Joshua, and yet even before his death it had become a major centre of Israelite activity, and seems to have served as a sort of capital town (Joshua 24). The evidence of archaeology is consistent with this, for Shechem did not share in the wave of destruction and decline that can be documented elsewhere in the thirteenth century BC. Others have drawn attention to an earlier story telling how Shechem was conquered by

Jacob and his sons, and try to integrate that into the armed struggle model by suggesting that when the invading tribes arrived several centuries later they found the city was occupied by people who were, literally, their relatives, and this is why they did not need to overthrow it (Genesis 34; 48:22). Either way, Shechem provides an example of a city that passed from being Canaanite to Israelite in a more or less peaceful way.

Overall, however, this understanding of the emergence of Israel has won few supporters. It is doubtful whether Israel's earliest nomadic life followed the kind of pattern that Alt suggested, and in addition it is very difficult on this understanding to explain why the story of the exodus should have come to occupy such a central place in the thinking of people who not only had not shared in the experience themselves, but who also, as outsiders entering a new land, would presumably have had their own traditions of their origins and forebears.

Social revolution

Yet another possibility that has been put forward is the idea that some inhabitants of Canaan could have been won over to Israel's side by a process of political and religious conversion. The family of the prostitute Rahab at Jericho may be an example of this (Joshua 6:22–25), as also may be another group associated with the city of Bethel (Judges 1:22–26). Then there is the rather odd position of the Gibeonites, who came and asked to be incorporated into the nation of Israel, and who were accepted by Joshua on the basis of a covenant treaty (Joshua 9).

Incidents like these have been taken as evidence that Israel's 'conquest' of Canaan was far more dependent on moral victories than on military might. Indeed some have asserted that there was no 'conquest' in any physical sense at all, but that what changed the population from 'Canaanites' into 'Israelites' was the result of some sort of social revolution, a 'peasants' revolt', inspired not by political considerations, but by moral and religious convictions. They point out that the understanding of God's character preserved in the stories of the covenant at Mount Sinai was quite different from other religious and political belief systems of the region. Moses had spoken of a God who was interested in people on a personal level, and was active in the events of everyday life for their benefit. From what is known of religion in Canaan, the gods were there to preserve the existing order both in the world of nature and in the world of politics. They were powerful supporters of the ruling classes, whereas the God of Israel was committed to supporting the oppressed and downtrodden – and had proved it in the events of the exodus. It is therefore not surprising that many Canaanite peasants should have been attracted by this new assessment of the human situation. Among scholars holding to this position, various explanations are given as to how this might have happened, whether as a result of a group who had been part of the exodus experience coming in and inspiring others to revolt through the sharing of their story, or as a more indigenous movement among the existing population of Canaan. On this understanding most, if not all, of the people who were later known as Israelites were originally Canaanites, and 'Israel' was not so much an ethnic group as a spiritual and political ideology.

This view has been criticized on the grounds that it owes more to a Marxist view of history than to any objective evidence. It also struggles to explain how, if the 'conquest' was an internal revolt, the characteristically 'Israelite' settlements were restricted to the relatively infertile hill country. If Canaan became Israel by overthrowing the original rulers, why did the victors not take over the best land, instead

'Canaanites' and 'Israelites'

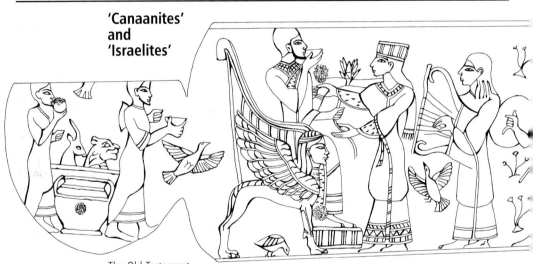

The Old Testament narratives draw a simple demarcation between people they call 'Canaanites' and the nation of Israel. Understandably, the nature of these Canaanites is never clearly spelled out, if only because the Old Testament historians were most interested in the Israelites, and as a result 'Canaanite' is mostly used as a blanket term to describe whoever were the inhabitants of Palestine before the emergence of Israel as a separate entity. So far as we know, there was no one group of people during the period of which we are speaking (Late Bronze Age) who would have described themselves as 'Canaanites'. Indeed, there is very little evidence to suggest that Canaan would have been thought of as a

definable territorial location. The Amarna Letters, for example, use the term but do not identify it. That may have been for the simple reason that both writers and readers already knew where it was anyway, though there is not absolute consistency in the way it is used, with some letters including a place like Ugarit within Canaan, while others exclude it. Most likely, 'Canaan' was at this time a general way of referring to the whole of Syria and northern Palestine.

If the land of Canaan itself is difficult to define with precision, then the nature of its population raises even more questions, and during the period when Israel was emerging as a nation it seems to have

of moving out to the margins? Supporters of this view also need to explain why, on the face of it, the Bible tells such a different story. Given the multifaceted nature of the Old Testament narratives, and the variable nature of the information they provide regarding early Israel, it might have been expected that if there was a successful internal Canaanite revolt of this kind, at least some indication of it would have remained embedded in the traditional stories. At the same time, it does address some facts that the other models find problematic:

■ There is evidence of a strong element of continuity between the culture of Canaan and what emerged as the culture of Israel. The Ugaritic texts, discussed below, show that early expressions of Israelite

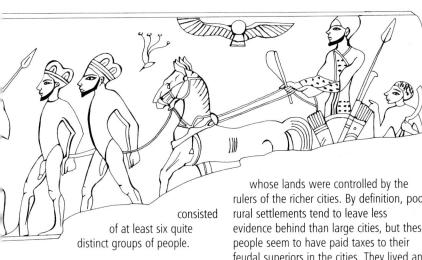

This ivory tablet, found at Megiddo, probably commemorates the victory of a Canaanite king. He is seated at the left on his throne, and before him is shown a queen or goddess and a musician with a lyre. The king appears again on the right in his chariot. Two prisoners are roped to his horse's bridle.

consisted of at least six quite distinct groups of people.

City states

Politically, the most obvious feature of this area was a large number of semi-autonomous city states. These were all heavily fortified, and must have had large armies. The different types of housing found in them also indicates a social structure in which the ruling classes lived off the production of the lower classes. Of course, the rulers were not independent, as they had to pay significant taxation to the Egyptians.

Rural dwellers

Not everyone lived in a city; in fact the majority of the total population did not, and many of them were peasant farmers whose lands were controlled by the rulers of the richer cities. By definition, poor rural settlements tend to leave less evidence behind than large cities, but these people seem to have paid taxes to their feudal superiors in the cities. They lived an insecure life, needing the protection of the armies from the cities, while resenting the control that their overlords imposed on them.

Apiru

These people have been mentioned in connection with the exodus stories. The Amarna Letters mention them raiding fields and rural settlements in Canaan. They seem to have been displaced people, maybe including criminal elements, who mostly found a niche for themselves around the cities, at some times working as mercenaries and at others raiding weaker communities on their own account.

faith had a lot in common with Canaanite religious language, and in addition the worship of Canaanite deities continued for centuries in later Israel. The other two models find it difficult to explain these similarities, and find themselves hard pressed to offer convincing explanations as to why people moving in from outside should so soon have adopted Canaanite ways of being. If the Israelites were originally Canaanites, that would not be a difficulty.

■ This explanation also correlates readily with the archaeological evidence from Canaanite cities. For whereas an invading force could be expected to have attacked buildings and fortifications, an internal revolt would be more likely to target rulers and their agents, leaving less evident destruction of their strongholds.

'Canaanites' and 'Israelites' *continued*

Pastoralists and nomads

There is evidence of people living in the more remote and hilly regions of the land, where the ground was less fertile but it was easier to survive without the interference of the city states. During the Late Bronze Age, this population was not as large as it had been previously, nor as it would become in the Early Iron Age with the development of recognizably Israelite settlements in this same region. At the time Israel was emerging, the people living here might have been nomadic pastoralists, or even groups of apiru – it is not possible to be more certain.

Shasu

The texts mentioning these people mostly place them around the fringes of Palestine, in Edom and generally to the south-east of Canaan. But they certainly seem to have had some connections with Canaan,

At about the time the Israelites were arriving in Canaan, the Philistines were settling along part of the coast. They came originally from Crete, and were known by the Egyptians as the 'Sea Peoples'. This relief, from the temple of the dead of Rameses III at Medinet Habu portrays a naval encounter between 'Sea People' and Egyptians. The Philistines can be recognized by their tall, feathered headgear.

The judges

Though the book of Joshua contains some of the most memorable stories in the entire Hebrew Bible, with its stirring tales of military prowess and individual bravery, the real struggle to bring Israel to birth continued long after the death of Joshua. Those promoting this new style of life were fortunate in being able to avoid confrontation with the various great world powers of the time. The Egyptians and the Hittites were both in decline, while the new power of Assyria was not yet ready to expand into Canaan. The real challenge was in Canaan itself, where the Israelite tribes held control of only a few areas of the country. To make matters worse, the Israelite settlements were isolated from each

---

especially following the decline of the power of Egypt.

Incomers

This would include Philistines and other 'Sea Peoples'. Unlike the others, who all seem to be from roughly the same ethnic background, these people were from totally different stock, originating from the area around the Aegean Sea. Presumably some of the ancestors of Israel could also be classified under this heading.

Though these groups were all different, they shared a similar culture, both in terms of the material remains they left behind and in relation to their religious world-view. The one thing they did not share was a common political or national identity, though throughout this time Egyptian dominance was declining and there was considerable upheaval and social change. As the power centres shifted, new villages emerged in the highlands, the influence of the city states was fragmented, and new alliances between villages emerged, in such a way that by about 1050–1000 BC the kingdom of Israel began to take shape.

In the past, discussions of the origins of Israel have taken account of the existence of this population diversity, but scholars have generally preferred to trace historical Israel to only one strand or another, debating whether all the nation came from slavery in Egypt (and therefore none of

them were Canaanites to start with), or conversely proposing that 'Israelites' were originally 'Canaanites', and therefore the exodus stories could not be trusted. The truth is likely to be more complex than that, for there seems to be evidence that elements from all these different groups did in time align themselves with the vision of nationhood propounded by Israel, and which traced its origins back to the stories of exodus and covenant at Mount Sinai. Even those whose ancestors did not literally share in those events were attracted by the underlying political and spiritual ideology which they represented, and 'Israel' the nation was therefore more the product of a shared vision of the future than an ethnic entity. At this point, the likely historical course of events corresponds almost exactly with the message of the later interpreters of Israel's history, the prophets, who regularly found themselves having to insist on the universal scope of both their nation and their faith, in the light of others who would have interpreted things more narrowly.

other by two powerful groups of existing Canaanite city states: one group, just to the north of Shechem, was centred on towns like Megiddo, Dothan and Beth-Shan; and another, to the south of Shechem, extended westwards from the northern end of the Dead Sea right across to the Mediterranean coast. On top of that, the Israelite tribes were not always able to banish the Canaanite rulers even in those areas where they had achieved some sort of dominance. The tribes of Manasseh, Ephraim, Zebulun, Asher and Naphtali were all forced to reach some compromise agreement with other elements in the land, and when this is added to the fact that several other groups were also trying to carve out their own territories, it is hardly surprising that the situation was so volatile and unstable (Judges 1:27–36).

All this is described in the Old Testament book of Judges. The book takes its name from the fact that its heroes are called 'judges'. This terminology would most obviously suggest they were concerned with the administration of law, and the Hebrew word for 'judge' is in fact very similar to titles given to government officials elsewhere in the ancient world – at Mari, Ebla and Ugarit. Some of the people mentioned in Judges

Life in the days of the judges

What was life really like in those early years when the character and identity of the nation of Israel were being established? Like any other emerging nation, Israel certainly had their troubles. Looking back from the perspective of a more settled period, the editor of the book of Judges felt that at times it verged on anarchy: 'all the people did what was right in their own eyes' (Judges 21:25).

It is not hard to find evidence to support such an opinion. The gruesome story of how a woman traveller was sexually assaulted and murdered in the town of Gibeah is no doubt a typical example of what was going on (Judges 19:1–30). But what happened as a result of this incident is of great significance in understanding the nature of emerging Israelite society at this time. For after the woman's male companion sent a message to all the other tribes, telling them what had happened, they were so outraged that they formed a large army to punish the tribe of Benjamin for allowing such a thing to happen in their territory, and in the struggle that followed, the tribe of Benjamin was all but exterminated (Judges 20:1–48). This seems to depict a situation where, under normal conditions, the different tribes of Israel were primarily concerned with their own affairs, but when the need arose they obviously had a strong sense of national solidarity, and could unite to confront a common threat – whether it came from outside enemies, or from internal subversion. But what was it that held them together like this? A clue may be found in the deep remorse that was felt after the Benjaminites had been subdued. For there was great concern that Benjamin should not be wiped out altogether: 'Israel must not lose one of its twelve tribes. We must find a way for the tribe of Benjamin to survive' (Judges 21:17). The alliance of twelve tribes – and no less – was clearly of some importance to them.

The sense of corporate identity implied by these stories can readily be understood by reference to the nature of tribalism as it can be traced more widely throughout the ancient world, and indeed in other cultures of more recent date. Groups of people conscious of belonging to one another tend to define that belonging by reference to different distinguishing marks at different times. The need for such

may well have had some administrative functions, though it can be misleading to compare the 'judges' of early Israel with figures in other cultures. Without exception, these other states all had a monarchy, and a much more sophisticated political apparatus than Israel had at this time. By contrast to the powerful kings who headed up the many city states of the land, the great judges of the Old Testament stories did not owe their position to a bureaucratic or hereditary appointment. It was, rather, something that stemmed naturally from their remarkable gifts of great wisdom, bravery and leadership – qualities that were demonstrated not in legal arguments about justice, but in the actual work of getting justice for their people. They were men and women of great political vision and religious devotion, and the stories about them show people who were determined that the promises of God and the commitment of the people, as expressed in the covenant made at Mount Sinai, should be enshrined in the very fabric of their new emerging society.

The Old Testament names twelve judges, but records details about only six of them. Of these, only one, Othniel, is linked with the tribes who eventually came to be associated with the southern part of the

definition typically only arises when the tribal identity appears to be threatened in some way, and the nature of the threat tends to determine how corporate uniqueness will then be described. It may be by reference to common ancestry, or different lifestyles, or religious taboos. In Israel, however, over and above individual tribal loyalties there was also a sense of commitment to being a part of the people of Yahweh, which could both incorporate and supersede such loyalties. During the twelfth and eleventh centuries BC, that was expressed in the form of a tribal league, then later from the tenth century onwards, in the form of the monarchy. The nature of the tribal league of this period can almost certainly be explained quite simply by reference to such fluid alignments among different elements of the population. However, other more complex models have been used to understand the nature of Israelite social organization at this time, and one of these in particular is worth noting here, if only because it has in the past exercised considerable influence over interpret-ations of Israel's early history.

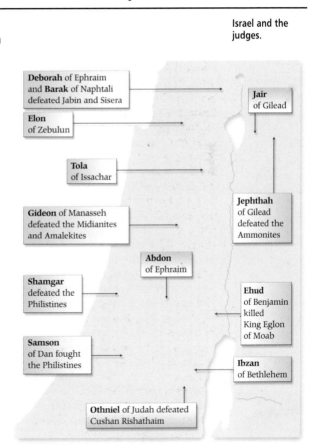

Israel and the judges.

Deborah of Ephraim and **Barak** of Naphtali defeated Jabin and Sisera

Jair of Gilead

Elon of Zebulun

Tola of Issachar

Jephthah of Gilead defeated the Ammonites

Gideon of Manasseh defeated the Midianites and Amalekites

Abdon of Ephraim

Shamgar defeated the Philistines

Ehud of Benjamin killed King Eglon of Moab

Samson of Dan fought the Philistines

Ibzan of Bethlehem

Othniel of Judah defeated Cushan Rishathaim

country (Judges 1:11–15; 3:7–11; Joshua 15:13–19). All the others are associated with northern tribes. This perhaps reflects the relative strength of Israel in different parts of the country at the time. But it could also suggest that the stories themselves were first handed on, and later written down, in the northern part of the country. The meaning that the editor of the book of Judges found in these stories is certainly similar to the message of the prophets who later flourished in that part of the land. The interpretative framework of the book of Judges implies that the real meaning of Israel's experience can only be understood from a religious viewpoint, and describes all the stories as following the same pattern, and teaching the same lessons (Judges 2:11–23):

■ When Israel was faithful to God, the nation prospered.

■ When Israel deserted their own God, Yahweh, and turned to other deities, they were unable to resist their enemies.

■ Finding themselves in great distress, the people of Israel turned again to God, who in turn provided a deliverer for them (a judge).

■ After the death of a judge, the same pattern of events was typically repeated all over again.

Life in the days of the judges *continued*

This is the work of the German scholar Martin Noth who in 1930 proposed a model derived from information about associations of tribes in ancient Greece and Italy, especially a group that was associated with the shrine of the god Apollo at Delphi. These groups came to be known as 'amphictyonies', from two Greek words which mean 'to live around'. They lived around a particular religious centre, and their common allegiance to the worship of their particular deities was the thing that bound them together and gave them mutual obligations to one another. Noth observed that many ancient communities were divided into a regular number of groups, or tribes, including in the Old Testament itself twelve Ishmaelite tribes (Genesis 25:13–16) and twelve Edomite tribes (Genesis 36:9–14), as well as those found in Israel. Unfortunately, nothing else is known about these near-neighbours of Israel, though Noth identified a number of distinctive features of the life of such an amphictyony, which he believed could also be found in the Old Testament.

A fixed membership
The Greek amphictyonies always had either six or twelve members. The reason for this

was perhaps a practical one, for with twelve months in a year it meant that each tribe could take it in turn to look after the central sanctuary on a regular basis. Whatever the origin of Israel's twelve tribes, it is certainly interesting that, though the actual names given to the tribes could vary, the number twelve is always preserved in the Old Testament.

A central shrine
The main focus of the Greek amphictyonies was the central shrine, and this also became a place for the administration of laws that were common to all the member states. By definition, an amphictyony must have such a central place of worship. But was there such a place in ancient Israel? The story in Joshua 24 seems to suggest that Shechem could have served as that kind of central sanctuary. But later, when the tribes united against Benjamin, they went not to Shechem but to Bethel (Judges 20:18) – and not long after, in the time of Samuel, Shiloh appears as the most important centre of worship (1 Samuel 1–4). The apparent absence of just one shrine could be due to the fact that, unlike other deities, the God of Israel could not be contained in just one

Every one of the stories about the judges is used to illustrate and give substance to this theological understanding of Israel's fortunes. For this reason, it has often been suggested that the narrative is less than accurate as history. Given the personal nature of much of the story, it is obviously impossible either to prove or disprove that, though the overall picture that emerges of life in Canaan at this period seems to match what is otherwise known of lifestyles at this time.

Deborah and Barak fight with 'Canaanites', a term generally used to denote the indigenous people of the land (Judges 4–5), while the others deal with various groups who were outsiders trying to gain access to the land for themselves: the Moabites (Ehud, Judges 3:12–30); the Midianites (Gideon, Judges 6:1 – 8:35); the Ammonites (Jephthah, Judges 10:6 – 12:7); and the Philistines (Samson, Judges 13:1 – 16:31). Most of these people were local heroes, fighting local battles. The story of Samson is almost a personal crusade against the Philistines, though the fact that he was able to marry a Philistine woman suggests that at this stage relationships between the two groups were reasonably friendly, and certainly not as hostile as they were later to become.

---

place, but was believed to be present everywhere, a presence that was more appropriately symbolized by the portable ark of the covenant. Perhaps, therefore, this sign of God's presence, which could be moved about from place to place, was itself the central focus for all the tribes. But if so, could it also have been a kind of administrative centre, served by its own officials? Martin Noth believed that it could, and he argued that the officials of the Israelite amphictyony were to be identified with the so-called 'minor judges' – that is, those of whom we know nothing more than their names (Judges 10:1–5; 12:8–15). He further suggested that the law which they administered is to be found in Exodus 20:22 – 23:33, the 'book of the covenant'.

An annual festival

In the Greek amphictyonies, each member state sent official delegates to an annual convention, which took place at the central shrine. This was partly a religious occasion, and partly an administrative council. The evidence for such an annual pilgrimage in the Old Testament is limited, though there is the story of how Joshua gathered the tribes together at Shechem, to remind them of their obligations under the covenant (Joshua 24), and the later story of Samuel's parents describes them undertaking an annual pilgrimage to the sanctuary in Shiloh – though there is nothing to suggest they were any sort of official delegates (1 Samuel 1:1–8). It is in fact very difficult to find evidence of such delegates in early Israel, though Noth believed that passages like Numbers 1:1–16 could have been lists of these people.

A common purpose

The job of an alliance like this was to defend the central shrine and to uphold the common interests and laws of the constituent states. There are two striking illustrations of such a common concern in the book of Judges. On the one hand, we have the story of how six tribes united under Deborah to oppose a common threat from the Canaanites (Judges 4–5), and on the other is the story of how eleven tribes acted against a gross violation of covenant law by the tribe of Benjamin (Judges 19–20). According to Noth, these two incidents document the development of the amphictyony, with an alliance of twelve tribes arising out of the

The story of Deborah and Barak provides a good illustration of the nature of Israelite society at this period. Their exploits against the Canaanites, led by Sisera, the army commander of Jabin, king of the city of Hazor, are vividly described in the great poem which was almost certainly written by an eyewitness of the events it describes (Judges 5:1–31). It was certainly written sometime in the twelfth century BC, and that takes us right back to the time of the judges themselves. Deborah and Barak were probably trying to break through the line of Canaanite city states that isolated the northern area of Galilee from the Israelite settlements around Shechem. For though Jabin's city, Hazor, lay to the north of Galilee, the battle itself took place just to the south-west of the Plain of Jezreel, and involved a coalition of Canaanite city states. Possession of this great plain was of vital importance: all the significant trade routes had to go this way, and whoever controlled this area effectively controlled most of the land. The outcome of the battle was victory for Israel. The Canaanite kings were not entirely routed, but their power was broken, and it was only a matter of time before Israel was able to overthrow Jabin and his influence (Judges 4:23–24).

Life in the days of the judges *continued*

six-tribe group headed by Deborah. But other interpretations are possible, especially if one is prepared to imagine that the stories have been rewritten in the light of social conditions in later Israel.

Martin Noth's reconstruction of life in the time of the judges has many attractions, not least being the way that it offers an all-embracing ideological framework within which to understand the biblical stories about early Israel and its organization. But it was always going to be difficult to match every detail of the Old Testament with the evidence from Greece and Italy. Not only did these Greek amphictyonies flourish in a time and place far removed from Israel in the period of the judges, but they may also be too complex to be appropriate for understanding early Israel. The most useful model for our purposes is probably not that of a religious league, but of a segmentary tribal system, comprising autonomous tribal units of diverse origins, who were able to act together without the need for a central organizational structure.

At the same time, Noth's theory did serve to highlight some of the key aspects of Israel's emerging national consciousness.

For it is certain that a shared faith in God was a major element in the alliance between the Israelite tribes, even though it may not have been expressed in just one central place. The power of the spiritual vision was no less notable for that, and though different tribes had their own leaders (typified by the judges) there was the underlying consciousness that God was the only real 'judge' of the people (Judges 11:27), and the devotion given to human leaders was therefore secondary and derivative (Judges 8:23; 9:1–57). It would be surprising if such a devotion was not given some tangible expression in the way the social and political institutions of Israel's national life were structured.

The rulers of the Canaanite city states had many sophisticated weapons, including chariots, and the Israelites were successful in this instance only because they were able to form an effective alliance. Deborah managed to unite six of the Israelite tribes – Zebulun, Naphtali, Ephraim, Benjamin, Manasseh and Issachar – and the one thing that brought them together was their common religious faith. In this sense, it was not an exaggeration for the editor of the book of Judges to claim that obedience to God would lead to success, while disobedience would lead only to failure. When the tribes were united by their common heritage derived from the covenant at Mount Sinai, they were an effective coalition. But when they began to drift away from the worship of the God of whom Moses had spoken, purely sectional and selfish interests came to be all-important, and they were powerless to make much headway in establishing their new society.

Israel and the religion of Canaan

Politically, the Canaanite city states were eventually displaced by the people who came to be known as Israel. But ideologically, what had been traditional Canaanite culture exerted an enormous influence on Israel for many centuries. The editor of the book of Judges saw the religion of Canaan as a more formidable force than its armies, and when Israel was tempted to adopt its values, disaster was the inevitable outcome: 'Then the people of Israel sinned against Yahweh and began to serve the Baals. They stopped worshipping the Lord, the God of their ancestors, the God who had brought them out of Egypt, and they... served the Baals and the Astartes. And so Yahweh lost patience with Israel and allowed raiders to attack them and rob them... and the Israelites could no longer protect themselves... They were in great distress' (Judges 2:11–15). This message sums up the perspective from which almost all the historical narratives of the Hebrew Bible were written, and was applied as a means of understanding the ever-changing fortunes

of the nation. Centuries after the time of the judges, all the great prophets, from Elijah to Jeremiah, were saying the same thing: that the people of Israel were going to ruin because of their love for the gods and goddesses of Palestine.

So who were these other deities, 'the Baals and the Astartes'? Some of the answers to that question have been unearthed by archaeologists at the tell of Ras esh-Shamra, on the coast of modern Syria, just opposite Cyprus. This was the site of the ancient Canaanite citadel of Ugarit. Its heyday was in the fifteenth and fourteenth centuries BC, something like 200 years before any likely date for the exodus, but there is every reason to believe that the religion practised in southern Palestine at the time of the emergence of early Israel was very similar to the religion of these people who lived further north. In an annex to the temple at Ugarit, archaeologists have made one of the most exciting discoveries of all

The Canaanite god Baal was regarded as a controller of the weather, and one on whom the fertility of the land depended. This claim conflicted with the Israelite belief that Yahweh was God of every aspect of life. This Baal mask dates from about 1300 BC.

Israel and the religion of Canaan *continued*

time, for in a large collection of clay tablets, we find the story of Baal and the other Canaanite gods and goddesses who are mentioned in the Old Testament. These tablets date from about the thirteenth century BC, and are written in a language that has come to be known as Ugaritic. It is one of the earliest-known scripts to have

On the coast of modern Syria, at the tell of Ras esh-Shamra, was once the Canaanite city of Ugarit. This picture is of an entrance to the great palace. Archaeologists have unearthed at Ugarit a great deal of evidence about Canaanite religion and civilization in the centuries leading up to the exodus.

used an alphabet, and though it is completely different from Hebrew in appearance, there are many underlying similarities in the two languages, in specific vocabulary and terminology as well as in general structure. These tablets contain much valuable and important information not only about the deities of ancient Ugarit, but also about religious practices of the time. In addition, the many religious objects also found here – altars, statues and so on – provide added insights into how these gods and goddesses were worshipped.

A number of key characters play a part in the various stories. There is El, the chief of the gods, and his female companion Asherah. But they take a back seat to Baal, the weather god, and his lover Anat, the goddess of love and war. One story tells how Baal was attacked by Mot, the god of barrenness and sterility. As in many ancient fertility myths, he overcomes Baal and destroys his powers of life and fertility, scattering his body to the four corners of the earth. While El, the father-god, leads the heavenly mourning for his lost son, Anat, the goddess of fertility, goes out to take her revenge:

She seizes Mot, the son of El,
with the knife she cuts him,
with the shovel she winnows him,
with fire she burns him,
with millstones she grinds him,
on the field she throws him.
The birds eat his remains,
the feathered ones make an end to what is left over.

Baal's power is then restored through the renewal of his sexual relationship with Anat – and that in turn ensures the fertility of the earth and its inhabitants for another season. The maintenance of the agricultural status quo appears to have been one of the main ideological purposes of this kind of religion. Without the rains that fall from October to April, agriculture would have been impossible, and so when the rains stopped in May it seemed as if Baal was dead, and needed to be revived. Some experts believe that the story of Baal's revival by Anat was the central feature of an annual New Year festival that was celebrated throughout Palestine, and perhaps more widely. On this occasion, held every autumn, the king and a temple prostitute would act out the story of Baal and Anat, to make sure that all would be well for another year. No doubt the same kind of rites were enacted in many local shrines: sexual acts with temple prostitutes feature prominently in Old Testament denunciations of Canaanite worship, and physical union with them was probably considered to be as much a part of the job of a farmer as were the actual operations of agriculture.

It is hardly surprising that there should be evidence of people within Israel adopting similar forms of worship. The Old Testament books in their final form were written with the benefit of hindsight, and later generations could look back and surmise that, if Israel had preserved the distinctive elements of faith in Yahweh, instead of going along with the indigenous religious practices of Canaan, things might have turned out differently. But in the earliest period, the issue was not quite so simple, even to those who wanted to be faithful to the values that could be traced back to Moses and the covenant. For though these stories depicted Yahweh as all-powerful in relation to life in the desert, that was no guarantee that such power would automatically extend to control of the weather and the fertility of fields and flocks. As a consequence, it is not difficult to find traces of a diversity of religious practices at this time. Some appear to have accepted the worship of Yahweh only with reluctance, if at all, and for all practical purposes continued the worship of traditional Canaanite deities. Others tried to hold both traditions alongside each other, while yet others worshipped mainly Yahweh, but played safe by using Canaanite shrines and Canaanite ritual in doing so. The extent to which this kind of thing happened can be seen in the way that even leading Israelite families, who were otherwise praised as faithful to the worship of Yahweh, could on occasion give their children names that would invoke the protection of these traditional deities. For example, one of the sons of Saul was named Jonathan ('Gift of Yahweh'), while another was Ish-Baal ('Man of Baal'), and the names of Baal and Anat were attached to many Israelite towns and villages.

Given the fluid cultural matrix out of which Israel emerged as a separate nation, it is not surprising that we should find evidence of such syncretistic ways in the Old Testament. The gods and goddesses of Canaan represented the inherited spirituality of at least some elements of the population that came to be called 'Israel', and in any case even incomers could hardly fail to have been impressed by the agricultural and economic success of the Canaanite city states – and if they claimed this was due to their religion, then at least such rituals would seem to be worth consideration. But those who created the Old Testament in its final shape could see that the worship of Yahweh and the worship of Baal could not be mixed, for there were fundamental differences between the two:

● Yahweh, the God of Israel, was a God who acted in history, and not a god of nature who was revealed only in the annual cycles of summer and winter. Though Yahweh's character could be disclosed in the context of relationships (as illustrated through the stories of the family of Abraham and Sarah and their successors), being a personal God did not necessarily imply that Yahweh had either gender or sexuality. Indeed, the claim that God is not so much asexual, as beyond sexuality, came to be one of the key distinguishing characteristics of Israelite faith.

● The rituals of traditional Canaanite religion were first and foremost magical rites. Though the behaviour of deities like Baal and Anat was in most ways regarded as unpredictable, there was also a belief that due to innate correspondences between human activity and the life of the gods and goddesses, it was to some extent possible for people to make the gods do their bidding. This was the reasoning behind the assumption that sexual intercourse between a farmer and the

Gezer was a well-defended city lying only a few miles from the main trade route between Egypt and Mesopotamia. Ten stone pillars, some more than three metres tall, formed the 'high place' which was of religious significance for the city.

deity's representative (usually in the shape of a temple prostitute) would produce more fruitful crops, by inducing the deities to have sex among themselves. By

Israel and the religion of Canaan *continued*

contrast, however, the God of Israel could not be bullied by magic. Yahweh had not been forced to call Abraham and Sarah, or to deliver the slaves from Egypt: those and other things like them had all arisen out of God's own spontaneous love and care for the people.

● Any magical understanding of ritual runs the risk of encouraging its practitioners to assume that religion has nothing to do with behaviour in normal life, but only with the special actions that take place in shrines and temples. This notion runs completely contrary to the Hebrew Bible's understanding of the personality of Yahweh. The God of Israel was not most concerned with the empty performance of hollow rituals, but with the way people behaved in everyday life. This lesson was hammered home over and over again by the prophets, as they declared that Israel's religious duty was not something that took place in a shrine, but in the market place: 'to do what is just, to show constant love, and to live in humble fellowship with our God' (Micah 6:8).

● In view of this, it is not surprising that Israel's God demanded exclusive worship. The gods and goddesses of Canaan were always tolerant of other gods, who were, in a sense, their own relatives. But the formative stories that gave Israel their sense of national identity all showed Yahweh demanding the exclusive commitment and obedience of the people (Exodus 20:1–3).

The deuteronomic history

Mention has already been made of the fact that the stories of Israel's history as they are now presented in the Hebrew Bible are the result of a long process of collection and edition that took place over several centuries. The fact that history is presented from a particular perspective does not, in itself, question the authenticity of the narratives. But in order to understand the stories as thoroughly as possible it is necessary at this stage to have some understanding of the purposes for which they were put together in their final form.

Back in 1943, Martin Noth proposed that the books of Joshua, Judges, 1–2 Samuel and 1–2 Kings were gathered together to form an epic history of Israel not long after the state of Judah and its capital Jerusalem had been destroyed by the Babylonians under Nebuchadnezzar (586 BC), and that in this edition the book of Deuteronomy, which immediately precedes these historical books in the Old Testament, was incorporated almost as a kind of introductory section to explain the theological basis on which Israel's history was to be understood. Hence he called this extended story 'the deuteronomic history'. He believed that this great reassessment of Israel's history took place sometime after 561 BC (the year when Jehoiachin, former king of Judah, was released from prison in Babylon, 2 Kings 25:27–30), but before the Persians came to power and overthrew the Babylonian empire (539 BC), a change which enabled the subsequent rebuilding of the Temple in Jerusalem to take place in about 520 BC.

This is a bold hypothesis to explain the origin of these Old Testament books, and it has repercussions for how the compilation of other books took place – something that is explored in more detail in Chapter 7. But it is also an attractive one, and a number of facts seem to speak in its favour:

● It is not at all unlikely that those who survived the destruction of Jerusalem would begin to look at their past history as a way of making sense of their present predicament. The book of Jeremiah mentions inhabitants of Judah who were exiled in Egypt, and who engaged in this kind of reflection, and there is every reason to suppose that the same thing would have happened in Judah itself. Not only that, but in the immediate aftermath of the fall of Jerusalem there must have been an added incentive to gather together the traditions of the nation for their own sake, simply as a means of preserving the ancient records for posterity. All these books refer to other ancient sources of information from which their own stories have been extrapolated or summarized, and all these other records have subsequently disappeared with the passage of time.

● At the same time, these Old Testament history books are more than just an anthology of extracts from older historical materials. For they also present a clear and coherent view of the meaning of the events that are recorded. The nature of this interpretative framework is made quite explicit in the book of Judges, but it is clearly present in many other passages too. It has not been superimposed on every detail of the narratives, but at strategic points the lessons of history are made plain: Israel was committed in a covenant relationship to God, and this placed upon them certain responsibilities. Accordingly, if the people were willing to accept these responsibilities and obey the Law of the covenant, they could expect the blessing that God had promised. On the other hand, deliberate disobedience would lead to failure and destruction. This message is often conveyed in the form of speeches at strategic points in the story (Joshua 23; 1 Samuel 12; 2 Samuel 7; 1 Kings 8:22–53), a literary device that is common to much ancient history writing.

● The fact that the covenant forms the basic framework within which Israel's history is understood in these books also gives a certain plausibility to Noth's claim

that Deuteronomy was the preface for the whole work. For the literary structure of Deuteronomy is closely linked to the covenant pattern which has been traced in Hittite and Assyrian sources. In addition, the speech with which the book opens (Deuteronomy 1–4) is almost a classic exposition of the theological perspective of the so-called deuteronomists. What is more, it seems to contain an explicit appeal and reassurance to the people for whom the exile proved to be such a great crisis: 'Yahweh will scatter you among other nations, where only a few of you will survive… There you will look for Yahweh your God, and if you search… with all your heart, you will find… When you are in trouble and all those things happen to you, then you will finally turn to Yahweh in obedience. God is merciful, and will never abandon you or destroy you, nor forget the covenant made in person with your forebears' (Deuteronomy 4:27, 29–31).

This understanding of the nature of the deuteronomic history has not been universally accepted by scholars, though it has won a considerable measure of support and most would acknowledge its existence, while debating various aspects of the perspective it appears to represent. Three major issues may be highlighted:

● Noth regarded the deuteronomic history as simply an explanation of the tragedy that had befallen the people of Israel, and he therefore understood it as an essentially pessimistic work. But this is not the whole story. The main emphasis is certainly on Israel's past, but not simply from an antiquarian standpoint. Indeed, it is questionable whether anyone in ancient Israel ever would have been interested in the past in the way that today's Western people tend to be, merely out of curiosity to know what happened. For the biblical writers, the past was always seen as the theatre of God's activity, and therefore it inevitably became far more than merely a collection of things that had happened: it was a mirror of the future, and a challenge to the people to face up to that future, particularly in relation to its spiritual dimensions. The prophets came to think of the failures of the past as an invitation to renewed obedience, and these history writers were inspired by the same perspective. Perhaps that is why they ended with the story of Jehoiachin's release, for that in itself must have generated renewed hope in the hearts of the people.

● Some have questioned whether there is such a thoroughgoing, unified presentation of the meaning of Israel's history in all these books. They point out, for example, that some passages of Samuel and Kings (like the succession narrative contained in 2 Samuel 9–20 and 1 Kings 1–2) seem to show very little trace of the deuteronomic point of view. They also ask whether the simple viewpoint of Deuteronomy itself, related to the earliest stages of Israel's history, is truly compatible with the elevated position of the king and the significance of the Jerusalem Temple in the later books. But these observations have more bearing on the complex way in which the various stories were gathered together. It is quite likely that the long job of writing a continuous history of Israel had already been started long before the dark days of the exile. Many scholars think that even before the time of Josiah (640–609 BC), the outline for such a narrative was already in existence, and even in the earliest parts of the history, it is universally agreed that some of the stories were first written down more or less as they happened. For the later editors were not so much concerned to rewrite the stories, but to present them in a way that would be most meaningful to the people of their own day.

● Scholars have often asked just who these so-called deuteronomists actually were. They have been identified in turn with groups of priests, prophets and wisdom teachers, though it can hardly be doubted that they had a good deal in common with the great prophets. Of these, Isaiah is the only one who is actually mentioned by name in the Old Testament histories (2 Kings 19–20), but the underlying message of these books is the same as theirs: the facts of Israel's history were taken as proof that the prophets were right. There are also a number of passages in the books of the prophets which are quite similar to parts of the deuteronomic history. Indeed, it is quite possible that these prophetic books were first gathered together by the same people who issued this great historical work. It is perhaps more than accidental that the Jews themselves came to regard the books from Joshua to Kings as 'the former prophets'.

4 'A King Like Other Nations'

'You have been our king from the beginning, O God; you have saved us many times' (Psalm 74:12). The words were written centuries later, but they sum up well enough the ideals of the early days of Israel's history, at least as seen through the spectacles of the final editors of the Hebrew Bible. Though the tribes may from time to time have their human leaders, in the end God was to be their only true sovereign. Even the great judges were not important in themselves, but were just men and women whom God had inspired to lead their people in times of special need.

The stories generally show the judges themselves recognizing this. When some of the tribes suggested to Gideon that his bravery and courage deserved the reward of a permanent position of power, he would have nothing to do with it. It was, he declared, impossible for his people to be ruled both by God and by a human king (Judges 8:22–23). His son Abimelech did not have the same scruples, and managed to persuade the people of the city of Shechem to make him their ruler, though in the event his success was short-lived (Judges 9). It was unthinkable that the monarchies of the Canaanite city states should have provided an acceptable model for the emerging Israelite culture: the belief that Yahweh was their ruler was not meant to be a pious fiction, but something that would be given practical application in the affairs of everyday life. The tribes were held together not by the institutions of a shared government, but by the experiences of a shared faith, symbolized by the ark of the covenant. Of course, there were already movements afoot that would both challenge and undermine the loosely knit tribal federation of this period, movements that were probably inevitable rather than necessarily being the outcome of conscious choice on the part of the people. Population growth and movement, and the consequent need to find more efficient ways of feeding larger numbers, not to mention climatic changes and the natural tendency of those in positions of leadership to want to better themselves, all contributed to the evolution of the Israelite state during the Early Iron Age (1200–1000 BC). The deuteronomic editors of these narratives in the Hebrew Bible had little to say about such matters, but chose instead to concentrate on stories that brought the Israelite tribes into conflict with other groups who were also trying to establish themselves in the land at this time. This was a way in which they could tell the old stories so as to address the circumstances of their own day all the more effectively. Their procedure in doing so does not in itself invalidate their narratives, though it does serve to underline the essentially selective nature of them. There is plenty of evidence to show that the Philistines in particular were making a powerful bid for exactly the same territory, and while relations between these two groups were somewhat fluid and flexible, and the Philistine threat was not the only factor that led to the emergence of an organized state with its own monarchy, there can be no doubt that this still acted as a powerful catalyst for social change at this period.

Samuel and the ark

There is a degree of uncertainty about the exact relationship between the Philistines and the Israelites at the earliest period of the tribal federation. It could even be that certain elements which eventually joined Israel may have originally been part of the 'Sea Peoples', just as the Philistines were. Samson, for example, is described as belonging to the tribe of Dan, though he married a Philistine woman and was involved with several others. There is no suggestion that by doing so he was stepping outside any accepted boundaries, and the squabbles with the Philistines that grew out of these relationships were essentially matters related to his own personal life rather than having any connection with larger tribal conflicts (Judges 13–16). Indeed, some evidence may point to the tribe of Dan having originally been connected to the 'Sea Peoples'. They seem to have used a similar type of pottery to the Philistines, and one later passage implies that they had a different god to the rest of Israel (Amos 8:14). Amos does not name this god, which means it is not possible to make a definite connection between Israel and the Philistines through this route. However, even David at a later stage had no hesitation in turning to the Philistines for support, which tends to suggest that he saw at least that group of them as not unsympathetic to his own ambitions (1 Samuel 21:10–15).

The relationship between the two groups might therefore be much more complex than was formerly supposed, though they did eventually emerge as competitors. As military opponents, the Philistines would certainly have been a strong and powerful force. They had adopted the political structures of the Canaanite city states to their own advantage, but they had one thing their Canaanite predecessors never had: a strong sense of national unity. Though they were independent, the Philistine cities could act in a concerted and unified way. This made them a formidable enemy, for in addition they were also technically more advanced than Israel, and knew how to use chariots and iron weapons in war.

Both politically and militarily, Israel was less well organized than the Philistines, and could offer no effective resistance to a more sophisticated military machine. After a devastating defeat near Aphek, the leaders of the Israelite tribes realized that they were powerless (1 Samuel 4:1–11). Not only were the rising generation of tribal leaders unable to emulate the brave exploits of those whose reputations survived from previous generations, but in the course of one battle in particular the ark of the covenant was captured, its shrine at Shiloh destroyed, and the Israelite army decimated (1 Samuel 5:1 – 7:1). This kind of defeat was not difficult for the deuteronomic editors of the traditions to explain, and was linked directly by them to religious mistakes, not least the assumption that it would be possible to get God on their side through such means as carrying the ark of the covenant into battle. Following the lead of the sons of Eli the priest (who were themselves killed in the battle), the people had forgotten the close personal nature of Israel's relationship to God, preferring to replace the dynamic understanding of the covenant with a more static spirituality which imagined that God could not only be contained in a box, but could also actually be manipulated by mere humans. With the box gone, the people found themselves militarily powerless and socially disenfranchised, as the Philistines took the leading place in the land. It is unlikely that the Philistines wanted to possess the whole land for themselves. More probably they were trying to take over the position once occupied by the Egyptians: they would be the rulers, and the Israelites and other groups living in Canaan would be their subjects. That did not make it any less painful for Israel. But what could they do to carve out a niche for themselves in this competitive situation? Samuel seemed powerless, yet he was the only surviving representative of the old order. And although the ark of the covenant took its own revenge on the Philistines and was eventually returned to Israel, the old fervour and enthusiasm did not return with it. It became clear that the old forms of loose tribal alliances were no longer adequate to address the challenges of changing circumstances. Moreover, the Philistines were not the only challenge that the Israelite tribes had to face.

Saul

The man who put new life into the Israelites was Saul. He enters the narrative through another chilling tale of gratuitous violence. Among other groups trying to establish themselves in the land at this time were the Ammonites, who were pressing in from the east side of the River Jordan. They attacked the people of Jabesh Gilead, and made it a condition of peace that the right eye of every citizen should be put out. It was not long before this news had travelled far and wide, and Saul heard it as he was on his way home from the fields. Like the judges before him, he was moved to fury by 'the spirit of God', whereupon he cut up the oxen he was driving and sent pieces of them throughout the whole district, with the gruesome message: 'Whoever does not follow Saul and Samuel into battle will have this done to their oxen!' (1 Samuel 11:7). Under Saul's leadership, a powerful army was raised from among the tribes of Israel to deal with this new threat, and Jabesh Gilead was liberated.

Up to this point, the story is quite similar to the tales told about the judges. But a new element is introduced into the narrative after Saul's great victory, for the people gathered at the shrine in Gilgal, and acclaimed him as their king (1 Samuel 11:13–15). According to the stories in Samuel, this was not a spontaneous action, but the culmination of much debate among the Israelite leaders. For the appointment of a king was not something to be taken lightly. After all, if it had previously been wrong for Gideon to be king, how could it now be right for Saul? The deuteronomic history reports this argument in some detail. Indeed, the two sides were put with such vigour that scholars commonly

---

'Has even Saul become a prophet?'

The question arises out of an incident recorded in 1 Samuel 10:5–13. After being anointed by Samuel, Saul went up to worship at the sanctuary of Gibeah, and as he was on his way he encountered a group of prophets who were shouting and dancing to frenzied music, in some sort of religious ecstasy. Quite unexpectedly, Saul himself was caught up in the same excitement, and he too joined in their dancing and singing. This was such an unexpected turn of events that bystanders spoke of Saul becoming 'a different person' under the influence of this religious enthusiasm, and many expressed their surprise that a reputable person like him should have become mixed up with this kind of behaviour.

The fact that this could happen to Saul will surprise no one, for there are plenty of well-documented examples of religious groups whose fervour and excitement leads them into wild and uncontrollable behaviour of this sort, often stimulated by music, as was the case here.

Many readers, however, are surprised to see people like this described as 'prophets'. For the typical prophet of the Old Testament is not a person who indulges in religious excitement, but someone with a message from God to the people, who expresses that message in clear language, appealing not to the emotions of their hearers, but to their reason and sense of religious commitment.

A number of observations can be made on this issue:

● Some have drawn attention to the statement in 1 Samuel 9:9, that 'at that time a prophet was called a seer'. A seer would be someone who tried to discover God's will by psychic or semi-magical means. Perhaps then, it is argued, the confusion is just a matter of terminology, and the great classical prophets with their incisive comments on social and political affairs simply evolved over a period of time out of such unsophisticated practitioners. There are certainly some statements in the Hebrew Bible that could be taken to support this view. Amos, for example, seems to distinguish himself from a 'prophet' who would give messages for money (Amos 7:14), while Micah 3:5–7 appears to make reference to the same sort of people.

● At the same time, some passages do seem to refer to ecstatic experiences of this sort in the lives of the great prophets. Even Jeremiah was described as a 'madman' (admittedly, by his enemies,

reckon they can trace two distinctive accounts of Samuel's role in the affair, which have been combined by the later editors:

■ The first is contained in 1 Samuel 9:1 – 10:16 and 11:1–15, and here Samuel is introduced as a relatively unknown local figure, who appoints Saul as king under God's direct guidance. The monarchy will save Israel from their enemies, and for this reason is generally looked on with favour in these sections of the story.

■ In another account, though, Samuel seems to be already well known as a national figure, and a man who disapproves of the appointment of a king because this would mean a rejection of God as the only true ruler of Israel (1 Samuel 8:1–22; 10:17–27).

Given the conscious literary artistry with which these narratives have been constructed, it is likely that the editors of the book of Samuel incorporated these different perspectives with the specific intent to

---

Jeremiah 29:26–27). Hosea was accused in much the same way (Hosea 9:7) – and some of the experiences of these later prophets (especially people like Ezekiel) were certainly most unusual. We also know of at least one occasion when the prophet Elisha gave his message to the accompaniment of music (2 Kings 3:15–19), while the behaviour of one of his colleagues provoked a king of Israel to call him 'that crazy fellow' (2 Kings 9:11).

● There are parallels to all this in other cultures of the time. The Old Testament itself provides descriptions of typical behaviour of the prophets of Baal, who sought to invoke divine power by a self-induced religious ecstasy (1 Kings 18:20–29). Given the close parallels between the culture of Canaan and that of the Israelites, it would not be especially surprising to find such similarities. There is little external evidence about the practices of such people in Canaan itself, though there is some from Mari in the form of a series of letters dating from the eighteenth century BC. They concern a wide variety of prophetic functions, one of the most important of which was the encourage-ment of a king in times of particular difficulty, especially the giving of advice in times of war. This aspect of the work of a prophet certainly features regularly in the Old Testament,

though their advice (as at Mari) was not always what their rulers wanted to hear (2 Samuel 12:1–15; 1 Kings 22:1–28).

Ecstatic enthusiasts frequently assume a new importance, especially at times of social uncertainty and cultural upheaval. When the accepted norms look to be changing and ordinary people feel out of control of their own lives, the prospect of being able to tune in directly to spiritual forces beyond this world is bound to offer a welcome sense of safety and security. No doubt ancient Israel was no exception, and it is not difficult to understand how guidance received from such sources should have been welcomed as providing inspiration at a time of great difficulty. Certainly, no period was more difficult for the emerging nation of Israel than the time of Saul. This function of ecstatic spirituality may later have been continued and refined in those prophets who were attached to the royal courts of Israel and Judah. The precise relationship of this kind of religious devotee with the great preaching prophets of the Old Testament is still uncertain, though both types of prophet obviously thought of themselves as the communicators of a message from God to the people.

highlight the tensions inherent in them. For between them they represent the contradictions to which the deuteronomic historians traced the ultimate collapse of their nation many centuries later. On the one hand, a strong leader was needed to consolidate the position of Israel as a national entity; but on the other, the existence of such a leader would inevitably weaken the conviction that God was Israel's only true ruler. This tension is clearly reflected in the stories about Saul, and to a greater or lesser extent is represented in the stories about all those who succeeded him.

In some respects, Saul is presented less as a king than as a kind of perpetual judge. It was certainly important that he should be seen to have the same popular appeal and military prowess that the judges had possessed. In practical terms, however, Saul had his difficulties. Up to this point, the main military force in Israel had been the large army of

volunteers from the tribes. It was with such a spontaneously recruited force that Saul had been able to avenge the people of Jabesh Gilead. But this sort of arrangement was only appropriate for great emergencies. It was not the way for a king to operate, nor was it likely to be an effective way of securing the nation's territory militarily. Given the nature of population movements in Canaan at this period, guerrilla warfare would be a far more effective strategy than large-pitched battles – and for that, a small body of professional soldiers would be much more suitable than a large force of untrained volunteers. So, like the rulers of the Canaanite city states before him, Saul formed his own personal army (1 Samuel 13:2; 14:52).

At En Gedi by the Dead Sea, a stream flows down a gorge to the shore. The whole area abounds in caves, and this is the region where David hid from Saul and his soldiers during the years of his exile from court.

By all accounts it was a successful move, for he was able to keep the Philistines at least out of the hill country, which provided greater freedom of movement for the Israelites (1 Samuel 13–14). But this sense of security was bought at a price. For though Saul lacked most of the trappings of other kings of the time, and even his headquarters at Gibeah was by no means a palace, he was separating himself from his people. His professional army owed its allegiance not to the tribes in general, but to Saul himself as its commander-in-chief. Since Saul appears to have had no resources of his own, he must have needed someone else to pay for the army – and that meant the tribes. Though there is no direct evidence for it in the Old Testament, he was probably forced to raise some kind of taxation from the people. It could well have been financial stringency that forced Saul to disregard Samuel's instructions about the goods of the defeated Amalekites (1 Samuel 15:1–35), but whatever the reason, as a result of this episode Saul came to be regarded as a headstrong, selfish man who put his own will and wisdom before the will of God, and who was too ready to jettison the old religious ideals when they interfered with his own state-building strategy.

In the event, Saul's efforts to bring coherence to his people failed. No doubt there were many reasons for this. The stories show him as a king who ultimately lost the popular support that had brought him to power, largely as a result of doing things that any king could have been expected to engage in: establishing an army, and trying to impose some centralized government on the land. Transforming a loose federation of tribes into a coherent state is not an easy task, and Saul did not have the diplomatic skill necessary to carry it out effectively. His popularity was further undermined by the emergence of one of his young subjects, a shepherd called David, who had the personal charisma that Saul lacked (1 Samuel 16–31). Overtaken by jealousy and suspicion, Saul eventually fell into a deep depression and by the end of his life was mentally deranged. He died a lonely and forlorn figure, taking his own life on the battlefield after a crushing defeat at the hands of the Philistines on Mount Gilboa. The complexity of Saul's personality eludes us, though he emerges as a tragic figure. He had great potential as the recognized successor to the judges, but the nature of the task to which he was committed was too great for him; he

Israel becomes a state

The deuteronomic historians emphasize the need for military security as a key catalyst that led to the emergence of Israel as a state, rather than it remaining a loosely federated group of tribes. It is not difficult to see why they would do that, for much of the later history of their people was determined by power struggles in the region, and their lack of military prowess turned out to play a significant part in the ultimate collapse of both Israel and Judah. There need be no question that the ability to deal effectively with others who were also trying to carve out territory for themselves played an important part in the development of the early monarchy. The Philistines were only one group who needed to be kept in check, and nearby states such as Edom, Moab and Syria all had vested interests in the land (1 Samuel 14:47; 2 Samuel 8:1–14), along with other tribal peoples like the Ammonites (1 Samuel 11:1) or Amalekites (1 Samuel 30:1). But other factors clearly played a part as well, and help to explain why the development of the monarchy – whatever its shortcomings might eventually turn out to be – was inevitable. When the stories of Israel's kings are placed alongside what is known of life in Canaan during the

Early Iron Age (1200–1000 BC), at least three other significant factors can be identified:

● Population growth seems to have been quite rapid at this time, and is of course an easy way for an emerging national entity to expand its territory and influence. But growing populations require more resources, and if those resources are not easily obtainable, social tensions are the inevitable result. In some Middle Eastern states at the time, populations were kept in check by crude forms of birth control, generally by disposing of unwanted infants. There is no evidence of that at any period of Israelite history, which meant that population movement was the most obvious way of dealing with the growing numbers. There is ample evidence that this was indeed what was happening at this time, but given the generally inhospitable nature of the terrain outside the central plains, and the unpredictability of the annual rains, the highland communities that emerged never had much chance of being materially self-sufficient. The land they were trying to farm was simply inadequate to produce the food required for a balanced diet, and in order to sustain a satisfactory lifestyle in such circumstances some kind of centralized arrangements for

was incapable of incorporating the old tribal ideals of his people within the structures of an emerging state, and his downfall was inevitable. In addition, he made very little headway against the well-organized armies of other groups such as the Philistines, which left him as a king without a kingdom. The three major city states of Jerusalem, Aijalon and Gezer still separated the centre of the country from the south, and to the north the strategic Plain of Jezreel was still controlled by the Philistines.

David

David was made of different stuff from Saul. He was a charismatic figure in every sense of the word, and would overcome tribal suspicions and resistance to the idea of a king, to unite the whole of Israel into a remarkably powerful alliance. The deuteronomic historians looked back on David knowing that he had turned out to be Israel's greatest national hero. He was the traditional composer of Israel's best-loved songs (the

---

Israel becomes a state *continued*

the exchange and distribution of different foodstuffs was necessary.

● The evolution of more complex societies in a marginal environment inevitably requires more sophisticated structures to deal with the kind of disputes that arise in relation to the fair distribution of resources. Some matters cannot be decided by informal meetings of tribal leaders, particularly when external factors such as the nature of the land, or the location of water are involved, for they generally transcend the ways in which territory is divided on a tribal basis. Arguments about equitable access to such resources invariably requires the development of more sophisticated systems of justice, accountable to some centralized individual or structure capable of enforcing decisions about such matters. When the book of Judges characterizes the early period as a time when 'there was no king in Israel; all the people did what was right in their own eyes' (21:25), it could easily have been this kind of free-for-all struggle for essential commodities that was implied. It is certainly striking that one of David's achievements is said to have been that he 'administered justice and equity to all his people' (2 Samuel 8:15).

● The increasing use of iron at this period was another feature that called for the

structures of a more centralized state. For reasons that no one quite understands, what is now known as the Late Bronze Age ended in Palestine about 1200 BC because the raw materials for making bronze were no longer easily obtainable. The move to new agricultural sites in the highlands of Canaan from about this time onwards required tough materials for tools, as the land itself was difficult to work and generally stony. Iron was the obvious choice, but Palestine had little indigenous iron ore, and none of it was of very high quality. This was not an insuperable obstacle, for the extensive international trading partnerships that existed made it relatively easy to import supplies from elsewhere. But in order to do that efficiently, and ensure the fair distribution of such implements as could be crafted, required a centralized body that would not only be able to deal with international traders, but that could also organize the manufacture of tools in urban centres and their efficient supply to those living in more remote areas.

Psalms), and the man about whom many of the most popular stories were told. All this is obvious from the way in which the books of Samuel introduce him to the narrative. In contrast to the stories of Saul, the accounts of David's life have been composed with great artistry and literary skill. The stories of his friendship with Saul's son Jonathan (1 Samuel 19–20), and of his unexpected defeat of the Philistine giant Goliath (1 Samuel 17) have remained firm favourites with Bible readers through many centuries and in all cultures. The sheer quantity of material relating to David's exploits also underlines his importance to the final editors of the Hebrew Bible: between 1–2 Samuel and 1 Kings, almost 70 per cent of the stories are about David, compared with only 20 per cent about Solomon, and even less about Saul.

David's rise to power

David was obviously a striking character. Not many shepherds become kings, and he must have had some extraordinary talent to rise so quickly to a position of such eminence in Saul's court. The features that impressed Saul also caught the imagination of the people, and it was not long before they were singing David's praises in the streets: 'Saul has killed thousands, but David tens of thousands' (1 Samuel 18:7). This kind of popularity aroused Saul to intense jealousy, and so he dismissed David from the court, giving him instead the command of 1,000 soldiers in his private army. But David could not be held back. His military exploits were amazing, and 'everyone in Israel and Judah loved David because he was such a successful leader' (1 Samuel 18:16). His admirers even included Saul's daughter Michal, who fell in love with David and married him (1 Samuel 18:17–27). But Saul became more and more envious, and set out deliberately to kill him. As a result, David was forced to go into exile, in the south of the country (1 Samuel 19–22).

There he was secure from Saul,

David extended the boundaries of Israel well beyond the kingdom ruled by Saul.

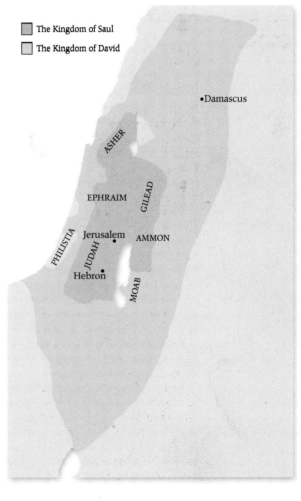

The Kingdom of Saul

The Kingdom of David

Damascus

ASHER

GILEAD

EPHRAIM

PHILISTIA

Jerusalem

JUDAH

AMMON

Hebron

MOAB

for between them lay a number of fortified Canaanite city states, including Jerusalem. In the south, David probably forged some sort of alliance with the Philistines (1 Samuel 22:1–2), for he was able to organize a court at Adullam and to protect himself and his troops by running a protection racket (1 Samuel 25). He also strengthened his position here by marriage alliances, and obviously became closely involved with Achish, the Philistine king of Gath (1 Samuel 27). Achish wanted to take David with him to the battle of Gilboa, where Saul met his death, but he was left behind when his loyalty was questioned by the other Philistine chiefs. They were right to do so, for David had been playing a double game with Achish (1 Samuel 29). But their suspicion of him turned out to David's advantage, for while the Philistines had been arguing about David, Amalekite raiders had attacked the town of Ziklag. On his return, David went out to avenge his own people. He took back all that the Amalekites had taken, and more besides, and then tactfully distributed it among the people of the towns where he was best known (1 Samuel 30).

Saul was finished and died in disgrace, having failed to win the allegiance and support of his people (1 Samuel 31). But David's position was assured. He had already established himself among the southern tribes, and he was now recognized as their leader. In effect, he became the king of Judah, reigning at Hebron. The southern tribes of Judah had always been isolated from the northern tribes and they had probably never been fully integrated into Saul's kingdom. So they had no qualms about accepting David: he had already shown his prowess in battle, and he continued to protect the people for a further seven and a half years (2 Samuel 2:10–11). But David was not satisfied with this. He knew that Israel would never be truly great until northern and southern tribes were fully united. In the north, Saul's son Ishbaal (Ishbosheth) had taken his father's place, but he had no popular support. In his fury against David, Saul had gone so far as to kill the priests who looked after the tribal sanctuary at Nob (1 Samuel 22), an action that was enough in itself to ensure that no son of his would ever be acclaimed by the tribes. Ishbaal's only real supporter was Abner, the commander of Saul's personal army, and when even he defected to David's side, Ishbaal was finished (2 Samuel 2:8 – 4:12). David agreed to become king of all the Israelite tribes, and the northern group pledged their allegiance to him (2 Samuel 5:1–5). The consolidation of a centralized state provided the infrastructure through which a new national identity could finally emerge, and David successfully established new conditions for internal social stability as well as the external security that was required to establish Israel as a dominant political force in the land.

A new king and new ways

A new kingdom needed a new capital. Hebron was too far south, and the north had no organization to speak of since the defeat at Gilboa and the murder of Ishbaal. So David found a new capital in Jerusalem. This was a particularly clever move, for the city had belonged to neither northern nor southern tribes, which meant that it had the potential to overcome any residual jealousies among the old tribal groupings. Strategically, the capture of this city by David's troops, who gained access to it by climbing up a water shaft (2 Samuel 5:6–10), also removed one of the last physical barriers to the unity of the kingdom, for Jerusalem had been one of the last remaining independent city states that had effectively isolated north from south during the time of Saul.

For all these reasons it could become 'the city of David' in a distinctive way. He constructed new fortifications, and built a palace for himself, and in the process established significant relationships with foreign powers, especially the Phoenicians, by employing craftworkers from all over the region (2 Samuel 5:11–12). Unfortunately, very little still remains of the Jerusalem of David's time, though there can be no doubt that he and his successor Solomon transformed it into a major administrative centre, probably aided by the considerable bureaucratic expertise of its original Jebusite inhabitants, who were now incorporated into the kingdom of Israel. This was just a small section of a fairly large foreign population that became a part of David's kingdom, for as he extended his influence in all directions he defeated Edomites, Moabites, Ammonites and Syrians, as well as Philistines, and their towns and people naturally pledged their allegiance to David.

The spoils captured in these military expeditions, and the taxes paid to him by conquered peoples, financed the construction of many fine buildings in Jerusalem. It also enabled David to increase the number of mercenaries in his personal army, and to establish a full royal court at his new palace. But he was always careful to preserve those all-important links with the looser tribal alliances that had preceded the emergence of the Israelite state. One of his earliest acts was to bring the ark of the covenant to Jerusalem. To the tribes, this had always been a central symbol of their commitment to one another, representing the story of the escape from Egypt, the covenant with God at Mount Sinai and the common worship of Yahweh that held them together (2 Samuel 6).

We need not doubt that David's religious commitment played an important part in all this. But the arrival of the ark of the covenant in Jerusalem also had social consequences, for it gave David's own position a special seal of approval. More than that, for in a sense, the ark installed in David's city now became David's personal possession. It certainly removed the power centre from the tribes themselves, and vested it in a state authority that could transcend the old tribal loyalties. In other words, David achieved what Saul had failed to do: he established his own position independently of the continued acclamation of the people. The nation was controlled by his own army, with his own city, and now he had his own national shrine at the centre of things.

David was undoubtedly a great leader. By combining military

prowess with inspirational leadership he secured for himself a significant place not just as a successful ruler, but also, through the royal ideology which evolved to underpin his dynasty, as a significant religious icon for future generations. Politically, David's rise to fame was facilitated by the relative weakness of Egypt and Assyria at the time, but his achievement was still remarkable nonetheless.

The old ways and new ideas

One of the most significant stories told about David in the Old Testament is of his adultery with Bathsheba and the murder of her

Jerusalem was captured by David, who moved his capital there from Hebron. Known ever since as 'the city of David', Jerusalem became and has remained the focus of devotion for the people of Israel. The original part of the city is in the foreground of the picture, on the spur of land leading up to the Temple Mount, and bordered on one side by the Kidron Valley.

husband Uriah (2 Samuel 11). This kind of behaviour has been typical of
royal households from time immemorial, and continues to be so. But
somewhat surprising is the bold denunciation of David's behaviour by
the prophet Nathan, and the apparently deep sincerity of David's
subsequent change of heart (2 Samuel 12:1–15). The inclusion of such a
personal story relates to the concerns of the deuteronomic historians,
who wanted to remind their readers that even David, the greatest of all
kings, was still subordinate to a higher power than himself, namely the
values of the covenant with Yahweh. But David's personal failings did
not threaten his position, as is underlined by the inclusion of an oracle

previously delivered by the same prophet Nathan, declaring that God had established a specially close personal relationship with David's family, ensuring that David's sons would succeed him in perpetuity, and David himself could enjoy special privilege as God's 'son' (2 Samuel 7:1–17).

Throughout the ancient world, kings were described in this kind of lofty language, and though on occasion it could imply a claim to divinity (as with the pharaohs of Egypt), more often it was just a general part of the metaphorical language used to highlight the uniquely privileged position of a monarch. Of course, it could easily be used as a way of legitimizing anything that a king might want to do, and that certainly happened from time to time in Israel, just as it did elsewhere.

Trade in Solomon's time.

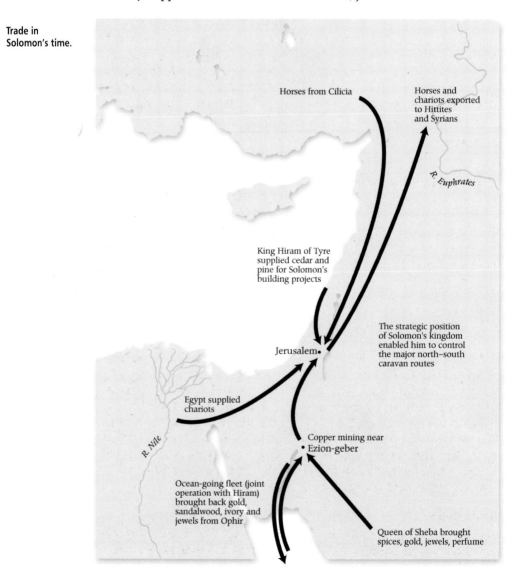

Horses from Cilicia

Horses and chariots exported to Hittites and Syrians

R. *Euphrates*

King Hiram of Tyre supplied cedar and pine for Solomon's building projects

The strategic position of Solomon's kingdom enabled him to control the major north–south caravan routes

Jerusalem

Egypt supplied chariots

R. *Nile*

Copper mining near Ezion-geber

Ocean-going fleet (joint operation with Hiram) brought back gold, sandalwood, ivory and jewels from Ophir

Queen of Sheba brought spices, gold, jewels, perfume

But the editors of these stories make it clear that continued divine approval of the royal family operated within a moral framework, whose values derived from the covenant relationship between God and people established at Mount Sinai. In effect, the kind of royal ideology represented by Nathan's oracle became a way of incorporating the king into the covenant, thereby investing him with special privileges. But by the same token, he was also faced with the moral requirements of the covenant, and his position as God's 'son' meant he could be punished by God, just as any other parent might punish their children for wrongdoing.

As the story unfolds, this lesson is reinforced in many different ways. The kings of David's dynasty did not live up to these high aspirations but, as Samuel had foreseen, became like the kings of other nations, more often concerned for themselves than for their covenant obligations to God and to their people (1 Samuel 8:10–18). However, this promise to David and his family was to assume great importance at a later stage in Israel's history, as frustrated political ambitions came to be transferred to a future hope for an ideal descendant of David, the Messiah.

Solomon

Towards the end of David's reign, the prospective heirs began to jockey for position. Revolts led by David's son Absalom (2 Samuel 13–19) and Sheba, a man from the tribe of Benjamin (2 Samuel 20:1–22), were crushed, and by the time of David's death his son Adonijah was the most obvious successor. He had the support of Abiathar the priest and of Joab, who was commander of the national army (1 Kings 1:5–10). But another son, Solomon, had more powerful friends. His mother Bathsheba had been David's favourite wife, and she was supported by Nathan, the priest Zadok and Benaiah, the commander of David's own private army. In the end, Solomon won, and with the exception of Abiathar the priest, who was sent off into exile, Adonijah and all his supporters were killed (1 Kings 1:11 – 2:46). Right from the start, Solomon's emergence as king was founded on court intrigues and military strength. Unlike his father David, and Saul before him, his position depended only on the fact that he was the head of state. He was indeed a king like the rulers of other nations, who did not need to seek the approval of his people because by now a ruling class had developed, in which Solomon was pre-eminent. This development was viewed ambivalently by the deuteronomic editors, who applauded the achievements which had led to the emergence of Israel as a powerful nation state, while at the same time raising serious questions about the kind of spirituality often invoked to strengthen the position of the kings.

The empire

Militarily, Israel's position had been secured before Solomon came to power, and though there is evidence to suggest that both the Edomites and the

Syrians recovered some territory during his reign (1 Kings 11:14–25), this was a period of consolidation rather than expansion. Solomon set about securing the position of the state and enhancing his own situation, and at this time poured vast resources into the development of the private army that his father had left to him. What had probably been in David's day little more than a personal bodyguard for the king now developed into a sophisticated fighting force, whose resources are listed as 1,400 chariots and 12,000 men and horses (1 Kings 4:26; 10:26). Chariots had once been the monopoly of the Canaanite city states, and it was this more than anything else that had prevented the tribes in the days of the judges from establishing their own settlements in the plains at the centre of the country. No doubt Solomon utilized the wider expertise of Canaanite culture in developing such weapons, for his own chariots were stationed exclusively in old Canaanite strongholds.

Alliances

Solomon adopted a policy of forging alliances with other neighbouring states as a means of consolidating his own position. Phoenicia, Arabia, Syria and Cilicia, and some states in north and east Africa, all became significant trading partners, while relationships with Egypt were cemented by Solomon's marriage to an Egyptian princess. This must have been an especially important alliance, for a special palace was built for this Egyptian wife. The pharaoh of the time also took it seriously, for he captured the city of Gezer and gave it to Solomon as a wedding gift (1 Kings 9:16–17), the archaeological evidence from Gezer showing both the destruction caused when the Egyptians destroyed it and Solomon's reconstruction of it in a distinctive style.

Another of Solomon's close allies was Hiram, king of Tyre. The Phoenicians had widespread trading links throughout the Mediterranean Sea, and they gave Solomon assistance to develop his own sea trade in the Red Sea and the Indian Ocean (1 Kings 9:26–28; 10:22). They also probably helped him with the expertise necessary to build and operate his own copper refineries on the Gulf of Aqabah. Solomon was also a horse dealer on a grand scale, trading with the Egyptians to the south and the Hittites in the north.

A ship from Solomon's merchant fleet.

The Temple

The profits from all this activity helped to finance the construction of many buildings in Jerusalem: Solomon's own palace, a palace for his Egyptian wife, a hall of audience for state occasions, a smaller judgment hall and, of course, the Temple.

David had originally wanted to build a permanent temple to house the ark of the covenant (2 Samuel 7:1–17). He had been unable to do so, but that did not stop him securing a site and gathering together items to

Solomon's Temple

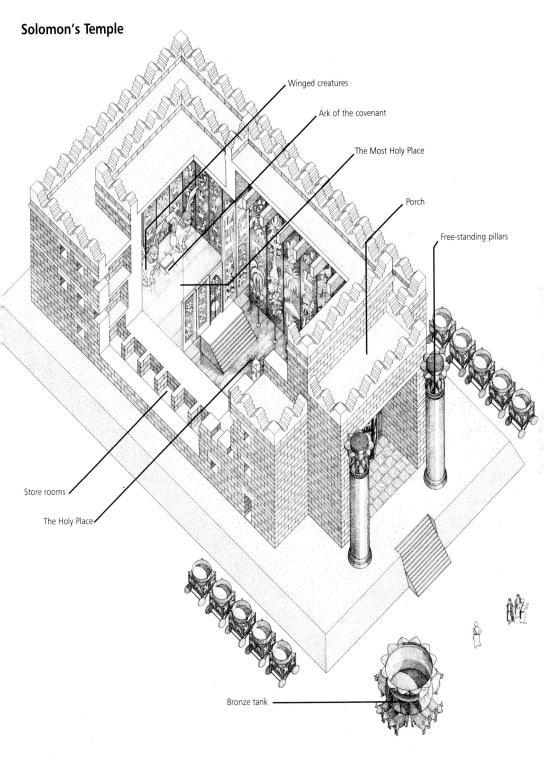

Winged creatures

Ark of the covenant

The Most Holy Place

Porch

Free-standing pillars

Store rooms

The Holy Place

Bronze tank

go into a temple (2 Samuel 24:18–25; 2 Chronicles 3:1). Solomon was remembered by later generations of Israelites largely because of his completion of this project. Like everything else that he attempted, the work was carried out on a lavish scale. The best materials were imported at great cost, and skilled craftworkers were brought in from Phoenicia. Throughout the region, the building of a temple was part of the process of establishing royal ideology and providing a religious legitimization for the existence of a state. The general design of the Temple Solomon had built in Jerusalem was typical of others throughout the region, and though it was to contain the ark of the covenant, which symbolized the presence of Israel's God Yahweh, the actual plan was identical to shrines in honour of Baal that have been discovered elsewhere in Palestine (1 Kings 5–7).

It is difficult to know exactly how Solomon viewed his Temple, though the similarities with temples honouring other deities certainly extend well beyond the architecture. For example, the Jerusalem Temple was consecrated at exactly the same time in the year as the Baal temple at Ugarit, just before the beginning of the all-important autumn rains (1 Kings 6:1, 37–38; 8:2), and Solomon assumed for himself some of the most important religious functions (1 Kings 3:15; 8:62–66), such as the offering of sacrifices and blessing the people (1 Kings 8:14–61). These were all functions that monarchs would naturally undertake, for they were a way of affirming their own position as head of state. But it is striking that, only a few pages before in the deuteronomic history, Saul and David had been expressly forbidden to do both these things, and Saul's attempt to do so had led directly to his downfall (1 Samuel 15:10–35), whereas in this narrative the editor makes no comment at all on these features of Solomon's kingship – presumably because of the

The stories about David and Solomon

The books of Samuel and Kings belong together, and are a compilation of different stories gathered by an editor or editors to make one great account of Israel's history, which probably included the books of Joshua and Judges as well. Quite often, the editors refer to their sources of information (e.g. 1 Kings 11:41). At other points, scholars have tried to uncover the origins of their stories. More often than not, this has proved to be an unprofitable exercise, but in the case of the stories of David and Solomon many people believe that such 'source analysis' can show that we are actually reading a kind of 'court

history' that was written down more or less at the same time as the events themselves happened.

The stories in 2 Samuel 9–20 and 1 Kings 1–2 are undoubtedly among the most vivid narratives in the entire Old Testament. They are well written and excitingly presented, with the kind of psychological appreciation of human relationships that gives an added plausibility and realism to what they say. In this respect they are quite different from what precedes or follows them – and even from the final chapters of 2 Samuel itself (21–24).

In 1926, the German scholar Leonhard Rost suggested that this section of Samuel and Kings was originally a self-contained

central importance later attached to Jerusalem and its Temple. Such criticism as there is was reserved for what many saw as Solomon's active promotion of the interests of 'foreign deities' (1 Kings 11:1–13). Looking back from a longer historical perspective, his careless disregard for the original values of the covenant could be seen to have been a major factor in his eventual downfall. Solomon may have been renowned for his wisdom, but it was not the kind of practical wisdom that led to a sympathetic understanding of his own people, or to an appreciation of the kind of king that Israel's faith would tolerate.

Arts and science

The 'wisdom' attributed to Solomon was in fact not just common sense and human insight. It was, rather, part and parcel of a great international intellectual movement of the day that is often simply referred to as the 'wisdom movement'. As such, Solomon's involvement with it was yet another indication of his royal status, not only within Israel, but also on the wider world stage. The writer of 1 Kings explicitly compares Solomon's 'wisdom' with that of other ancient rulers: 'Solomon's wisdom surpassed the wisdom of all the people of the east, and all the wisdom of Egypt. He was wiser than anyone else' (1 Kings 4:30–31). The nature of this intellectual endeavour becomes clearer when we learn that 'he composed 3,000 proverbs and more than a thousand songs. He spoke of trees and plants... he talked about animals, birds, reptiles, and fish' (1 Kings 4:32–33). This is comparable to the intellectual pursuits of kings and philosophers throughout the history of ancient Egypt and Mesopotamia, who compiled encyclopaedic descriptions of the world and all its affairs, covering subjects as diverse as astrology, mathematics, politics and zoology. The knowledge thus gained was sometimes distilled

story, compiled in order to prove that Solomon was the legitimate heir to David's throne. There is no doubt that the accession of Solomon is surprising, for he was a relatively minor son, and apart from a short notice of his birth in 2 Samuel 12:24–25 there is no mention of him before he became king. He also came to power through a court intrigue and by murdering his opponents, something which Rost suggested must have stirred many loyal Israelites to start asking awkward questions. In response, a supporter of Solomon set out to justify his position as legitimate heir to the throne – and, in the nature of things, he must have done so at an early date in Solomon's reign.

There was a well-established tradition of such political apologetic among other nations at the time, especially the Hittites. So, encouraged by international contacts, and the new opportunities for artistic endeavour provided by Solomon's court, Solomon's friend took the older traditional stories about David's reign, and showed how the elder sons Amnon, Absalom and Adonijah, had all disqualified themselves by their disregard for the covenant traditions (2 Samuel 13:8–14; 16:22; 1 Kings 2:13–17). This was why Solomon emerged as David's successor, and the brutal events which brought him to power were a regrettable but necessary evil.

Rost hailed this narrative as the beginning of real history writing in the ancient world, though recent scholars have

into pithy sayings, such as we find in the Old Testament book of Proverbs, parts of which are said to have been composed by Solomon himself (Proverbs 10:1; 25:1). In a later period, professional wisdom teachers could be found as religious advisers, occupying an official position comparable to that of a priest (Jeremiah 18:18), though at this stage the pursuit of 'wisdom' was probably a secular interest.

All this activity stimulated the development of other literary skills in Israel. We know that Solomon had his own official archivists who recorded the events of his reign (1 Kings 11:41), and it is also widely believed that the stories of Samuel, Saul and David were written down in a continuous narrative at this time (though not in their final form). It is certainly not unlikely that a successful king would want to record the events that led up to his accession to the throne. Many scholars have also postulated that as a reaction against all this self-centred artistic and intellectual endeavour, other writers during Solomon's reign wove the traditional stories handed down by the tribes into a great epic account of Israel's earliest history, which later was incorporated into the books of the Torah. The purpose of this was to emphasize again how Abraham, Moses and the early tribes had prospered not because of their own efforts, but because of their humble dependence on the love and goodness of God.

Balancing the books

For a variety of reasons, there was growing ill-feeling and resentment against the style of Solomon's rule. Some still regretted the replacement of voluntary tribal associations by the apparatus of a state, while the emerging underclass that was inevitably created saw no reason why they should actually pay for the king's extravagant lifestyle through

---

The stories about David and Solomon *continued*

been more hesitant. They point out, for example, that these stories contain much that is unfavourable to David and Solomon, and therefore perhaps what we now have is an expurgated version of a series of stories that originally disapproved of the Davidic dynasty. This argument carries less weight if the original intention was apologetic, for in such a situation, unfortunate facts have to be faced, and explained away in some way or another rather than ignored altogether. But it has also been suggested that much of the material is more like a novel than historical narrative. It certainly includes some surprising details, such as the conversation that Amnon had with Tamar as he raped her (2 Samuel 13:1–22), though features

like that do not necessarily call into question the general impression created by the narrative. It simply shows that it was written in the first instance by a journalist rather than an annalist, which in turn perhaps suggests that it was not really the official court record of David, but a popular account of Solomon's origins, designed to win the support of the average person in the street for their new king.

taxation. Taxation, however, is an inevitable part of the infrastructure required to support any state, and Solomon's trading activities could never have generated sufficient funds to finance what needed to be done. On occasion, he tried to pay off his creditors by giving them land or cities, as with Hiram of Tyre (an offer which was refused, 1 Kings 9:10–14).

The administrative framework for the collection of taxes already existed, for David had inaugurated a modest system whereby twelve different districts of his territory would support his court with provisions for one month each year. Solomon extended this to provide the means for collecting taxes, and each district was placed in the charge of a single officer (1 Kings 4:7–19). The idea had little appeal for the people, not so much because they were reluctant to pay their dues, but more because of resistance to the idea of a privileged elite being served and paid for by the ordinary citizens. But this is all part and parcel of how a state needs to operate, and though the deuteronomic editors might hint that it was a Canaanite way of doing things, and therefore an erosion of the traditions represented by the ancestral faith of Israel, it was an inescapable consequence of the kind of political entity that Israel had now become.

Worse was to come, however, for the taxation raised in the districts was still not enough to balance Solomon's books, and so he introduced what the Old Testament euphemistically calls 'forced labour' – in other words, slavery (1 Kings 5:13; 11:28). There has been debate as to whether Israelites were included in such schemes, but whoever the workers were, the whole idea turned out to be one of the key factors in precipitating a coup under the leadership of Jeroboam, one of the officers in charge of the taxation districts. This plot was uncovered, and he fled into exile in Egypt for a while (1 Kings 11:26–40), but the movement that he represented was too deeply rooted to be stopped. The tribes in the northern part of Solomon's kingdom – the original tribes who had chosen Saul as their leader – had had enough. Not only did they regard Solomon's demands as excessive, but they believed them to be unfair, for the southern tribes – who first made David their king – appear to have been excluded from the taxation districts altogether (1 Kings 4:7–19).

The seeds of Solomon's destruction germinated in the same soil as many revolutionary political movements: the exploitation of an underclass by the rulers. Later generations regarded that not only as incompetent government, but also as a gross violation of the standards of the covenant, by which all rulers would be judged – and by those standards Solomon was a miserable failure, no matter how successful he might otherwise have been.

After Solomon

When Solomon died he was succeeded by his son, Rehoboam. But by then an irreversible change of mood had come over the northern tribal grouping: they had had enough of dynastic kingship, and they were looking for a return to a simpler ideal of statehood in which the people, and not an elite ruling class, would decide their own fate. As we have seen, the exact details of the evolution of the Israelite state are among the most hotly debated subjects in Old Testament scholarship. But however it might be accounted for, it seems indisputable that there was by this period a deeply ingrained conviction among much of the population that the true calling of the nation was to form an egalitarian social community based on the understanding of God's own personality as revealed through the stories of the covenant forged at Mount Sinai.

So when Rehoboam went north from Jerusalem to Shechem to secure the allegiance of the northern tribes, their local leaders announced the terms on which they would be prepared to acknowledge him as their king (1 Kings 12:1–7). Rehoboam's oldest and most experienced advisers told him to listen sympathetically, but he rejected their advice and warned the northern leaders that worse was to come: 'My father placed heavy burdens on you; I will make them even heavier. He beat you with a whip; I'll flog you with a horsewhip!' (1 Kings 12:14). He regarded them as rebellious subjects, and got ready to force them back into line. But it was too late: Jeroboam had already returned from Egypt, and the people had acclaimed him as their king. It was an

---

The psalms and Israel's worship

The psalms were fundamental to Israelite worship, and in many respects can be understood as providing a detailed account of the religious activities at the Jerusalem Temple in the period before the exile to Babylon. Two points in particular have contributed much to our understanding of this subject:

● Many of the psalms can be understood not just as hymns, but as more comprehensive liturgies. Not only do they reflect the praise and penitence of the worshippers – they also contain God's response to that worship (e.g. Psalms 2; 12; 20; 21; 45; 50; 81; 89; 91; 95; 108; 110; 132). Moreover, these responses are often similar in both style and substance to the messages of the Old Testament prophets, and on this basis it has been suggested that in the Temple at Jerusalem there was a group of prophets who worked alongside the priests in leading the people in worship. When it was first made,

this claim was a surprise to many Old Testament scholars. In the nineteenth century it had often been taken for granted that in Old Testament times the prophets and the priests were firmly opposed to each other, with the priests being concerned with the mechanical performance of rites of 'religion', while the prophets concerned themselves with a more dynamic spirituality, bringing a living word from God to their people. It is certainly true that most of the prophets had hard things to say about the meaningless performance of empty religious rituals. But this perception of a sharp division between priest and prophet often owed more to the intense anti-Catholic views of Protestant (especially German Lutheran) scholars than it did to the evidence of the Hebrew Bible itself. Even Amos, who is often thought to be one of those most fiercely opposed to religious rituals, apparently delivered his messages in the context of organized worship at Bethel, while the book of Jeremiah not only lists prophets and priests

irreversible change, and from this point onwards the northern tribes had their own king and their own kingdom (Israel) while the descendants of David in Jerusalem ruled over a much smaller kingdom in the south (Judah). Israel's golden age was past, and the future would witness gradual dissolution and decline until both kingdoms would eventually disappear.

Society and religion

The years between Saul and Solomon saw the establishment of a distinctively Israelite society for the first time. Despite the problems that it caused, the idea of a monarchy was accepted, and even when the ten tribes broke away under Jeroboam they did little to change the outward forms of the state established by Solomon; they simply explained them in a different way. So it is to be expected that the events of these years should have set the pattern for Israel's life for many years to come. In spite of the tensions that surfaced among different factions in the population, the reigns of David and Solomon were looked back upon with affection by all later generations. Though the deuteronomic editors of Israel's history books could see much to be ashamed of in the activities of them both, that did nothing to diminish the esteem in

together as leaders of the community (Jeremiah 18:18), but also gives other indications of the association of prophets with the Jerusalem Temple (e.g. Jeremiah 5:30–31; 23:11; 26:7, 16; 27:16; 29:26). Scholars have described these people as 'cult prophets' in an effort to distinguish them from figures such as Amos or Jeremiah. In Jeremiah's time, most of them were giving false reassurance to the people, and as a result their office disappeared after the Babylonian exile. But the book of Psalms gives some indication that at an earlier period they had a full and perfectly legitimate part to play in the worship of God at the Temple.

● A number of scholars have also claimed on the basis of the psalms that the king played a significant role in the worship at the Temple. This is intrinsically likely anyway, as involvement in public ritual was a key way in which rulers could establish and reinforce the legitimacy of their reign. There was a good deal of diversity in the ways that ancient people thought of their kings. Some of them were

Many different instruments were used in worship at the Jerusalem Temple, one of which was the harp. Here, a musician seated on a folding stool plays a harp.

which they were held, David being credited with the authorship of much of the Old Testament book of Psalms, while Solomon was thought of as the founder of the 'wisdom movement' in ancient Israel. Regardless of their weaknesses, these kings and their successors in Jerusalem exerted a considerable influence on the religious and cultural life of their people. The important religious message of the various books traditionally connected with David and Solomon will be considered in some detail in later chapters. But it is appropriate here to notice some aspects of the picture they provide of religious life and culture in ancient Israel.

The psalms

The Old Testament book of Psalms consists of 150 separate pieces of religious poetry or songs, arranged in five separate sections, or 'books'. The way in which the psalms are numbered is slightly different in the Hebrew Bible from in the Greek (Septuagint) version, and Christian Bibles all follow the Greek scheme. Psalms 1–8 are the same in both, but then Psalms 9–10 in the Hebrew Bible were combined into just one, Psalm 9, in the Septuagint. From that point on, the numbers do not correspond until the final section of the book, where they come together again at Psalm 147. The Greek Bible also included a Psalm 151, which

---

The psalms and Israel's worship *continued*

regarded as divine or semi-divine beings, whose well-being was crucial to the continued prosperity of their people. The king's involvement in religious ritual might be connected with the cycle of the seasons, as appears to have been the case in Babylon, for example, where the king appeared in the annual New Year Festival acting out the part of a god, whose ritual death and resurrection then symbolized the death and renewed vitality of nature. Israel never thought of their kings as divine, though the royal ideology of the House of David did insist that they enjoyed a special position as a result of God's blessing upon them (Psalm 2:7). Whether there was an annual festival in Israel at which the king underwent a ritual humiliation and restoration along the lines of the Babylonian festival is more debatable, though it seems likely that the annual celebration of the New Year was a major religious event in Israel, albeit centred on the enthronement of God, and the celebration of Yahweh's continued sovereignty over the forces of chaos and

disorder that continually threatened Israel's precarious existence. Others, however, have denied this, preferring instead to see the New Year festival in Israel (the feast of Tabernacles) as an occasion for solemn renewal of the covenant made at Mount Sinai, or even as an annual celebration of the establishment of the royal family of David. Beyond inferences that can be drawn from some of the psalms, and cryptic passages elsewhere, there is little hard evidence to show just what religious functions the king might have carried out in ancient Israel, though he is unlikely to have been exclusively, or even mainly, a religious functionary. Religious imagery and ritual could be used to bolster the king's position, but the overall impression given by the Old Testament is of men whose activities had some interaction with religious worship, but whose main sphere of operation was elsewhere, in the judicial and diplomatic functions of the ancient monarch.

was never included either in the Hebrew Bible or in any version of the Christian Old Testament. This was ascribed to David, and consists of a reflection on the story of David's choice as king (1 Samuel 16:1–13). Though Psalm 151 is known from the Greek version, the Dead Sea Scrolls contain sections of two psalms in Hebrew which seem to have formed the basis for it, so presumably it was originally translated into Greek, rather than compiled in that language. Its date is impossible to determine.

As a collection, the book of Psalms was probably brought together for use in the worship of the restored Temple that was built in Jerusalem about 520 BC, after the Jewish exile in Babylon. Naturally, some of the psalms were written at that time (e.g. Psalm 137), though the majority were not, and it is widely agreed that they mostly originated in the worship of God by ancient Israel during the period from about 1000 BC to 586 BC. Many of the psalms have titles, but these were not a part of the original compositions, and are rightly relegated to footnotes in modern versions of the Bible. Some of these titles contain musical directions, indicating the tune to which particular compositions were to be sung, or the musical instruments that might be used to accompany them. Others indicate that a particular psalm was connected with David, the sons of Korah, sons of Asaph, and others. The precise meaning of such ascriptions is often unclear. Even the term 'a psalm of David' could just as easily mean 'a psalm for David', and may not necessarily have been intended as a claim that he was its author. Such a title could also indicate that the psalm in question originally belonged to a collection of songs issued by the Davidic royal house in Jerusalem, or that it was written for the king there, who was of course always David's descendant. There is no compelling reason for rejecting the possibility that some of these psalms could go back to David himself, though in the nature of such things it will never be possible to know for certain.

Life is always a kaleidoscope of conflicting experiences and emotions – and we find this variety reflected in the contents of the Old Testament psalms. Not all psalms are the same. Some of them are majestic hymns of praise to God, reflecting the joy of the jubilant worshipper who is at peace with God and with the world (Psalms 145–150). By contrast, others reflect the darker moments of human experience. Feelings of guilt feature in some of them (Psalms 51; 130), while others consist of songs of protest complaining about unjust suffering (Psalms 13; 71). Some psalms give a glimpse of how the whole nation might react in a time of national disaster or uncertainty (Psalms 44; 74; 80; 83), while others invite us to share in the great ceremonial events of national life, such as the coronation or wedding of a king (Psalm 45), and yet others contain intimate expressions of heartfelt gratitude to God by an individual worshipper who had been delivered from some personal trial (Psalms 30; 92; 116).

In the early years of the twentieth century, the psalms were classified along these lines by a German scholar, Hermann Gunkel, who proposed five main categories: hymns of praise, individual songs of lament, community laments, individual songs of thanks, and royal psalms. This classification has stood the test of time, though it is in some respects unsatisfactory. For example, Gunkel tended to make too sharp a distinction between individual and community psalms: a

number of psalms that begin as the words of a single person go on to speak not just of an individual, but of the whole nation of Israel (Psalms 51; 102; 130). It might also be questioned how distinctive the category of 'royal psalms' actually is, for all the royal psalms could easily be fitted into other categories, the only thing that binds them together being their reference to the king.

Their diversity and versatility suggest that the psalms must have been used in a number of different

A number of the psalms depict Jerusalem as a place of security, and encourage people to pray for the peace of the city.

ways. Gunkel, for example, assumed that they were mostly personal expressions of piety, the sort of poetry that any worshipper might use to express their deepest feelings about life and about God. Others have argued that the psalms do not reflect individual experiences, but the experience of the whole nation of Israel over a long period of time. It has even been suggested that they are a kind of spiritual temperature chart of Israel's history from the earliest days up to the time after the exile. Both these elements are no doubt present, but what is fundamental to the varied thoughts of the psalms is a deep religious experience that their authors knew to be relevant to the whole of life. For the sense of God's reality can come as readily from nature (Psalms 8; 104) as from Israel's history (Psalms 78; 105) or from the writer's own private experiences (Psalms 31; 130).

Wisdom

Just as David was traditionally associated with the types of religious poetry we find in the book of Psalms, so Jewish tradition has linked Solomon with the so-called 'Wisdom' books of the Hebrew Bible, and the deuterocanonical books of the Christian Old Testament actually contain one such book, called the Wisdom of Solomon.

Paradoxically, there is only one book in the Hebrew Bible that mentions Solomon in its title, the Song of Solomon – and that is not a wisdom book at all! Moreover, it probably has no direct connection with Solomon, other than the fact that his name occurs in it a number of times (Song of Solomon 1:1, 5; 3:7–11; 8:11–12). Indeed, the way he is mentioned in these passages rather suggests that he was not the author of it. Its exact origins are uncertain. It contains at least one Persian word (4:13) and one word that may be Greek (3:9), which would suggest it was written sometime after the rise of the Persian empire in 539 BC. But it also has features that suggest a much earlier origin, while there is some evidence of similar poetry in the nations surrounding Israel, dating from long before the time of Solomon. It is quite likely, therefore, that it is really an anthology of poetry, rather than a continuous composition written at one particular point in time. Its subject (sexual love) is certainly timeless, and it consists of a collection of erotic poems in which a woman and her lover exchange intimate details about their relationship. Many readers of the book, both Jewish and Christian, have been alarmed by its frankness, and have preferred to think of it as a symbolic writing, representing the relationship between God and the people of Israel, or between Christ and the church. But such ideas were certainly not in the minds of those who first included it in the Hebrew Bible. For them, God was the creator of all things, including sex and relationships, and a collection of love poems was therefore no more out of place than the story of God's dealings with Israel in the great events of their national history.

Solomon's name and influence has more often been connected with two other Old Testament books: Proverbs and Ecclesiastes. Along with the book of Job, and (from the deuterocanonical books) the Wisdom of Ben Sira and Wisdom of Solomon, these are usually classed together as 'wisdom' books. Their message is explored in detail in later chapters, but knowing a little of their origins will help us here in understanding the nature of Israelite culture.

What is wisdom?

There is no short, simple answer to this question. When Solomon is described as a 'wise man', the description seems to include many different characteristics. To be wise was 'to know the difference between good and evil' (1 Kings 3:9), but it also included political skills to deal with his own people and diplomacy in international relations (1 Kings 5:7, 12), as well as possession of the sort of knowledge we would associate with a botanist or zoologist (1 Kings 4:33). In addition to all that, Solomon's wisdom also included the ability to write poetry (1 Kings 4:32) and sensitivity in resolving legal disputes (1 Kings 3:16–28).

From this, it seems that when the ancients spoke of 'wisdom' they included all those elements in a person's character and upbringing that enable them to be a mature and successful member of society. In order to find a meaningful place in society, there are certain things we need to know. Nowadays, much emphasis tends to be placed on educational achievements, or proficiency in particular skills which will equip people to perform a specific job. No doubt vocational training had its place in the life of the ancient world, but being fully human involved much more than that – and this is what forms the substance of the wisdom literature of the Old Testament. These wisdom books reflect a broad cross-section of moral insights, intellectual thinking and social skills that would equip a person to live in an informed and mature way. The influence of several specific life situations can be traced in this literature.

THE FAMILY

In recent Western culture, it has often been assumed that the state should prepare children for life, both in terms of vocational training and in moral and religious teaching. But in most other cultures, it is in the context of the family that children can learn by both precept and example the distilled wisdom of previous generations. Here, they discover effective ways of relating to other people, and what to avoid if they want to have a happy and fulfilled existence. All of this is based on

---

The wisdom books

Like the Psalms and most of the messages of the prophets, the wisdom books are written in poetry. In Hebrew poetry the most important feature is not its metrical form, but a device known as 'parallelism', in which the ideas that are communicated are the most important thing. In the simplest form of poetry ('synonymous parallelism'), the second line of a typical couplet simply repeats in different words the thought of the first line:

> Who has the right to go up Yahweh's hill?
> Who may enter God's holy Temple?
> (Psalm 24:3)

'Antithetic parallelism' can make the same point by placing one part of the couplet in a positive form, while expressing the other negatively:

> Good people will be remembered as a blessing,
> but the wicked will soon be forgotten.
> (Proverbs 10:7)

There are a good many other more subtle and intricate forms of verse, and sometimes there is a parallelism just of form, and not of meaning.

Many other literary devices are used in the wisdom books, including riddles, parables and autobiographical advice, as well as dialogue (as in Job). The acrostic is also occasionally used, that is a poetic composition in which each couplet or section begins with a different letter of the alphabet, starting with the first letter and working through to the end. Psalm 119 is the most striking example of this in the Old Testament, but Proverbs 31:10–31 also uses the same device.

Proverbs
This book is a collection or anthology of practical wisdom. The title (1:1) attributes the book to Solomon, though it is only in two places (10:1 – 22:16; 25:1 – 29:27) that Solomon is explicitly connected with its teaching. Other sections are attributed to Agur (30:1–33) and Lemuel (31:1–9), both characters of whom nothing else is known. Yet other sections are presented as anonymous compositions, which is exactly what we would expect in view of the likely origins of the kind of practical advice that the book contains.

Many of the wisdom sayings in Proverbs go back a long way into Israel's history, and were obviously composed long before the book itself was edited in its present form. The earliest date that could possibly be

the experience of their parents, and before them of their grandparents, who in turn inherited much from their own forebears. The family was the place where children learned social skills in ancient Israel, and many of the sayings in the book of Proverbs originated in this context and have the form of advice given by a parent to a child (e.g. Proverbs 4:1, 3–4, 10, 20).

THE VILLAGE

In addition to being a part of a family, we all belong to a larger community in the place where we live, and much of the 'wisdom' that equips us for life is derived from relationships in that context. Again, this is something that has become increasingly alien to many Western people, who live in physical isolation from others, often relying on the television or the Internet to provide them with a sense of 'community'. Even in the West, though, there are still many places which have the

given to this final editing would be the sixth century BC, since Hezekiah (king of Judah from 715 to 687 BC) is mentioned in 25:1. But it is more likely that the final editing of Proverbs was not completed until around the third century BC.

The book is mostly concerned with advice about relationships in different areas of life. As such it contains the sort of guidance about good manners and sensible behaviour that could have originated in any society. But the editors have gone out of their way to emphasize that the true meaning of such wisdom could only be found in a living relationship with God: 'To have knowledge, you must first have reverence for Yahweh' (1:7).

Ecclesiastes

This is a very different kind of book from Proverbs. Whereas Proverbs takes an optimistic view of life, and makes a positive assessment of its potential, Ecclesiastes is essentially negative and sceptical. If the wisdom books are indeed based on the distilled experiences of real people, its negative cynicism need not come as a surprise. There can be few people who could not at some time identify with the questions posed by the author of Ecclesiastes, who in the opening words asks whether life has any real

meaning, or whether instead it is 'all useless' (1:2). The author vacillates between these two, and though there is an underlying belief in God, there is also the honest recognition that faith sometimes seems to give little meaning to the details of everyday activities. There is no mention of Israel's history here, nor of the nation's experiences in events like the exodus, which other authors of the Hebrew Bible would have referred to as some sort of answer to the writer's questions. Instead, the author concedes that, while the mere reiteration of traditional religious dogmas is sometimes powerless to solve life's most pressing problems, ultimately the meaning of it all is known to God, even if the human mind finds it impossible to comprehend. In practical terms, 'all we can do is to be happy and do the best we can while we are still alive. All of us should eat and drink and enjoy what we have worked for. It is God's gift' (3:12–13).

The apparent unbelief of Ecclesiastes has caused problems for both Jewish and Christian readers of the book. But it does bear witness to two facts that are of fundamental importance. It reminds readers that there is a dimension of human life which cannot be understood by the exercise of rational thought, and it testifies to the reality – and acceptability – of doubt and

In Israelite communities, the city or village gate was the place where the elders sat. There, judgments were passed, and business transacted.

sense of community that is widespread elsewhere in the world. In Israelite villages, everything happened at the city or village gate. Justice was dispensed there, and it was also the place where the great issues of life were debated. It was the place where people went to exchange views and ideas, and some of this kind of 'wisdom' is also contained in the wisdom books of the Hebrew Bible. In one of his speeches, the hero of the book of Job says that he had regularly taken his place at

The wisdom books
continued

uncertainty about God's ways, even in the midst of a community of believing people.

Ecclesiastes identifies its author as 'David's son, who was king in Jerusalem' (1:1). This was probably meant to indicate Solomon, though there are compelling reasons against supposing that he had any connection with it:

● The author often writes from the point of view of an oppressed subject rather than that of an absolute monarch like Solomon (4:1).

● He also seems to have lived in a province of a great empire like that of the Persians, for the book contains a warning against the spies of the rulers (5:8).

● Political upheavals are mentioned, but of a kind that were not experienced in Solomon's time (4:13–16).

● The Hebrew language in which Ecclesiastes is written shows clear signs of the influence of Aramaic, which was the language of the Persian empire. This suggests a date in the third or second century BC.

Job

The book of Job falls into two parts, with a prologue and epilogue written in prose (1–2; 42:7–17) and the rest in poetry. The prologue and epilogue contain an old story about an otherwise unknown individual

called Job, who was an upright and God-fearing person and also 'the richest man in the east' (1:3). But then in a series of inexplicable calamities he lost all that he had and was himself afflicted with a painful and disfiguring disease. This part of the story depicts God as the president of a heavenly court, and explains Job's sufferings by reference to an accusation brought against him by the prosecutor, who is named as Satan. The charge was that Job's spiritual commitment was not genuine, and so his sincerity was put to the test as a means of verifying his faith, and at the end of the story (42:7–17) Job's proverbial patience was rewarded by renewed prosperity and happiness. Some features of this story (such as the part played by Satan) suggest a fairly late date in Jewish history, though other features seem to set it in a very early historical context. Perhaps it was an ancient story that was adapted by a later wisdom writer, to provide an opportunity for the exploration of the place of suffering and evil, which is the theme of the major part of the book.

Job is clearly not a wisdom book in the same sense as Proverbs. Whereas much of the homespun advice of Proverbs implies that doing good will automatically lead to success and prosperity, Job puts a series of question marks against that kind of

the city gate with those who went to debate and ponder on life's great mysteries (Job 29:7), thereby perhaps hinting that much of the argument contained in that book had been well rehearsed in such a setting in many an Israelite settlement. Proverbs also refers to the discussions at the city gate (24:7; 31:23, 31), and no doubt much of the advice contained in that book had its origins in the same context.

THE ROYAL COURT

The sort of advice that was given in the family and at the city gate would not have been unique to Israel. People of all cultures have their equivalents, and the ancient world was no different from the modern one in that respect. One of the results of Solomon's great expansion of trade and international diplomacy was that the people of Israel became familiar with the 'wisdom' traditions of the surrounding nations. Just as the Queen of Sheba came to Jerusalem to find out about Israelite

---

easygoing optimism. In Job's case, doing good had evidently led to exactly the opposite outcome, and the conventional view connecting goodness with prosperity was so deeply entrenched in the culture that the only way his friends could think of to try to help him was by suggesting that maybe he was not as good as he thought he was – otherwise why would he have suffered at all? Job knew this to be untrue, and rejected their diagnosis out of hand. But this was not the only problem with which he had to contend, for in the midst of it all he found himself wrestling with the same problems as the writer of Ecclesiastes. Far from finding God in these adversities, Job felt abandoned by the very God whom he had so diligently served. Where was God, he asked – indeed, what sort of a God would leave someone as upright as Job to suffer the unpredictable fate determined by a meaningless and evil universe?

Job's friends had no answer to that question, nor is any answer given to it in the book. When the writer eventually records God's answer to Job's questions, it does not include an explanation either of Job's suffering or of the apparent meaninglessness of life itself. Instead, in an impressively majestic poem it draws attention to the grandeur and greatness of both God and the world, and in doing so

redirects Job's thoughts away from himself and towards the glory of God and the created world (38–41). In the face of this self-revelation of God's character and personality, Job recognizes that the only response to make is one of trust and worship. The 'why' of human suffering was not answered as an intellectual question; indeed it is never answered in that way anywhere in the Bible. Job's friends might have been looking for an easy explanation of the presence of so much evil and undeserved suffering in the world, but the writer of the book of Job rejects all simple understandings. Here, the presence of evil in God's world remains an inexplicable enigma, but there is a message for those who struggle with it. As Job realized that he could never resolve his own predicament, and was forced to rely on God alone, he found his broken heart was healed as God burst into his life and surrounded him once more with constant care and love. In the end, renewed and consistent trust in God is the only way to deal with the vicissitudes of human life.

Other wisdom passages in the Hebrew Bible

In addition to those works that can readily be identified as belonging to this genre, scholars have often claimed that materials

wisdom (1 Kings 10:1–13), Israelites themselves were no doubt busy discovering the wisdom of other races. There was a good deal of such wisdom literature available elsewhere, especially in Egypt. One Egyptian text has many striking similarities to parts of the Old Testament book of Proverbs, and it was probably in such international circles that the knowledge of 'trees and plants... animals, birds, reptiles, and fish' (1 Kings 4:33) was handed on. Solomon specialized in such 'wisdom', and in this form it was probably a more intellectual pursuit than the moral advice that was handed on from generation to generation in the family and the village community. The more intellectual nature of such knowledge has led to the suggestion that from the time of Solomon onwards there may have been in Israel a group of professional wisdom teachers, whose job it was to study and teach such subjects in specialized schools. The much later book, the Wisdom of Ben Sira, certainly originated in such a context, though by then (c. 180 BC) the

The wisdom books
continued

originating from wisdom schools can be traced elsewhere in the Old Testament. They point to some of the oracles of the prophets, especially in Amos and Isaiah, which seem to propound similar views to those found in the wisdom literature. We have already noted the theory that the 'succession narrative' (2 Samuel 9–20; 1 Kings 1–2) could have been moralistic 'wisdom' writing, and the same is possibly true of the stories of Joseph (Genesis 37; 39–50), which portray him as an ideal example of a person who lived his life according to the kinds of rules found in the book of Proverbs. It has also been suggested that the portrayal of the heroine of the book of Esther may owe something to such motives. There is nothing to prove any of these speculations, and it is unlikely that any of these stories came into existence purely as a means of demonstrating the value of practical wisdom. However, at the same time, the book of Job does provide a specific example of how an older story could be taken up and reinterpreted in this way, and if the concerns of the wisdom books were deeply embedded in the fabric of Israelite society, then it would be surprising if the same lessons were not articulated in other types of Old Testament literature.

Wisdom in the deuterocanonical books
Two books in the deuterocanonical collection deriving from the Greek Old Testament also fall into the category of wisdom writings. These are the Wisdom of Solomon and the Wisdom of Ben Sira (sometimes known as Ecclesiasticus). Wisdom 9:7–18 seems to imply that Solomon was its author, though without actually naming him, but few in the ancient world regarded it as his composition, and in addition the general cultural and historical circumstances reflected in it, not to mention the style and substance of its teachings, all indicate a much later date. There is no significant evidence to suggest it was ever compiled in any language other than Greek, and indeed it contains many technical terms that were typical of Greek philosophical speculation in the centuries immediately preceding the Christian era. The most obvious place to locate it would be among the Jewish community at Alexandria in Egypt and, since it seems to be unacquainted with the work of Philo of Alexandria, perhaps sometime in the first century BC. The teachings of the Wisdom of Solomon indicate familiarity with concepts drawn from Plato (7:22–24; 11:17; 14:3; 16:21; 17:2; 19:2) as well as the ideas of the Stoics (8:20; 17:11), though the author does not always use them in a technical philosophical

main subject of study would have been the Hebrew scriptures themselves. But at an earlier date, Jeremiah 18:18 mentions 'the wise' alongside priests and prophets as leaders of the nation, and of course from the time of Solomon onwards there were many professional diplomats, who must have been taught reading, writing and other intellectual skills by someone. There may well have been schools in ancient Israel in which knowledge was pursued for its own sake, though in the absence of specific evidence it is not possible to be certain.

way. Its aim appears to have been to encourage Jewish believers to continue in their faith, knowing that even in a culture dominated by a different and apparently more sophisticated world-view, their ancient stories and traditions still made sense. In the process, its message also appealed to those who were not themselves descended from the Israelite people, but who may have been attracted by the ideals of biblical faith, inviting them to abandon the worship of false gods and commit themselves to the covenant faith of Yahweh.

The prologue to the Wisdom of Ben Sira (Sirach) says that it was originally written in Hebrew and then translated into Greek by the author's grandson, and there is no reason to doubt this as copies of sections of the original Hebrew text are known. It is less clear to what extent the two versions were identical, as the translator himself says he made some substantial alterations. The translation itself is precisely dated, to 'the thirty-eighth year of the reign of Euergetes', that is Ptolemy VIII Euergetes Physcon (170–116 BC), which would make the date of the original composition perhaps about 180 BC. All of this seems plausible, and fits the contents of the book, which means this is the only writing of the entire Old Testament which can be precisely dated and attributed to a specific author, whose full

name was Jesus ben Sira (50:27) and who lived in Jerusalem. The work itself is a striking example of the international character of the wisdom movement, for it combines elements of Greek philosophical thinking with traditional concepts from the Hebrew scriptures in a new and creative synthesis. As is often the case with this sort of literature, it is hard to trace a single line of argument running through from start to finish, though the general theme of it is clear: that true wisdom is found in the Torah, and exercised through trust in God. The way in which Ben Sira personified the figure of Wisdom, connecting it with concepts found in the wider culture of the day, provided an important framework within which Christians could later explain their beliefs about Jesus of Nazareth as both human and divine. As with the earlier wisdom books of the Hebrew Bible, however, the main emphasis is on practical morality and acceptable forms of behaviour in the context of everyday life.

5 The Two Kingdoms

A kingdom divided

What happened after Solomon's death is often referred to as 'the division of the kingdom'. As a statement of fact, that is what happened: the extensive empire ruled over by Solomon was split into two. To a large extent, however, this split seems to have been the natural culmination of an ideological division that had existed for much longer. The northern tribes, led by Ephraim, and the southern tribes, led by Judah, had only ever been truly united by their common allegiance to David. Both groups looked on him as a leader following in the footsteps of the judges, whose position was therefore assured only because God had chosen and equipped him. His continued rule was valid only insofar as he lived up to the responsibility that was involved in such a lofty calling. Solomon had come to power in different circumstances altogether, and became king for no other reason than that David was his father. He was part of an established dynasty, and that factor in itself raised new questions about his relationship to the national self-understanding. The fact that Solomon had violated so many of the values associated with the Sinai covenant, together with the fact that he was not a northerner, helped considerably to revive deeply ingrained rivalries and suspicions between the two groups of tribes.

Back to the old ways

When the tribes in the north saw their chance to opt out of the vast bureaucratic state centred on Jerusalem, they lost no time in choosing to do so. They were not motivated purely by political expediency, nor even primarily by a feeling of outrage at the injustices that Rehoboam promised to impose on them, though both of those considerations no doubt played a part. But over and above all this, the narratives reflect a deeply rooted desire to get back to the old ways, to retrace their national footsteps and go back to their traditional roots. As we have already seen, there is considerable debate about the extent to which different elements of the population had been a part of the actual events of the exodus from Egypt. But it is clear that, by now, significant numbers of people had adopted that story as their own, and wanted to see the values embedded in it being worked out in the realities of political life. Though there were many good economic and social reasons why Israel had become a state with a king, looking back it seemed as if the days of the judges had represented some kind of golden age when the tribes had at least made the effort to live with the spontaneous belief and action that had been enshrined within the covenant, even if they had not always carried it through to perfection. Of course, the changing political realities made it impossible just to turn the clock back and return to the way things had been in those early days. Then, the judges had been leaders of their own tribes, and it was exceptional for them to unite all the tribes. In the new climate, that was impractical, and whatever new leader might emerge needed to be a national figure. Equally, though, he must never succeed to the throne just because his father had been king before him. Every king must demonstrate that he had been called and equipped by God for the job at hand – and he would stay as king only for as long as he was seen to be carrying out God's will among the people.

This view was accepted in theory by the people of the southern state of Judah: they too believed that God should be the ultimate ruler of the nation. But the political context in which they found themselves had led to the emergence of a permanent royal family, and they were firmly convinced that God's rule would now be exercised only through the royal house of David. The old ideals represented by the stories of the judges had found their fulfilment in the promise to David and his successors, and therefore it was both pointless and unnecessary to try to ascertain God's direct will in each different generation. This view doubtless owed a great deal to the political – even geographical – situation of the southern kingdom, especially the position of its capital Jerusalem. For it is striking that once Omri, king of Israel, had founded his own royal capital in Samaria, the northern state too came to accept the concept of a royal family – first Omri's own family, and later that of Jehu and his successors.

ISRAEL
Samaria

Jerusalem

JUDAH

The divided kingdom.

Political changes

A casual reading of the books of Kings may suggest that Judah was by far the more important of the two kingdoms – and, in its lasting religious influence, it has certainly proved to be. But this reflects the choice of material made by the editors of the deuteronomic history, who were writing to encourage and challenge the remnants of the people of Judah in the aftermath of Babylonian domination, and for that purpose the history of their own nation was obviously more relevant than events in the rival kingdom of Israel. But in the two centuries following the death of Solomon, there is no question that the northern kingdom of Israel had more territory, a larger population, and was in every way the more wealthy, more civilized, and even at times the more religious of the two. Israel was therefore a greater force in the international politics of the time. Its strategic location within Palestine ensured that the superpowers of the day would always be interested in what was going on there, and while this ensured its citizens a prosperous lifestyle, it also made it more vulnerable to invasion. Life in Israel was a good deal less secure than it was in Judah, whose capital, Jerusalem, was well away from all the main trade routes, and therefore of less interest to the rulers of surrounding states. As a result, the kingdom of Israel had a shorter and more turbulent history than the kingdom of Judah,

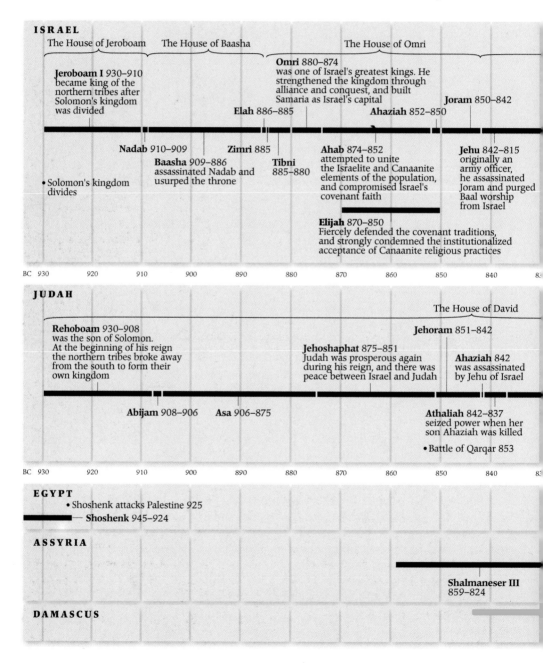

ISRAEL

The House of Jeroboam The House of Baasha The House of Omri

Jeroboam I 930–910 became king of the northern tribes after Solomon's kingdom was divided

Omri 880–874 was one of Israel's greatest kings. He strengthened the kingdom through alliance and conquest, and built Samaria as Israel's capital

Joram 850–842

Elah 886–885

Ahaziah 852–850

Nadab 910–909

Zimri 885

Ahab 874–852 attempted to unite the Israelite and Canaanite elements of the population, and compromised Israel's covenant faith

Jehu 842–815 originally an army officer, he assassinated Joram and purged Baal worship from Israel

Baasha 909–886 assassinated Nadab and usurped the throne

Tibni 885–880

• Solomon's kingdom divides

Elijah 870–850 Fiercely defended the covenant traditions, and strongly condemned the institutionalized acceptance of Canaanite religious practices

BC 930   920   910   900   890   880   870   860   850   840   8

JUDAH

The House of David

Rehoboam 930–908 was the son of Solomon. At the beginning of his reign the northern tribes broke away from the south to form their own kingdom

Jehoshaphat 875–851 Judah was prosperous again during his reign, and there was peace between Israel and Judah

Jehoram 851–842

Ahaziah 842 was assassinated by Jehu of Israel

Abijam 908–906   **Asa** 906–875

Athaliah 842–837 seized power when her son Ahaziah was killed

• Battle of Qarqar 853

BC 930   920   910   900   890   880   870   860   850   840   8

EGYPT

• Shoshenk attacks Palestine 925
— **Shoshenk** 945–924

ASSYRIA

Shalmaneser III 859–824

DAMASCUS

and almost 200 years after Jeroboam was first acclaimed as king of Israel, the whole of his kingdom was wiped out, and its subjects taken away to Assyria to become the so-called 'ten lost tribes'.

In the shorter term, too, the decision of the northern tribes to go their own way led to considerable social and economic changes in the life of the people of the two kingdoms.

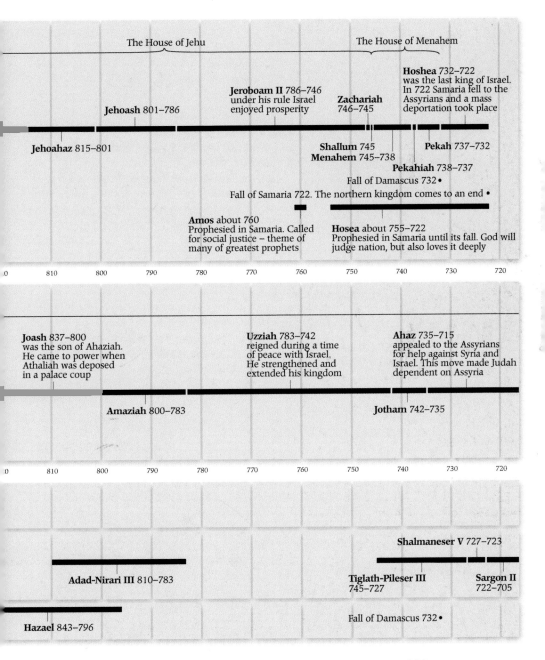

The House of Jehu

The House of Menahem

Hoshea 732–722
was the last king of Israel.
In 722 Samaria fell to the
Assyrians and a mass
deportation took place

Jeroboam II 786–746
under his rule Israel
enjoyed prosperity

**Zachariah
746–745**

Jehoash 801–786

Jehoahaz 815–801

Shallum 745
Menahem 745–738

Pekah 737–732

Pekahiah 738–737

Fall of Damascus 732 •

Fall of Samaria 722. The northern kingdom comes to an end •

Amos about 760
Prophesied in Samaria. Called
for social justice – theme of
many of greatest prophets

Hosea about 755–722
Prophesied in Samaria until its fall. God will
judge nation, but also loves it deeply

| 0 | 810 | 800 | 790 | 780 | 770 | 760 | 750 | 740 | 730 | 720 |

Joash 837–800
was the son of Ahaziah.
He came to power when
Athaliah was deposed
in a palace coup

Uzziah 783–742
reigned during a time
of peace with Israel.
He strengthened and
extended his kingdom

Ahaz 735–715
appealed to the Assyrians
for help against Syria and
Israel. This move made Judah
dependent on Assyria

Amaziah 800–783

Jotham 742–735

| 0 | 810 | 800 | 790 | 780 | 770 | 760 | 750 | 740 | 730 | 720 |

Shalmaneser V 727–723

Adad-Nirari III 810–783

**Tiglath-Pileser III
745–727**

**Sargon II
722–705**

Hazael 843–796

Fall of Damascus 732 •

LOST TERRITORY

The people of Israel and Judah were no longer able to hold separately the large empire that they had held together under David and Solomon. The province of Aram (Syria) in north-east Palestine had already been lost in part during the reign of Solomon, and it soon became a powerful nation

in its own right, based on the city state of Damascus. It was a serious rival to both Israel and Judah, and frequently invaded the Israelite territory to the east of the River Jordan. All but one of the Philistine city states regained their freedom from Judah in the south, though by this time they were no longer a military threat. The Ammonites also took this chance to free themselves from Israelite rule, and the Moabites probably did the same. Judah fared slightly better than Israel, and still retained some kind of control over the trade routes through the Gulf of Aqaba in the south, and Rehoboam built new fortifications in many of his cities (2 Chronicles 11:5–12).

But the loss of all this territory left both Israel and Judah as very second-rate powers. In the time of David and Solomon, the united kingdom had been the major power centre in the whole area, whereas from now on the two kingdoms were little more than pawns in the political games of the superpowers based in Egypt and Mesopotamia. The strength of both kingdoms was considerably

King Shoshenk I of Egypt invaded Judah about five years after the division of the kingdom. His conquests in Palestine are listed here at the temple of Karnak (modern name for Thebes). King Rehoboam gave him treasures from the Temple to persuade him not to attack Jerusalem.

weakened by the invasion of Shoshenk I, pharaoh of Egypt (945–924 BC), who moved in about five years after the separation of the two states, eager to re-establish the authority that Egypt had enjoyed in Canaan before the emergence of Israel as a nation. The Old Testament only mentions this campaign in relation to Judah, and relates how Rehoboam was forced to give him treasure from both the Temple and palace, to stop Shoshenk (called Shishak in 1 Kings 14:25–28) from actually attacking Jerusalem. This seems to have worked, for in an inscription in the temple of Amun at Thebes, Shoshenk makes no mention of towns in Judah being taken. He does, however, mention a number of towns in Israel, and an Egyptian inscription found at Megiddo suggests that he must have overrun most of Palestine. In an interesting detail of his temple list, he mentions a place called 'the Field of Abram', which is the only reference outside the Bible to connect a person of that name with Palestine. Of course, Shoshenk did not want to occupy the country, though no doubt he left troops at strategic places. A later king of Judah, Asa, faced an attack from the same quarter led by a man called Zerah, who is described as a Sudanese but was probably an Egyptian officer left in charge of troops in south Palestine at the time of Shoshenk's invasion (2 Chronicles 14:9–15).

PETTY SQUABBLES

The fact that the two kingdoms were also fighting each other further reduced their chances of being able to retain all their original territory. They were at war for something like fifty years, fighting over the border territory that was just to the north of Jerusalem (1 Kings 14:30; 15:16–22). This was perhaps inevitable, for Jerusalem's original appeal to David had been its unique position midway between the two groups of tribes. But now what had been a tactical advantage became a strategic liability, as Judah's capital was too near the border with the northern kingdom, and that made it especially vulnerable to attack. Rehoboam, Abijam and Asa (kings of Judah), and Jeroboam, Nadab and Baasha (kings of Israel) were squabbling over the land in this area for a considerable time. Baasha of Israel managed to move in as close as five miles from the city of Jerusalem, and when it looked as if he would advance further, Asa of Judah appealed for help to Benhadad, king of Damascus. This king already had a treaty with Baasha, but Asa must have made him a very attractive proposition, for he sent an army to attack the towns in the north of Israel, thereby forcing Baasha to withdraw his army from the frontier with Judah. It was not the last time that Judah adopted such tactics, but they eventually discovered to their cost that it was a very short-sighted policy.

SOCIAL UNREST

The northern kingdom of Israel also turned out to be politically unstable. In theory, they thought it was right to try to reinvent the pattern of a loose tribal federation in which every leader of the people should be individually chosen as a result of their personal charisma and religious commitment. But, as a political and social institution, this was simply unworkable. At best, it meant that Israel became what Albrecht Alt called 'a kingdom based on revolution by the will of God'. In practice, what this more often meant was that the nation was torn apart over the issue of the kingship. For one thing, it was open to any military adventurer to try to seize the throne, whether or not he had any religious support, or indeed any leadership skills. In addition, it was only natural that those kings whose reigns had been properly accredited should in due course want their own sons to succeed them, especially if they had built up personal fortunes. As a result, Israel was in constant turmoil and in the course of the first fifty years, the throne was seized three times by a usurper who assassinated his predecessor. Jeroboam reigned for twenty-one years, but only one of the six kings who followed him reigned for more than ten years (Baasha), and some lasted only a matter of months.

Religious problems

It was all very well for Jeroboam to come to power in the north on a wave of popular enthusiasm, but he soon needed to get down to the business of running the kingdom. In doing so, he faced many formidable obstacles, not least of which was that there was no obvious capital city that might form the administrative centre of his government. The Old Testament mentions three capitals where he operated in turn: Shechem, Penuel and Tirzah (1 Kings 12:25; 14:17). There may have been a simple military reason for this, as he was forced to retreat from one to the other in the face of Shoshenk's invading armies. But it is more likely that there was a popular resistance to the very idea of having a capital city, on ideological grounds. For it had been through the possession of his own personal city that Solomon had been able to behave with such disregard for the sensitivities of the people and their inherited traditions. At least if Jeroboam had no fixed capital, there was less chance that he would build up a state apparatus to work for his own personal benefit.

But it was essential that at least one of the functions of the city of Jerusalem should be located at a permanent site in the north. The Temple built at Jerusalem to house the ark of the covenant was part of the trappings of statehood that reinforced the power and prestige of the monarchy. But it had also provided a significant and important link with the spiritual heritage of the people, and it was only to be expected that the tribes in the north, motivated and inspired by a fierce devotion to the covenant which the ark symbolized, should want to go on pilgrimage there. Yet, politically, it was essential that Jeroboam should stop them from doing so, for to allow this would have been tantamount to an acknowledgment that Jerusalem still had a hold over the loyalty of the northern tribes, and the free passage of pilgrims from one state to the other would only increase the risk of subversive action to undermine Jeroboam's position as king.

On top of that, a significant proportion of Jeroboam's territory was rural and remote. That had worked to his advantage in seceding from the south, for the support base of the Jerusalem kings had to a large extent been among urban city dwellers. In addition, however, these rural communities also seem to have been the places where traditional forms of Canaanite religious practices had flourished, independently of what went on in Jerusalem. Yahweh was certainly worshipped, but often through rituals and belief systems that reflected not the underlying rationale of the covenant traditions, but the inherited spiritual ideology of traditional Canaanite practice. It was important for Jeroboam somehow to unite these two different religious traditions, and he came up with an idea that he believed would solve several problems at once.

He would displace the old loyalties to the Temple in Jerusalem by building his own new religious centres. The sites he chose were at Dan in the extreme north, and Bethel in the south near to the border with Judah. These had a long history connected to traditional Canaanite spirituality, yet both of them also had important connections with events in the earlier history of the people of Israel (Genesis 12:8; 28:19; Judges 18:30; 20:18–28; 1 Samuel 7:16).

However, Jeroboam's actions in establishing these places of worship were to earn him the lasting condemnation of the deuteronomic historians. For at these two shrines, Jeroboam placed golden bulls (1 Kings 12:28–33). This was a bold effort to bind the different elements of the population together, and to reconcile Canaanite beliefs with the distinctive faith of Israel. It would not be too difficult to associate these bulls with the traditional worship, because Baal himself had often been represented as a bull. At the same time, however, it was possible to think of these bulls as thrones for the invisible God of the covenant, Yahweh, just as the ark of the covenant also represented God's invisible presence in the Temple at Jerusalem. From one perspective, this could be seen as a stroke of genius, but as the editors of the books of Kings looked back on it all they regarded it as an incredibly foolish move. When judged from the perspective of the deuteronomic history as outlined, for example, in the first chapter of Judges, this represented a dilution of the worship of Yahweh with alien practices, and Jeroboam's best efforts were therefore doomed to failure for, like Saul before him, he had overstepped his authority. He had conspired to undermine the very convictions that had brought him to power in the first place, and the prophet who announced his accession now pronounced his doom. Though he had been God's choice, Jeroboam had lost God's approval, and he would have to go, to be replaced by a king who would be more sensitive to the requirements of the covenant faith (1 Kings 14:1–16).

A bronze bull calf from about the 12th century BC. Jeroboam placed golden bulls at the shrines of Dan and Bethel as a counter-attraction to the Temple at Jerusalem.

New alliances

Jeroboam's immediate successor was his son Nadab, though he was not accepted by the people, and had the approval of no religious leaders. He lasted for little more than a year before Baasha came to power (1 Kings 15:25–32). The people recognized him as the right man, and he had a relatively long reign of twenty-four years, though the judgment of the historians was that he too followed in Jeroboam's footsteps and 'led

Israel into sin' (1 Kings 15:34). Like Jeroboam, he was also rejected by a prophet speaking in the name of Yahweh (1 Kings 16:1–7), and when he died his son Elah tried to succeed him. He in turn reigned for less than two years, but lacked any popular support, and Zimri assassinated him in a military coup, seizing the throne for himself (1 Kings 16:8–14). He was not the right man either, and survived for only seven days (1 Kings 16:15–20). This kind of instability naturally weakened the position of the nation of Israel. But the man who got rid of Zimri was to be one of Israel's greatest kings. Not only did he re-establish much of the nation's prestige, but also he did it so successfully that when he died his son was recognized as the most appropriate person to follow him. The father was Omri and the son was Ahab.

Prosperity again

The Moabite Stone, put up by King Mesha of Moab in Omri's day. Its inscription includes information not included in the Old Testament account.

The Hebrew Bible says very little about Omri for, in the view of the editors of 1 Kings, he was even more wicked and irreligious than any of his predecessors (1 Kings 16:21–28). As with so many of Israel's rulers, his social and political achievements are mentioned only briefly, and those who are interested to learn more about them are told that 'Everything else that Omri did and all his accomplishments are recorded in *The History of the Kings of Israel.*' Statements like this remind us that the deuteronomic historians were basing their narratives on sources that were much older than their own day, but are

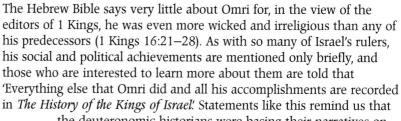

of little help in uncovering details that we might now be interested in, for none of these other ancient sources still survive. By contrast, Omri's son Ahab features very prominently in the Old Testament story, though here again we are told far more about his religious outlook than about political affairs during his reign (1 Kings 16:29 – 22:40). Despite the relative lack of information about them, however, there can be no doubt regarding the greatness of Omri and his son. For under their rule, Israel once again became a force to be reckoned with.

INTERNATIONALLY

Omri and Ahab strengthened the kingdom's position with a number of new alliances and fresh conquests. They put an end to the long-standing but pointless warfare with Judah, and this led to a new period of prosperity and peace in the southern state also. Jehoshaphat, king of Judah, took control of many trading routes in the south, and the new friendship between the two states was eventually sealed by the marriage of Ahab's daughter, Athaliah, to Jehoshaphat's son, Jehoram

(1 Kings 22:41–50; 2 Kings 8:18). Israel made peace in the same way with the Phoenicians of Tyre. This alliance was also sealed with a marriage: this time, Ahab himself married a Phoenician princess called Jezebel (1 Kings 16:31). Omri also managed to regain control over Moab. The Old Testament says nothing of this, but it is documented on a large black stone inscription erected by king Mesha of Moab after he had finally managed to release his kingdom from Israel's grasp again, following the death of Ahab (2 Kings 3). Naturally, much of this inscription dwells on Mesha's victory rather than on his previous submission to Omri. But it says quite plainly that 'Omri, king of Israel, humbled Moab for many years.'

INTERNALLY

Omri secured his own position by building a new capital. This is what David had done by capturing Jerusalem, but Omri went one better and chose an entirely new site, with no previous settlement on it. It is almost certain that he was trying to imitate David's success, for just as Jerusalem had been chosen because of its central position between the northern and southern tribes, so Samaria was roughly midway between the mainly Canaanite cities nearer the coast, and the predominantly Israelite towns further inland. This was to be Omri's own city, just as Jerusalem had been David's own city, and under Omri and Ahab it was built up into a fine place, well fortified and with many elegant buildings. Like Jerusalem, it also had a temple, and this came to be regarded as Ahab's greatest mistake: 'He sinned against Yahweh more than any of his predecessors. It was not enough for him to sin like King Jeroboam; he went further… and worshipped Baal' (1 Kings 16:30–31). Viewed from a less hostile angle, Ahab's religious observance was probably more concerned with politics than with spirituality as such. Like Jeroboam before him he had the problem of uniting the Canaanite and Israelite elements of his population. What went on in Samaria was mainly, if not exclusively, for the benefit of the Canaanites, and it was even organized like a traditional city state. But the city of Jezreel was still of great importance, and it could well be that Ahab had in effect two capitals: Samaria for the Canaanites, with a temple dedicated to traditional Canaanite deities, and Jezreel for the Israelites, with a temple for their God, Yahweh. It is certainly significant that both Ahab's sons had distinctively Israelite names (Ahaziah and Joram), something that could not have been said even for a great hero like David.

The ruins of Ahab's palace look down from the hill on which once stood the city of Samaria, capital of the northern kingdom of Israel.

Decay and collapse

The tensions that Omri and Ahab created between their state and the inherited covenant faith of their people soon became overpowering, and the stories about them highlight better than any other section of the deuteronomic history the kind of internal conflicts between different ideologies of statehood that were never successfully reconciled throughout Israelite history. The divergence between the inherited assumptions of Canaanite culture and the radical views reflected in the covenant from Mount Sinai are highlighted especially by the stories featuring Ahab's wife Jezebel. Her role in Ahab's monarchy can be interpreted in several ways, all of which probably reflect different aspects of her aspirations. Their marriage was a political alliance as much as anything else, and Jezebel's enthusiasm for promoting Canaanite religious practices may easily have had political overtones: if Israel's official religion was the same as that of her own kingdom of Tyre, that would not only have cemented relations between the two, but might even have emphasized the superiority of her own people over the Israelites. In addition, though, she emerges as a woman deeply committed to her husband, and with high ambitions for him – and some of the stories certainly illustrate the different philosophies of kingship that prevailed depending on whether the pattern of the Canaanite city states was adopted, or whether the covenant principles of Yahweh formed the basis of political power. The king would always have enjoyed more personal power and prestige under the traditional Canaanite structures than in the Israelite view. The idea that a peasants' revolt was one of the key elements leading to the emergence of Israel as a nation may well have been overstated, but the theme was certainly one that recurred repeatedly in later years, and nowhere is this more clearly illustrated than in the stories of Ahab and Elijah. Elijah was a fierce defender of the covenant traditions, and he realized that the kind of institutionalized acceptance of Canaanite practices that was now being proposed was something quite different from the casual adoption of traditional religious practices that still went on in village shrines throughout the land. This time, it was a direct threat to the very fabric of the nation because, if successful, Jezebel's plan would undermine all that the nation was supposed to stand for.

Ahab managed to survive, and was succeeded in turn by his two sons Ahaziah and Joram (1 Kings 22:51–53; 2 Kings 3:1–27). But there was nothing they could do to prevent the disintegration and eventual collapse of the royal house of Omri. It was not long before a revolution was instigated by devotees of the covenant faith of Israel. They had chosen an army officer by the name of Jehu to be the next king of Israel, and he was anointed in the aftermath of a great battle between Israel and Syria at Ramoth-Gilead (2 Kings 9:1–13). Joram had been wounded in the battle and had returned to Jezreel to recuperate. Jehu therefore left the battlefield, and with a band of his own men headed straight for

Jezreel. When he got there he found that by a stroke of luck Ahaziah, the king of Judah (not to be confused with King Ahaziah of Israel, Ahab's son), was also there visiting Joram. Since he too was a relative of Ahab, Jehu had no hesitation in assassinating both of them, along with Jezebel the queen mother (2 Kings 9:14–37). He followed up this bloodbath with an appeal to the city rulers of Samaria to come over to his side, which they did, and signify their allegiance to him by presenting him with the heads of seventy members of Ahab's family who were left there (2 Kings 10:1–11). Not content with that, Jehu managed to trick all the priests of Baal into entering the temple in

Elijah and the religion of Baal

Elijah is a significant character in the Old Testament. The stories about him are reminiscent of the account of Saul's encounter with a group of ecstatic prophets (1 Kings 18:4, 13), and he certainly had that mystical quality about him which instilled in people a mixture of fear and admiration in equal amounts. His movements could at times be unpredictable and beyond human comprehension (1 Kings 18:12), though these things are not the most distinctive marks of his personality. For he was first and foremost a man with a message, driven by the conviction that the God whom he knew and worshipped was not just a God who had lived and worked in the past, but one who was present with the people here and now, and who had a distinctive understanding of the important issues in their national life. In this respect, Elijah was the forerunner of the great prophets whose messages are presented in the books of the Old Testament that bear their names.

The precise nature of the conflict between Canaanite values (represented by Baal worship) and the ancestral faith of Israel is made clear in three stories from the life of Elijah:

● Elijah came from Gilead, from the very edge of the desert in the east of the country (1 Kings 17:1–7). His lifestyle was spartan, his clothes were rough, and he was immediately recognizable as an enthusiast for the style of life described in the stories about Moses and the tribes in the desert in the period following the exodus. He was a miracle worker (1 Kings 17:8–24), and significantly perhaps, his miracles were mostly concerned with the fertility of the land, especially the holding back or sending of rain. This was supposed to be the special function of the Canaanite Baal, but Elijah was determined to prove that it was really his own God, Yahweh, who controlled the rain. So he challenged 450 prophets of Baal and 400 prophets of Asherah to a contest on Mount Carmel. This was a high ridge near the territory of the Phoenicians, which had belonged to Israel during the days of David and Solomon. The altar to Yahweh built there then had by now reverted to the honouring of Baal, and Elijah was determined to sort out once and for all the religious priorities of his people. He challenged the prophets of Baal and Asherah to bring fire from heaven, presumably the lightning that would normally come before a rain storm. After much religious ecstasy, they were both exhausted and unsuccessful, but where they failed Elijah succeeded, not by following their practices, but by a simple prayer to his own God. As a result, the long period of drought ended with deluges of rain (1 Kings 18:1–46); it was Yahweh, and not Baal, who controlled the weather.

● In spite of that, Jezebel still held the power, and she was all the more determined to track down the elusive Elijah. He felt (mistakenly) that he alone was left as a faithful representative for the

Samaria, and there had them all butchered on the spot (2 Kings 10:18–31). Though the editors of Kings depict Jehu as a fanatical worshipper of Yahweh, his purge was obviously based more on political expediency, for the same tensions between different religious ideologies persisted throughout his reign and also that of his son Jehoahaz (2 Kings 13:6). Jehu's lack of commitment to serious change alienated his religious backers, who withdrew their support – and 100 years later the prophet Hosea denounced the violence that accompanied his rise to power as being incompatible with the authentic covenant faith of Israel (Hosea 1:4–5).

Elijah and the religion of Baal *continued*

God of Israel. In fear of his life he ran away from Jezebel right to the south of Judah, then south again from Beersheba to Mount Sinai. This was the place where Moses had taken the escaping slaves, and was the very centre of his people's faith. This was where the covenant had been made, and where God's people could still gain fresh inspiration. In an experience infused with much emotion and mystery, Elijah was reminded that though Yahweh did indeed have power over the forces of nature, that was not the centre of Israel's faith, but God's supreme activity was to be seen in the events of everyday life, not only through the deliverance of the slaves from Egypt, but also in the ongoing concerns of Elijah's contemporaries. Elijah was sent back to stir up a political ferment in both Syria and Israel, which would lead to the overthrow of the house of Omri and its allies (1 Kings 19:1–18). Commitment to the covenant faith did not make him a mere reactionary: it transformed him into a political activist reminding his people by his social involvement that the God of Mount Sinai was still their only true leader.
● The story of Naboth's vineyard brings out the meaning of all this in social terms (1 Kings 21:1–29). When Ahab wanted to have this piece of land to extend his own garden, he knew it was impossible. For in Israel, land belonged not to individuals, but to God – and particular people only held it in trust because God had given it to them. This was quite different from the traditional Canaanite norm, as Ahab well knew. After all, his father Omri had been

able to buy the site of Samaria outright from a Canaanite. But Ahab was still too committed to the Israelite ideals to accept that land could be seized by the king just to suit his own inclinations, and so he sulked for what he knew he could never rightly possess. His wife Jezebel, on the other hand, took a different view. She regarded the life and property of every subject as belonging to the king, and so she had no hesitation in having Naboth killed, and confiscating his property for her husband's use. It was Elijah who boldly denounced the queen's action – just as Nathan had done when David acted on the same principles of self-interest (2 Samuel 12:1–15). For Elijah, religious belief was concerned with common life and politics, and even the queen was not above the Law of the covenant from Mount Sinai. For in the covenant community, every man and woman stood equal. This meant that economic and social justice had to be a concern of God's representatives just as much as more apparently 'religious' matters connected with ritual and worship. This theme was taken up by all the great prophets of the Hebrew Bible, but it first emerges in the testimony of Elijah, who pronounced the death sentence on Jezebel and the whole house of Omri, and declared that God would ultimately intervene to restore justice and freedom to the people.

Whatever its weaknesses, it is not difficult to see why Jehu's revolution succeeded. Though Omri's dynasty had been remarkably successful, it was suffering from so many tensions that its collapse was inevitable:

■ The strongest opposition had been evoked by the Baal worship at Samaria, instigated by Jezebel and encouraged by Ahab. The fact that Jehu joined forces with a fanatical religious movement led by Jehonadab, son of Rechab, shows just how strong the reaction was (2 Kings 10:23–24), for these Rechabites were trying to opt out of civilized, settled life altogether. They neither built houses, nor cultivated the soil, nor drank wine (Jeremiah 35:6–10). All these things were regarded as part of a typical Canaanite lifestyle, but they wanted to get back to the kind of life the escaping slaves had with Moses in the desert. They were convinced that the settled life of farming could never be reconciled with Israel's ancestral faith, and so it must be abandoned.

■ There was also a certain amount of social unrest and injustice in the land, much as there had been towards the end of Solomon's reign. This time it had been caused partly by a great famine during the time of Ahab, which had increased the number of poor people and led to a radical division in society between the rich merchants and the poor

The hills of Samaria, which formed part of the northern kingdom of Israel.

peasants. The story of how Ahab took over Naboth's vineyard was by no means unique, and many small farmers found themselves being displaced by rich and powerful princes at this time.

■ Externally, too, Israel was under pressure. New enemies were making their presence felt, especially Assyria (based in Mesopotamia) and Syria (based in Damascus). The Assyrians had pressed as far west as the Mediterranean Sea during Ahab's reign, and at that time a casual alliance against them was formed by the king of Damascus, in partnership with Ahab and the king of Hamath. They all met Assyria at the Battle of Qarqar, just north of Hamath, in 853 BC, and managed to repel the Assyrians. Ahab's military strength at this time can be judged from the fact that though he could provide only half as many troops as Syria (but the same as Hamath), he had 2,000 chariots, which was more than Syria and Hamath put together. Israel obviously had fewer people than Damascus, but far greater material resources. But Benhadad, the king of Damascus, was not interested in a lasting peace with Ahab, and, though there is some debate about it, the Old Testament appears to suggest that Ahab was killed in battle against the Syrians at Ramoth-Gilead (1 Kings 20:1–34; 22:29–40). His sons were powerless to regain this lost territory, and no doubt lost the support of the army for that reason – which goes a long way towards explaining why the swashbuckling Jehu, fast driving and ready for desperate action, was so readily accepted as the new king of Israel.

The Assyrian obelisk, the famous 'Black Obelisk' of Emperor Shalmaneser, depicts Jehu of Israel paying tribute as leader of a vassal state. It is the only known portrait of an Old Testament figure.

Growing insecurity

As things turned out, Jehu himself was relatively powerless in political terms. He naturally lost the support of the powerful alliance with Phoenicia, and since he had also murdered the king of Judah, Ahaziah, any residual backing he might have expected from Jerusalem also vanished. Power was seized in Judah by Athaliah, the mother of Ahaziah of Judah and daughter of Ahab. She murdered all the other possible claimants to the throne, except for one child, Joash, who was rescued by the priest Jehoiada. Athaliah reigned in Jerusalem for six years, and is dismissed by the editors of Kings for the same reasons as Ahab: she, too, was compromised in relation to Canaanite ways of doing things, including religious practices. In due course, she was deposed in a palace coup led by Jehoiada, and Joash was installed as king (2 Kings 11:1–21).

During this period of

uncertainty and weakness, Israel was under pressure from the Syrians of
Damascus, as illustrated by a broken basalt monument recovered from
the city of Dan. This seems to describe the same battle as 2 Kings 8:28–
29, and appears to imply that the Aramean Hazael killed both Ahaziah of
Judah and Joram of Israel. 2 Kings 9:15–29 suggests that Jehu murdered
them, although 2 Kings 8:29 does mention that Joram was already
suffering from wounds received in battle with Hazael. Whatever the full
story, the fact that Hazael was able to place his inscription in Dan itself
makes it obvious that Israel could easily have been overcome at this time
by the Syrians, had they not also been faced with the armies of the
Assyrian king Shalmaneser III (859–824 BC). This was the king who had
been successfully repelled by the coalition of which Ahab had been a
part, but shortly after Jehu came to power, he was back with a vengeance.
He had a carefully calculated plan for extending his own empire, and
made annual military expeditions. Some territories he conquered
altogether, but from most he simply collected tribute. In 841 BC he
moved systematically through the whole area: Damascus was besieged,
and much of the Syrian kingdom was invaded, while Phoenicia and Israel

Countries in
conflict.

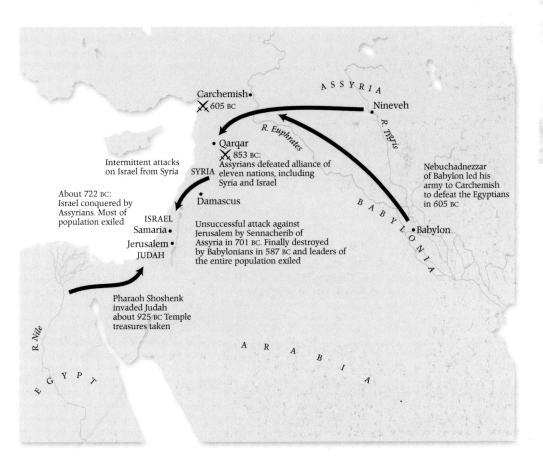

both had to pay tribute to keep the Assyrians at bay. Shalmaneser kept meticulous records, in which he describes all this in great detail. Not only does he mention that he took tribute from Jehu of Israel, he also lists what he was given, and depicts Jehu himself bowing down low to present these gifts. This is a most interesting record for the picture of Jehu preserved on Shalmaneser's Black Obelisk is the only surviving contemporary portrait of any Israelite named in the Hebrew Bible.

Before the end of Shalmaneser's reign, a revolt back in Nineveh weakened Assyrian power. But this was of no advantage to Israel, for it simply gave Hazael yet another chance to get even, and under Jehu's son Jehoahaz, Israel became almost a province of Syria (2 Kings 13:1–9, 22–23). The whole of Israel east of the River Jordan was occupied, and the Syrians pressed into Judah in the south. Joash, the king in Jerusalem, prevented Hazael from attacking the city only by offering him a part of the treasure from the Temple (2 Kings 12:17–18). In little more than 100 years, the states of Israel and Judah had been reduced from the great empire that Solomon held to satellites of the city state of Damascus.

New prosperity and false security

International relations were in such turmoil at this period that by the time Jehu's grandson, Jehoash, came to the throne in Israel things were quite different. The power of Assyria was building up again under Shalmaneser's grandson, Adad-Nirari III (810–783 BC), and his renewed interest in Palestine was to enable both Israel and Judah to regain some of their former glory. According to the Assyrian annals, Israel was again forced to pay tribute, along with the Edomites and Philistines – but not, apparently, Judah. Damascus was worst hit by this renewed Assyrian advance. The Old Testament describes how 'Yahweh gave Israel a saviour, so that they escaped from the hand of the Syrians' (2 Kings 13:5), and this might well be a reference to the Assyrian king Adad-Nirari III. In any event, the Assyrian attack on Damascus gave Jehoash the chance he was looking for, and he soon began to recover Israel's lost territory to the east of the River Jordan. Amaziah, the king of Judah, also recovered land from Edom at this time, but then foolishly declared war on Israel, and as a result Judah was so decisively defeated that Jehoash of Israel actually raided Jerusalem itself (2 Kings 14:1–16). With this, Amaziah lost the confidence of his own people and was soon assassinated (2 Kings 14:17–22). But, as had always been the case in Judah, his place was taken by his son Uzziah.

National revival

There followed then two of the longest and most prosperous reigns in all Israelite history: Jeroboam II of Israel (786–746 BC) and Uzziah of Judah (783–742 BC). They reigned for over forty years each, and though the Old Testament gives no specific details of their military activities, the two kings between them extended their borders almost to the original reach of Solomon's united kingdom (2 Kings 14:23 – 15:7).

Uzziah repaired the fortifications of Jerusalem, reorganized his army and equipped it with new types of weaponry. He introduced new agricultural practices to the land, and was even able to reopen part of Solomon's copper refineries on the Gulf of Aqaba (2 Chronicles 26:1–15). This led to a revival of trade through the Red Sea, and since the two kings of Judah and Israel were at peace with one another, between them they must have controlled all the major trade routes of the area.

The splendid buildings constructed by Jeroboam II in Samaria demonstrate well enough the prosperity of the northern state. Many people became very rich as a result of the increased opportunities for international trade, and they also became very religious, for they concluded that their new-found wealth must be a sign of God's favour upon them. In this optimistic atmosphere they came to believe that their position was assured, and their kingdom was impregnable, and began to

---

The book of Amos

A prophet is commonly thought of as a person who predicts the future. But this was not the way the great Hebrew prophets saw themselves. They were essentially God's messengers, sent to remind their people of the covenant made at Sinai, and to apply it to the everyday life of their towns and villages. They were not fortune-tellers or psychics, but politicians and preachers.

They did occasionally write some parts of their message down (e.g. Jeremiah 30:2; 36:1–2), but it is unlikely that any prophet actually wrote the books now found in the Old Testament. Indeed, these writings are not really 'books' in the sense of having a connected argument from start to finish, but are much more like an anthology of ideas, linked together by editorial sections typically containing historical and biographical notes or stories highlighting selected incidents from the prophet's life. The book of Amos contains all these types of material.

The person and the message

Though Amos himself came from the town of Tekoa, which was just south of Jerusalem in Judah (1:1), his message was for the people of the northern kingdom and he delivered it in one of the religious sanctuaries set up by the first Jeroboam, at Bethel (7:10–17), and possibly also in Samaria itself (3:9 – 4:3). While he was in Bethel, Amaziah, the priest of the sanctuary, tried to send him back to Judah, telling him that his own people should pay for his services. He obviously thought Amos was some kind of professional prophet, who was looking for a full-time job attached to a permanent place of worship. We know that there were such full-time prophets in both Israel and Judah, some of whom seem to have had an official position alongside the priests (Jeremiah 35:4–5), while others were court officials who would say anything that the king wanted to hear (1 Kings 22:1–28). But Amos was not this kind of person. He is described as a simple shepherd, who was not delivering his challenging messages to tickle the ears of his political masters, but because God had shown him the rotten state of Israelite society, and he felt impelled to do something about it (3:3–8; 7:10–17). Amos saw a complete breakdown of morality and covenant faith not only in Israel, but also in the nations with whom it was most closely associated: Syria, Philistia, Tyre, Edom, Ammon, Moab and Judah. (1:3 – 2:5). Of course, all but Judah had never pledged themselves to

look forward with eager anticipation to the coming of a great 'day of Yahweh', when Israel would finally be victorious over all enemies. But not everyone thought like that, for during the reign of Jeroboam II many people once again began to question whether all this high living was compatible with the covenant faith of Israel. Some scholars believe that in reaction against it, a new edition of Israel's early history was written, this time reflecting the memories that had been handed down in the northern tribes (unlike the similar early history of Solomon's day, which essentially drew on the collective memory of the southern tribes). If so, this narrative (which emphasized the work of Moses) would later be incorporated into the books of Genesis and Exodus (often referred to as 'E' because of the constant use of the divine name 'El' or 'Elohim', in distinction from the Solomonic collection – 'J' – where the term 'Yahweh' predominated). Whether or not that hypothesis is correct, there can be no doubt that there was strong disapproval of Israel's style of life at this time, for it was towards the end of Jeroboam II's reign that the prophet

---

The book of Amos
continued

observing the values and standards of the covenant faith, but Amos still condemned them in God's name for they had refused to treat each other with the kind of dignity that befits human beings. The things Amos complains about are what today would be described as violations of human rights: acting with great cruelty, taking whole communities into slavery, breaking treaties and exacting merciless revenge on neighbouring states.

All this was just a prelude to God's judgment of Israel. Israel might not have done any of these things, but they had still broken the covenant relationship with Yahweh in very fundamental ways. Though the northern state had ostensibly been founded on a conviction that all members of the community were of equal worth and value, this had never become a social reality. Instead, some had become rich on the back of others, and continued to increase their wealth at the expense of the rest. People were selling themselves into

The prophet Amos, the earliest whose words are systematically recorded in the Old Testament, was a shepherd. His message to Israel was an uncompromising warning that God's judgment would come unless they brought back justice into their society.

Amos delivered his strident messages, in which he declared that Israelite society was rotten to the core. Though many were rich and prosperous, others were penniless and oppressed (Amos 8:4–6). The great shrines like Bethel were full of worshippers, but it was all just empty ritual – and for people like that 'the day of Yahweh', when it came, would not be a time of triumph but a day of doom (Amos 5:18–27).

Assyria on the move

It was not long before Amos's dire predictions were to become a painful reality. The moral disintegration that began in Jeroboam II's reign led to social and political disintegration in the years after his death, with a rapid succession of weak kings, assassinations and revolts. At the same time, the power of Assyria was increasing again with the accession to the throne of Tiglath-pileser III (745–727 BC). He had a new expansionist policy, which he hoped would avoid the failures of his predecessors, whereby instead of merely taking tribute from defeated nations, he would incorporate

---

slavery because they could not repay trivial debts (2:6–8). The rich were feasting themselves and playing in idle luxury, while others were homeless (3:9 – 4:1; 5:10–13). These features are all well documented as regular characteristics of life in an advanced agrarian society, as an economic elite come to possess most of the land, thereby rendering others homeless, while an increasingly powerful merchant class prospers by trading in the necessities of life, as well as in luxury

goods. Whether this social structure had permeated the entire nation is unclear, and there is some evidence that in more rural parts life was more egalitarian. But in the urban centres, where power was based, there is plenty of evidence to support Amos's picture.

Judgment and hope

Paradoxically, in the middle of all this there was a great religious fervour. The shrines were full of worshippers, all carrying out their ritual observances with meticulous care. They would make sure they did not violate the weekly day of rest – but as soon as it was over, they could hardly wait to get back to what Amos regarded as the legalized robbery that went on in every market place. It was this false confidence in religion that incensed Amos more than anything. The rich believed they were prospering because they were very religious – but, if only they had had the eyes to see it, they would have realized they were wealthy because they had disregarded the basic requirements of their covenant faith. This is the context in which Amos declared God's total lack of interest in such empty ritual: 'go to the holy place in Bethel and sin, if you must! Go to Gilgal and sin with all your might! Go ahead and

conquered states into the Assyrian empire. To ensure that they did not then revolt again, the leading elements of the population would be moved away to other parts of the empire, and replaced with settlers similarly displaced from elsewhere. The first mention of an Assyrian invasion of Israel occurs in the account of Menahem's reign (2 Kings 15:17–22). He tried to keep the kingship within his own family by paying tribute to Tiglath-pileser, but his son Pekahiah reigned for only two years before he was removed by an anti-Assyrian revolt led by Pekah. He in turn went on to form a new alliance against the Assyrians with Rezin, king of Syria. They tried to persuade Jotham, king of Judah, to join them, but he refused, and when a new king came to power in Jerusalem, they declared war on Judah (Isaiah 7:1–9). This move struck terror into the people of Jerusalem, and brought into prominence one of the Old Testament's greatest prophets: Isaiah. He advised the new king, Ahaz, that this threat to his security would come to nothing, and promised that before the newly born child Immanuel could tell the difference between good and bad, both

The use of ivory in decorations and furnishing was a typical feature of the self-confidently affluent society of Israel in its final years.

bring animals to be sacrificed… offer your bread in thanksgiving to God… This is the kind of thing you love to do' (4:4–5). But God had other ideas: 'Yahweh says, "I hate your religious festivals; I cannot stand them!… I will not accept the animals you have fattened to bring me as offerings"' (5:21–22). These had not been the things that characterized Israel's experience of

God in the desert.

The covenant relationship forged at Sinai was concerned not with religious ritual, but with a personal relationship between God and the people, a relationship of love and concern that should have created a new society marked by the same qualities. So Amos pleaded in God's name, 'Stop your noisy songs; I do

Syria and Israel would collapse (Isaiah 7:10–25). As it turned out, Isaiah was right, but Ahaz did not believe him. It was perhaps on this occasion that in desperation he offered his son as a sacrifice to try to change what looked like the inevitable course of events (2 Kings 16:3–4). He certainly made strenuous efforts to win Assyrian backing, and in response to his appeal they attacked Damascus, killed Rezin and took away his people (2 Kings 16:5–9). This turned out to be a short-sighted move, for Ahaz had bought short-term security at the expense of his own continued independence. He went to Damascus to pay homage to Tiglath-pileser, and brought back from there the plan for an altar that was erected in the Temple at Jerusalem, as a sign of submission to the Assyrian empire and its gods (2 Kings 16:10–18). As Isaiah had warned, it was a foolish idea to go to the Assyrians for help.

Meanwhile in Israel, things were going from bad to worse. Pekah's position was weakened because the Assyrians took over yet more of his territory, and he was assassinated by Hoshea (2 Kings 15:29–30). Hoshea

---

not want to listen to your harps. Instead, let justice flow like a stream, and righteousness like a river that never goes dry' (5:23–24).

Not that Amos expected to be heard, for in his opinion the real trouble was that the worship at Bethel and Gilgal was not the worship of Israel's covenant God at all. Yahweh's name might be invoked, but what was going on was the worship of Canaanite deities, with their rather different view of society (2:7–8; 5:26–27; 8:14). Evidence of this kind of syncretism has been found in a series of drawings on storage jars of this same period, from Kuntillet Ajrud in the northern Sinai, and an inscription which mentions a blessing 'by Yahweh of Samaria and his Asherah'. In Amos's view, this was a step too far. Israel's leaders were no longer able to tell the difference between truth and lies. But it would all come to an end – and soon. Just as God had intervened in Israel's history before, so the same thing would happen again, only this time it would be Israel that would be totally destroyed, with the people taken away into exile, and their cities devastated (5:1 – 9:10). The prosperity of the day of Jeroboam would indeed culminate in 'the day of Yahweh'. But instead of a day of great blessing, it

would be a day of judgment and despair (5:18–20).

The last paragraph of Amos (9:11–15) gives just a slight ray of hope, and because of this some scholars believe it was added later by the book's editor, to alleviate the blackness of Amos's message. That may well be, though it is worth noting that this final section does not really contradict what he says. Amos knew that the nation was heading for a great disaster, but he also knew that events were in God's control: 'I will give the command and shake the people of Israel like corn in a sieve. I will shake them among the nations to remove all who are worthless' (9:9). It was precisely because of this that Amos felt an element of mercy and love would always be found even in judgment. For this was the same God who had rescued the people from Egypt, and who had shown overpowering love for them in so many ways throughout their history. It was inevitable, therefore, that though the present looked bleak, beyond the storm clouds of God's anger Amos could still dimly see the clear rays of God's love.

The book of Amos
continued

The Assyrian ruler Sargon II, who completed the siege of Samaria and deported much of the population of Israel to other parts of his empire.

for his part realized that the kingdom was in grave danger of disappearing entirely, and so he surrendered – unwillingly – to the Assyrians, but then, as soon as the immediate danger was past, he began plotting against them. He saw his chance to break free when Shalmaneser V replaced Tiglath-pileser III, and he appealed for support to the pharaoh of Egypt (2 Kings 17:1–4). Egypt, however, was powerless to help, and when Shalmaneser moved his armies against Israel, no one was in a position to stop him. Samaria fell after a siege lasting two years (2 Kings 17:5–6), and in his annals Sargon II (Shalmaneser's successor) reports that he removed 27,290 people from Israel and replaced them with others from elsewhere in his empire. An Assyrian officer was put in charge of the land, and Israel was finished.

The Assyrians

The Assyrian empire was based in northern Mesopotamia, chiefly around the cities of Nineveh, Asshur and Kalah. The people of this area had exerted a strong influence in that region for a long time, and their existence can be traced back to a time well before Israel emerged as a nation. But it was not until the early days of the Hebrew monarchy that the Assyrians began to take an interest in the lands that lay to the west of their home.

Tiglath-pileser I (1115–1077 BC) was the first king to try to move westwards. But he had not thought out his strategy with sufficient care, and though he got as far as the northern part of Syria he was unable to establish a firm power base in that region. In the next few centuries, the Assyrians concentrated on setting up a strong administrative structure, into which conquered territories could easily be incorporated. They also developed a well-

trained and highly disciplined army, ready to move at a moment's notice. The description of them in Isaiah 5:26–29 vividly reflects the impression that these troops made on those who saw them: 'here they come, swiftly, quickly! None of them grows tired; none of them stumbles. They never doze or sleep. Not a belt is loose; not a sandal strap is broken. Their arrows are sharp, and their bows are ready to shoot. Their horses' hooves are as hard as flint, and their chariot-wheels turn like a whirlwind. The soldiers roar like lions that have killed an animal and are carrying it off where no one can take it away from them.'

Ashurnasirpal II (883–859 BC) rebuilt the Assyrian capital at Kalah, and established a firm control over his Mesopotamian territories, and this new security gave his son Shalmaneser III (859–824 BC) the chance to expand his empire to the west. He was the emperor whose forces met Ahab and his Syrian allies at the battle of Qarqar in 853 BC. But it was almost another century before the toughest emperor of them all came to the throne: Tiglath-pileser III (745–727 BC). He was also acclaimed as king of Babylon in southern Mesopotamia, and turned out to be an expert military strategist. He saw that the key to imperial expansion was the establishment of a clearly defined policy. Though many of the records from his reign are confused and uncertain, he obviously had a clear strategy for annexing other states, which was carefully followed in the case of Israel (though there was some flexibility, for neither Judah nor the Philistine city states were ever dealt with in precisely the same way):

● First, he would try to make a treaty with other rulers, persuading them to acknowledge his sovereignty in exchange for certain limited privileges.

● Any hint of revolt by such vassals would be dealt with at once – usually by direct invasion, followed by the annexation of a good deal of their territory, and the installation of a new king to rule over what was left in accordance with Assyrian instructions.

● Any further resistance would lead to the whole state being taken over and turned into an Assyrian province, with its native leaders being deported to other parts of the empire.

Tiglath-pileser III represented the zenith of Assyrian power. Some of his successors still had expansionist ideas, and Esarhaddon (681–669 BC) even annexed Egypt. But by the end of Esarhaddon's reign, Assyria's imperial power was spent and though the reign of his successor, Ashurbanipal (669–627 BC) saw the establishment of a remarkable library of cuneiform texts at Nineveh, it also witnessed an extended civil war in Babylon, and revolts in other parts of the empire. By the end of his reign, the empire was beginning to disintegrate and its collapse was inevitable.

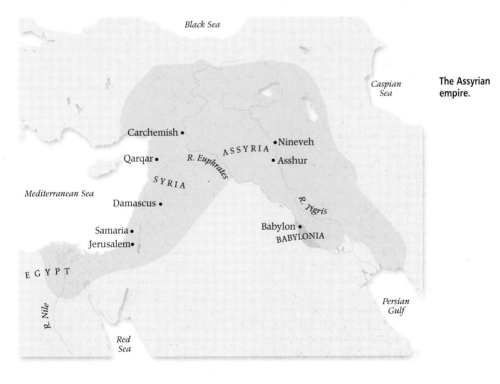

The Assyrian empire.

143

Hosea and the fall of Samaria

The indecision and opportunism of the last few kings of Israel are both reflected in the book of Hosea. Hosea began his work as a prophet after Amos, but probably before the end of Jeroboam II's reign, and he continued until after the Assyrians had captured Samaria. The disorders and constant revolts of the people against their kings are all vividly described here: 'In the heat of their anger they murdered their rulers. Their kings have been assassinated one after another, but no one prays to me for help' (7:7). The people thought they could do without God, and so Israel 'flits about like a silly pigeon; first they call on Egypt for help, and then they run to Assyria! But I will spread out a net and catch them like birds as they go by. I will punish them for the evil they have done' (7:11–12). Yet, in spite of the impending doom, Israel seemed to be quite unaware of what was happening: 'Yahweh says, "The people of Israel are like a half-baked loaf of bread. They rely on the nations around them and do not realize that this reliance on foreigners has robbed them of their strength. Their days are numbered, but they don't even know it"' (7:8–9).

Hosea's life and message
Very little is known about Hosea himself, though like Amos he was probably a member of the emerging upper classes, who unlike some of the others was greatly concerned about the social consequences of economic change. He was obviously a country person who could refer with the knowledge of experience to the morning mist and the dew (13:3), to the fragrance of the cedar trees of Lebanon (14:6), to corn and wine and olive oil (2:8), and to the work of ploughing and harvesting (10:11–13). Along with all this, Hosea displays a strong nostalgia for the life of the desert, for he loved not only his own countryside, but also its history, and he could look back with excitement to the old stories of Jacob and Moses and the exodus

(11–13). Whereas Amos was logical and impartial, Hosea was too deeply attached to his own homeland to imagine that God did not have a special affection for this place and its people. He loved the land, he loved the people and he was sure that God loved them too.

Hosea's message is inextricably interwoven with his own personal story, which starts with his marriage to a woman called Gomer. Some interpreters believe that this woman was a temple prostitute whom Hosea tried to win over to his own understanding of God's way of relating to people, though it is just as likely that she was his wife and her unfaithfulness was quite unexpected. In any event, Hosea and Gomer had three children, each of whom were given symbolic names that would convey a message about the fate of the nation. The first was called Jezreel, as a statement that God would still avenge Jehu's massacre there; the second was called Unloved, to declare that Israel seemed to have gone beyond God's love and forgiveness; and the other was called Not-my-People. Gomer subsequently left Hosea to live with another man (1:2 – 2:5), and in the next recorded event from Hosea's life, he goes to the market place and sees a prostitute who has fallen into some sort of slavery from which she can be released for a small payment. Moved by her plight, the prophet buys her and takes her to live with him (3:1–5). Some interpreters believe this was a different woman altogether from Gomer, though if the details of the story are compared to Hosea's subsequent message about God's relationship with Israel, it makes more sense to assume that this prostitute was in fact Gomer, who had presumably therefore been abandoned by the man she was living with.

Certainly this personal tragedy was the key to Hosea's message for the nation. Just as his love for Gomer had been rejected and despised, so had God's love for Israel. If an ordinary mortal like Hosea could feel so deeply grieved when his partner left him, how must God then feel over the unfaithfulness of Israel? Because of his personal involvement in this way, Hosea was able to see deeper into the nature of Israel's wrongdoing than Amos. Amos denounced the great public evils of the people, but Hosea saw behind them the breakdown of commitment to the covenant ideal in the everyday relationships found in homes throughout the land.

God and Israel

The people of Israel believed they would gain prosperity and good harvests by observing the traditional fertility rites of Baal worship. But from Hosea's standpoint, these rituals involved the very same sexual indulgence that had ruined his own home life. Just like Gomer, Israel was saying, 'I will go to my lovers – they give me food and water, wool and linen, olive oil and wine' (2:5). This, said Hosea, was the typical thinking of the Canaanite mentality, worshipping Baal for what they could get out of him, like prostitutes who would have sex for money. But in fact, Hosea knew that it was Israel's own God, Yahweh, who provided all these things: 'She would never acknowledge that I am the one who gave her the corn, the wine, the olive oil, and all the silver and gold that she used in the worship of Baal' (2:8). This was not what religious devotion in Israel should have been like. The worship of Yahweh was to grow out of gratitude for the undeserved love that had already been showered upon the nation. So Hosea returns over and over again to what God had done for Israel. Sometimes he uses imagery drawn from his own relationship with Gomer. At other times, he thinks in terms of God as the parent (mother) of the people and Israel as a recalcitrant son: 'the more I called to him, the more he turned away from me. My people sacrificed to Baal; they burnt incense to idols. Yet I was the one who taught Israel to walk. I took my people up in my arms, but they did not acknowledge that I took care of them. I drew them to me with affection and love.

I picked them up and held them to my cheek; I bent down to them and fed them' (11:2–4).

There was little sign of hope in Amos's message, and for him, the 'day of Yahweh' was almost entirely a day of punishment. But Hosea speaks of God making 'Trouble Valley' into 'a door of hope' (2:15). God still loved these people, and in due course Israel would return: 'She will respond to me… as she did when she was young, when she came from Egypt. Then once again she will call me her husband – she will no longer call me her Baal' (presumably a reference to the use of Canaanite practices in the worship of Yahweh, 2:15–16). To be sure, Gomer had suffered the consequences of her action, and so would Israel: 'Samaria must be punished for rebelling against me. Her people will die in war; babies will be dashed to the ground, and pregnant women will be ripped open' (13:16). Still, God would never give up Israel, any more than Hosea could give up his own wife: 'How can I give you up, Israel? How can I abandon you?… My heart will not let me do it! My love for you is too strong' (11:8).

In return, God was looking only for the unreserved commitment of the people. Unlike Baal, Yahweh was not primarily interested in religious rituals, but instead was seeking a renewed style of personal relationship: 'What I want from you is plain and clear: I want your constant love, not your animal sacrifices. I would rather have my people know me than burn offerings to me' (6:5–6). What was required was a return to the old simplicity that had characterized the life of the slaves who escaped from Egypt. They knew how much God had done for them, and because of that faithfulness and love they knew they could unreservedly commit themselves to God's care. Israel had come a long way since those days, but God's love was unchanging – and that message was to become increasingly important to the Bible writers as time went by.

Dating the Old Testament story

At first glance, it might seem easy to give dates to the events recorded in the Old Testament. There are certainly many lists of ancestors and descendants of prominent people, as well as complicated comparative datings at a number of points in the narratives. But it is extraordinarily difficult to condense all this material into one consistent chronological system. There are a number of significant problems:
● Different ancient versions of the Old Testament actually have different figures at many points. The Hebrew Bible is not always the same as the Greek version (the Septuagint).
● We do not wholly understand the basis on which the Old Testament's dating system operates. For instance, it usually refers to numbers of years within a given king's reign. But do these years include the year in which he became king, or is 'the first year' of a reign actually the first full year after the king's accession? Lack of certainty on this point can lead to considerable differences in dating, even over a short period of time.
● In the earlier Old Testament books, people are often credited with amazingly long lifespans, regularly running into hundreds of years. There are similarly extravagant claims in many records from ancient Mesopotamia, but we do not know precisely how to understand them in relation to our own calendar. It seems likely that such calculations were based on a shorter year than our twelve-month period, but in the absence of more certain knowledge we can deduce very little from them.
● Many scholars feel that the figures given in the Old Testament are stylized, and perhaps even symbolic. For example, when viewed as a whole the time scheme looks to have been designed so as to give special prominence to four important events in Israel's history: the exodus, Solomon's building of the Temple, the end of the Babylonian exile and the Maccabean reconsecration of the Temple. We also find the frequent use of the number forty, which perhaps suggests that it stands for something – maybe just indicating a long time, or a generation (though a literal generation would be much shorter than that). This figure occurs frequently in the stories of the judges, and if we add together all the time indications found there, we have a period in excess of 300 years. Yet we know from other evidence that, whatever understanding of the emergence of early Israel is adopted, the time between Moses and Samuel can hardly have been more than half that length.

There are obviously many uncertainties in trying to assign accurate dates to events in this literature. But from the time of the great empires founded by the Assyrians and the Babylonians, we have detailed records written by their own annalists, and these often mention people and events also described in the books of the Hebrew Bible. Moreover, the Assyrian and Babylonian records can easily be dated in absolute terms. This means that it has been possible to work out a general chronological framework for the Old Testament, by using these other materials and combining them with the dating methods found in the Bible story. Naturally, different scholars make their own judgments on such complex issues, though the dates used in this book are widely recognized as being accurate to within about ten years or less for the stories of the early monarchy, while the dates given for events and people during the Assyrian and Babylonian periods (and later) are much more accurate than that.

6 Judah and Jerusalem

Danger and uncertainty

With Israel gone, and Samaria reduced to a heap of ashes, life in Judah changed dramatically. Jerusalem was no longer protected from Assyria by its remote location. The border of the Assyrian empire was now less than twenty miles away, and Judah's security was threatened. Ahaz had only made things worse by actually offering to subject himself to the Assyrians, in exchange for protection against the kings of Damascus and Israel. Isaiah had been unable to prevent this, but he had no doubt of the likely outcome of such political madness, and in a characteristically picturesque message he declares that the people of Jerusalem 'have rejected the quiet waters from the brook of Shiloah' (near Jerusalem), in exchange for 'the flood waters of the River Euphrates, overflowing all its banks. They will sweep through Judah in a flood, rising shoulder high and covering everything' (Isaiah 8:6–8). Instead of trusting in God, Ahaz and his people had deliberately courted disaster in their cowardly submission to the Assyrians.

Ahaz himself was too cautious to allow that to happen during his reign. But he was sowing the seeds of eventual collapse.

POLITICALLY

Ahaz's acceptance of Assyrian rule was inept, but it also had immediate and serious social repercussions for his people. The halcyon days of Uzziah were gone for ever: much of Judah's territory had been lost, and along with it, a large slice of the royal income. That in itself would have been bad enough to lead to a major economic recession for Ahaz, but his problems were increased by considerable numbers of refugees trying to escape from the northern kingdom of Israel. He was forced to extend Jerusalem, building new houses and defences to settle these people. In such a situation it was perhaps inevitable that people should be tempted to get whatever they could for themselves with no thought of the wider social and moral consequences.

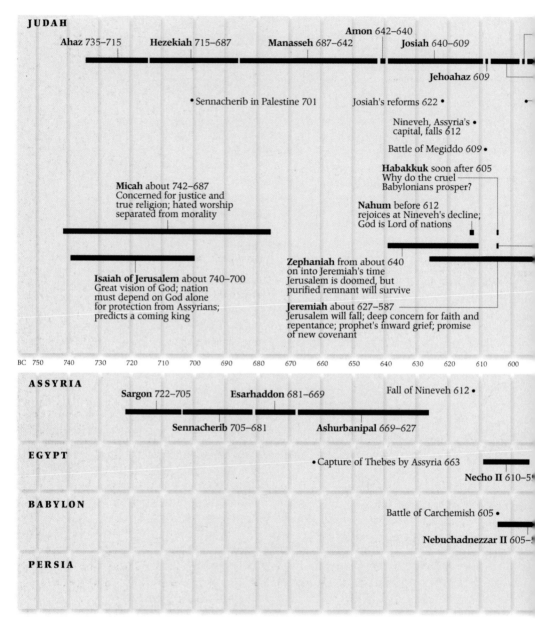

JUDAH

Ahaz 735–715   Hezekiah 715–687   Manasseh 687–642   Amon 642–640   Josiah 640–609

Jehoahaz 609

• Sennacherib in Palestine 701   Josiah's reforms 622 •

Nineveh, Assyria's •
capital, falls 612

Battle of Megiddo 609 •

Habakkuk soon after 605
Why do the cruel
Babylonians prosper?

Micah about 742–687
Concerned for justice and
true religion; hated worship
separated from morality

Nahum before 612
rejoices at Nineveh's decline;
God is Lord of nations

Zephaniah from about 640
on into Jeremiah's time
Jerusalem is doomed, but
purified remnant will survive

Isaiah of Jerusalem about 740–700
Great vision of God; nation
must depend on God alone
for protection from Assyrians;
predicts a coming king

Jeremiah about 627–587
Jerusalem will fall; deep concern for faith and
repentance; prophet's inward grief; promise
of new covenant

BC 750   740   730   720   710   700   690   680   670   660   650   640   630   620   610   600

ASSYRIA

Sargon 722–705   Esarhaddon 681–669   Fall of Nineveh 612 •

Sennacherib 705–681   Ashurbanipal 669–627

EGYPT

• Capture of Thebes by Assyria 663

Necho II 610–5

BABYLON

Battle of Carchemish 605 •

Nebuchadnezzar II 605–

PERSIA

RELIGIOUSLY

Ahaz was encouraging this. Not only was he officially promoting the
worship of Assyrian deities, even in the Temple itself, but he also
allowed many other forms of traditional Canaanite spirituality to
prosper. The arrival of northern refugees probably just added to the
pressure for more such syncretistic diversity, but all these things added
together meant that the distinctive message of Israel's own faith was
once again in danger of being lost. Isaiah was deeply concerned about

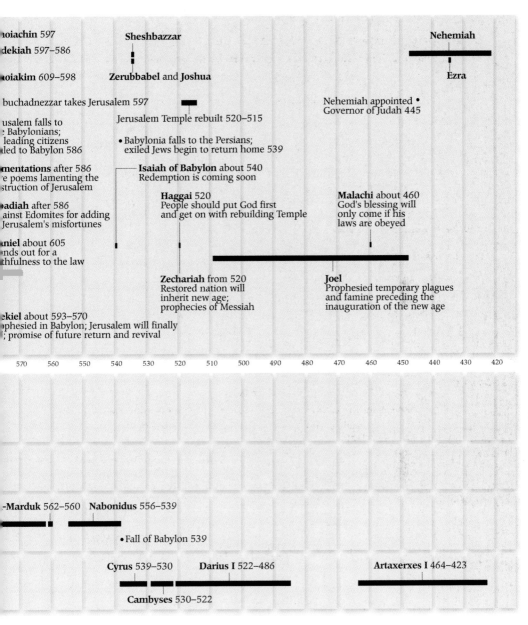

oiachin 597
dekiah 597–586

Sheshbazzar

Nehemiah

oiakim 609–598

Zerubbabel and **Joshua**

Ezra

buchadnezzar takes Jerusalem 597

Jerusalem Temple rebuilt 520–515

Nehemiah appointed •
Governor of Judah 445

usalem falls to
e Babylonians;
leading citizens
led to Babylon 586

• Babylonia falls to the Persians;
exiled Jews begin to return home 539

mentations after 586
e poems lamenting the
struction of Jerusalem

Isaiah of Babylon about 540
Redemption is coming soon

adiah after 586
ainst Edomites for adding
Jerusalem's misfortunes

Haggai 520
People should put God first
and get on with rebuilding Temple

Malachi about 460
God's blessing will
only come if his
laws are obeyed

uniel about 605
nds out for a
thfulness to the law

Zechariah from 520
Restored nation will
inherit new age;
prophecies of Messiah

Joel
Prophesied temporary plagues
and famine preceding the
inauguration of the new age

ekiel about 593–570
ophesied in Babylon; Jerusalem will finally
; promise of future return and revival

| 570 | 560 | 550 | 540 | 530 | 520 | 510 | 500 | 490 | 480 | 470 | 460 | 450 | 440 | 430 | 420 |

-**Marduk** 562–560 **Nabonidus** 556–539

• Fall of Babylon 539

Cyrus 539–530   **Darius I** 522–486

Artaxerxes I 464–423

Cambyses 530–522

all this, not least because of his opinion that the social and political
collapse of the northern kingdom had been caused by its failure to pay
due attention to the demands of the Law from Mount Sinai. He could
see the same things happening in Judah, where there was plenty of
religious activity, but little evidence of its impact in everyday life.
Isaiah's messages at this period bear a remarkable resemblance to the
dire warnings that Amos had given: 'Listen to what Yahweh is saying
to you… "Do you think I want all these sacrifices you keep offering to

me?... I am tired of the blood of bulls and sheep and goats... I am disgusted with the smell of the incense you burn... I hate your New Moon Festivals and holy days; they are a burden that I am tired of bearing... Stop all this evil that I see you doing... and learn to do right. See that justice is done – help those who are oppressed, give orphans their rights, and defend widows'" (Isaiah 1:10–11, 13–14, 16, 17).

The same message was emphasized by the prophet Micah. But whereas Isaiah belonged to the upper classes, Micah was a farm worker who saw even more clearly what was wrong with society, because he had experienced its injustice for himself. Judah, he said, was rotten from top to bottom, and even the national leaders 'hate justice and turn right into wrong... building God's city, Jerusalem, on a foundation of murder and injustice' (Micah 3:9–10). They might manage to persuade their own prophets to promise that 'wine and liquor will flow' for them, but messages like that were just 'lies and deceit' (2:11). By imagining that God's approval and support could be secured by religious observances alone, people had got their standards mixed up. For Micah, though, the real basis of the covenant society was not empty ritual, but justice and equality: 'What shall I bring to Yahweh, the God of heaven, when I come

Isaiah described Judah as God's vineyard. He expected a good harvest, but the grapes it produced were sour.

to worship...? Shall I bring the best calves to burn as offerings...? Will Yahweh be pleased if I bring... thousands of sheep or endless streams of olive oil? Shall I offer... my firstborn child to pay for my sins? No, Yahweh has told us what is good, and this is what is required: that we should do what is just, show constant love, and live in humble fellowship with our God' (Micah 6:6–8).

Like Amos before him, Micah saw little hope for people whose view of God's nature was so alien to the covenant faith: 'Twist and groan, people of Jerusalem, like a woman giving birth, for now you will have to leave the city and live in the open country. You will have to go to Babylon... Zion will be ploughed like a field, Jerusalem will become a pile of ruins, and the Temple hill will become a forest' (Micah 4:10; 3:12).

There were times when even Isaiah felt the same. In a dramatic picture, he describes Judah and Jerusalem as God's vineyard which had great potential, though only ever produced sour grapes. So the vineyard must be destroyed: 'I will take away the hedge round it, break down the wall that protects it, and let wild animals eat it and trample it down' (Isaiah 5:5). Ahaz was not disposed to listen to this kind of message. He believed he had already secured a measure of prosperity for his people, though in reality he was undermining the foundations of society. Instead of trusting in God, he was terrified of the Assyrians, and insisted on relying on his own political judgment. Judah had lost its independence to Assyria, and Isaiah could see no hope as long as Ahaz was king. So he withdrew from public life, and until the death of Ahaz he gave his teaching only to a small group of his own personal friends.

False confidence

Ahaz was succeeded by his son, Hezekiah. By the time he came to power, the Assyrian emperor Sargon II had become preoccupied with other problems in the east and north of his empire. This meant the states in Palestine had a little more freedom, and they lost no time in trying to turn that freedom to real political advantage. Egypt's power was also increasing at this time, and the Philistine city states were soon plotting with the Egyptians to get rid of Assyrian domination once and for all. Naturally, they tried to get the support of Judah, and no sooner was Hezekiah enthroned in Jerusalem than Philistine ambassadors came to ask for his help. But Isaiah warned them that Assyria's power was far from broken: 'Howl and cry for help, all you Philistine cities! Be terrified, all of you! A cloud of dust is coming from the north – it is an army with no cowards in its ranks' (Isaiah 14:31). Undaunted, the Egyptians tried to persuade Hezekiah to join their revolt, and Isaiah repeated his message. In a dramatic anticipation of what would happen to the rebels, the prophet took off all his clothes and walked naked round the streets of Jerusalem. This, he said, was 'a sign of what will happen to Egypt and Sudan. The emperor of Assyria will lead away naked the prisoners he captures from those two countries. Young and old, they will walk barefoot and naked, with their buttocks exposed, bringing shame on Egypt' (Isaiah 20:3–4). Hezekiah had more sense than his father, and listened carefully to Isaiah's advice. It was just as well he did, for in a short time the Assyrian army had moved in strength against both the Philistines and the Egyptians, who proved incapable of defending themselves, let alone Judah, and their power collapsed just as Isaiah had predicted it would.

Reform in Jerusalem

Hezekiah was still tempted to make his own bid for freedom, but he now realized that he would need to move carefully. So he began in a low-key way by reforming the religious practices of his people (2 Kings 18:1–8). Isaiah and Micah had both complained that the worship of their own God Yahweh was being mixed up with the worship of other deities. Some of this was certainly the continuation of traditional Canaanite practices of the kind that had long been popular, especially in the northern kingdom of Israel. But, in addition, Ahaz had created an altar to the Assyrian gods in Jerusalem. There is some debate about Ahaz's motivation, for as a general rule the Assyrians did not

Facing page, top:
King Hezekiah
faced a constant
military threat
from Assyria.
As part of his
preparation for a
possible siege,
he had a water
tunnel dug to
bring water from
outside the
Jerusalem city
wall to the Pool
of Siloam inside
the city. This
constant water
supply stood the
city in good
stead when
Sennacherib's
army invaded.

Right:
King Hezekiah
sought to re-
establish the
Temple as the
only centre of
worship in Judah,
so strengthening
links between
king and
worshippers. He
also invited
Israelites from
the old northern
kingdom to go to
Jerusalem. He
was aware that
such action
would attract the
attention of
Assyria, and he
developed the
defences of
Jerusalem in
preparation for
possible reprisals.

insist on this as a sign of political subservience, and it may be that this kind of thing is to be understood more generally as an indication of Judah's openness to the wider culture of the region. Hezekiah soon saw that by getting rid of these things, he could not only please religious fanatics like Isaiah, but it would also be a way of re-establishing a distinctively Judahite culture. A number of features of Hezekiah's reforms seem to indicate there was some political intention behind them:

■ As well as clearing the Jerusalem Temple of all the paraphernalia of alien worship, he also tried to close down even legitimate places of worship elsewhere in the country. That would ensure the Temple in Jerusalem would be the only place where the people could worship Yahweh. Of course, this Temple had always been Judah's national shrine, but when Solomon first built it, it also became an instant symbol of the king's own power. Hezekiah knew that if he could persuade his people to worship only in his own Temple, that was bound to strengthen their loyalty to him and to his successors.

■ Hezekiah's own people were not the only ones who were invited to worship in Jerusalem. He also sent a message to those who were left in what had been the territory of northern Israel (2 Chronicles 30:1–12). This state was now part of the Assyrian empire, and therefore had no official ties with Israel's national faith. But Hezekiah knew that many of its inhabitants still held to the loyalties of the old Israelite tribes, and if they could be tempted to travel south to worship in Jerusalem, that may begin to undermine the Assyrian power on his doorstep. Hezekiah certainly made strenuous efforts to link his reign with the corporate memory of the old kingdom in the north, even calling his son Manasseh, which was the original name of one of the ten northern tribes.

■ As well as reorganizing religious worship, Hezekiah also made military preparations for the inevitable Assyrian backlash. He built new defences in Jerusalem and many other cities (2 Chronicles 32:5;

152

Isaiah 22:9–11), reorganized the army, built new store cities, and rationalized his civil service (2 Chronicles 32:5–6, 27–29). In Jerusalem itself he built the Siloam Tunnel, to make sure the city would have plenty of water in the event of a siege (2 Kings 20:20; 2 Chronicles 32:30; Isaiah 22:9–11). Hezekiah was determined that, when the right opportunity presented itself, he would have a good chance of seizing a real and lasting independence from the Assyrians.

His chance came with the death of Sargon II. Soon after that, both the king of Babylon and a new Egyptian pharaoh sent a message asking Hezekiah to help overthrow the Assyrians. Isaiah warned against this, but his words fell on deaf ears (Isaiah 30:1–7; 31:1–3). The only ruler in Palestine who was opposed to this plan was the Philistine king of Ekron, but Hezekiah soon overcame his opposition by giving his support to some sort of revolt among his own officials. The Assyrian king Sennacherib describes how 'the officials, the

Below:
'Sennacherib's prism', an Assyrian document inscribed on stone, describes the siege of Jerusalem from the invader's point of view. Sennacherib speaks of shutting Hezekiah in Jerusalem 'like a bird in a cage'.

politicians, and the people of Ekron, had thrown Padi, their king, into fetters... and handed him over to Hezekiah the Jew'. After this, all the Philistine city states seem to have fallen in with this new anti-Assyrian alliance.

The Assyrians move in

It was entirely predictable that Sennacherib would not tolerate this kind of revolt, even on the edge of his empire. He marched south through Palestine, and Egypt and the Philistines collapsed at once. Then he moved against Judah, using the same tactics that his predecessor Shalmaneser V had adopted against the northern kingdom of Israel. First, he would weaken Hezekiah's position by taking over much of his territory. In this instance, instead of making the towns and villages of Judah a part of his own empire, he handed them over to various Philistine kings, but the end result was the same: Hezekiah had no supporters to whom he could appeal for help. By the time the Assyrians moved in the direction of Jerusalem, Hezekiah was, in Sennacherib's own vivid imagery, 'like a bird in a cage'. Hezekiah could see there was no chance of escape. The best he could hope for was to

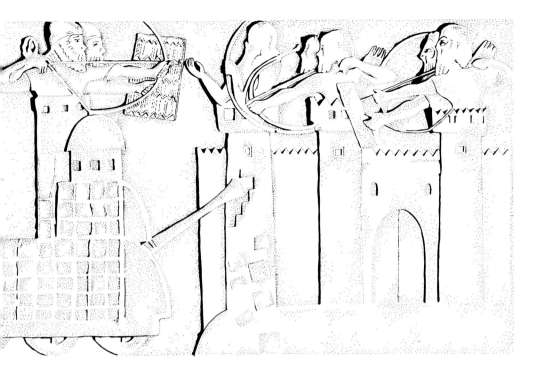

save the city itself by paying Sennacherib a huge tribute. The Assyrian king was prepared to accept this, and so Hezekiah sent large quantities of gold and silver treasures to the town of Lachish, where Sennacherib was encamped with his army.

It is not altogether clear what happened next. The Old Testament continues with the story of a siege of Jerusalem which ended in complete failure (2 Kings 18:17 – 19:37). The Assyrian army apparently camped outside the city in force, in the hope that the people would depose Hezekiah and so save themselves from the hardship of a long siege. Then, just as the fall of the city seemed imminent, the Assyrian army suddenly withdrew, after many of its soldiers had died in some mysterious way. The Assyrian records have a detailed account of Sennacherib's activities in Judah, but make no mention of this event. That in itself is not too surprising, for their official annals regularly ignored defeats. Most scholars believe that the Old Testament story is authentic enough, but they differ about when it actually happened. Though it seems unlikely that he would have besieged Jerusalem just after receiving a large payment of tribute, some think this must have been a part of Sennacherib's campaign in 701 BC. Others have noted that the story mentions 'King Tirhakah of Sudan', and since a king of that name ruled in Egypt from about 689 BC, it is therefore possible that this incident took place later, perhaps as a result of another attempted revolt by Hezekiah. On the other hand, Assyrian sources provide no evidence for such a second expedition by Sennacherib into Palestine.

The irresistible weight of Assyrian military might is directed towards a walled city in this relief from the palace of Ashurnasirpal II at Calah. Archers on the ramparts attempt to defend the city against others in a siege tower.

Assyria's final fling

Comparatively little is known of what was going on in Judah in the
years immediately following Sennacharib's invasion. Sennacherib himself
was soon murdered, and his successor was Esarhaddon, who was to be
one of Assyria's most powerful rulers (2 Kings 19:37; Isaiah 37:37–38).
When he died, his empire was divided between his two sons.
Ashurbanipal (669–627 BC) reigned at Nineveh, and Shamash-Shanakin
at Babylon. During this period, the Assyrians eventually achieved their
greatest ambition. Ashurbanipal finally managed to crush Egypt, and
capture its capital city, Thebes, which meant that Assyria now
dominated the whole of the Fertile Crescent, including the rival superpower of Egypt. But Ashurbanipal was not primarily a great warrior. He
had no need to be: his predecessors had already established the empire
on a firm foundation. He was able to turn his attention instead to the
enrichment of Assyrian culture, and his palace at Nineveh became a
great centre of both the literary and the visual arts. His artists produced
some of the most striking work anywhere in the ancient world, and his
scribes gathered an amazing library of literature. Not only did they
catalogue the events of recent history with great precision, but they also
gathered together the ancient traditions of Mesopotamia, which went
back right to the very dawn of civilization. Their writing methods may
seem primitive to us today, for they used the material that lay ready to
hand: river mud. First they formed the mud into conveniently sized
blocks, then they wrote on them with wedge-shaped sticks while the
mud was still wet. Once this 'cuneiform' writing was complete, the
blocks could be baked solid in the heat of the sun. This meant their
books were bulky, but it also ensured they would be virtually indestructible, and even today it is still possible to piece together mud blocks that
have been broken for centuries. It is due to this royal library at Nineveh
that we have so much detailed knowledge of the ancient civilizations of
the area and of their national traditions.

There was little to say about life in Jerusalem and Judah at such a
time as this. Hezekiah's successor, Manasseh, had no room to flex his
nationalistic muscles. He was no match for Assyria's power, and was in
complete subjection to it. The Assyrian records mention him only as a
source of building materials and troops, and confirm that he continued
to pay regular taxes. The Hebrew Bible makes no direct mention of
Assyrian power during Manasseh's long reign, but the reality of it is
reflected quite clearly in the description of affairs in the Jerusalem
Temple (2 Kings 21:1–18). Judah's own national faith was once more
neglected, and all sorts of alien ceremonies were promoted, including
star worship. Like Ahaz before him, Manasseh was forced to express his
subservience to the Assyrians by worshipping their deities, but this time
he made sure there would be no protests from people like Isaiah: those
who disagreed with his policies were put to death (2 Kings 21:16).
Because of this, the editors of the deuteronomic history eventually came

to regard him as the most incorrigibly wicked of all the kings. His son Amon continued the same unhappy policies (2 Kings 21:19–26).

Reform and renewal

Then came an unexpected opportunity for change. Things suddenly began to move on the fringes of the Assyrian empire. The Egyptians regained their independence, while the kingdom of Lydia in the north-west, and the Medes in the east, began to harass the Assyrians, and at the same time, hordes of Asian raiders (Scythians) swept down from the north. The internal stability of the empire had already been shaken by feuding between Ashurbanipal and his brother and this, combined with all the external factors, had an unsettling effect. Within a few years of Ashurbanipal's death, the Assyrians found themselves fighting for survival against the Babylonians and the Medes.

As before, the weakening of Assyrian power led to the revival of national hopes in Judah. This time, they centred around Amon's son, Josiah, who became king in Judah while he was still only a boy (2 Kings 22:1–2). As soon as he grew up, Josiah set about reasserting his country's independence. Assyria's problems now looked serious, and he saw a real chance of restoring the kingdom to something like the glory of the days of David and Solomon. His achievements fell short of that, but nevertheless Josiah had considerable success in extending his territory. Archaeological evidence shows that he controlled land as far north as Galilee, and his influence extended east of the River Jordan into Gilead. He also had some power over the Philistine states in the west, and all of this was consolidated with at least two marriages. This territorial expansion went hand in hand with a thoroughgoing religious reformation. This was now following a predictable pattern, for Hezekiah's earlier move for independence had also started with the removal of non-Israelite religious symbols. In the event, Josiah was far more successful than Hezekiah and even managed to remove altars and images related to Assyrian beliefs from the territories of the former northern kingdom of Israel. At this time, the sanctuary established at Bethel by Jeroboam I was destroyed, along with many local shrines and their priests.

But the central feature of Josiah's reform was the recovery of a book of the Law in the Temple at Jerusalem. The account in 2 Kings does not suggest this book was the cause of the reform, for it only came to light after workers had moved in to renovate the Temple. But once discovered, it played a significant part in the subsequent course of events (2 Kings 22:3–20). The Old Testament narrative does not directly identify this book, but from what is said, three main ideas seem to have dominated it:
■ Israel could only ever be one united people, and therefore the political division between Judah and Israel was meaningless.
■ The central plank of Israel's faith must be belief in only one God, Yahweh.
■ Israel's one God must be worshipped in only one place.

A lost book

Up to this point, Josiah's reforms had probably been more concerned with getting rid of Assyrian objects than with promoting the worship of Israel's God Yahweh. But this book provided a new, positive impetus. At times of political crisis and uncertainty, people often try to go back to the old ways, even today. In Josiah's time, many nations in the ancient world were taking a fresh look at their own national heritage, and for the same reasons. So when an ancient book was discovered in Jerusalem, it was naturally treated with special reverence. As it happened, this book also played right into Josiah's hands, for its main ideas seemed to give a religious backing to the political moves he was already making. He was trying to restore Judah's control over the former territory of the whole of the united nation of Israel; he was getting rid of Assyrian gods; and he needed to strengthen his personal position by insisting that the religious allegiance of the people should be given to his own royal Temple in Jerusalem.

There can be no doubt that this law book was the book of Deuteronomy. Some scholars have occasionally suggested that, far from being an ancient book, Josiah had actually arranged to have it written for precisely the reasons just mentioned. But this is highly unlikely. It is not intrinsically improbable that such documents would be stored in the Temple, for temples in the ancient world often served as repositories for significant national archives. Moreover, if Deuteronomy had been newly written in Josiah's time, it would have reflected his own situation much more clearly than it does. In particular, it would surely have identified the one place where God should be worshipped as the Temple in Jerusalem. But in fact, Deuteronomy does not do this – and in any case, it was not a new idea, as Hezekiah himself had tried to strengthen his own position by a similar stratagem long before the time of Josiah.

Deuteronomy does not in itself support the centralization of worship in Jerusalem, and it actually has many close links with the dynamic view of kingship that had been followed more self-consciously in the northern kingdom of Israel. For this reason, many scholars believe that the 'one sanctuary' mentioned in Deuteronomy was not Jerusalem, but the place where the ark of the covenant had been kept during the earliest period of Israel's emergence as a nation (Deuteronomy 12:5). The whole book clearly emphasizes the lessons that had been forcefully presented by northern prophets like Amos and Hosea: that the nation's prosperity could only be assured if they were willing to return to the old ways, and recognize the demands for justice and equality that had been such an important part of the covenant made at Mount Sinai. This is something that the people of Judah had forgotten, preferring to emphasize the promises given to David and to his successors. Instead of asking what they had done to deserve the punishment that was being handed out to them by Assyria, they reassured themselves with the belief that Jerusalem was God's chosen city – Zion – and so nothing could ever happen to it. It was impregnable, and would always be that way. Even Isaiah had agreed with this point of view, and though he regarded Assyria's iron hand as the agent of God's punishment, he still could not believe that Judah's day was finished (Isaiah 1:10–20; 2:6–21; 5:26–30; 9:1–7; 11:1–16; 14:1–2). But now, as Josiah and his people read this old book, they could see very clearly that unless they changed their ways, Judah and its people were indeed at an end. So, in a solemn ceremony, itself reminiscent of the events of Mount Sinai, the people of Judah pledged their allegiance once again to the long-forgotten ideals of their ancient faith (2 Kings 23:1–3).

The Babylonians

While all this was going on in Judah, the Assyrians were fighting desperately to hang on to the fragmented remnants of their once-great empire. The Babylonians were now more powerful than ever, and it was only a matter of time before they had captured all the main Assyrian cities. The defeated Assyrians tried to re-establish themselves at Haran, but they were soon ejected from there as well. Some thirteen years after Josiah's reformation in Judah, the Assyrians made a last-ditch effort to regain this town. This time, their old enemies the Egyptians came to help them. Necho II, now pharaoh of Egypt, could see that his real rival was no longer the king of Assyria but Nabopolasser, king of Babylon. There was absolutely no reason at all why Judah should have become involved in all this, but for some inexplicable reason Josiah decided that he would try to stop the Egyptians from reaching the beleaguered Assyrian army. He was unable to do so, and died in the attempt at Megiddo. The sense of loss that swept the nation can be judged from the fact that, centuries later, a poem mourning his death was still being repeated as part of the regular liturgy for worship (2 Chronicles 35:25). Indeed, there is some evidence that it was at this time that the books of Kings were first compiled, as a tribute to the achievements of Josiah. It is certainly striking that in these books he is the only king who manages to pass the test of loyalty to Yahweh, and all the others are judged by their failure to achieve what he did.

Politically, Judah came under Egyptian domination for a while at this time, but nothing could stop the advance of the Babylonians. Four years after the final collapse of Assyria, the Babylonian army met the Egyptians in battle at Carchemish, and decisively defeated them. At this Jehoiakim, a king of Judah who had been put in power by the Egyptians, was forced to transfer his allegiance to the Babylonian Nebuchadnezzar (2 Kings 24:1). Like his predecessors, he continued to keep his eyes open for a suitable opportunity to reassert his own independence, and when Babylon was defeated by the Egyptians some four years later, he decided to take his chance. But he had seriously misjudged the situation. Nebuchadnezzar moved in strength through the whole of Palestine, and besieged Jerusalem with his army, determined to replace Jehoiakim with a king who could be trusted. As it happened, the job was done for him, for Jehoiakim died during the course of the siege, and was replaced by his son Jehoiachin. He realized that resistance was futile, and surrendered to Nebuchadnezzar. Not surprisingly, the Babylonian did not trust him and took him off into exile in Babylon, along with many of the leading citizens and a large quantity of the treasures from both palace and Temple.

Three prophets

Three of the shorter prophetic books seem to have originated during the reigns of Josiah and Jehoiakim: Zephaniah, Nahum and Habakkuk. Virtually nothing of a personal nature is known of the prophets whose messages they contain, but they were all concerned with one subject: the way that God was using nations like Assyria and Babylon to punish Judah and encourage the people to be true to their own faith.

Zephaniah

Zephaniah is identified as a descendant of Hezekiah (1:1), and he probably delivered his messages in the earliest days of the reign of Josiah. Judah and Jerusalem, he declared, were being brought to ruination by the worship of traditional Canaanite gods like Baal, as well as the astral deities of the Assyrians (1:4–6). But Zephaniah did not blame Josiah himself for this state of affairs. Instead, he singled out his court officials (1:8–9), which suggests that Josiah was still a boy and his great religious reforms were a thing of the future. Probably, therefore, Zephaniah delivered his messages sometime between 640 and 622 BC, and this date would also fit in well with the theme of the poem which ends the book (3:14–20). For this is a celebration hymn, following the deliverance of Judah and Jerusalem from some particular enemy – possibly the Scythians, who were advancing south towards Egypt at about this period. However, the jubilation with which the book closes is not reflected in the rest of the prophet's messages.

Zephaniah warned his people against a false confidence in the security of Jerusalem just because of God's promises to David. The 'day of Yahweh' would be coming soon enough – and it would not be a day of rejoicing for the people of Judah, any more than it had been for the people of Samaria (1:7–18). They would experience God's anger, along with the other nations. Even Assyria, which God had used to punish the people of Israel, would in turn be destroyed because of their pride and self-satisfaction (2:13–15). But like Isaiah before him, Zephaniah saw that God could both punish the people, and yet still show love for them. Though Jerusalem was doomed, 'a humble and lowly people' would survive (3:12), and through them God's promises would come true.

Nahum

This book belongs to a period nearer the end of Josiah's reign, either just before or just after the collapse of the Assyrian capital Nineveh in 612 BC. Nahum too saw that, though Assyria had been the instrument of God's punishment for the people of Judah, they had over-reached themselves – and they would be punished in their turn. The collapse of Nineveh (Nahum 2–3) is described in such vivid language that some scholars have argued the prophet must actually have witnessed the scene. But others believe that his apparent realism is a purely imaginary – though remarkably accurate – description of the city's fall, and was probably composed even before the Babylonians finally moved in. Either way, the message of the book centres around the conviction that Yahweh, and not the Assyrians, is the one who determines the course of history and can use the nations at will. The knowledge that God was in control was an important lesson for the people of Judah to learn, for they had suffered so much at the hands of Assyria, which otherwise might have seemed very unfair.

Jeremiah and the fall of Jerusalem

Even before Josiah's reformation in 622 BC, another young prophet by the name of Jeremiah had already begun his work. He belonged to a family of priests from Anathoth, a village located about four miles northeast of Jerusalem. Like the other prophets, he was convinced that God

Because of the poetic form of the book, and its dramatic content, some have suggested that Nahum's messages were compiled in this way so as to be used liturgically in the Temple at Jerusalem, to celebrate Nineveh's downfall, and to remind the worshippers of God's great power.

Habakkuk

This book tackles a similar set of questions, though from a more reflective perspective. Habakkuk lived slightly later than Nahum, in the reign of Jehoiakim. By the time he delivered his messages, Egypt had been defeated at the battle of Carchemish (605 BC), and Habakkuk now had a chance to reflect on the Babylonian style of government. He was not impressed with what he saw. Things in Judah were bad enough, and society was collapsing in moral and political anarchy (1:2–4). God was rightly using superpowers like Babylon to discipline the people of Judah. But were the Babylonians any better? They 'catch people with hooks, as though they were fish. They drag them off in nets and shout for joy over their catch! They even worship their nets and offer sacrifices to them, because their nets provide them with the best of everything' (1:15–16). So, asked Habakkuk, how could God tolerate this kind of inhumane wickedness, while dealing so sternly with the lesser evil that was going on in Jerusalem?

He found the answer to that in the conviction that the Babylonians would themselves be punished by God. Like Nahum, Habakkuk had no difficulty in believing that God was personally in charge of history, and could therefore use even evil nations to accomplish good. But such people would never be allowed to get away with their wrongdoing: 'You are doomed! You founded a city on crime and built it up by murder. The nations you conquered wore themselves out in useless labour, and all they have built goes up in flames. The Lord Almighty has done this. But the earth will be as full of the knowledge of God's glory as the seas are full of water… Yahweh will make you drink your own cup of punishment, and your honour will be turned to disgrace' (2:12–14, 16). Of course, Habakkuk realized that this kind of answer to the problem of evil in the world is not much direct use to those who are actually suffering. But he also included some practical advice for his people: 'Those who are evil will not survive, but those who are righteous will live because they are faithful to God' (2:4). There is some debate as to the precise meaning of these words, but almost certainly the Hebrew expression used in this passage should be understood as referring to God's own faithfulness, first experienced in the events of the exodus and repeated many times in the nation's history since then. It was in these words that St Paul and Martin Luther later found the heart of biblical faith, and of course the commitment of which they spoke is essentially a human response to the personal faithfulness of God. This confidence in God was eloquently expressed by Habakkuk in the closing verses of his book – and it was to be needed in the dark days that lay ahead for Judah: 'Even though the fig trees have no fruit and no grapes grow on the vines, even though the olive crop fails and the fields produce no corn, even though the sheep all die and the cattle stalls are empty, I will still be joyful and glad, because the Lord God is my saviour. The Sovereign Lord gives me strength, and makes me sure-footed as a deer, and keeps me safe on the mountains' (3:17–19).

had spoken personally to him, and entrusted him with a message for the people. He was to be 'a prophet to the nations', communicating the will of God in the midst of much international turmoil (Jeremiah 1:5). This was certainly an appropriate time for the emergence of such a person, for by the year of his call (627 BC) Assyria's power was crumbling and independence for Judah once more seemed a real possibility. But Jeremiah could not share in the mood of national optimism. He saw many things wrong in his nation: the people had chosen to ignore the covenant laws of God, and would have to face the inevitable conse-quences of such disobedience. One day he saw an almond tree in blossom. The Hebrew word for 'almond' had a similar sound to another Hebrew word that meant 'watching', and Jeremiah saw this tree as a sign that God was watching over the people, looking for the appropriate time to carry out the sentence of destruction (Jeremiah 1:11–12). When he saw a pot of boiling water on a fire that was fanned by a wind from the north, he realized that this, too, had a message in it. God's anger was about to boil over against Judah: 'Destruction will boil over from the north on all who live in this land, because I am calling all the nations in the north to come. Their kings will set up their thrones at the gates of Jerusalem and round its walls, and also round the other cities of Judah. I will punish my people' (Jeremiah 1:14–16).

Misplaced trust

Things soon began to change with the religious reforms instituted by Josiah. Jeremiah no doubt was in favour of all this: he certainly wanted to get rid of foreign religious influences, and some of his messages may well have been delivered in support of Josiah, for they angered his relatives in Anathoth, who decided to try to kill him (Jeremiah 11:18–23). Their reaction would have made sense if Jeremiah was supporting Josiah's closure of all the sanctuaries except the Temple in Jerusalem, for as priests they would presumably be in danger of losing their jobs. Jeremiah soon realized that Josiah's reforms were not going to have much lasting effect on the way of life of the people, and by the time of Jehoiakim things were as bad as they had ever been. But Jeremiah also came to think that Josiah's emphasis on the Jerusalem Temple had actually undermined the faith that was emphasized in the ancient law book uncovered there, for instead of facing up to their responsibilities under the covenant Law, the people developed a pathetic and misguided confidence in their religious institutions. They came to imagine that as long as they performed the prescribed rituals in the Temple, God would actually preserve them from their enemies and all would be well.

In the end, events proved Jeremiah was right. But in the short term, he was disappointed and depressed. The people refused to listen to his message, and he was puzzled himself, because it appeared not to be coming true. Instead of the doom that Jeremiah had predicted, Judah was enjoying a period of great prosperity. Under Josiah the nation's territory was enlarged and there seemed to be no shortage of money for grand new building projects. Under the circumstances, people like Jeremiah were unlikely to be taken seriously, and then when Nineveh was destroyed in 612 BC his message seemed to be quite discredited.

The end is coming

However, within a very short period of time the picture had changed quite radically. Three years later, Josiah was dead and the Egyptians had taken over the land of Judah. The prosperity that had gone before had been attributed to the fact that things had been set right in the Temple at Jerusalem. So what had gone wrong now? Why had God not saved these apparently faithful people from the power of Egypt? In this situation, Jeremiah's messages began to look less unrealistic, and when under Jehoiakim the reforms of Josiah virtually disappeared, the stage looked set for the scenario of disaster that Jeremiah had so vividly described. Even Jehoiakim himself could see that, and he made a concerted effort to get rid of opponents like Jeremiah. At least one prophet, Uriah, was killed, and Jeremiah himself was brought to trial (Jeremiah 26:7–24). He escaped death, but still continued to deliver his messages of doom and destruction, and was beaten up and put into the stocks for a night. Even that did not stop him. God had spoken, and he could not refuse to communicate the message: 'When I say, "I will forget Yahweh and no longer speak in God's name," then your message is like a fire burning deep within me. I try my best to hold it in, but can no longer keep it back' (20:9). But he was still banned from delivering his messages in public at the Temple, and so he withdrew from public life for the rest of Jehoiakim's reign, and distributed his messages by getting his friend Baruch to write them down and then take them into the streets to read them aloud. At this time, Jeremiah's messages were no longer general declarations of disaster, but definite predictions of the impending end of Jerusalem, and especially of the destruction of its Temple. Jeremiah had no doubt that the idea that God was bound to protect the Temple and city was false.

But Jeremiah was not only struggling against opposition from his enemies. He also had his own problems with the message God had given him. If it was correct, why did no one else accept it? After all, Jeremiah had not refused God's call, even though he wanted to do so. He had laid himself open to disbelief and ridicule, and had become involved in endless arguments (15:10–21). He had given up the ordinary human joys of home and family to speak on God's behalf, and he was tempted to feel that God had somehow deceived him (20:7–18). This was a hard time, and some of the most striking passages of the book of Jeremiah are concerned with this kind of self-examination. But it was also a significant period of spiritual learning for this most open-hearted of all the prophets, and the record of his personal journey of faith and self-discovery at this time has become one of the most inspirational sections of the entire Bible for more than one generation of spiritual searchers. The story of Jeremiah provides one of the most outstanding models of what it means to trust God in a personal and living way.

Dark days in Jerusalem

When Nebuchadnezzar captured Jerusalem in 597 BC, he placed a new king, Zedekiah, on the throne there. But things did not change. Instead

of learning their lesson, the people of Jerusalem concluded that they were specially favoured by God, because they had escaped the ultimate fate of being carried off into exile. Jeremiah had no time for this easy optimism: he knew that what had happened was a just punishment for the people's wrongdoing, and that worse was to come. He pointed to two baskets of figs in the market, one containing good figs and the other full of rotten figs. The good ones, said Jeremiah, were the exiles in Babylon. The bad ones were the people left in Judah – and everyone knew what happened to figs that were too bad to eat (Jeremiah 24).

The people of Jerusalem were deported to Babylon in stages. At first only the leaders were taken in the days of King Jehoiachin, while Zedekiah was put on the throne as a puppet ruler. Only after his revolt was the city finally destroyed. Jeremiah characterized this intervening time as being like a basket of figs, of which the good ones stood for those already in exile, and the bad ones for the leaders who remained.

Zedekiah hardly knew which way to turn. Jeremiah advised him that the only sensible thing to do was to accept Babylonian domination. He wanted to listen, but he was a weak man and when the Egyptians tried to persuade him to join a revolt against Babylon there was no shortage of other prophets who advised Zedekiah to do so. Jeremiah, however, refused to change his mind. In a dramatic presentation of his message, he appeared wearing a wooden yoke on his shoulders, as a mime to show what would happen to the nation (Jeremiah 27). He was confronted in the Temple by a prophet called Hananiah, who ridiculed Jeremiah's message, and to prove his point he proceeded to smash Jeremiah's yoke. Determined not to allow his message to be subverted in this way, Jeremiah quickly replaced the wooden yoke with an iron one (Jeremiah 28). In the event, Jeremiah was right. The Babylonian army moved up to crush the rebellion masterminded by Egypt, and Judah was finished. After a siege of eighteen months the city of Jerusalem fell to Nebuchadnezzar. Zedekiah tried to escape, but he was captured. His family was killed before his eyes, and then he was blinded and carried off to Babylon along with most of the leading people of the land. This time the Babylonians made sure of their victory by systematically destroying all the main buildings in Jerusalem, including the Temple. A palace official named Gedaliah was made governor of Judah, and from this point on there would never be a king again (2 Kings 25:1–26).

Jeremiah's dreadful predictions had come true, and even the Temple lay in ruins, its treasures plundered. Still, Jeremiah was confident that

God's promises could not be overthrown so easily and, like Habakkuk before him, he knew that there would be a future for his people. Even while Jerusalem was under attack, Jeremiah had purchased a piece of land in his native village, as an expression of his confidence for the future (Jeremiah 32:1–15). The action nearly cost him his life, for as he was leaving the city to go and view the property he was arrested on suspicion of being a traitor (Jeremiah 37:11 – 38:13). Yet his trust in God was not founded on a crudely materialistic expectation. He had already made it plain that his people's future and the real meaning of the faith from Mount Sinai was not to be found in the Temple. All the institutions connected with that were only of limited value. God was not most truly to be found in the ritual of sacrifice, but in a personal and living relationship of trust and commitment. The exiles in Babylon were to learn that soon enough, but it was an insight that had already been given to Jeremiah. For he saw beyond and through the disaster and destruction, to a new relationship that God would establish with humankind. God had remained faithful to the covenant made at Mount

Other traditions related to Jeremiah

In addition to the book of Jeremiah contained in the Hebrew Bible, the deuterocanonical books with their origins in the Greek Bible (Septuagint) also include two writings connected to Jeremiah: Baruch and the Letter of Jeremiah.

Baruch

A person named Baruch is mentioned in the book of Jeremiah, where he is the prophet's friend and secretary, responsible for writing down his messages and distributing them when Jehoiakim had silenced Jeremiah himself (Jeremiah 36:4–8). The book of Baruch is presented as a compilation of such teachings, the first section (1:1 – 3:8) in prose and the rest (3:9 – 5:9) in poetry. The opening sentence dates these messages to 'the fifth year' of the exile, written in Babylon and delivered to the exiles in that city. Since Jehoiachin is mentioned and Temple worship still appears to be continuing (2:26), the natural implication seems to be that the exile in question was the first deportation of 597 BC, which would place this book in 593 BC. However, none of this can be reconciled with what is otherwise known of Baruch from the book of Jeremiah. There, he was still with the prophet even after the fall of Jerusalem in 586 BC (Jeremiah 43:5), and the natural implication of that passage is that he was taken to Egypt, along with Jeremiah. Other historical references are confused and contradictory, and some scholars have concluded that the book is not even a single piece of writing, but combines two or three originally separate pieces. Some passages appear to reflect a later stage again, around the time when the Babylonian empire was collapsing and there was a real prospect that the exiles might be able to return home (4:5 – 5:9). The book of Baruch is known only in Greek, though the terminology used in some sections seems to indicate that it may have been translated from a Hebrew or Aramaic original. There are many connections with the books of Jeremiah, Lamentations and Isaiah 40–55, which suggests it was written later than them, while some passages have links with Daniel, which was not written until the second century BC. Possibly it was written about the same time as Daniel, at another time of great persecution for the Jewish people,

This seal may have belonged to Baruch, friend and secretary of the prophet Jeremiah.

Sinai, but the people had been unable to respond to this freely shared love. They had not managed to live up to the high ideals of the past, and what they needed now was a 'new covenant' that would both fulfil and supersede the original one. This time it would be a covenant that not only asked them to be obedient to God, but also actually gave them the moral power to do so: 'The new covenant that I will make with the people of Israel will be this: I will put my law within them and write it on their hearts. I will be their God, and they will be my people... all will know me, from the least to the greatest. I will forgive their sins and I will no longer remember their wrongs. I, the Lord, have spoken' (Jeremiah 31:33–34).

Other traditions related to Jeremiah *continued*

encouraging them to remain faithful to their heritage, and maybe also, like Daniel, it incorporated materials that had been originally written earlier, but edited and applied to the new situation.

The Letter of Jeremiah

This is neither a letter, nor does it have any direct connection with Jeremiah. It consists of a polemic against the worship of idols, in the context of a time when the Jewish people were still trying to work out how and why God's judgment on them should have lasted for so long even after the exile. It may originally have been written in Hebrew, because a play on words in verse 72 would only have made sense in that language, though it is most likely that it originated among the people of the Babylonian exile, for whom it must have seemed as if the deities of other nations, with their grand visual representations and statues, were more powerful than Yahweh. Since the book is mentioned in 2 Maccabees 2:2, it cannot have been compiled later than about 100 BC, and the best guess as to its date would place its composition sometime in the second half of the second century BC.

The Lachish Letters

The last days of Judah are depicted vividly in the book of Jeremiah, where the prophet's message reflects the disarray and confusion of the people as they could see the Babylonians coming, and yet were powerless to do anything about it. Unlike the edited accounts of history we get in the books of Samuel and Kings, this is the kind of first-hand evidence that helps to bring past events to life. The situation described by Jeremiah is also documented in one of the most remarkable finds ever made by archaeologists in a Bible city: the Lachish Letters.

The city of Lachish lay to the south-west of Jerusalem, and its history began long before Israel ever emerged as a nation. It was an important city from the earliest period, and has been more thoroughly excavated than most Israelite towns. The material found there has been of great importance in helping to understand the development of the Hebrew language, while the discovery of traditional altars and other religious objects using Canaanite designs has added to our knowledge of the kind of practices so often denounced by the prophets. The city was destroyed by Sennacherib in 701 BC, and then later Nebuchadnezzar captured it in about 587 BC, just before the final collapse of Zedekiah's Jerusalem. The Lachish Letters relate to this sequence of events.

The letters themselves are actually what archaeologists call 'ostraca', that is, scraps of broken pottery with messages written

The Assyrian king Sennacherib receives the surrender and booty from the Judahite town of Lachish. The siege of the town was graphically documented by the Assyrians in a series of reliefs in Sennacherib's palace at Nineveh.

The Lachish Letters
continued

on them. A total of twenty-one of these ostraca were found, mostly in what appears to have been the guardroom of the city gate. Not all of them are now legible, but the majority of those that are were addressed to a man named Yaush, who was probably the military commander of Lachish at the time. Many of the messages were written by someone called Hoshayahu, who seems to have been

Fragments of a letter, written on pottery by a military commander at an outpost near Lachish, bear witness to a desperate state of affairs as the Assyrian army advanced.

the officer in charge of a military outpost to the north of Lachish. The same name is found in Jeremiah (42:1; 43:2), though there is no way of knowing whether they were the same person. Still, the letters do provide a fascinating insight into the same situations as were described by Jeremiah:

● Jeremiah 34:1–7 reports a message given by Jeremiah to Zedekiah while Nebuchadnezzar's army was moving against Jerusalem. At the same time, 'The army was also attacking Lachish and Azekah, the only other fortified cities left in Judah' (Jeremiah 34:7). Azekah was almost

halfway between Lachish and Jerusalem, and in one of the Lachish ostraca Hoshayahu writes, 'We are watching for the signals from Lachish... for we cannot see Azekah.' Azekah was perhaps midway between Hoshayahu's post and Lachish, and was therefore used as a signalling station. But at the time of writing, it had apparently fallen to the Babylonians.

● The name Jeremiah is found in two of the letters, though there is no reason to identify this person with the Old Testament prophet in either case. There is, however, a clear reference to 'the prophet' in at least two of these letters, and the same term may also be found in a further two. Someone who could be referred to as 'the prophet' without further explanation must have been a high-profile public figure, and it has been proposed that the person indicated here must have been Jeremiah himself. Of course, that is impossible to prove one way or the other, and it has also been suggested that 'the prophet' could be Uriah, since the same letter also refers to 'Coniah, son of Elnathan' going to Egypt, and according to Jeremiah 26:22 Jehoiakim sent a man called Elnathan to bring Uriah from Egypt to face death in Jerusalem. This identification is more problematic, for the letters did not originate in Jehoiakim's reign, but later in the time of Zedekiah. Nevertheless, even though the exact identity of 'the prophet' remains uncertain, references like this do indicate that such prophets as Jeremiah were playing an important part in national affairs at this period in Judah's history.

Other more fanciful efforts have been made to link these texts more closely to the prophetic movement, its supporters and detractors, in Jerusalem. But their greatest value is the insight that they give us into the people of Jeremiah's day, and their reactions as they faced the inevitable end of their nation at the hands of the Babylonian army.

The prophets

People who are described as 'prophets' clearly played a crucial role in the history of the two nations, Israel and Judah, and in addition their messages dominate the Old Testament as we have it today. They are among the greatest religious teachers of all time, and have had a profound impact not only on the life of those who knew them, but also, through their writings, on the life of every subsequent generation of Bible readers.

In the nineteenth century, it was fashionable to suppose that it was through the activity of the prophets that an originally primitive and superstitious faith was transformed into the high ideals of morality that are now found in the Hebrew Bible. But it is obvious that approaches of this kind said more about the religious perspectives of those who proposed them than about the prophets themselves, and biblical prophecy is a much more complex and diverse phenomenon than that kind of simplistic explanation might suggest.

Four different Hebrew expressions are conventionally translated as 'prophet'. Some passages seem to suggest that the terminology changed with the passage of time (1 Samuel 9:11), but in reality we cannot now tell the technical difference between these terms. The fact that the terminology is so diverse, however, clearly suggests that prophets differed from each other, and that prophecy was not just a single social and religious phenomenon. People who could be called prophets operated in many different social contexts: as diviners (1 Samuel 9:1–25); as ecstatics, often in groups who were distinguished by special marks and clothing (1 Samuel 10:5–8; 19:18–24; 1 Kings 20:35–43; 2 Kings 1:8; 2:23–24; 4:38; 6:12); as royal court prophets (1 Samuel 22:5; 2 Samuel 12:1–15; 24:11; 1 Kings 20:35–43); as war prophets (Judges 4:4–9; 1 Kings 20; 22:1–28); as cultic prophets (1 Samuel 10:5–8; 2 Kings 4:18–25); as 'false' prophets (1 Kings 22; Isaiah 9:15; Jeremiah 6:14; Ezekiel 13:2; Micah 3:5–6).

Some prophets seem to have operated in more than one way. For instance, when Samuel tells Saul about his lost asses he is a seer with psychic powers (1 Samuel 9:11, 19–20), but he then goes on to give specific messages about the kingship in a more spontaneous kind of prophetic utterance (1 Samuel 10:1–8). Yet others, like Amos, claim not to have been real 'professional' prophets at all (Amos 7:12–15).

Several models have been used by scholars to try to explain the form and function of Hebrew prophecy. Here we shall notice just four of the more significant approaches.

A history of religions approach

In view of our ever-increasing knowledge of social and religious situations throughout the ancient world it is natural to compare Old Testament prophets to similar characters elsewhere. One of the earliest exponents of this view was the Scandinavian scholar Alfred Haldar. According to him, prophecy was a phenomenon found in the context of organized religion (the cult). A close analysis of texts from Babylon (Old Babylon, 1894–1595 BC) showed that they distinguished between two types of prophet. On the one hand were the *Mahhu*, priests or prophets who specialized in wild, ecstatic, trance-induced behaviour. But alongside them were the *Baru*, who specialized in divination, that is, they would be asked a specific question, the answer to which they would discover by throwing dice, or by astrological speculations, or by offering sacrifices and examining the entrails of the dead animals in order to discover the will of the gods.

Haldar claimed to find Old Testament evidence for this pattern, mainly in the dual functions of Samuel. He believed that other isolated passages provide evidence for the work of 'divination corporations'

(Isaiah 21:6–10) or sacrificial inspection (Psalm 5:3). But this view of the nature of prophecy is difficult to substantiate from the Old Testament:

● Although the Old Testament does provide evidence for wild behaviour on occasion (1 Samuel 10:9–13), and of prophets giving specific answers to questions (1 Samuel 9:3–20), it is not the most obvious or common form of Old Testament prophecy. There is a good deal more evidence for a more 'rational' kind of prophecy. Indeed, when Jeremiah finds a message in a potter's workshop (Jeremiah 18:1–12), or in a basket of figs (Jeremiah 24), it is at least arguable that his message is essentially the result of rational deliberation on the everyday happenings of life, and has nothing at all to do with special emotional or religious experiences.

● Even when prophets do answer specific questions ('divination'), the Old Testament provides no evidence that they manipulated special objects such as dice or sacrifices in order to arrive at an answer (1 Samuel 9:17–20; 1 Kings 22).

● To use such technical means of divination required special training and a lot of practice. Again, there is no Old Testament evidence of the prophets being trained at all, and a fair amount to the contrary (e.g. Amos 7:12–15).

Others have looked to Egypt and Syria as sources of possible models for Old Testament prophecy. Mari is another society in which there was evidently a kind of 'prophecy'. Texts from there speak of 'prophets' who were religious functionaries, of trance prophets, and of yet others who brought messages to the attention of the king and who were therefore a specialized kind of bureaucrat. At one time or another, all this material has been regarded as a possible 'source' of Old Testament prophecy, and there is no doubt that much of it can help us to a better understanding of the Old Testament. But there is unlikely to be any direct line of connection between them:

● The social functions performed by diviners, ecstatics and so on can arise in any society, ancient or modern, quite independently of external direct contact.

● There is in the Hebrew Bible a much wider diversity than in any of the comparative materials so far identified. There tends to be less emphasis on divination here than elsewhere, and Samuel's example is quoted so frequently only because there are no other biblical examples of this kind of thing.

● In general, the Hebrew prophets were concerned more about the great sweep of history and the meaning of human life in the grand sense, than about the trivialities of everyday life.

A psychological approach

Julius Wellhausen (1844–1918) argued that the prophets were essentially inspired individuals, who changed the form of Israelite religious belief. The presence of apparently irrational prophetic behaviour in certain Old Testament stories seemed to suggest that a useful perspective on the prophets would be gained by asking what it was that made them such exceptional people. This line of enquiry was especially associated with the work of Hermann Gunkel (1862–1932), who concluded that the key to understanding the prophets was 'ecstasy'. By this he meant the kind of irrational, over-emotional behaviour that is familiar from many contexts the world over. There are many contemporary examples of such things, not only in the Judeo-Christian religious tradition, but also in Sufism and many aspects of the New Age.

Gunkel described the prophetic experience in the following way: 'When such an ecstasy seizes him, the prophet… loses command of his limbs; he staggers and stutters like a drunken man; his ordinary sense of what is decent deserts him; he feels an impulse to do all kinds of strange actions… strange ideas and emotions come over him… he is seized by that sensation of hovering which we know from our own dreams.' Scholars of this earlier generation often referred to what they knew of Canaanite prophecy to back up their theories, though in reality they knew next to nothing about that apart from what is reported in 1 Kings 18. But like many things connected to the emergence of Israel as a nation, this kind of simple explanation does not match all the facts. Of course, a passage like that shows the prophets of Baal producing ecstatic hysteria by a series of self-inflicted moves – music, shouting, dancing, drink, drugs and so on. But then there are other narratives which show Israelite prophets doing exactly the same things (1 Samuel 10; 2 Kings 2). Because of the apparent difficulty of reconciling such descriptions with the kinds of messages delivered by the great prophets of the Old Testament, Gunkel concluded that prophecy must have evolved from this kind of ecstatic mass hysteria to become an altogether more rational phenomenon. But it is possible to assess the evidence differently. Some, for example, have tried to identify the ecstatics with 'false prophets', contrasting them with the 'real' prophets who were rational speakers, though this is very difficult to do as there are many indications that the great prophets could also have unusual psychical experiences (Jeremiah 4:19; 23:9; Ezekiel 1:1 – 3:15). Others have tried to distinguish the experiences of the great prophets from the content of their messages, surmising that the messages were delivered in a rational way after the experiences, but with no particular reference to what had gone before. But all such rationalizing explanations are unsatisfactory. The Old Testament itself makes none of these distinctions, and all the prophets mentioned there have unusual experiences of one sort or another. The way in which the experiences are related to life situations seems to depend on the circumstances of the moment, and although analysis of ecstasy and other related emotional states can shed some light on prophetic experience, it is clear that a full understanding of the prophets is not to be found there.

A literary approach

It was the search for a meaningful life situation that led Claus Westermann to begin to analyse the literary form of the prophetic messages in the Old Testament. In the ancient world, the way a person spoke was determined by their context to a much greater extent than it is today. By analysing the forms of prophetic speech it is therefore possible to locate it in various contexts, such as the law court (Amos 7:16–17; Micah 2:1–4), the wisdom school (Jeremiah 17:5–8), the context of worship (Habakkuk; Isaiah 40–55), or the royal court ('Thus says...' is a royal messenger speech-form). That being the case, it can be argued that the prophets must have been essentially ordinary people, whose background lay in the official functions of these different life situations. It has even been suggested that the descriptions of 'visions' and other 'ecstatic' experiences could perhaps be stylistic devices, rather than literal descriptions of things that happened.

This way of looking at the prophets and their messages has added enormously to our understanding of them. But by itself, it can lead to a one-sided view of their functions:

● It is to some extent a reaction against the extreme 'ecstatic' view: instead of prophets being seen as innovators, they are here viewed as conventional persons operating within the normal structures of society. But the fact is that the element of 'ecstasy' is still there in the Old Testament, and cannot be disposed of quite so simply.

● Then there is the question of a jump from literary form to life situation. A person who uses a legal form is not necessarily a lawyer, but may be just a good communicator, using language that will be especially evocative and challenging to those who hear.

The prophets
continued

A theological/cultic approach

A century ago, Wellhausen was arguing that the prophets had broken completely with cultic worship in ancient Israel, and were attempting to introduce morality into what had hitherto been a barren and empty form of ritualism. Today, many scholars would argue the exact opposite, suggesting that the religious life of Israel had started with a covenant based on a distinctly moral view of God, and that the prophets were closely associated with this covenant ideal and with its celebration in the context of worship. There can be no doubt that the idea of a 'covenant' is at the heart of the Old Testament faith. All these books centre on the unmistakable conviction that God had burst into the lives of the people of Israel as an act of unmerited love ('grace'), and that as a result of this the people were called upon to respond by loving obedience in return. When we talk of 'the covenant', this is all we mean: the responsive obedience of the people, consequent upon their experience of God's grace. In historical terms, that experience had been demonstrated most

dramatically in the events of the exodus and what followed, and this is a major theme in the messages of many of the greatest prophets. It was also celebrated regularly in the great worship festivals that marked the progress of Israel's religious life. Some scholars in the past have no doubt exaggerated the role of the prophets in this religious worship. But it certainly makes sense to see them as guardians of the covenant faith. It explains why they spoke in full expectation that people would listen, for they were calling them back to their spiritual roots.

No one of these models by itself can fully explain Old Testament prophecy. The whole phenomenon is so diverse that perhaps we need to speak individually of particular prophets rather than trying to speak of them all in one breath. But they were all conscious of having been in the presence of God in some mystical sense, and then of speaking or acting in God's name as interpreters of the covenant faith in relation to the events of their own day and to the lives of their contemporaries.

7 Dashed Hopes and New Horizons

The period following the Babylonian invasion of Judah was one of the most important in the entire history of the Israelite nation and faith. The previous millennium had seen many striking changes, as Israel first emerged as a nation, soon to become a significant political entity, and then to sink into economic and spiritual decay, so that in the years immediately prior to the fall of Jerusalem, the state of Judah had become a relatively unimportant middle-eastern kingdom. Politically, the nation was finished. Yet by the Christian era the religious beliefs based on the life of this ancient people had achieved a worldwide influence, and large groups of their descendants were making a significant contribution to the life and culture of major cities throughout the known world.

This amazing transformation, in which Judaism arose phoenix-like out of the ashes of the old kingdom of Judah, can only be explained after a careful analysis of the new currents of thought that swept through this faith community in the centuries immediately following the Babylonian exile. These centuries were an incredibly creative time, as the lessons of the past were assessed. and their spiritual power was harnessed to a new cause. Unfortunately, less is known about this period in Israel's history than the one that immediately preceded it, and there are many decades in the exilic age about which virtually nothing at all is known. Even such scraps of information as can be gathered from the Old Testament and other sources are often confused and incomplete. Interpreting them is sometimes a matter of pure guesswork, and always a process of painstaking deduction from partial and incomplete evidence.

Facing up to disaster

The nature of the problem can easily be identified by enquiring about life in Judah itself in the days immediately following Nebuchadnezzar's invasion. The general outline of events is reasonably clear: the royal family was deported to Babylon, along with most of the leading citizens, after which a palace official called Gedaliah was made governor of Judah, with his capital at Mizpah (2 Kings 25:18–24; Jeremiah 40:7–12). This fact suggests that neither the destruction nor the deportation was as extensive as has often been imagined: there would have been little purpose in appointing Gedaliah if there were no territory and no population over which he could rule. But at the same time, it is not at all clear what his status actually was. Was he, for example, regarded as a Babylonian official, and Judah a Babylonian province? Or was the social structure much less rigid than that? We simply do not know.

What we do know is that his existence soon provoked opposition and it was not long before he was assassinated by a man called Ishmael, who was a member of the former royal family (2 Kings 25:25–26; Jeremiah 40:13 – 41:3). As a member of the Jerusalem aristocracy Ishmael had managed to escape the Babylonians by fleeing to the neighbouring state of Ammon. He was not the only one, and once the Babylonian armies had left the scene other such people came out of hiding and allied themselves with Gedaliah. They imagined that they would be able to continue the grand lifestyle which they had enjoyed previously, but that dream was never realized. For though Ishmael

At the time of Nebuchadnezzar II, the main entrance into Babylon via the Processional Way was through the Ishtar Gate. The brick surface of the gate was decorated with reliefs of animals which were coloured with bright glazes. This head of a serpent-dragon represents the city god Marduk.

himself was put to flight after his murder of Gedaliah (Jeremiah 41:11–15), those who were left at his head-quarters now feared a Babylonian reprisal, and so they decided to go and live in Egypt, where they would be able to obtain employment as mercenary soldiers (2 Kings 25:26; Jeremiah 41:16–18). Jeremiah did not want to go with them. When he had been offered a choice earlier, he had decided to stay in Judah rather than go to Babylon, and nothing had happened to change his mind (Jeremiah 42–43). He felt that his people had suffered enough, and God would soon restore their fortunes. But to be sure of that they must stay in their own land. By going abroad they would forget the God of their ancestors. Jerusalem was the place where they had lost their true faith, and it was where they must try to regain it. In spite of this firm conviction, however, Jeremiah was forced against his will to join the exiles in Egypt, and he spent the rest of his life there. No doubt those who took him to Egypt felt they had done the right thing, for it seems that the Babylonians did indeed return to Judah, and a further deportation in 582 BC may well have been a reprisal for the chaos that followed the murder of Gedaliah (Jeremiah 52:30).

We know virtually nothing of life in Judah for at least the next forty years, though what little we do know suggests that its people were profoundly disillusioned by what had taken place. Considering the high expectations they had held, this is hardly surprising. They had convinced themselves that there was no possibility that Jerusalem could fall to an alien army, because it was God's city whose safety was guaranteed because of the divine covenant with David's family. As they faced up to the realities of their predicament, it must have seemed to these people as if very little was left of Judah's great national heritage.

Not everyone, however, accepted that Israel's national faith could explain the tragedy. Some people gave up their faith altogether. One way of coming to terms with it all was to think of these sad events as a battle between Israel's God and the Babylonian gods, and on that reckoning the gods of Babylon had apparently won. Others felt they had been misled all along by the very prophets who claimed to speak in the name of their own God, Yahweh. Those who took Jeremiah to Egypt believed

The book of Lamentations

The depth of feeling about this national tragedy is reflected with great pathos in the book of Lamentations. The book consists of five poems, the first four of which are arranged in an acrostic pattern based on the letters of the Hebrew alphabet. This is an unusual literary device in the Old Testament, and though it may have been used here simply as an aid to the memory, it is more likely to be connected to the deeply felt message of these poems. They are essentially an adaptation of the mourning songs that were conventionally sung at every funeral, and their literary form (covering all the letters of the alphabet) may well be intended to reflect the all-embracing character of the tragedy which left the people emotionally and morally distraught.

The people were forced to accept the truth of what prophets like Jeremiah had been saying all along: that the havoc now wrought upon Jerusalem was the work of God, and it had been brought about by the disobedience and unfaithfulness of their own people. Though 'No one has ever had pain like mine, pain that Yahweh brought on me in the time of God's anger' (1:12), nevertheless 'Yahweh is just, for I have been disobedient' (1:18). This first poem

could well refer to the situation in Jerusalem after 597 BC, but before the final destruction some ten years later. But the whole book offers a striking insight into the despair that now engulfed those whose arrogance and vanity have been depicted so graphically in the book of Jeremiah. His message of doom had been opposed by false prophets, and their teaching now lay exposed for what it really was: 'Your prophets had nothing to tell you but lies; their preaching deceived you by never exposing your sin. They made you think you did not need to repent' (2:14).

The pitiful trust of the people in the sanctity of their capital city and its institutions is clearly reflected here too: 'No one anywhere, not even rulers of foreign nations, believed that any invader could enter Jerusalem's gates. But it happened because her prophets sinned and her priests were guilty of causing the death of innocent people. Her leaders wandered through the streets like the blind, so stained with blood that no one would touch them' (4:12–14). Jeremiah had seen all this coming long before the final tragedy, and now those who opposed him had been forced to agree. As they realized what they had done, and what it all meant, their unbridled despair and grief knew no boundaries.

that the Babylonian invasion had been the fault of people like him, who had encouraged them to abandon the worship of the traditional deities of Canaan. If the land had belonged to these other gods and goddesses for centuries, they reasoned, then why should anybody be surprised if the land met with such disaster once they were no longer honoured? For people who thought this way, the path to renewed prosperity could only be found in an enthusiastic return to the old ways of the Baal religion: 'We will offer sacrifices to our goddess, the Queen of Heaven, and we will pour out wine offerings to her, just as we and our ancestors, our king and our leaders, used to do in the towns of Judah and in the streets of Jerusalem. Then we had plenty of food, we were prosperous, and had no troubles. But ever since we stopped sacrificing to the Queen of Heaven... we have had nothing, and our people have died in war and of starvation' (Jeremiah 44:17–18).

Jeremiah, of course, strongly resisted such an opinion, and argued once

---

The book of Lamentations *continued*

Yet, even in the midst of such shattered dreams, the broken remnants of a once-proud nation could still see cause for hope: 'The thought of my pain, my homeless-ness, is bitter poison; I think of it constantly and my spirit is depressed. Yet hope returns when I remember this one thing: God's unfailing love and mercy still continue, fresh as the morning, as sure as the sunrise. Yahweh is all I have, and that is where I put my hope... good to everyone who trusts the promises, so it is best for us to wait in patience – to wait for God to save us' (3:19–26). That in itself could never relieve the anguish that these people felt, but it did give them the confidence to pray for restoration, and that prayer is the theme of the fifth and final poem in the book: 'Bring us back to you, Lord! Bring us back! Restore our ancient glory' (5:21).

Author and date

In the Hebrew Bible, Lamentations appears as an anonymous work. But other traditions, mostly within Christian circles, have attributed it to Jeremiah himself. The main reason for this seems to be found in 2 Chronicles 35:25, where it is stated that 'Jeremiah composed a lament for King Josiah... The song is found in the collection of laments.' But

Lamentations has no connection at all with this early period of Jeremiah's life, and it in fact makes much better sense when understood as the composition of those very elements of Jerusalem society that had been originally opposed to all that Jeremiah stood for. Various aspects of the political outlook reflected in Lamentations seem to suit Jeremiah's opponents rather than the prophet himself. For example, it is strongly anti-Babylonian (1:21–22; 3:59–66), and suggests its authors had relied on Egypt for help (4:17), something that Jeremiah consistently opposed (Jeremiah 37:5–10). It is also difficult to imagine Jeremiah referring to Zedekiah as 'the source of our life, the king whom Yahweh had chosen, the one we had trusted to protect us from every invader' (4:20). To the prophet, he had been one of the 'bad figs' (Jeremiah 24:8–10).

Nevertheless, the book certainly stands as a vindication of Jeremiah's message, as it reveals how even those who had been implacably opposed to him were forced to admit their guilt in the face of God's judgment. These five poems probably reflect the ways they did this in Judah itself, in the period immediately following 586 BC, and before the collapse of the Babylonian empire in 539 BC.

again that it was the other way round: this was precisely the kind of worship that had led to the disaster in the first place and doing more of what had caused the problem would never solve anything (Jeremiah 44:23). But who could the people believe? This was a crucial question for the restructuring of Jewish society. Eventually, it was Jeremiah's argument that won the day, for his interpretation of Israel's history was embodied in the stories of the Old Testament itself. The idea that obedience and loyalty to Israel's own God led to success and prosperity is the organizing principle of the books of the deuteronomic history, which almost certainly were issued in a new revised edition in Judah during these years immediately following the Babylonian invasion. In previous times of rapid cultural change, the people had regularly looked to their past to help them redefine the nature of their nation, and that seems to be the context in which the historical narratives of the Hebrew Bible were first compiled. As they began to rebuild their shattered lives at this time, it was only to be expected that they would review the past once more, in an effort to see where they had gone wrong and thereby identify things to be avoided in the future.

By the rivers of Babylon

Far more is known about the life of the exiles who were taken off to Babylon than about those who were left behind in Judah. They seem to have been settled mostly in the border regions between Babylonia and Assyria, perhaps as part of some official policy to reclaim derelict sites that had been devastated during the many wars between these two powers. The names of some of the Jewish settlements certainly seem to imply that: places like Tel Abib ('mound of the flood', Ezekiel 3:15), Tel Harsha and Tel Melah (meaning 'mound of broken pottery' and 'mound of salt' respectively, Ezra 2:59). Unlike the Assyrians, who forced the exiles from Samaria to mingle with other races, the Babylonians generally allowed exiles to maintain their own ethnic identity, and organize their own communal life together. The Judean deportees therefore enjoyed considerable freedom to continue their traditional customs, both social and religious. The fact that Jehoiachin was there no doubt helped to develop this community spirit. He was one of those taken from Jerusalem in the first deportation of 597 BC, but since he was also the last true member of the royal family of David, it was to be expected that the exiles would focus their national allegiance on him. His exact position is not absolutely clear. According to 2 Kings 25:27–30, Nebuchadnezzar's successor, Amel-Marduk, released Jehoiachin from prison and gave him a distinctive position at the Babylonian court. That was in 561 BC, though even before that the Babylonian annals describe Jehoiachin as 'king of Judah'. Perhaps, therefore, his imprisonment was little more than a nominal house arrest. His presence in Babylon was certainly important for the exiles: they counted the years of their exile in relation to him, and his sons and grandsons continued to play an important part in Jewish affairs for a considerable time (1 Chronicles 3:17–24; Ezra 1:8; 2:2; Ezekiel 1:2). But he seems to have been a figurehead rather than a ruler in any sense and the Jewish community itself was organized by groups of elders (Ezekiel 14:1–11; 20:1).

On the whole, life in Babylon was probably quite comfortable – even prosperous – for the exiles from Judah. Jeremiah's advice to some who were clamouring to get back to Judah captures it well: 'Build houses and live in them; plant gardens and eat what they produce. Take wives and have sons and daughters; take wives for your sons, and give your daughters in marriage... seek the welfare of the city where I have sent you into exile, and pray to the Lord on its behalf' (Jeremiah 29:5–7). From a slightly later period than this, we have detailed business records relating to the activities of a Jewish firm run by the Murashu family in Nippur, and the Old Testament itself suggests that within a relatively short space of time many of the exiles had become economically well-off (Ezra 1:6; 2:68–69). They adopted Babylonian language (Aramaic), and were soon giving their children names reflecting Babylonian customs. Yet though they were secure, they were not always happy. No matter how comfortable life in Babylon might be, it was not the same as the homeland they had left behind. The despair and dereliction felt by these people made such an impression on them that, like the story of their slavery in Egypt centuries before, it achieved a permanent place in their national consciousness:

> By the rivers of Babylon we sat down;
> there we wept when we remembered Zion.
> On the willows nearby we hung up our harps.
> Those who captured us told us to sing;
> they told us to entertain them:
> 'Sing us a song about Zion.'
> How can we sing a song to the Lord in a foreign land?
> May I never be able to play the harp again
> if I forget you, Jerusalem!
> May I never be able to sing again if I do not remember you,
> if I do not think of you as my greatest joy! (Psalm 137:1–6)

By the standards of international justice of their day, the Babylon-ians had been relatively benevolent. But the exiles still hated them, and the same poem which contains such a moving expression of Jewish anguish ends on a note of hatred that is unparalleled anywhere else in the Bible: 'Babylon, you will be destroyed. Happy are those who pay you back for what you have done to us – who take your babies and smash them against a rock' (Psalm 137:8–9). The messages of the prophet Ezekiel paint a similarly bleak picture. He himself was one of the exiles, and he knew that this dreadful experience had sapped all spiritual

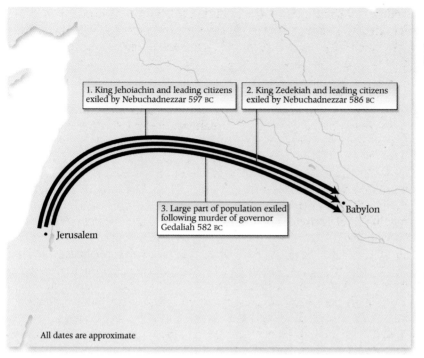

The exile from Judah.

1. King Jehoiachin and leading citizens exiled by Nebuchadnezzar 597 BC

2. King Zedekiah and leading citizens exiled by Nebuchadnezzar 586 BC

3. Large part of population exiled following murder of governor Gedaliah 582 BC

Babylon

Jerusalem

All dates are approximate

Ezekiel

Ezekiel's career was roughly contemporary with that of Jeremiah. Both of them came from priestly families, but Ezekiel was far more conscious of his background, and he maintained a much closer interest in the Jerusalem Temple than Jeremiah ever had. Ezekiel was one of those who were taken to Babylon in the first deportation of 597 BC, and his carefully dated messages were given between 593 and 571 BC.

The book of Ezekiel falls neatly into four sections:

● Messages concerning the people of Jerusalem before the city was destroyed in 586 BC (1:1 – 24:27)

● Oracles against foreign nations (25:1 – 32:32)

● Messages given in Babylon, mostly relating to the return of the exiles to Judah (33:1 – 39:29)

● A priestly blueprint for a future reconstructed Jewish state (40:1 – 48:35)

The book and its message are nothing like as straightforward as this neat literary structure might suggest. Indeed, the book's contents are so diverse that it is not difficult to imagine many different people having been involved in its composition. At one time the prophet is a person who has strange visions of winged animals and of wheels with eyes (Ezekiel 1:4–28), while at another he seems much more like Jeremiah, pronouncing doom on a wicked Jerusalem and laying a new emphasis on a personal relationship between God and the people (15:1–8; 20:1–49). Then there is a prophet whose messages to other nations reflect an extensive grasp of the intricacies of international politics (25:1 – 32:32), and in addition there is a priest who plans with great detail for the operation of a new temple with even stricter ritual than it had before (40:1 – 48:35). Because of this, some scholars have regarded the book as a compilation of the work of several different people. As long ago as the first century AD, the Jewish historian Josephus mentioned 'two books' of Ezekiel

vitality out of his people. They were, he said, like a valley full of dead bones, with no life in them at all (Ezekiel 37). They were quite powerless to do anything to help themselves: their only hope for new life now lay with the prospect that God might yet do something new among them.

Ezekiel was not the only one who saw the situation in these terms. For it is widely believed that during the exile in Babylon, the Jewish leaders began to reassess the state of their people by looking back into

---

Ezekiel *continued*

(*Antiquities of the Jews* 10.5.1). The balance of probability, however, is that all these messages originated with just one complex and multifaceted person.

Ezekiel was called to be a prophet in Babylon in 593 BC. He had a vision of a fiery cloud from the north containing a chariot drawn by four winged creatures of a kind familiar from many Babylonian sculptures and inscriptions (1:4–28). There was a throne on this chariot, and on the throne was the God of Israel, Yahweh. In the vision, Ezekiel was given a scroll to eat, which contained the message he was to deliver: 'cries of grief… and wails and groans' (2:10).

These messages are contained in the first section of the book, and were addressed to the people of Jerusalem in the dark days of the reign of Zedekiah. Ezekiel depicts the moral and spiritual decline of Jerusalem society with such realism that it is hard to believe he was not there, but in Babylon. Indeed, some scholars think Ezekiel must have paid visits to Judah at this time, though it is more likely that he had some kind of psychic experience, the most obvious possibility being a form of astral projection or out-of-body experience. Ezekiel's experiences as a prophet are much closer than those of the other great prophets to the behaviour of those bands of ecstatics who are mentioned in the early period of Israel's history. He obviously had a psychic personality, for after receiving his initial vision, he lay in a trance for a full week (3:15). In view of all this, his extraordinary accuracy in portraying life in Judah could well have been due to such experiences rather than being drawn from actual observations made on the spot. At the

same time, Ezekiel was not an irrational prophet, and his essential message was not significantly different from Jeremiah's: Jerusalem would be destroyed shortly, and its people taken off into exile. He saw no immediate hope of a return, though there are hints that the exile might be limited to about forty years (4:6).

In spite of his declaration of doom and destruction, Ezekiel's message to the exiles in Babylon after the events of 586 BC was a positive one. He had no doubt that the nation had brought ruin on itself, but he was equally convinced that the nation's fate was not in their own hands. It was God's loving actions that had made them a nation in the first place, and it was this same power that would restore them, even giving them the ability to repent and start afresh: 'I will give you a new heart and a new mind. I will take away your stubborn heart of stone and give you an obedient heart. I will put my spirit in you and I will see to it that you follow my laws and keep all the commands I have given you. Then you will live in the land I gave your ancestors. You will be my people, and I will be your God' (36:26–28). God was personally concerned for the people, just like a good shepherd caring for their sheep. No matter how far they might be scattered, God would retrieve them and lead them to new life: 'I will take them out of foreign countries, gather them together, and bring them back to their own land… I myself will be the shepherd of my sheep, and I will find them a place to rest' (34:13, 15).

Two distinctive features of Ezekiel's messages are worth special notice:
● When he looks forward to the restoration of a kingdom of Israel under a

their past. We have already seen how the deuteronomic history emerged in Judah itself at this time, for precisely the same reasons. But the emphasis of that history on a close connection between the people's obedience and the blessing of God could easily lead to the false conclusion that the exiles themselves were responsible for their own destiny. The message of prophets like Amos and Hosea, and even Jeremiah, could be misunderstood to suggest that good behaviour was

---

prince of the royal family of David, he often describes it in terms that clearly go beyond a literal nationalism. The earlier prophets had often hoped for better things to come, but they generally believed that it was at least theoretically possible that the new and better age would come through a restored monarchy in Jerusalem, and a new king who would actually obey God's will, unlike his predecessors who had found that so difficult. Ezekiel, however, implies that the inauguration of a golden age, when God and the people would live in complete harmony, could not be achieved by any ordinary king. It would have to be the direct work of God acting in person. This kind of thinking led eventually to the development of a new type of Jewish religious literature, the so-called apocalyptic books, and we can see traces of its beginning in passages like Ezekiel 38–39. Here the prophet describes how the enemies of Judah under a mysterious leader called Gog would attack Palestine, only to be annihilated with torrents of fire and brimstone raining down from the sky. After this the exiled Jews would be restored to their own land, and the spirit of God would be poured out on them. The same kind of extravagant language is used when Ezekiel describes a wonderful life-giving stream flowing from the restored Temple in Jerusalem out to the Dead Sea, and changing the Judean desert into a land of great fertility (47:1–12).

● Ezekiel's messages also contain a detailed plan for a renewed Temple in Jerusalem (40:1 – 48:35). Not only does he describe the building itself, but he also lays down the rules that should regulate its worship. Some scholars have seen this as

the symptom of an arid legalism which they believe to have been rampant in the exilic age. The same influences are said to be found in other prophets of the period, and this interest in religious ritual is often contrasted with the convictions of the truly 'great' prophets like Amos and Hosea, who declared that God's will was not fulfilled through cultic practices, but as part of ordinary everyday behaviour. But this sharp differentiation between worship and life misrepresents Ezekiel's message. It owes more to modern Protestantism than anything else, and as a result the significant features of Israel's worship have often been misunderstood. Ezekiel was not emphasizing the performance of religious ritual for its own sake, but he knew that the renewal of the spiritual life of the nation was not something the exiles could accomplish for themselves. Even in the days immediately following the exodus from Egypt, obedience to God's covenant Law had not been easy. Failure and disobedience were an inescapable reality, and it had not been the innate goodness of the tribes that had made them a great nation, but the unchanging presence of God. Right from the start, that presence had been represented by the formal institutions of worship, from the simple tent of worship in the desert to the elaborate Temple in Jerusalem. Far from being an aberration, these things were a permanent symbol of the centralities of Israel's faith, representing not only God's own faithfulness and power, but also the path to forgiveness for those who had lost their way. It was for this reason that the same symbols must be an essential part of the restored community.

Nothing can live in the salt waters of the Dead Sea. But the prophet Ezekiel saw a vision of a new temple in Jerusalem with a river flowing from it towards the Dead Sea. As the water reached the sea, it turned the salt water to fresh, and the sea produced an abundance of life.

a way of blackmailing God into blessing Israel. But at the earliest period of Israel's history, that kind of moral quid pro quo had been only one side of the story. The prophets' demand for obedience to God's Law had itself been based on the unsought goodness of God's love in events like the calling of Abraham and Sarah, or the exodus from Egypt. The prophets had rightly declared that the roots of the nation's religious problems were to be found in the culture of Canaan.

The Pentateuch

It is widely believed that the historical reassessment which took place among the exiles in Babylon had strong connections with the compilation of the first five books of the Hebrew Bible, the Torah or Pentateuch – though if the book of Deuteronomy was indeed originally a preface to the deuteronomic history, it would be more accurate to speak here of a 'Tetrateuch', consisting of Genesis, Exodus, Leviticus and Numbers.

In Jewish thinking, the Pentateuch was always traditionally regarded as the work of Moses, though no one today would argue for that. At least five reasons can be given for believing that the writing of these books was a much more complex process that took place over many centuries.

Anachronisms
Deuteronomy 34 tells the story of Moses' death, which at least makes it unlikely that he wrote this section, though Philo (*On the Life of Moses* II.291) and Josephus (*Antiquities of the Jews* 5.8.48) both claimed that he did. More significantly, however, a number of other incidental features of some of the stories in these books reflect the perspective of a later age. For instance, Genesis 36:31–39 lists the kings of Edom who ruled 'Before there were any kings in Israel'. Or again, a couple of incidents in Abraham's life are said to have taken place when 'the Canaanites were still living in the land' (Genesis 12:6; 13:7). In another place, part of the land of Canaan itself is given the name 'Philistia', though it was never called that until after the arrival of the Philistines (Genesis 21:34; Exodus 13:17).

Duplicate stories
The same story has sometimes been recorded in two different versions. For example, Beersheba is given its name twice (Genesis 21:31; 26:33), as is Bethel – once when Jacob was running away to Haran (Genesis 28:19), and again when he was coming back (Genesis 35:15). Similarly, in the story of the covenant-making at Mount Sinai, Moses is said to have gone up the mountain three times, though there is no mention of him ever coming down (Exodus 24:9–18).

Inconsistencies
For example, in the story of creation, Genesis 1:26–31 suggests that people were created after all the animals, whereas in Genesis 2:7–20 a person is created first, and the animals are later created to be companions for the human. Or in the story of the great flood, the number of animals to be saved in the ark is either one pair of each species (Genesis 6:19–20), or seven pairs (Genesis 7:2). Joseph appears to have been taken off to Egypt by both Ishmaelites (Genesis 37:25) and Midianites (Genesis 37:28) – and, in the same story, was it Reuben (Genesis 37:22) or Judah (Genesis 37:26) who was the good brother who tried to rescue him?

Legal differences
The laws set out in Deuteronomy are sometimes different from laws about the same things contained in other books of the Pentateuch. For example, in Exodus 20:24 sacrifices can be offered to God 'In every place that I set aside for you to worship me'; but in Deuteronomy 12:14, 'you must offer them only in the one place that

But as the stories of an even earlier period were revisited, it became apparent that the time before that had hardly been perfect. Perhaps, then, there was a lesson here for the exiles as they struggled to come to terms with their national disaster.

Inspired by such thoughts, it seems likely that religious leaders in Babylon set out at this time to write a history of the very earliest experiences of their nation, beginning from creation itself. They did

---

Yahweh will choose in the territory of one of your tribes'. Exodus 28:1 suggests that only Aaron's family had the necessary priestly qualifications to offer sacrifices, while Deuteronomy 18:6–7 allows any Levite to do so. The actual methods to be adopted also vary: in Exodus 12:8–9 the Passover lamb must be roasted, while in Deuteronomy 16:7 it is to be boiled.

God's name

According to Exodus 6:2–3, Moses was the first person to know God's personal name 'Yahweh', though Genesis 4:26 states that from the very earliest times people had used this name in their worship. Alongside this, there are many other passages which call God by the name 'El' or 'Elohim', and it has been proposed that these different names indicate different ideas about God's character: in the stories that use the name Yahweh, God can be represented almost as a kind of superhuman person who speaks and meets with people in everyday circumstances, while in those where the name Elohim predominates, God appears more remotely through intermediaries such as dreams or messengers.

These five features are not all that important when considered separately, but taken together they have generally been regarded as a conclusive demonstration that the Pentateuch was certainly not the product of just one author, whether that might have been Moses or indeed anyone else. According to the most widely accepted view, the Pentateuch in its final edited form was compiled from four separate documentary sources,

conventionally labelled J, E, D and P: J being the source using the name Yahweh, E using the name Elohim, D being Deuteronomy and P a priestly source, dealing mainly with religious matters connected with worship, sacrifice and so on. This theory was put forward in its classical form by the nineteenth-century German scholars, K.H. Graf and J. Wellhausen, and for that reason is often referred to as the Graf–Wellhausen theory. Wellhausen also believed that these source documents represented an evolutionary development from primitive to more sophisticated views and therefore could be used as a way of understanding the whole course of Israel's national history, beginning with J (950–850 BC), which was followed in turn by E (850–750 BC), D (621 BC) and P (c. 450 BC).

In the early decades of the twentieth century, scholars set out with great enthusiasm to 'recover' and 'reconstruct' these four apparently lost documents. They concluded that J had originated among the southern tribes in the time of Solomon, and E among the northern tribes in the time of Elijah, and the two had been joined together sometime after the fall of Samaria in 722 BC. D was generally identified with the law book recovered in the time of Josiah, though possibly of a northern origin. It was certainly quite a different kind of 'source' from the others, for whereas J and E could apparently be traced more or less extensively throughout the Pentateuch, D appeared to be restricted to just the book of Deuteronomy. Finally, P was regarded as an exclusively priestly collection, containing mainly the details of organized cultic ritual, and anything

not compile this narrative from nothing, any more than the deutero-nomic historians did with theirs. On the contrary, they had at their disposal the full riches of their nation's heritage, going back over many centuries. As they retold these familiar stories, they could see that the problem of human disobedience was nothing new, but was actually an intrinsic part of human life itself. Yet, in spite of that, God's living presence had been with their people. From the very

---

The Pentateuch
continued

connected with it – though also including certain other materials of a narrative type. This understanding of the matter prevailed in one form or another for most of the twentieth century. There were always those who pointed out the limitations of this or that detail in Wellhausen's analysis, but scholars who rejected it entirely were isolated individuals, usually regarded as eccentrics. The situation today, however, is quite different, and probably no significant scholar would now accept the theory as Wellhausen proposed it. It is still worth understanding, though, as his presentation of these hypothetical sources has provided the frame of reference within which other approaches have been explored. It will only be a matter of time before his theory is formally declared to be finished, but in the meantime scholars are generally preferring to explore other methods of understanding these pivotal books within the Hebrew Bible. There are a number of reasons for such a radical rejection of what at one time would have been regarded as the unassailable conclusion of scientific scholarship:

● Wellhausen's view was firmly based on a particular philosophical understanding of history and its development. Along with other thinkers of his day, he believed that human society had gradually evolved from primitive beginnings to the sophisticated thinking of his own time. Wellhausen therefore took it for granted that Israel's religious experience must have started off as a simple nature worship (animism), which later evolved into the high moral standards of the Old Testament prophets, based on belief in only one universal God (monotheism), having passed through the

intermediary stage of henotheism (commitment to only one God, though in a context of belief in the existence of many). This evolutionary theory has since been totally discredited, and it is arguable that the literary analysis which Wellhausen built upon it has, therefore, been left with no credible ideological foundation.

● Since Wellhausen's day, knowledge of life in the ancient world in general, and of Canaan and Israel in particular, has changed almost beyond recognition. Wellhausen and his contemporaries were writing before the development of the techniques of systematic archaeology. It was not difficult for them to look at the Old Testament as a kind of theological source book, rather than as a body of literature to be understood with reference to the social circumstances within which it was compiled. Viewed in this way, it seemed plausible to think that Israel's religion could have evolved from a primitive animism to an elevated monotheism in the course of just a few hundred years. But the more that becomes known about the world in which Israel became a nation, the more implausible it is to imagine that Israel's faith should be thought of in these terms. According to Wellhausen's theory, for example, almost all the details of Israel's ritual worship were the invention of the P writer, late in the period of Babylonian exile. But the discoveries at the site of ancient Ugarit, for example, have shown that even quite technical terms used in the Hebrew Bible were in common use in Canaan long before Israel became a nation, let alone the time of the exile. Far from reflecting later stages in the development of religious thought, much of

earliest days in the desert, God had been there, even at times of disobedience. The thing that brought the tribes from Egypt to their own land was not their own goodness, but the love of God. So a new hope and concern began to emerge from the lessons of history. As they looked at their own meagre resources, they could see no hope, but when they reminded themselves of God's resources, anything seemed possible.

---

the Pentateuchal material reflects precisely the circumstances of the period of which it purports to tell. Of course, this does not prove that it was all written down at an earlier period, but it certainly demonstrates that the assumptions on which Wellhausen based his argument were simply mistaken.

● Criticisms of this sort have not prevented Old Testament scholars continuing to refine and articulate more fully the theory that Wellhausen put forward. Even today some are still arguing about the dates of the various so-called source documents. But their conclusions vary widely, with even the J source being dated in periods as far apart as the ninth century and the post-exilic age. Others have suggested there was no such thing as an E source, while yet others argue that the four-source theory is inadequate, and the Pentateuch in fact contains many more sources than that. Some have further claimed to be able to trace J, E and P not only in the Pentateuch, but also in Joshua, Judges, Samuel, and even Kings. Much of this debate has been engendered by the surprising fact that the so-called sources are not actually consistent in their use of the different names for God, even though this was supposed to be one of their most characteristic features. Considering that scholars have been trying to define the nature and contents of these source documents for more than a century now, it is not unreasonable to expect them to have come to some sort of conclusion on the matter. The fact that they have so strikingly failed to do so raises serious questions about their very existence.

A number of scholars have noted the strength of this particular criticism, and have accordingly directed their energies elsewhere. Gerhard von Rad, for instance, argued that this section of the Old Testament (which for him extended into Joshua/Judges – what he called the 'Hexateuch') was centred around two major themes. One was the exodus/entry into the land; the other was the covenant ceremony at Mount Sinai. Both of these were originally related to religious celebrations in the life of early Israel, and he suggested that the continuous narrative we now have grew out of the confessions and creeds that were so often repeated in worship. This process took place, he argued, in the time of Solomon. Martin Noth also proposed his own rather different thematic origin for the same materials. But all such attempts have still been firmly based on a Wellhausen-type source analysis, and they have not successfully avoided the general criticisms noted above.

● Recent discussion of this issue has emphasized the importance of treating the Pentateuch as real literature. Wellhausen and his followers worked with a very restricted view of how ancient literature was actually written. Their understanding has often been colourfully described as a 'scissors and paste' approach, which tended to assume that the final editors of the books sat down with four documents in front of them, and chopped bits and pieces from here and there, which were then glued together to make a 'new' book. Moreover, they were not joined seamlessly, but in such an incoherent fashion that we can still unpick them and identify the original source documents. That sort of idea could appear to make sense to the

A new beginning

The stories of Israel's past reminded the exiles of what God had done for their nation. Even at times of great despair, Yahweh's love had never failed them, and they could be sure that God would not abandon them now. It was not long before things began to stir in Babylonian politics that were regarded as the personal actions of God.

The Pentateuch
continued

scholars of a previous generation, but more sophisticated understanding of how literature comes into existence – especially a national archive like the Hebrew Bible – shows that it is quite inadequate. Traditional ways of handing on ancient stories, frequently by word of mouth, simply do not operate like this. In addition, if these books are the inspirational masterpieces that most scholars believe them to be, then it is unlikely that editors capable of producing such works would not themselves have noticed the apparent discontinuities in their narratives. Could it therefore be that the features once presumed to betray the presence of ill-fitting source materials were from the very start consciously intended to perform some kind of literary or stylistic function in the presentation of the story? For instance, some believe that the use of different names for God can be explained in this way, by supposing that the term Yahweh was used when the writer was talking of Israel's own national God, with the term Elohim being reserved for contexts in which a more abstract, cosmic picture of God was in view. Even the existence of duplicate stories is not necessarily an indication of badly assimilated source materials, for the texts from Ugarit display a very similar phenomenon, and in that case the frequent repetition of the same material has been indispensable to scholars trying to guess what might have been originally there in texts that are now broken.

The obsession with uncovering hidden sources behind biblical documents dominated scholarship for many generations, not only in relation to the

Pentateuch, but also other parts of the Hebrew Bible. The outcome of all this can be clearly seen in any of the traditional books of introduction to both Old and New Testaments, which tend to be preoccupied with questions of origin, date and authorship, often to the exclusion of anything else. But this way of looking at things was a product of the time of the European Enlightenment, when 'scientific' method was applied to everything in the mistaken belief that science was somehow neutral and objective, and therefore gave greater access to the truth than other forms of investigation. The science of the day was dominated by the theories of people like René Descartes (1596–1650) and Francis Bacon (1561–1626), and the starting point was generally based on the assumption that to understand anything it had to be dismantled, and split into its component parts which could then be studied in isolation under the microscope. That approach has long since been discredited in scientific enquiry, for it is now recognized that the sum of the parts is often more than that of the individual elements, and true understanding needs to begin by investigating things within the holistic context from which they gain their meaning, and to which they in turn contribute. The same thing is true of literature. The meaning of a book must begin with the text as it stands, because no matter how much a work of literature may have been edited or rewritten, its ultimate meaning is to be found in the form it now has. The search for possible sources may help to illustrate the perspectives of different editors who have worked on it, but the Pentateuch is a

When Nebuchadnezzar died in 562 BC he was succeeded by a number of very weak and inept rulers. Only Nabonidus had a reign of any length (556–539 BC), but he made himself very unpopular by neglecting the worship of Marduk, the traditional god of Babylon, and choosing to live in a self-imposed exile at Teima in the Arabian desert, leaving his son Bel-shar-usur (the Belshazzar of the book of Daniel) to look after things in the capital. This was a very unsettled period in

connected story with its own message, and the real significance of that message is going to be found not by taking it to pieces, but by careful study of its nuances and themes as they have been presented to the reader by those who compiled it in its final form.

The outcome of all this is that in the final decades of the twentieth century there was a comprehensive re-examination of almost all the basic issues in Pentateuchal scholarship. This was motivated partly by dissatisfaction with the traditional Graf–Wellhausen theory, but more especially by the realization that in the literary world at large there are other, more promising methods of analysis than source criticism. Some would like to think that the collapse of what was once the scholarly orthodoxy justifies a return to belief in a Mosaic authorship for the Pentateuch. But that would be going well beyond the evidence now available. The narrative itself gives no reason at all to link his name with all these books, and such scattered references as do connect Moses with them all relate to clearly defined parts of the narrative, rather than to the Pentateuch as a whole (Exodus 24:4–8; Numbers 33:2; Deuteronomy 31:19–29). Writing was widely used in the ancient world long before the emergence of Israel as a nation, so there is no intrinsic reason why some elements now incorporated in the Pentateuch should not have been written down in the earliest period. Indeed, some scholars confidently trace features such as the ten commandments back to the age of Moses. But later, even those things connected with Moses himself needed to be reinterpreted and applied to

new situations. In addition, as new elements joined the population of Israel, their own stories handed on over many centuries would also be incorporated into what became Israel's national heritage. The inauguration of the monarchy and the transformation of the tribal confederation into a state must also have necessitated a considerable reinterpretation of Israel's traditional values and ideals, in order to suit the new circumstances.

It now seems quite likely that, instead of passing through several written stages, all this took place in a more or less haphazard fashion until the Pentateuch itself was written in its present form. It certainly makes good sense to think that this epic story of Israel's earliest days was reissued during the period of the early exile, as a means of explaining the failures of the past and to help chart a new course for the future. But the stories and laws were not freshly created at that time. The new element was the perspective that the experience of the exile had given, and with that hindsight the story of God and the people of Israel could become a source of renewal for the nation's life and an inspiration for the rediscovery of that ancient faith whose origins could be traced back to the covenant at Mount Sinai.

During the exile, the Babylonian empire went through a period of decline. Emperor Nabonidus, seen in this relief worshipping the sun-god, rejected the national religion and spent much of his time in retreat in the desert.

The Cyrus Cylinder gives details of the reforms this Persian ruler undertook in Babylon after he had overthrown the Babylonians in a bloodless take-over. In Isaiah's prophecy, Cyrus is seen as the unwitting agent of Yahweh in establishing the conditions for the exiles' return to Jerusalem.

Babylonian history, and life for the exiles may well have become more difficult. There is a strong tradition in Jewish literature of how the exiles were subjected to harsh treatment, almost amounting to official persecution. In the Hebrew Bible, the stories contained in Daniel 1–6 tell how Daniel and his friends were subjected to the most harrowing treatment during this time, and a similar picture is painted in various additions to the books of Esther and Daniel which were contained in the Greek Old Testament, as well as in books like Judith and Tobit. If this was a time of discomfort for the Jews in Babylon, it was short-lived. For by now, the power of the Babylonian empire was spent, and when a little-known king from southern Persia emerged as a new leader, it was only a matter of time before he was able to take over the whole of the country. His name was Cyrus, and in 539 BC the people of Babylon actually welcomed him as their king, and he took control of the city without the use of force.

Cyrus set about the restoration of Babylonian society. The temples which Nabonidus had neglected were restored to their former glory, and Cyrus himself shared publicly in the worship of the god Marduk. But he had a different outlook from his predecessors, and of all the ancient rulers with whom the Jews had to deal, Cyrus was the most liberal and humane. He did not see politics in terms of armed conflict between various national religions, but instead recognized the right of all nations to worship whatever deities they wished. Not only that, but he also gave his citizens the right to live wherever they chose. This was a massive reversal of the policies that had dominated Mesopotamian society for many centuries, but he was determined to make it work. He inherited a population with many ethnic groups who had been uprooted from their own lands and settled in Babylon against their will, and not only did he encourage these displaced people to go back home, but he also made available financial resources to enable them to do so. The Cyrus Cylinder contains details of all this, while the book of Ezra preserves the text of an official document issued by Cyrus that dealt specifically with the plight of the Jewish exiles.

Back to Jerusalem

Though Cyrus had issued an edict allowing the Temple in Jerusalem to be rebuilt at the beginning of his reign, there was no great rush by the exiles in Babylon to return to Judah. Indeed, Josephus (who, of course, was writing centuries later) reports that when they were given the

---

Isaiah of Babylon

The advance of Cyrus was seen by a Jewish prophet in Babylon, whose inspirational messages are to be found in Isaiah 40–55. As they stand, of course, these messages are part of the book which reports the life and teaching of another prophet named Isaiah, who lived in Jerusalem some 150 years earlier during the days of Ahaz and Hezekiah. But there are some compelling reasons for regarding these later sections of the book as coming from this later period:

● Isaiah 40–55 contains no mention at all of any personal details about the prophet Isaiah. This is in strong contrast to Isaiah 1–39 which relates a number of stories about the prophet himself, especially his dealings with king and people in Jerusalem.

● The style and language of Isaiah 40–55 is also quite different. These chapters use what is possibly the most sophisticated Hebrew in the entire Old Testament. In addition, these messages do not have the form of the short, pointed sayings that were typical of most of the prophets, but consist instead of sustained lyrical passages, celebrating God's sovereignty in creation and history. Because of their distinctive poetic structure, it has been thought that these messages may have originated in the context of worship. Perhaps they reflect the way that God's kingship was celebrated in the Temple at Jerusalem during the heyday of the kingdom of Judah. But they are not just hymns, for they also contain many specific historical references, directly related to the message of the prophet himself.

● The fact that these specific references are based on the experiences of the exiles in Babylon is one of the strongest reasons for assuming they are the work of a prophet who lived at this time. The fall of Jerusalem is clearly stated to be a past event (51:17–23) and the fall of Babylon is imminent (43:14–15; 47:1–15). The people are encouraged to think they will soon be set free (48:20), and Cyrus himself is mentioned by name as the person who would bring this about (44:28 – 45:4). Other passages clearly envisage Cyrus's triumph, without actually naming him (41:2–4; 48:1–16).

It seems likely, therefore, that the messages of Isaiah 40–55 were given to the exiles in Babylon just before 539 BC, when Cyrus's triumph was assured and it looked as if his policies were about to provide new opportunities for the renewal of the old state of Judah.

For the sake of convenience, the prophet who delivered these messages is generally referred to as Isaiah of Babylon, Second or Deutero-Isaiah. Of course, his personal name would not necessarily have been Isaiah, though there is a continuity between these messages and those of his illustrious predecessor. Indeed, Isaiah himself had gathered a group of disciples around him, so that the messages he gave could be

chance to go back home, they did not want to leave the comfortable life they had established in exile (*Antiquities of the Jews* 11.1.3). But it was important to the Persians that their repatriation policy should be set in motion. While they undoubtedly had humanitarian reasons for introducing it, the benefits of having loyal and grateful subjects at strategic parts of their empire can hardly have escaped their notice, and since Palestine was near to the border with Egypt it was important for them to re-establish a friendly state there.

Sheshbazzar was appointed governor of Judah. His name was thoroughly Babylonian, though that does not mean he was not a Jew. Apart from the fact that he made a start on rebuilding the foundations of the Temple, nothing is known of him (Ezra 5:16). We are better

---

Isaiah of Babylon
continued

safeguarded for later generations (Isaiah 8:16), and it is quite possible that these later messages could have come from the same circle of disciples. What they were saying was a fresh application of old truths to new circumstances, which would be why they had no hesitation in including them all in the same book as the messages delivered previously by Isaiah in Jerusalem. If this individual was indeed one of the great prophetic figures of the Old Testament story, it has often been thought strange that we evidently possess no explicit information about him (though, in the context of the day, we can at least be sure that it would almost certainly have been a male). But in reality we know almost nothing about most of the prophets, apart from the messages that are recorded in their books. In any case, the relative anonymity of this prophet in Babylon is consistent with the whole outlook of these messages, for he was concerned first and foremost with the might and power of God, rather than with himself. The change that he believed was about to take place would not be initiated by exiles: it could only be the work of God, a 'new exodus' to be compared with that under Moses, in which the escaping slaves (like the exiles) had been powerless, but were miraculously delivered by their all-powerful God (Isaiah 43:14–21).

A powerful God
Cyrus is seen as the instrument of this deliverance that was to come, but the people are warned against placing their trust in him. The real power that would restore the Jewish people could only come from God. The glorious return to their homeland was envisaged as a worldwide movement, to include also those who had fled to Egypt (49:12). God's power would not be restricted by geography or national boundaries, as had sometimes been thought by Israel in the past. This prophet was convinced that his God was not one among many, but the only true God: 'Yahweh is the everlasting God who created all the world, and never grows tired or weary' (40:28). It was important for him to emphasize this, for some of the exiles had come to regard their plight as a direct result of the weakness of Israel's God when faced with the apparent 'power' of the gods of Babylon. Those who clung to the old covenant faith may even have been in the minority (Ezekiel 20:3; Daniel 1–6), but Isaiah of Babylon knew they were right.

His contempt for the gods of Babylon was unbounded. In satirical vein, he points out how their own worshippers actually made them from the very same wood as they used to burn on the fire. To him, such an attitude was just blind ignorance: 'Such people are too stupid to know what they are doing. They close their eyes and their minds to the truth. The maker of idols hasn't the wit or the sense to say, "Some of the wood I burnt up. I baked some bread on the embers and I roasted meat and ate

informed about a further group of exiles who returned a little later under the leadership of Zerubbabel (another Babylonian name, this time certainly a Jew) and Joshua. Joshua was a priest, but Zerubbabel was the grandson of Jehoiachin, the last truly legitimate king of the royal family of David. He also held an official Persian appointment, and he could have been Sheshbazzar's successor as governor. The appointment of a member of the old Judahite royal family may have been a conscious effort by the Persians to persuade more Jews to return. Zerubbabel certainly appreciated that, with Persian help, a new Jewish state could emerge from the ashes of the past. With the disappearance of most of the familiar features of the earlier kingdom, however, there was just one thing that united the new settlers with

---

it. And the rest of the wood I made into an idol. Here I am bowing down to a block of wood!"' (44:18–19). That is not the kind of God who had been revealed in the formative events of Israel's history. Their God had been, and still was, a God of real power, the God of all creation: 'I am... the Creator of all things. I alone stretched out the heavens; when I made the earth, no one helped me' (44:24).

God's people and their land

With this emphasis on God's universal sovereignty, we might have expected God's special relationship with Israel to have been forgotten, or at least pushed into the background. But it was not. The fact that God's power extended over the whole world meant that the exiles could go back to their homeland without worrying whether God would have the power to take care of them. Many of them probably needed this kind of encouragement, for even after Cyrus gave them permission to return there was a natural temptation to prefer the safety and security of the life they knew over the hazards and unknown perils of a long journey and a strange land. But to those who would trust God, it was all a great spiritual adventure: 'From the distant east and the farthest west, I will bring your people home. I will tell the north to let them go and the south not to hold them back. Let my people return from distant lands, from every part of the world' (43:5–6). God had done it long centuries

before in the exodus from Egypt, and would do it again for no other reason than a continuing and great love for these people: 'Watch for the new thing I am going to do. It is happening already – you can see it now! I will make a road through the wilderness and give you streams of water there' (43:19). Jerusalem may be a ruined wasteland, but it would soon be restored to its former glory: 'I will show compassion to Jerusalem, to all who live in her ruins. Though her land is a desert, I will make it a garden, like the garden I planted in Eden. Joy and gladness will be there, and songs of praise and thanks to me' (51:3).

God's servant and God's world

Despite this renewed emphasis on God's concern for the people, this Babylonian prophet was convinced that God's love was not restricted to Israel alone. Just as the whole world was the arena of God's activity, so all the people of the world would now be the object of God's love. This is the message of one of those passages that have been called 'the servant songs': 'Yahweh said to me, "I have a greater task for you, my servant. Not only will you restore to greatness the people of Israel who have survived, but I will also make you a light to the nations – so that all the world may be saved"' (49:6).

There are four of these servant songs, and they seem to be separate and self-

their forebears, and that was their faith in God. In exile, that faith had been centred on customs like circumcision, and keeping the sabbath day, as well as prayer and the reading of the Torah. But now the Temple could be rebuilt, and its repair and renovation were to be Zerubbabel's main tasks.

The Temple ruins had probably continued to be a place of worship throughout the period since Nebuchadnezzar's destruction. Even in the aftermath of the invasion, Jeremiah 41:4–5 mentions worshippers who had come from the territory of the former northern kingdom of Israel on pilgrimage to the site. No doubt people from that quarter, as well as the Jewish population left behind in Judah itself, had continued to worship there all along. There is some evidence to suggest that the Babylonians

---

Isaiah of Babylon
continued

contained poems, though no doubt still the work of the prophet himself, and certainly an integral part of his message (42:1–4; 49:1–6; 50:4–11; 52:13 – 53:12). In these songs, the prophet talks of a specific individual, 'the servant', through whom God's plans for a great and glorious future will come to fruition. But who was this servant? Elsewhere the prophet talks of the nation of Israel as the servant of God, and the person mentioned in the servant songs is often described in the same language as is used of Israel. Israel is 'my servant... the people that I have chosen' (41:8), and so is the servant of the songs (42:1). Both of them were specifically created by God's personal action (Israel, 43:1, 7, 15, 21; 44:2, 21, 24; the servant, 49:5), and were endowed with God's own spirit (Israel, 44:3; the servant, 42:1). This has led many scholars to conclude that when Isaiah talks of the suffering servant it is simply another way of referring to God's people, Israel. But, at the same time, things are said about the servant which are explicitly denied about Israel. The servant 'will not lose hope or courage' (42:4), nor has he 'rebelled or turned away' from God (50:5), as the nation so often did. In addition, he suffers patiently – not for his own wrongdoing like the nation, but for the wrongs of others (53:3–5). Most significant of all is the fact that, while the nation needed restoration, the servant is sent to restore and renew Israel (49:5–6; 53:4–6). It is therefore difficult to see how

the prophet could have identified this servant of God with the nation itself.

Who then was this enigmatic servant? Some people think the prophet had a particular living individual in mind, possibly Jehoiachin or someone like Jeremiah, or conceivably even himself. But it is more likely that he was thinking of some future person in whose life the ideals of Israel's ancient faith would become a reality, and through whom God's intentions for the people of Israel and the wider world could be brought to pass. He is never actually called the Messiah in the Old Testament, nor did the Jewish people ever think to equate the two. But these passages exerted a powerful influence on the Christian understanding of Jesus as the Messiah of Old Testament expectation. In particular, the account of the servant's suffering in the last song (52:13 – 53:12) has some extraordinary correspondences with the death of Jesus himself. In theological terms, the understanding that salvation can be found through suffering, service, weakness and vulnerability is undoubtedly the most profound legacy from this prophet in Babylon.

had actually given some formal control over the territory of Judah to people from what had formerly been the northern kingdom of Israel. For whatever reason, these people naturally offered their assistance to Zerubbabel. But he would have none of it, for to him these people were not real Jews. They may have thought they were worshipping the covenant God of Israel, but they had not shared in the experience of the exiles in Babylon, and therefore were not regarded as true descendants of the ancient tribes. These other people were of uncertain (and partly non-Jewish) racial origins, and their worship of Yahweh was therefore suspect.

The people of Samaria and their friends in Judah realized that the newcomers from Babylon were bent on forming their own Jewish state, in which the people who already lived in the land would have no place. So, having had their offer of cooperation turned down, these people felt they had no option but to oppose the plans of the returned exiles. They succeeded in delaying work on the Temple for something like ten years or more, by persuading the Persian officials responsible for the western empire that something illegal was afoot. By this time, Darius I was the emperor, but Cyrus's original permission still stood, and the work was allowed to proceed (Ezra 5). The new Temple was much poorer than Solomon's had been, but its completion was a milestone in the life of this beleaguered community (Ezra 3:12).

The return of the exiles.

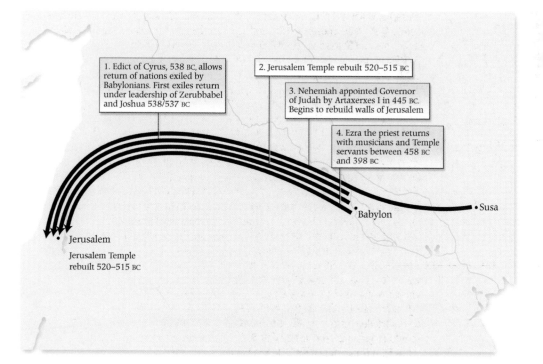

1. Edict of Cyrus, 538 BC, allows return of nations exiled by Babylonians. First exiles return under leadership of Zerubbabel and Joshua 538/537 BC

2. Jerusalem Temple rebuilt 520–515 BC

3. Nehemiah appointed Governor of Judah by Artaxerxes I in 445 BC. Begins to rebuild walls of Jerusalem

4. Ezra the priest returns with musicians and Temple servants between 458 BC and 398 BC

Susa

Babylon

Jerusalem

Jerusalem Temple rebuilt 520–515 BC

Confusion and despair

The new Temple was completed in about 515 BC. Now at last the people had a new hope, and no doubt they went about their worship with joy and expectation, believing that the new age which they had been promised must surely be at hand. In the event, however, the reality was to be quite different. We have no absolutely certain knowledge of life in Judah from 515 BC until 444 BC, though there is no reason to suppose that conditions improved, either religiously or economically. A number of prophetic messages reflect life at this time. The book of Obadiah is a short poem deploring the advantage that the Edomites had gained out of Judah's national disaster – and also assuring the Jewish people that better times were on the way. The book of Joel also probably relates to this period. Its immediate occasion is a plague of locusts, which led to a great famine – something which Joel assured his hearers would be just a temporary setback, and they could soon look forward to the

---

Haggai and Zechariah

Zerubbabel and Joshua were encouraged in their work by the prophets Haggai and Zechariah, and their messages provide a vivid insight into the mood of despair and apathy that prevailed among the people at this time. The wave of euphoria that accompanied Cyrus's rise to power subsided soon after his death, for his son Cambyses (530–522 BC) did not share his father's ideals. He was more interested in military conquest, and during his campaign against Egypt in 525 BC it is likely that he plundered Judah for food supplies. This would have been bad enough in good

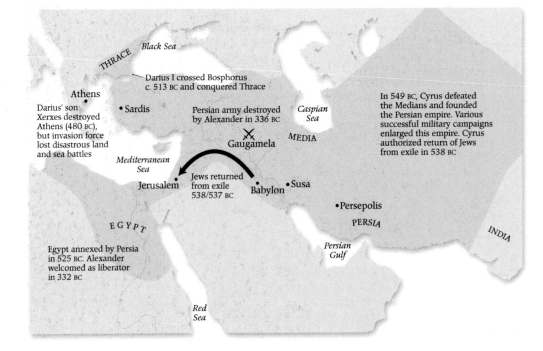

The Persian empire.

In 549 BC, Cyrus defeated the Medians and founded the Persian empire. Various successful military campaigns enlarged this empire. Cyrus authorized return of Jews from exile in 538 BC

Darius I crossed Bosphorus c. 513 BC and conquered Thrace

Persian army destroyed by Alexander in 336 BC

Gaugamela

Darius' son Xerxes destroyed Athens (480 BC), but invasion force lost disastrous land and sea battles

Jews returned from exile 538/537 BC

Egypt annexed by Persia in 525 BC. Alexander welcomed as liberator in 332 BC

THRACE · Black Sea · Athens · Sardis · Caspian Sea · MEDIA · Mediterranean Sea · Jerusalem · Babylon · Susa · Persepolis · EGYPT · PERSIA · INDIA · Persian Gulf · Red Sea

inauguration of the new age for which they were all longing. The same picture of despondency seems to be reflected in the final section of the book of Isaiah (Isaiah 56–66), which some therefore see as the work of yet another prophet (Third or Trito-Isaiah). These messages may well have been the work of followers of Isaiah of Babylon, for their general outlook is similar to his idealism, yet they seem to reflect the despair of this later age.

The only certain source of information from this period is the book of Malachi, and this shows that, though the Temple was standing again, the spiritual realities that it was supposed to represent were still not being taken seriously. The priests themselves were neglecting their proper duties, and the true covenant religion of Yahweh had become mixed up with magical practices (Malachi 3:5). The prophet regarded popular religion as little more than a form of practical atheism: "'You have said terrible things about me,' says Yahweh... "You have said, 'It's

Emperor Darius I, from Media, continued Cyrus's policy of supporting the exiles' return. In his time the Temple was rebuilt at Jerusalem.

times, but Haggai's messages show that the returned exiles were living at poverty level, and their crops were blighted by drought and disease. This in itself made it hard to establish a stable society, but in addition, there was a military coup back in Persia while Cambyses was on his way home from Egypt. He committed suicide and Darius, one of his generals, seized control of the army. He returned to Persia and in due course emerged as one of the most powerful Persian emperors of all time. But while all this was happening, the whole situation must have seemed very confused and uncertain to the Jewish community in and around Jerusalem. Were these upheavals signs of the beginning of the new age that they had spoken of back in Babylon? Or was it an indication of worse yet to come?

Haggai began speaking to the people in 520 BC, early in the reign of Darius. He urged them to make the rebuilding of the Temple a real priority. They had built houses for themselves, so why should they neglect God? If God was not worshipped adequately, they could hardly expect prosperity. But if they were prepared to put God first, then literally anything could happen. Zerubbabel was already there as God's chosen representative, and the symbol of God's own presence – the

useless to serve God. What's the use of doing what God says or of trying to show the Lord Almighty that we are sorry for what we have done?"" (Malachi 3:13–14). As in the past, this neglect of Israel's covenant faith was leading to great social evils, and Malachi declared that God would step in to judge this rotten community, especially 'those who give false testimony, those who cheat employees out of their wages, and those who take advantage of widows, orphans, and foreigners' (Malachi 3:5). In addition to all that, the community of returned exiles was losing its true identity as some of the men were leaving their Jewish wives for more attractive younger women who belonged to the racially mixed population that had tried to stop the rebuilding of the Temple. This was regarded as a very serious matter, for it threatened the very existence of the fragile Jewish settlement as a distinctive ethnic entity, and for that reason Malachi was convinced that it would only be a matter of time before God would have to deal with these evils (Malachi 4).

Haggai and Zechariah continued

Temple – should also be reinstated as the centre of national life. When that happened, the scene would be set for the new age that the exiles had hoped for: 'On that day I will take you, Zerubbabel my servant, and I will appoint you to rule in my name. You are the one I have chosen' (Haggai 2:23).

Zechariah was a contemporary of Haggai, and his messages are essentially similar in tone and content. He encouraged the completion of the rebuilt Temple, and in a series of visions he depicted the new age that God would soon bring about. He too saw a special place for Zerubbabel in all this (4:6–10; 6:9–15), but he also emphasized that Zerubbabel's success depended not so much on the fact that he was descended from King David, but on the fact that God was with him in a special way: 'You will succeed, not by military might or by your own strength, but by my spirit. Obstacles as great as mountains will disappear before you. You will rebuild the Temple, and as you put the last stone in place, the people will shout, "Beautiful, beautiful!"' (4:6–7).

The precise meaning of these statements made about Zerubbabel is unclear. The language used is undoubtedly similar to what would later be called 'messianic', though at the same time it can hardly have

been understood in that way for Zerubbabel seems to have retained the confidence of the Persians. There are also hints that the high priest Joshua came to occupy an even more important place than Zerubbabel in the new community. In the days of the old kingdom of Judah, the Temple in Jerusalem had been under the personal direction of the king, but with the disappearance of the kingly office, functions previously associated with the kings were now carried out by the priests. Indeed, in preparation for his new responsibilities, Joshua was actually crowned in what looks like a coronation ceremony (Zechariah 6:9–15). This was probably a significant development in Jewish thinking, for some 400 years later the Dead Sea Scrolls anticipated the coming of a priest who would be the Messiah, and who was at least as important as the 'secular' Messiah who would be descended from David. The same idea is also found in the letter to the Hebrews in the New Testament. Unfortunately, we have so little definite knowledge of the time of Haggai and Zechariah that it is no longer possible to trace the possible connections of this idea in any greater detail.

Renewing the covenant

It was not too long before moves were afoot to reform and re-establish the life of the Jewish community in Jerusalem. This took place through the work of Nehemiah and Ezra. There is some debate as to which of these two came first, and for the sake of clarity the arguments about that are dealt with separately below. One thing there is no doubt about is that Nehemiah was responsible for political reorganization, while Ezra's concern was more directly related to matters of religious practice.

Building the walls

Though he had risen to a position of some eminence in the Persian royal court, Nehemiah was himself a Jew, and when he learned about the deprivation of his people in Judah and Jerusalem, he asked the Persian king, by now Artaxerxes I, to let him go there and help to rebuild the community. So he was appointed governor of Judah in 445 BC (Nehemiah 1–2). There had probably been a succession of such governors ever since the days of Sheshbazzar about 100 years before, and though we know nothing of them or their work, the brief report of their activities included in the book of Nehemiah suggests they had been more concerned with their own comfort than with the well-being of their people (Nehemiah 5:15). The reaction of both upper-class Jews and the people of Samaria to Nehemiah's appointment certainly suggests that his predecessors did not share the commitment and religious idealism that were to be a hallmark of Nehemiah's work.

Nehemiah had a specific commission from the Persian emperor to rebuild the city of Jerusalem itself. But when he got there, he found that most of the Jews were satisfied with things as they were. From a social perspective, they had turned out to be model immigrants, for they had integrated almost entirely with the rest of Palestinian society. They had established strong trading links with the people of Samaria, to the mutual benefit of both groups, and this had led to cooperation over a wide range of other issues. Of course, the people of Samaria were not total foreigners, for they too could trace their ancestry back to the original Israelite tribes. The only difference was that whereas the Jews from Babylon regarded themselves as ethnically pure, these other people had, over many generations, married people of other races. Even so, they still worshipped the same God as the exiles from Babylon, and the two men from Samaria who turned out to be Nehemiah's most vociferous opponents – Sanballat and Tobiah – both felt that they had the same religious faith as their Jewish neighbours.

Nehemiah refused to condone all this; to him, integration between Jews and other people could only mean one thing: the loss of their distinctive Jewish identity. He believed that these people had abandoned the idealism that originally motivated their return from Babylon, and the fact that he also saw the rich sections of the community exploiting the poor only made him all the more determined to change things. He therefore challenged the moral standards of the Jewish business community, though he could see that as long as there was easy access from Samaria to Jerusalem, nothing was likely to change. If there was ever to be an ethnically pure Jewish community then it would need to have its own political identity centred in the city of Jerusalem itself. Among other things, that meant Jerusalem would need to be properly fortified, with its own city walls, not only to remind people like Sanballat and Tobiah that it did not belong to them, but also to give the Jewish population a city they could be proud of. Not surprisingly, Sanballat and Tobiah were deeply opposed to all this. Quite possibly they themselves had exercised some sort of jurisdiction over Jerusalem before Nehemiah's arrival, but in addition they enjoyed friendly relations with the leaders of

The rebuilding of the walls and gates of Jerusalem provided not only security, but a sense of identity.

the emerging community and felt it was quite unjust for them to be excluded in this way by an outsider. Still, Nehemiah managed to gather together a group of workers from the area surrounding the city and they got down to the task, with half of them doing the construction work while the other half guarded the unfinished wall. In the amazingly short time of fifty-two days, the wall was built (Nehemiah 6). It was not as extensive as the wall that had surrounded the city before 586 BC, but its completion gave a great boost to the morale of the inhabitants. For the first time since Nebuchadnezzar had destroyed their city, Jerusalem and its people had their own self-contained society, and a new opportunity to establish their distinctive national and religious identity.

Some twelve years after his arrival, Nehemiah went back briefly to the Persian capital Susa to report back to Artaxerxes (Nehemiah 13:6). He must have felt that he had made some progress, but on his return he discovered that things had not changed as much as he thought. In his absence, people who were not considered ethnically pure had come to live in Jerusalem, and the sabbath day was not being properly observed. On top of that, the worship at the Temple was not as strict as Nehemiah would have liked it to be, and some of the priests were so poor they had been forced to leave their posts to go to work on the farms, just to make a living. At the same time, Eliashib the high priest had given a suite of rooms in the Temple to Tobiah, the Samaritan whom Nehemiah hated the most! But that was not the worst thing, in his view, for many Jewish people were again marrying foreigners, including even the high priest's own grandson who had married the daughter of Sanballat (Nehemiah 13:4–31).

Handing on the Law

Nehemiah was determined to change all this. But it was a Jewish priest by the name of Ezra who issued the most far-reaching challenge to the people of Jerusalem. He too was a Persian state official, who came to Jerusalem with royal authority to reorganize religious affairs. He was accompanied by a further group of returning exiles from Babylon, who also brought with them a considerable financial endowment for the Temple in Jerusalem (Ezra 7:1–26). But they brought more than that, for Ezra was a 'scholar in the Law of the God of Heaven' (Ezra 7:12), and his interpretation of this law was to have a profound and lasting influence on the whole way of life and national identity of the community.

It is not absolutely clear from the Old Testament just what this law was, but it is reasonable to suppose that it would be substantially identical to the Torah as we know it today. The exiles in Babylon had never been able to construct their own temple, because they believed such a thing was prohibited. This meant that most of their traditional worship had been discontinued, but in order to carry on distinguishing themselves from other ethnic groups they had laid great emphasis on things like keeping the sabbath day, observing their own special food regulations and circumcision – all of which were laid down in the Law. The exiles clearly knew a good deal more about this than the people living in Judah itself. It is no cause for surprise to be told that they were unable to read it for themselves, because the Law itself was written in Hebrew, whereas the people now spoke Aramaic, which was the official language of the Persian empire. As Ezra read it aloud to them, a group of priests (Levites) then 'gave an oral translation of God's Law and explained it so that the people could understand it' (Nehemiah 8:8). The rough translation made by these Levites was the forerunner of many such translations, known as Targums. At first, a Targum was only an oral translation, but in due course the wording of these translations became more fixed, and the term Targum came to mean just the Aramaic version of the Old Testament. But the ignorance of the people in Judah went deeper than that, for they were apparently not at all familiar with the requirements of the Law. When they heard it for themselves, they were deeply moved and decided they must do something to reinstate the religious festivals which it mentioned (Nehemiah 8:9–18). Ezra, however, was determined to tackle other matters which he regarded as problematical, especially the question of Jews who were married to people of different ethnic origins. He was more diplomatic than Nehemiah, but also more ruthless, and he forced the Jews to agree to divorce all such partners. From the perspective of today's readers, Ezra's attitude can easily seem intolerant and bigoted, and given the way in which these and other sections of the Bible have subsequently been used to justify ethnic cleansing, there is certainly a broader issue here that needs to be explored – something that we will return to in a later chapter. But in the historical context of his own day, Ezra's view on such matters was not as unreasonable as it can be made to seem. In many of the marriage laws of ancient Greece and Rome, for instance, a man was not even allowed to marry a person outside his own class, let alone someone from a different race.

Whatever verdict history may eventually deliver regarding Ezra's attitudes, it is probably true that the community in Judah would not have survived as a distinctive entity without his efforts. But it is equally certain that the people paid a high price for their survival. For this new emphasis on ethnic purity and the accompanying insistence that a detailed observance of rules and regulations was somehow central to true spirituality was easily transformed into the kind of self-righteous legalism and hypocrisy that was roundly condemned by Jesus (Matthew 23:1–36), and which the Christian writer Paul later felt to be so contrary to the original intention of the covenant relationship between God and the ancient people of Israel.

Two dissidents

Not everyone was happy to accept this new emphasis on racial purity, the Law and the Temple. When Stephen, one of the leaders of the earliest Christian church, argued that the building of the Temple had been a mistake because 'the Most High God does not live in houses built by human hands' (Acts 7:48–50, quoting Isaiah 66:1–2), he had a long line of Jewish protest behind him. But at this earlier period, more criticism was focused on the policy of rigid separation from other races.

The book of Ruth may have been published at this time, as a protest against Ezra's actions. The fact that the Jews placed it in the third section of the Hebrew Bible (the Writings) certainly suggests that it was among the later books to be written, though in the Christian Old Testament it is placed after Judges, because its story is set in that age. It tells how Elimelech, a native of Bethlehem, emigrated to Moab at a time of famine, accompanied by his wife Naomi and his two sons, both of whom married Moabite women. The father and

the two sons all died in Moab, and Naomi returned to Bethlehem along with her daughter-in-law Ruth. There, Ruth met Boaz, who was a relative of her husband's family, and they got married. As a result, Ruth, a Moabite woman, became the great-grandmother of King David.

Like other parts of the Old Testament, this story may have originated in earlier times, though the opening phrase of the book, 'Long ago, in the days before Israel had a king', shows that it was written down much later. Though there is no positive evidence to prove it, it is plausible to think that it could have been written as a protest against the legislation of Ezra and Nehemiah: if a Moabite woman married to an Israelite could have been the ancestor of King David himself, then surely there was nothing wrong with mixed marriages!

The book of Jonah may also have originated in the same context. A prophet called Jonah is mentioned briefly in the time of Amos (2 Kings 14:25), but the book contains none of his messages. It tells the story of how Jonah was sent by God to go to Nineveh, the capital city of the Assyrian empire. Jonah, however, did not want to go, and boarded a ship going in the opposite direction. When a great storm blew up, the crew decided he must be the cause of it and at his own suggestion they threw him overboard, whereupon he was swallowed by a large fish which later deposited him on dry land. Jonah was once more sent to Nineveh to announce the destruction of the city, and this time he did so. His message resulted in such a dramatic and thoroughgoing change of heart on the part of Nineveh's people that God withdrew the threat of judgment.

Jonah was dispirited at this, and went to sit alone outside the city. A plant grew up to give him much-needed shade from the sun, only to disappear as quickly – much to Jonah's annoyance. But his frustration at this then becomes the occasion for the book's message to be emphasized: 'God said to him, "This plant grew up in one night and disappeared the next; you didn't do anything for it and you didn't make it grow – yet you feel sorry for it! How much more, then, should I have pity on Nineveh, that great city. After all, it has more than 120,000 innocent children in it, as well as many animals!"' (Jonah 4:10–11).

There are some indications that this book was written after the city of Nineveh had fallen (in 612 BC), and a few Aramaic expressions seem to date it in the Persian period. Its message would certainly be a corrective to the narrow exclusiveness of many Jews at that time. Like Jonah, they were often prepared to go to any lengths to avoid sharing their faith with others, preferring that non-Jews should be destroyed rather than change their ways and become the recipients of God's blessing.

Ruth, a Moabite woman, caught the attention of Boaz as she gleaned in his field near Bethlehem, and they were married. This mixed marriage resulted, three generations later, in the birth of King David. Was the account of their marriage written down centuries later as a protest against the racial reforms of Ezra and Nehemiah?

The history of the Chronicler

The books of 1 and 2 Chronicles were also written during this post-exilic period. In them, we have yet another interpretation of the story of ancient Israel, this time starting with Adam, the first man (1 Chronicles 1:1) and ending with Cyrus the Persian (2 Chronicles 36:22–23). The first nine chapters of 1 Chronicles consist entirely of various family and tribal lists and genealogies, and the story proper begins with the death of Saul, the first king of Israel (1 Chronicles 10). But he is mentioned only as a prelude to the story of David, and the main interest of the author of these books (generally referred to as 'the Chronicler') centres on the history of the southern kingdom of Judah from the time of David onwards.

Inevitably, therefore, the stories of the books of Chronicles parallel those of the deuteronomic history. Indeed, at many points the Chronicler shows that he has actually used the books of Samuel and Kings in the writing of his own story. This fact should make it easy to uncover his own special reasons for telling the story yet again, simply by comparing the Chronicler's accounts of events with the same ones described in the earlier books. Unfortunately, it seems likely that he was using a slightly different version of Samuel and Kings from the one that is now part of the Old Testament. We know of the existence of such a version from the Dead Sea Scrolls, a collection of scriptural and other writings preserved by a Jewish sect in the century immediately preceding the Christian era. But because of the doubt concerning the edition of Samuel and Kings used by the Chronicler, reconstructing his own historical method is not a straightforward business. Chronicles also contains other historical information not found in Samuel and Kings, much of which is of independent value in helping us to understand the events of Israel's earlier history.

On the whole, however, the Chronicler sets out not so much to record the facts about the past, as to comment on their meaning and significance, and though there may be doubt about some of the details, his main concerns are not difficult to discern. He looks back to the reigns of David and Solomon as a golden age in Judah's history. The kings who followed them were all disobedient to God's Law, and the northern kingdom of Israel is scarcely mentioned at all, for it was believed to be incorrigibly corrupt right from its inception. The deuteronomic picture of Solomon and David certainly provides a more realistic and balanced account of their reigns than we have in Chronicles. There is no extensive evidence to suggest that the Chronicler necessarily invented his facts: he simply omitted significant elements from the story, and emphasized other aspects that to him were more important. So, for instance, there is no mention here of David's struggle for the kingdom against Ishbaal, Saul's son, nor of David's adultery with Bathsheba, or indeed anything else that might show David in a bad light. The same is true of the narratives about Solomon. The court intrigues that brought him to power are not mentioned, nor are his extensive marriage alliances with other states, or his promotion of many aspects of traditional Canaanite spirituality. The Chronicler does not actually deny that any of these things took place, but simply chooses not to mention them. Instead, David and Solomon are both praised especially because they built the Temple, and David's preparations for doing so, as well as Solomon's execution of his father's plans, are described in far greater detail than in the earlier history books. Then, against this background, the later kings of Judah could all be depicted as men who led their country to ruin because they neglected this all-important feature of Judah's national life.

The fact that Cyrus's edict is mentioned in the last paragraph of 2 Chronicles has led some to suggest that the two books may have been written to provide support for the work of Zerubbabel in rebuilding the Temple after the exile. The fact that the issue of ethnic purity, which was so important later, does not feature in Chronicles may also support such a date. On the other hand, this may be too early, for the list of Jehoiachin's descendants in 1 Chronicles 3:17–24 goes well beyond the time of Zerubbabel, and possibly takes us to about 400 BC. In that case, the two books could have been written in support of Ezra's reforms. They certainly stress some of the same things, and of course in that political climate the total ignoring of the life of the northern kingdom of Israel could be seen as an encouragement to the people of Jerusalem to have no dealings with their descendants who now lived in Samaria. On the other hand, some scholars have argued that we should not try to link Chronicles up to specific events and situations in this way, but simply see it as the product of a number of different political and theological currents in the post-exilic Jewish community.

Ezra and Nehemiah

The date of 1 and 2 Chronicles is closely bound up with their relationship to the books of Ezra and Nehemiah. Many scholars believe that all four of them together were originally intended to be a history of the Jewish people from creation itself right up to the Chronicler's own day. If that is the case, then we would need to think of all four books as having been written about 400 BC, or possibly even later. The only substantial reason for seeing a connection between 1–2 Chronicles and Ezra/Nehemiah is the fact that the closing words of 2 Chronicles are identical to the opening paragraph of Ezra, but in other ways their concerns are rather different. In particular, the deep interest of 1 and 2 Chronicles in David's family is not reflected in Ezra or Nehemiah.

The style and general organization of material is also strikingly different. Whereas 1 and 2 Chronicles contain a coherent, well-organized account, Ezra and Nehemiah contain a very disjointed collection of stories and other materials. Temple records are quoted (Nehemiah 7:5–73; 12:22–23), as is the decree of Cyrus, both in Hebrew (Ezra 1:2–4) and in Aramaic (Ezra 6:3–5). Various other Aramaic letters are also included (Ezra 4:9–22; 5:7–17; 6:3–12; 7:12–26), while the actual story of Ezra's exploits is partly contained in the book of Ezra (7–10) and partly in Nehemiah (8:1 – 10:39). Some of this material has the appearance of being extracts from Ezra's own diary (Ezra 7:27 – 8:34; 9:1–15), and likewise much of Nehemiah's story appears in the form of extracts from his own personal diary (Nehemiah 1:1 – 7:73, and sections of 11–13).

Then, as the stories stand, there are complex issues involved in understanding the relationship between these two men. According to Ezra 7:7, Ezra went to Jerusalem in the seventh year of Artaxerxes' reign, and Nehemiah in his twentieth year (Nehemiah 1:1). That would place Ezra's arrival in 458 BC, and Nehemiah's in 445 BC. But this seems to imply that Ezra's reforms were a miserable failure, for when Nehemiah arrived he certainly found all the same abuses that Ezra fought so strenuously to overcome. There are other facts which further complicate matters. For instance, when Nehemiah arrived he set to work building a wall round Jerusalem, though Ezra 9:9 implies that there was already a wall there when Ezra arrived. There is also the fact that in Nehemiah's time, the high priest was Eliashib (Nehemiah 3:1), whereas in Ezra's time it appears to have been his son, Jehohanan (Ezra 10:6; Nehemiah 12:11, 22). Various attempts have been made to overcome this problem. Some suggest that Ezra perhaps came in the reign of Artaxerxes II, which would place his arrival in 398 BC, and therefore long after the time of Nehemiah. Others emphasize the fact that their careers do seem to have overlapped at some points (Nehemiah 8:9; 12:26, 36), and on that basis it has been suggested that the correct date for Ezra was not the seventh year of Artaxerxes I, but the thirty-seventh, which would make it 428 BC. All three possible dates for Ezra – 458, 428 and 398 BC – have supporters today, and it is difficult to decide which is likely to be correct. In our account of the work of these two men, we have assumed that Nehemiah did precede Ezra, but probably not by a long period of time.

Perhaps the reason for this confusion can be found in the disjointed nature of the narratives of these two books. For, as we read them carefully, they seem to be not so much a continuous story of Ezra and Nehemiah, as the sort of preliminary collection of information that a historian might make before writing the final polished account. The first six chapters of Ezra are more or less continuous, but between them and chapter seven there is a time gap of at least sixty years, and possibly more. The further fact that some parts of Ezra are written in Aramaic, while other parts are in Hebrew, also reinforces this impression of a collection of notes rather than a carefully crafted story. If this is a correct understanding of the nature of Ezra and Nehemiah, it would then be possible that 1 and 2 Chronicles were written early during the period of the exile, and that these other materials were gathered together by some later author – perhaps a follower of the original Chronicler – as a means of bringing the story up to his own day. We have so little knowledge of this period that it is difficult to be certain. But this does not detract from the usefulness of these books, for all scholars are convinced that Nehemiah and Ezra contain important and valuable historical materials from the period which they describe.

Exiles in Egypt

The Jewish community in Jerusalem was not the only context in which the God of Israel was being worshipped at this time. We have already noticed that the inhabitants of Samaria felt themselves to be a part of the faith community of Israel, and a series of Aramaic documents discovered at the island of Elephantine, near Aswan on the River Nile, provide a fascinating glimpse of life in another Jewish community at roughly the time of Nehemiah and Ezra.

At the time of these documents, Egypt was a part of the Persian empire and the Jews who lived here were a military settlement, perhaps guarding the southern frontier of Egypt and the trading post of Syene where traders from further south met the ships of Egyptian traders on the Nile. These Jews may well have been in this area long before Cambyses the Persian conquered Egypt in 525 BC, but they certainly had a military function rather than being (as some have supposed) the descendants either of a group of religious dissidents who left Jerusalem in protest at Josiah's reforms (621 BC), or of those Jews who took Jeremiah to Egypt after the fall of Jerusalem in 586 BC.

There are many different kinds of documents in this collection, including deeds for property, marriage contracts, and other legal transactions, but the most interesting ones are those which describe the religious observances of this group. For it is clear from them that the kind of Judaism being practised in this Egyptian garrison was very different indeed from the Judaism that was being taught at the same time in Jerusalem by Nehemiah and Ezra.

● In spite of the deuteronomic law stipulating that sacrifices were to be offered only in Jerusalem, there was a Jewish temple in Elephantine at which sacrifices were offered. The priests who officiated there are not said to have belonged to the tribe of Levi, nor is there any evidence that they knew the Torah.

After their temple had been destroyed in 410 BC, the governors of Judah and Samaria advised them to limit their sacrifices to meal offerings and incense. This could have been a gesture intended to show that the Elephantine temple was inferior in status to that in Jerusalem, though it could just as easily have been because animal sacrifices were particularly offensive to the Egyptians. Various explanations have been offered to account for the existence of this temple. Perhaps the deuteronomic law of a single sanctuary applied only in Palestine – or possibly the Jews of Elephantine had left Palestine before the reforms of Hezekiah and Josiah had really taken a grip. We simply do not know, though some scholars have suggested that there may be a veiled reference to this Egyptian temple in Isaiah 19:19, which reads, 'When that time comes, there will be an altar to Yahweh in the land of Egypt and a stone pillar dedicated to God at the Egyptian border.' Very little is known about this temple, except that it had pillars of stone, five gateways made of carved stone and a roof of cedar wood. But there is not the slightest suggestion that the Jews of Elephantine thought there was anything wrong in having such a temple outside Jerusalem. Indeed, when it was destroyed they appealed for help in its rebuilding both to the Jewish leaders in Jerusalem, and to the people in Samaria who were so hostile to Nehemiah.

● Though this temple was definitely dedicated to Yahweh (or Yaho, as God is called here), other deities had some part in it. Some believe there were five gods and goddesses worshipped here, represented by the five gates of the temple, others that

This papyrus letter was written by Jews who were living in Elephantine in southern Egypt near Aswan. It mentions Sanballat, governor of Samaria in the time of Nehemiah. Documents found at Elephantine show that Jews who lived there at that time continued to worship Yahweh.

Exiles in Egypt
continued

there were only two or three, of whom Yaho was certainly one. Most of the others mentioned in the texts are clearly of Canaanite origin. Throughout the history of both kingdoms, traditional Canaanite religious practices had survived in Israel and Judah, in spite of the prophets' denunciations of such things. The extent of syncretism is highlighted by those exiles with whom Jeremiah met in Egypt, who justified their worship of 'the Queen of Heaven' by reminding him that this was 'just as we and our ancestors, our king and our leaders, used to do in the towns of Judah and in the streets of Jerusalem' (Jeremiah 44:17).

● One of the most interesting texts is the so-called 'Passover Papyrus'. This dates from 419 BC, and contains a decree said to have been issued by Darius, laying down regulations for the celebration of the festival of Passover. This suggests that the annual observance of Passover was not as regular in early times as it came to be in later Judaism. But the very existence of this text is itself unusual, though it is of the same type as other edicts contained in the books of Ezra and Nehemiah, which also give directions for the establishment of Jewish religious practices.

It is naturally tempting to try to establish clear links between these documents and the Old Testament narratives. There is, for example, mention of a person by the name of Hanani, as well as a Jehohanan and a Sanballat, all of whom feature in the stories of Nehemiah and Ezra. But there is no way of being certain that they indicate the same people. One of the things that is quite clear from these texts is that there were some people who believed it was possible to be a good Jew without necessarily following the rigid lines that had been drawn in Jerusalem. In the next few centuries, this strand of Judaism was to be increasingly important in many parts of the Mediterranean world, not least in Egypt itself.

8 The Challenge of a New Age

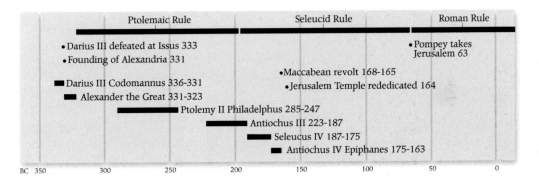

	Ptolemaic Rule	Seleucid Rule	Roman Rule

- Darius III defeated at Issus 333
- Founding of Alexandria 331
- Pompey takes Jerusalem 63
- Maccabean revolt 168-165
- Jerusalem Temple rededicated 164

■ Darius III Codomannus 336-331
■ Alexander the Great 331-323
■■■■ Ptolemy II Philadelphus 285-247
■■■■ Antiochus III 223-187
■■■ Seleucus IV 187-175
■ Antiochus IV Epiphanes 175-163

BC 350   300   250   200   150   100   50   0

The history books of the Hebrew Bible only take their story as far as the times of Nehemiah and Ezra, and relate nothing of later events. But the period covered by the Old Testament does not end there, for life in Judah continued and the changing attitudes and experiences of this period are reflected in some of the later books. Though we have very little specific knowledge regarding what life was really like in Judah in the seventy or eighty years following the work of Ezra, the community that he founded on the twin principles of religious and racial exclusivism probably continued along much the same lines. Judah was still a Persian province, but it was allowed to mint its own coins, and enjoyed other privileges that the community based in Samaria never had. During this period the differences between Jerusalem and Samaria eventually forced the two populations of Palestine to go their own separate ways.

As they read the ancient stories of Abraham and Sarah, and their successors, the people of Samaria recognized them as their own story, and the God of whom they spoke was worshipped with as much fervour in Samaria as by the settlers in Jerusalem. Yet, in spite of the fact that they still felt themselves to be a legitimate part of the great national and spiritual movement that could be traced back through the traditional stories of the Israelite nation, the reality was that they would never again be allowed to worship at the Temple in Jerusalem. It is one of the great ironies of Old Testament history that, at the very earliest period of the

emergence of Israel as a nation, anyone who could embrace the vision of an egalitarian society based on the worship of Yahweh was welcomed as a legitimate participant, whereas by the end of the story the narrow ethnic definitions promulgated by Ezra were used to exclude even those who, on any reckoning, were undoubtedly the close relatives of those returning exiles who were now resettling the land of Judah. It was therefore inevitable that, as they reassessed their own national life in the light of changing circumstances, the people of Samaria would need to develop their own distinctive beliefs and culture. It is unclear whether the people who are called 'Samaritans' in the New Testament were the ethnic

A high priest from the small community of Samaritans still living in Israel today. Their origins reach back at least to Sanballat and Tobiah in Nehemiah's time and possibly even to the racially mixed community who survived the fall of Samaria and the northern kingdom to the Assyrians. Though kept at a distance by mainline Judaism, the Samaritans have always looked on themselves as heirs to the Old Testament traditions.

descendants of the people led by Tobiah and Sanballat, or whether they were in fact a completely new sect that emerged in the days just before the beginning of the Christian era.

Either way, the people of Samaria got their chance to establish their own national identity in 333 BC. This was the year when the Persian king Darius III Codomannus was defeated in battle at Issus in north-west Syria. The victor was a young, enthusiastic warrior from Macedonia, Alexander the Great. Having overcome the main Persian army, he moved south towards Egypt, and the Samarians saw this as an opportunity to enhance their own national security by cooperating with the Greeks. As a result, they were given permission to build a temple for themselves on Mount Gerizim, though their emerging independence soon disappeared when, for some unknown reason, they revolted against Greek rule and their city was then made into a Greek military colony.

A new empire

Alexander's progress was spectacular. Egypt offered no resistance to him, and in 331 BC he was able to found a new city on the Nile delta. This was the city of Alexandria, and it was to have a considerable influence not only on Egypt, but also on the Jewish people living in various parts of the Mediterranean world. It later became an important centre of early

Christianity. The establishment of such new cities played a key part in Alexander's strategy. For he was not just out for political power: he also had an almost fanatical fervour about spreading Greek culture and the Greek language. He was remarkably successful in doing so, and although his empire did not last long as a united political entity, the cultural world that he created, based on all things Greek (generally referred to as 'Hellenism') lasted for nearly 1,000 years. Though Alexander himself died young as a result of some kind of disease in 323 BC, by then his empire stretched from Greece in the west to the borders of India in the east. But it did not survive intact, and after much feuding among Alexander's generals, Judah – or Judea as it was now to be called – came under the control of Ptolemy, who established himself and his successors as a new ruling dynasty in Egypt. From about 320 BC until 198 BC, the Jews came under the jurisdiction of these Greek rulers of Egypt (collectively known as the Ptolemies). Their policy with regard to conquered peoples was not much different from that of the Persians before them, and was based on an essentially pragmatic approach that sought to promote anything that would be mutually advantageous to both the rulers and their subjects, though there is evidence that Ptolemy I forced many Jews to emigrate to the city of Alexandria, which was at the time underpopulated. Many others went voluntarily, however, and there was soon a thriving Jewish community in this new Egyptian city. During this time, priestly families in Jerusalem collaborated closely with the Ptolemies and, in effect, became their agents in collecting taxes and ensuring public order.

In cultural terms, this was a period of considerable change, as Jewish people encountered a way of life that was quite different from anything they had met before. On the whole, it seems that Greek ways of doing things were combined with traditional Hebrew culture on a purely pragmatic basis. The Greek language, for example, was now the essential medium for both commerce and diplomacy, and was widely adopted within Palestine itself as well as by Jewish people living elsewhere. Though Aramaic continued to be spoken in Judea in particular, this was not to the exclusion of Greek, though the use of Hebrew as a living language disappeared for good. Of course, Hebrew was the language in which the Jewish scriptures were written (with just one or two very short passages in the latest books in Aramaic). It was this significant change that led to a demand that the books of the Hebrew Bible be translated into Greek, and it was during this period that the Septuagint was produced. The *Letter of Aristeas* tells how this was accomplished, and claims that the Jews of Egypt managed to persuade the Egyptian king, Ptolemy II Philadelphus, to sponsor the project. Though details of how the translation was produced are no doubt embellished, it is not at all unlikely that such a project would have received official support, for Ptolemy II had a policy of promoting traditional culture, and facilitated the establishment of a considerable library in Alexandria. The story tells of how he sent to

The empire created by Alexander the Great's fourth-century conquests included Judea. For the next centuries the dominant influence in the whole Eastern Mediterranean was 'Hellenism' – a culture based on Greek language.

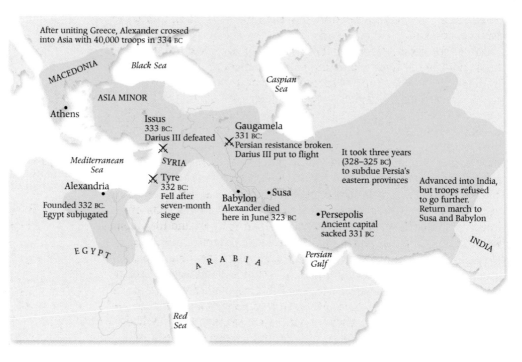

After uniting Greece, Alexander crossed into Asia with 40,000 troops in 334 BC

MACEDONIA

Black Sea

Caspian Sea

ASIA MINOR

Athens

Issus
333 BC:
Darius III defeated

Gaugamela
331 BC:
Persian resistance broken.
Darius III put to flight

It took three years
(328–325 BC)
to subdue Persia's
eastern provinces

Advanced into India,
but troops refused
to go further.
Return march to
Susa and Babylon

Mediterranean
Sea

SYRIA

Alexandria

Tyre
332 BC:
Fell after
seven-month
siege

Susa

Babylon
Alexander died
here in June 323 BC

Persepolis
Ancient capital
sacked 331 BC

INDIA

Founded 332 BC.
Egypt subjugated

EGYPT

ARABIA

Persian
Gulf

Red
Sea

The Greek empire.

Jerusalem for seventy men who knew both Hebrew and Greek, and locked them up in seventy cells while each one produced their own translation. When the work was finished, to everyone's amazement the seventy men not only expressed the same ideas, but also used the very same Greek words to do so — whereupon Ptolemy was so impressed that he was immediately convinced of the divine origins of both the Hebrew originals and their Greek translation. In reality, the process of translating the traditional scriptures into Greek was more humdrum than that, though the importance of the Septuagint can hardly be exaggerated, and its existence had far-reaching consequences not only for the spread of Judaism in the Mediterranean world, but also for the earliest Christian believers, who adopted it as their own Bible.

Jews and Greeks

At the time Alexander died, Ptolemy had not been the only one of his generals to have designs on Judea. Seleucus, who ruled from Antioch in north Syria, was not too happy that Judea and Lebanon should belong to the Ptolemies of Egypt, and throughout the third century their respective successors were constantly at loggerheads over possession of this territory. For the most part, this manifested itself in diplomatic efforts to out-manoeuvre one another, though there were several military skirmishes as well. The matter was finally decided in 198 BC, when the

Seleucid Antiochus III defeated Scopus, the general of Ptolemy V, at the battle of Paneon.

Antiochus was welcomed by the leaders in Jerusalem, some of whom (most notably the high priest Simon and members of the Tobiad family) had given him active support in his opposition to the Ptolemies. In return, the Seleucids adopted a tolerant policy towards the Jews, and Antiochus not only reduced their taxes, but also made a generous grant for the restoration of the Temple in Jerusalem, and formally affirmed their right to live according to their traditional laws and customs. All this ensured the continuation of the generally happy coexistence of Jewish values alongside Hellenistic culture, with mutual advantage to both sides. Unfortunately, Antiochus did not show the same wisdom in dealing with the rising power of Rome. Having extended his influence from Syria into the territory to the south, he tried to expand his empire westwards, something which the Romans took far more seriously. In 190 BC he was defeated in a land and sea battle at Magnesia, near Ephesus, and the peace treaty that he was subsequently forced to sign represented a considerable loss of face, for it required him to abandon completely his territory in Asia Minor. The humiliation of this was bad enough, but it also had financial repercussions, for this territory had always been the wealthiest part of the Seleucid empire and its loss pushed him to the brink of bankruptcy. He was soon desperate for money and just a year after signing the treaty with the Romans, Antiochus himself was killed in Elam while in the act of robbing a temple. Temples in the ancient world often served as banks where people could leave cash or jewellery in safe keeping, and the Temple in Jerusalem was no exception. Antiochus himself never sought access to its wealth, and in the early part of the reign of his son and successor Seleucus IV nothing changed. However, it was not long before the rise of dissenting factions among the ruling families in Jerusalem necessitated military intervention, in the course of which Seleucus dispatched his chancellor, Heliodorus, to plunder the Temple there. His attempt was evidently unsuccessful (2 Maccabees 3), but it alerted the Seleucids to the existence of substantial treasures in Jerusalem, while the knowledge of growing internal tension within the Jewish hierarchy encouraged them to keep a much closer eye on what was going on in this southern part of their domain.

Emerging tensions

There had been underlying tension in Jewish society long before the Seleucids had first gained control of Judea. Two leading families – the Tobiads and the Oniads – were behind all this, the one representing a more traditional Jewish orthodoxy and the other being eager to accept, as well as promote, the new Hellenistic culture. The climax of this power struggle happened to coincide with the murder of Seleucus IV and the accession of a new king, Antiochus IV Epiphanes. A member of the Oniad family called Jason bribed Antiochus to make him high priest in Jerusalem in place of his brother Onias. This suited Antiochus, for Jason was committed to the same policies of Hellenization as he was himself, and so with Jason's appointment, a thoroughgoing plan was set in motion to establish Jerusalem as a Greek city. Even the priests in the Temple were soon hurrying through their work in order to have time to go to the wrestling arena (2 Maccabees 4:13–15). The Greeks wore no clothes on such occasions, and to avoid possible embarrassment when they took part, the Jewish men even went so far as to try to disguise the fact that they had been circumcised (1 Maccabees 1:10–15; 2 Maccabees 4:7–17). All this was too much for those who wanted to remain true to the traditions of their people, and it was not long before Jason was deposed and replaced by Menelaus, a member of the Tobiad family, who was appointed by Antiochus for no other reason than the fact that he had offered a bigger bribe than Jason – something that could only inflame passions among the religious groups in Jerusalem (2 Maccabees 4:23–50).

Meanwhile, Antiochus had set his sights on Egypt. The ruler of Egypt, Ptolemy VI, was only a boy, and Antiochus defeated his army without difficulty (1 Maccabees 1:16–19). Desperate for money, he went to Jerusalem and robbed the Temple before returning home to Syria. But he was soon travelling south again, and in the spring of 168 BC he returned to Egypt. This time, he found the Romans had already arrived there, and they soon sent him packing. In the meantime, a rumour had spread in Jerusalem that Antiochus was dead, whereupon Jason seized the opportunity to try to get rid of Menelaus. Antiochus was in no mood for compromise. He had already been humiliated by the Romans, and he was determined to keep his grip on Judea. So he moved to Jerusalem again, and took what treasure was left in the Temple, assisted this time by Menelaus himself (2 Maccabees 5:1–20). Antiochus's visit to Jerusalem on this occasion was accompanied by great slaughter and destruction, and some of the inhabitants were forcibly removed and taken into slavery (2 Maccabees 5:11–14). But things went much further than that, and Antiochus also introduced stringent measures to restrict and control traditional expressions of Jewish spirituality. Circumcision, sabbath-keeping, and the reading of the Law were all banned, and in a very short time Antiochus was insisting that worship of the Greek god Zeus should be included in the rituals of the Temple. To add insult to injury, he opened the Temple to the whole population of the land, including those who were not ethnically Jews (1 Maccabees 1:41–50; 2 Maccabees 6:1–6). With this, Antiochus embarked on a comprehensive policy of enforced Hellenization, insisting that all elements of the population must be united by their acceptance of the Greek religion and Greek way of life.

National pride and religious zeal

The reasons for Antiochus's determination to stamp out all things distinctively Jewish are not altogether clear. The nearest comparable effort was 1,000 years earlier, in Pharaoh Akhenaten's attempt to eliminate from Egypt the worship of every god except Aten and himself. But this kind of attempt to annihilate an entire religion was not at all typical of ancient empires. People who believed in many deities did not usually think it was either worthwhile or necessary to try to get rid of any particular ones. Antiochus may to some extent have been motivated by an elevated sense of his own importance, perhaps regarding himself as an incarnation of Zeus. His epithet 'Epiphanes' literally means 'a manifestation of God', though some writers deliberately corrupted it to 'Epimanes', meaning 'madman'. Either or both possibilities could go some way towards explaining his actions, though he does not seem to have been the kind of person who would have had the capacity for sustaining the grand ideological vision implied by claims to divinity. Far from having any all-embracing strategy, he was the sort of ruler who reacted to events spontaneously, motivated by short-term pragmatism more than anything else. At this time, he was virtually bankrupt, his kingdom was in a shaky condition, and in addition it may well have been that Jewish leaders such as Menelaus and Jason were themselves supporting, if not actually proposing, these policies of extreme Hellenization.

No doubt Antiochus's actions had no one single explanation, but can be traced to all these factors in the social circumstances of the day. In and of itself, the influence of Hellenism had proved to be fairly neutral in relation to traditional Jewish values, and for more than a century the people of Judea had lived happily within this cultural matrix, as indeed their compatriots in other cities around the Mediterranean Sea continued to do. But the way in which Antiochus went about things in Palestine stirred up more resistance than anyone could possibly have bargained for. Jewish resistance was fanatical, and was only strengthened when Antiochus insisted that pigs (unclean animals to the Jews) should be offered in honour of Zeus. On 25 Kislev 167 BC, Antiochus inflicted the greatest indignity possible by having the altar of daily sacrifice in the Temple itself replaced by an altar to Zeus, on which pigs were sacrificed. At the same time, he issued orders that throughout the land people should be forced to offer similar sacrifices in their own communities. Though there was some support for this, the majority of the people were completely unprepared to take part in such ceremonies (2 Maccabees 6:7–31). The strength of their resolution was matched only by the cruelty of Antiochus's soldiers, who on one occasion skinned and fried alive an entire family who refused to submit to this compulsory Hellenization (2 Maccabees 7).

Such passive resistance may have been morally worthy, but it was hardly effective, and an armed resistance movement soon sprang to life. It began at the village of Modein, near Lydda, when a priest by the name of Mattathias was ordered to offer a sacrifice on a Greek altar. As he refused to do so, another man stepped forward in his place, whereupon Mattathias killed both him and the Seleucid officer who had given the

Antiochus IV Epiphanes, ruler of the Seleucid empire that controlled Judea, attempted to eliminate the distinctives of Jewish life and religion, but met with fierce resistance. The Seleucids wanted to make Jerusalem a purely Greek city, but the Jews fought strongly to retain the right to keep their Law.

order (1 Maccabees 2:1–26). That action marked the beginning of one of the most remarkable resistance movements in Jewish history. Mattathias and his family fled to the hills and began a sustained guerrilla war under the leadership of Judas, one of his five sons. Judas was nicknamed 'The Hammer' (*Maccabi*), and from that the whole movement came to be called 'the Maccabean revolt'. There was one particularly despicable act by Seleucid soldiers which ensured support from other groups. Jews generally had no interest in becoming involved in an armed struggle, and among them was a large ultra-religious group (the Hasideans) who had tried to isolate themselves from the conflict by retreating into the Judean desert. The Seleucid army pursued them, and challenged them to battle on the sabbath day. Naturally, they refused, for they would not work on the sabbath (1 Maccabees 2:29–38). When Antiochus's forces systematically murdered them, it became obvious that passive resistance was going to be useless – and equally obvious that if all Jews continued to observe the Law with that degree of strictness, there would soon be none of them left. So the Maccabees decided that they would sometimes need to be prepared to break the Law, and fight even on the sabbath (1 Maccabees 2:39–41).

This realistic policy attracted many new supporters, including the Hasideans themselves. Under the daring leadership of Judas, the rebels enjoyed some amazing successes, and it was not long before the weary Antiochus was forced to reverse his policies (2 Maccabees 11:27–33). The Jewish Law was reinstated as the foundation of Jewish society, and the Temple itself was cleansed and rededicated on 25 Kislev 164 BC, exactly three years to the day from its first violation (1 Maccabees 4:36–59; 2 Maccabees 10:5–8). The annual feast of Hanukkah (still observed today) was inaugurated to celebrate the occasion. The Hasideans were happy, for they had won the freedom to practise their own religion and keep their own laws. But Judas's family (the Hasmoneans) wanted more than that. This limited victory had given them the taste for power, and it was not long before they had more or less thrown off Seleucid rule and established themselves as a ruling dynasty in Judea. Under their leadership, Judea enjoyed a period of relative political independence until the Roman general Pompey took the city of Jerusalem in 63 BC. This period saw a continuation of the many complex internal struggles among different factions within the Jewish leadership, with some Hasmoneans seeming to favour the very things that Judas and his generation had fought so hard to overthrow. As a result, they soon lost the support of the Hasideans, who in turn disappeared as a single identifiable religious grouping. Some of them found the corruption and Hellenizing policies of the Hasmonean kings intolerable, and withdrew into the Judean desert, just as they had done in the days of Antiochus, and it was probably a movement of this kind that led to the foundation of the Essene community at Qumran by the shores of the Dead Sea. Other Hasideans did not go that far, but regrouped as a protest movement operating within mainstream Jewish society. Many scholars believe that they were connected with the rise of the Pharisees in the centuries before the birth of Jesus. The Hasmoneans, for their part, often seem to have favoured the Sadducees – another religious grouping which features in the New Testament stories of Jesus – though they themselves were perhaps the precursors of the intensely anti-Roman zealot movement that emerged in Palestine during the first century AD.

Keeping the faith

Throughout this period – and even more so in the centuries that followed – it became a major preoccupation to work out how the people of Judah could remain faithful to their ancestral beliefs while playing their full part in the rapidly changing world of their day. At the time of Ezra, it had seemed as if it might be possible for a renewed Jewish state to forge its own identity under the relatively benevolent oversight of Persia. The arrival of the Greeks did not bring any significant change of policy, though the realities of the much enlarged world-view that was now open to them meant that many Jewish people were happily experimenting to discover how their traditional practices might be adapted so as to be thoroughly at home in the new Hellenistic culture, while not losing touch with their roots in the past. This was bound to be a risky business, and three books in particular seem to have originated in this period as warnings against the possible dangers involved: Esther, Judith and Tobit.

The book of Esther was part of the Hebrew Bible, while Judith and Tobit were among those included in the Septuagint, which also included various additional passages in the text of Esther itself, not found in the Hebrew Bible. From a literary perspective, they all clearly belong to the same genre, and are what today might be called historical novels. That is, while they reflect an authentic perception of life at the time to which they relate, they were not intended to be historical narratives as such.

Esther

The story of Esther is set in Susa, the royal residence of the Persian empire, during the years when many Jews were returning from exile in Babylon. Esther herself was a Jewish woman who became queen to the Persian king Xerxes (486–465 BC), and then discovered that Haman, one of the king's leading advisers, was plotting to annihilate all the Jews. By a mixture of charm and cunning, Esther (whose husband knew nothing of her Jewish ancestry) managed to turn the tables on Haman, and he was executed while Mordecai (one of her own Jewish relatives) was promoted to high office in his place. This book was certainly one of the latest to be written, for it is found in the final section of the Hebrew Bible (the Writings). Its message seems to match the circumstances of either the later period of the Persian empire, or the early period of Greek rule, both of which raised similar questions, namely the importance of preserving Jewish distinctiveness even in the face of a relatively benevolent overlord. As later history would demonstrate, it was much easier to be fervent in devotion to traditional spiritual practices when such things were under threat. Esther's experience was meant to show that even those who were apparently well disposed to the Jewish cause could not always be trusted, and things might change literally overnight. It was always necessary to be vigilant, while at the same time recognizing that it

The book of Daniel and the Maccabean crisis

The story of these stirring and difficult times for the Jewish people is recounted in 1–2 Maccabees, which was not part of the Hebrew Bible but came into the Christian Old Testament textual tradition through the Septuagint. There is, however, one book of the Hebrew Bible which appears to reflect and comment on it: the book of Daniel. This is an obscure and complex book. Indeed, it is more like two books, for the first section contains a number of stories about a young Jew named Daniel who, along with his friends, faced opposition to his religion and way of life during the exile in Babylon (Daniel 1–6). But then the character of the book suddenly changes, and instead of telling stories about real people in plausible real-life situations it presents a series of grotesque visions. These depict the exploits of various mythological animals, and contain complicated speculations about the chronology of other Old Testament passages as they relate to the reigns of various unspecified kings (Daniel 7–12). In addition to this division in the book's contents, Daniel also has a linguistic division, for it is written in two languages, neither of which corresponds exactly to the two major sections of the book's message: Hebrew is used in 1:1 – 2:4 and 8:1 – 12:13, with Aramaic in 2:4 – 7:28. In addition to this, the vocabulary of Daniel is sprinkled with Persian, and even Greek, loanwords.

What, then, does this book mean, and why was it written? The answers to these two questions are very closely connected, for our understanding of the book's message will determine when we think it was written. We must therefore examine the two aspects of this book in some detail.

Stories about Daniel and his friends

This section of the book of Daniel is probably one of the best-known parts of the entire Bible. It recounts the adventures of a young Jew called Daniel who was taken off to exile in Babylon by Nebuchadnezzar in the course of an otherwise unknown attack on Jerusalem in 605 BC (1:1). He stayed there until at least after the triumph of Cyrus in 539 BC (6:28), and during this time Daniel and his friends were given the unexpected privilege of being educated in the king's own court. This, however, presented them with problems right from the start. For one thing, they were expected to eat food that was forbidden in Jewish tradition (1:3–17), and they were also required to worship a great statue that Nebuchadnezzar set up. They felt unable to do that and still remain faithful to their own religion, so as a punishment Daniel's three friends – Shadrach, Meshach and Abednego – were thrown into a furnace to be roasted alive. When they were miraculously saved from destruction, even Nebuchadnezzar himself was forced to admit the great power of their God (3:1–30). Daniel later found himself in a comparable situation during the reign of King Darius, thrown into a den of lions because he insisted on

was God alone who could ensure the nation's continuing safety. Paradoxically, the name of God is not actually mentioned in the Hebrew text of Esther, though the underlying logic of the story depends on the assumption that it was as a result of God's continuing care for the people that they were saved. The various additions to the story found in the Greek version include specific references to God, as well as other passages highlighting the role of dreams and visions, and also emphasizing how Mordecai's and Esther's prayers contributed to their final deliverance.

worshipping his own God – but again, he was unexpectedly delivered and Darius was forced to accept the supremacy of the God of Israel (6:1–28).

Many other stories about Daniel are found in other Jewish literature, including three significant additions to this book which are contained in the Greek version, but not in the Hebrew. The Prayer of Azariah (otherwise known as the Song of the Three Jews) consists of a poetic celebration of the experience of Daniel's three friends in the furnace, and includes extensive accounts of their prayers on that occasion. Another is the story of Bel and the Dragon, which shows Daniel exposing the deception of the priests by an idol called Bel, during the reign of Cyrus, and then causing a sacred serpent to burst – an action for which he is again thrown into a den of lions. Fed by the prophet Habakkuk, who is dispatched by God to keep him safe in such circumstances, Daniel eventually escapes what seems like certain death and the king is forced to accept the supremacy of Israel's God. The third addition, the story of Susanna and the Elders, comes at the end of the Greek text, though it seems to belong more naturally at the beginning of the story as it introduces Daniel as a child, showing him as one endowed with special wisdom and spiritual insight, whose timely intervention prevents the wrongful execution of Susanna, who has been falsely accused of seducing two elders of the community.

Apart from the stories of this book, nothing at all is known about Daniel. Some have suggested he may have been an ancient legendary figure, perhaps to be identified with the Daniel mentioned in Ezekiel 14:14, whose exploits are also recorded in the texts from Ugarit. But these stories are not told as part of a historical narrative. They are all intended to be moralistic presentations of the kind of experiences that were probably typical of Jewish life not only during the time of the Babylonian exile and the Persian empire, but also through into the Hellenistic period. They mostly emphasize that faithfulness to Israel's ancestral traditions would, in the end, lead to salvation, and the tables would be turned on Israel's opponents as they suffered the fate they had planned for others. There is also, however, an underlying emphasis on the horrific nature of the persecution that might need to be endured before deliverance would come, and it is this feature that, when combined with the historical allusions of the second section of the book, suggests that what may have been traditional stories of an earlier generation were brought together around the time of Antiochus IV's policy of enforced Hellenization, as a way of encouraging continued commitment to the faithful observance of Jewish Law and customs.

Visions of the future

The two sections are linked together by visions of four great empires. There is a story of how Nebuchadnezzar had a dream that he could not understand and, in the way of ancient Oriental rulers, he sent for his advisers to explain it to him (2:1–13). Where they failed, Daniel succeeded, and

Judith

The book of Judith is set in Judea after the return from the Babylonian exile, and concerns the resistance of the inhabitants of the town of Bethulia to a foreign general named Holofernes. Details of the story are taken variously to refer to Assyrians, Persians and Babylonians, but the core of it lies in Bethulia's resistance, inspired and led by Judith, a courageous widow who distracts Holofernes by her beauty and then, when he is drunk, decapitates him and takes his head back to the elders of the town.

In the preface to Judith in his 1534 translation of the Bible into

The book of Daniel and the Maccabean crisis *continued*

told Nebuchadnezzar that the dream was about four great empires, represented by a statue made of four different metals: gold, silver, bronze and iron. Nebuchadnezzar's own empire was the first of them (the golden one) and the others were to be empires that would follow on in turn (2:24–45). The fourth one would be the most terrifying of all, for 'it will shatter and

A Persian and a Median nobleman depicted on a frieze among the ruins of Persepolis. The second and third of the four empires in the apocalyptic vision in Daniel 7 have been identified with the Medes and Persians.

crush all the earlier empires' (2:40). But it will also have a weakness, for 'it will be a divided empire… part of the empire will be strong and part of it weak' (2:41–42).

The first of the visions in the second half of the book is very similar to that. This time, the four empires are depicted as four animals: a lion, a bear, a leopard and a fourth animal modelled on a goat. Again, the fourth one is to be even more terrifying than the others: not only did it have teeth

of iron with which to crush its victims, it also had a number of horns, capable of inflicting much terror. Indeed, the horns contended among themselves, until finally 'a little horn' with 'human eyes and a mouth that was boasting proudly' sprang up and 'tore out three of the horns that were already there' (7:1–8).

The precise identity of these kingdoms has been one of the most hotly disputed issues in the whole of Old Testament interpretation. But the book itself states clearly enough that the first empire was Nebuchadnezzar's (2:37–38), and if we start there the identity of the others becomes plain. The story of Belshazzar is probably meant to be a part of the first empire, for he is described as Nebuchadnezzar's son (5:2), but then comes a ruler of a different race, 'Darius the Mede' (5:31), and it therefore seems reasonable to suppose that he was the representative of the second empire. We certainly know that the power of the Medes was increasing in the years after Nebuchadnezzar's death, and they eventually joined with Cyrus the Persian in 550 BC, and thereafter were able to take over the Babylonian empire. Cyrus's Persian empire is the next one to feature in Daniel (6:8), and can therefore reasonably be identified with the third empire of the visions, which would make the fourth one the empire of the Greeks, founded by Alexander and subsequently divided among his successors. The symbolic language used of the fourth beast seems to allude clearly enough to the events following Alexander's death. One vision tells how 'at the height of his power his horn was broken. In its

German, Martin Luther suggested it was to be understood as an allegorical presentation of 'the victory of the Jewish people over all their enemies, which God at all times wonderfully guarantees... Judith is the Jewish people represented as a chaste and holy widow, which is always the character of God's people, while Holofernes is the godless or unchristian Lord of all ages.' Though to call it an allegory is an over-statement, that is still a fairly appropriate way of summarizing its message. Judith reflects and represents all that is most to be admired in the heroes and heroines of the books of the Hebrew Bible, and the way

In one of his visions, Daniel sees a raging goat moving so fast that its feet do not touch the ground, while hitting its enemy with great force. The description is of Alexander the Great, whose initial conquests were made with such lightning speed that they stunned the Persian opposition. The illustration is of Greek cavalry from Alexander's sarcophagus.

place four prominent horns came up, each pointing in a different direction. Out of one of these four horns grew a little horn, whose power extended towards the south and the east and towards the Promised Land... It even defied the Prince of the heavenly army, stopped the daily sacrifices offered to him, and desecrated the Temple. People sinned there instead of offering the proper daily sacrifices, and true religion was thrown to the ground' (8:8–9, 11–12). This corresponds so exactly to the events surrounding Alexander's death, the subsequent division of his empire among four of his generals, and the way in which one of those kingdoms later inflicted great persecution on the Jewish people under Antiochus IV Epiphanes, that it is impossible to imagine it could refer to anything else.

This impression is reinforced by later visions which describe the precise events leading up to Antiochus's arrival in Jerusalem, including the story of his visits to Egypt, his humiliation at the hands of the Romans, and his construction of 'The Awful Horror' in the Temple itself (11:21–31) – presumably the statue of Zeus he set up there. The Maccabean revolt which followed is also implied here: 'those who follow God will fight back... God's people will receive a little help, even though many who join them will do so for selfish reasons. Some of those wise leaders will be killed, but as a result of this the people will be purified' (1:32, 34–35). The fact that the hope of purification is in the future may well indicate that the book itself was written while the war was still in progress. It is perhaps slightly odd to find the brave efforts of Judas and his band of guerrillas described as only 'a little help',

in which she disposes of Holofernes has striking similarities to the stories of the exodus and of David and Goliath (1 Samuel 17), while her own personal disposition can be favourably compared to the stories about Sarah in Genesis 12–17.

The date of this book's composition could be more or less any time from about the fifth century BC onwards, though various political and religious allusions can be understood as referring to events and attitudes otherwise known from the second century BC, and that is where most scholars would place it.

The book of Daniel and the Maccabean crisis *continued*

Although Median influence grew after the reign of Nebuchadnezzar, it would have required the combined efforts of Medes and Persians to have toppled the Babylonian regime. Here a Median attendant leads two horses.

but some have concluded from this that the book of Daniel may have been the work of a Hasidean, who was still a bit uneasy about the Maccabean approach.

Despite the fact that this identification of the kingdoms of the book of Daniel makes the best sense out of other aspects of its message, some have argued otherwise. They point out that there never was a separate Median and Persian empire – and therefore the fourth empire would not be Alexander's Greek empire, but Rome. Others have wished to identify Alexander with the fourth empire, but used the same argument to suggest that

Daniel's historical sense is inadequate, and that he simply got it wrong when he seemed to infer that the Medes and the Persians were two separate kingdoms. But neither of these inferences is necessary:

● The Medes did develop their power even before the end of the Babylonian empire. Indeed, their position began to strengthen just after the death of Nebuchadnezzar in 562 BC. They subsequently united with the Persians under Cyrus in 550 BC, after which the two combined were able to achieve their imperial ambitions. They would probably

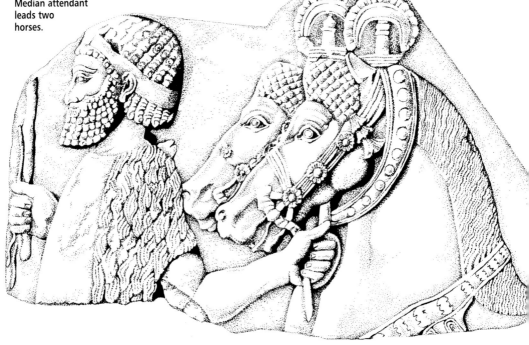

Tobit

The story of Tobit is set in Nineveh during the reign of the Assyrian king Shalmaneser IV (782–772 BC), and consists of two interwoven stories. The first shows Tobit as a man who is faithful to the traditional customs of Jewish spirituality, even when such things were unpopular. After ensuring that another Jew had been buried with proper concern for the regulations of the Torah, he found himself ritually impure and therefore needing to remain in the open air overnight. While sleeping, some bird droppings fell into his eyes, inflicting him with a blindness

---

not have been able to succeed separately, and in some places Daniel seems to reflect this quite clearly (5:28; 6:8; 8:20).

● We must also recognize that Daniel was using here a traditional literary scheme to describe these four kingdoms. It was quite common at the time to depict the activity of great nations by using the symbolism of the four metals gold, silver, bronze and iron. This literary device in effect required Daniel to have four kingdoms rather than three – whatever the facts might actually be. So he accommodated them by giving the Medes a semi-autonomous position which, had he been writing in a more historical style, he would probably not have done.

The book and its message

Interpreters of the book of Daniel are virtually unanimous in regarding it as a message of encouragement to those people who were suffering for their faith under the oppression of Antiochus IV Epiphanes. The visions of the second part of the book assure readers that, though things might seem to be out of control, their future – indeed, the whole of history – is in the control of a loving and all-powerful God. For the final terrifying beast is not overcome by their own efforts, but by God's personal intervention (8:25; 12:1–3), just as the great statue mentioned earlier in the book had been destroyed by a stone without any human assistance (2:31–35). That stone did not disappear, but 'grew to be a mountain that covered the whole earth' (2:35), and after these great empires have done their worst,

God 'will establish a kingdom that will never end. It will never be conquered, but will completely destroy all those empires, and then last for ever' (2:44).

This assurance that the world was not out of control must have meant a great deal to the beleaguered Jews in the early second century BC. But the book contains even more specific encouragement than that. For the stories about Daniel and his friends in the first section of the book have also obviously been selected with an eye to the circumstances that faithful Jews now had to contend with. Indeed, the prominence of Nebuchadnezzar in these stories may be intended as a conscious reference to Antiochus himself:

● The form of Nebuchadnezzar's name here is not the same as that found elsewhere in the Old Testament. But the word used in Daniel may have been intended to symbolize Antiochus. In Hebrew, as in many other ancient languages, names and words often had a numerical value, for each letter of the alphabet was also a number. It is unlikely to be a coincidence that when the numbers represented by 'Nebuchadnezzar' are added up they come to exactly the same figure (423) as the numbers of the name 'Antiochus Epiphanes'.

● The issue of food, which features so largely in the opening story of Daniel (1:3–16), was one of the crucial points in the whole argument about Hellenism. Much of the opposition that sparked off the Maccabean revolt was concerned with the unwillingness of faithful Jews to eat pork and other unclean foods.

from which no one could cure him, and which soon reduced him to poverty. Tobit sent his son Tobias off to Media to recover some money which he had left there. On the way, he met the angel Raphael, who accompanied him on the journey, in the course of which he also encountered a magic fish whose entrails then hold the key to the story's resolution. For on his arrival in the city of Ecbatana, Tobias met up with a Jewish woman named Sarah, who was a distant relative of his family. Married seven times, none of her marriages had ever been consummated because her husbands had all been attacked and killed first by a

---

The book of Daniel and the Maccabean crisis *continued*

● The worship of the great statue set up by Nebuchadnezzar (3:1–18), and the story of Bel found in the Greek text, also highlighted the same issues as Antiochus's action in setting up an image of Zeus in the Temple at Jerusalem. Indeed, in both cases it may be implied that the images were actually statues of the kings themselves. Even the story of Nebuchadnezzar's subsequent madness (4:19–33) may have been intended to be reminiscent of the commonly held belief that Antiochus was mad, because he thought of himself as an incarnation ('Epiphanes') of Zeus.

● Other details of the stories in the early chapters of Daniel are also similar to the conditions prevailing in the early Hellenistic age. Belshazzar, for example, falls from power because he defiled the sacred objects taken from the Temple in Jerusalem (5:1–4), in much the same way as Antiochus repeatedly robbed the Temple. The people of a later age would also recognize those Jews who collaborated with the unbelieving Seleucids in the duplicitous figures of the spies and informers who plotted against Daniel and ensured that he was shut up in the den of lions (6:1–14).

The book in its context

The book of Daniel is unlike any other Old Testament book. Its detailed descriptions of visionary experiences are found nowhere else in such proliferation. But books written in this style were to become increasingly popular in the two centuries before the start of the Christian era, and in the New Testament the book of Revelation is of a

similar type. These books have come to be known collectively as 'apocalypses', from a Greek word which means 'a revealing of secret things'. A number of special features make them readily recognizable and distinguish them from other literary genres:

● They are essentially literary works. In this respect they are quite different from the messages of the earlier prophets, who always used plain language that could be readily understood by anyone. The prophets also frequently used pithy poetic sayings that could easily be remembered, whereas the apocalyptic books are complex prose compositions. They contain long connected discourses, with many quotations and obscure allusions, and everyday events are invariably described in a symbolic way, often with many references to real or imaginary animals and monsters.

● They also often portray God as a transcendent, remote figure. Indeed, their whole emphasis is on the life of heaven rather than the everyday world of human experience. Events in this world are mentioned, but usually they are important only insofar as they are thought to reveal something about what is happening in some other, spiritual world. Because of this, the apocalyptic writings often emphasize dreams, visions and communications given to people by angels. God's plan for the nations is fixed and unchanging. The Old Testament prophets often gave the impression that the future course of history in some way would depend on how people responded to their messages. But for the apocalyptic writers,

demon called Asmodeus. Everyone thought Sarah must be responsible for what was happening, and when Tobias arrived she had been contemplating suicide. Raphael arranged a marriage between the two, and Tobias was able to banish the demon through the use of the fish's magic entrails. Raphael recovered Tobit's money, and the three of them then returned to Tobit's house in Nineveh, where his sight was restored using the gall from the same fish, after which Raphael returned to heaven – and the story ends with Tobit living into a long old age.

Almost certainly, this book was written in the early second century,

---

nothing could ever change the predetermined course of history as it moved to a final climax.

● This final climax is also to be revealed in a distinctive way. The new age is never thought of as part of the ongoing life of this world, but is either something that exists only in a different, heavenly world, or something that breaks into this world from outside by the direct personal intervention of God. This, too, is significantly different from the future hopes of most of the Old Testament prophets. For they generally expected a new age to dawn as a result of God's actions in the course of ordinary history, and insofar as an intermediary might be involved, it would be a human prince of the royal family of David rather than the kind of supernatural figures who appear in some apocalyptic books.

The apparent differences between apocalyptic and what seems to be the mainstream of Old Testament thinking have led many people today to regard all this as a rather eccentric and unprofitable sideline of later Jewish religious thought. It has often been dismissed as the result of alien influences being incorporated into the Jewish faith as a result of the exile. But there is more to it than that:

● The growth of apocalyptic must be understood within its own historical context. It is easy for readers who are detached from the hard realities facing the people of Judea at this time to dismiss their ideas as bizarre or irrelevant. The rise of apocalyptic was, however, directly related to changing

cultural circumstances and the corresponding need for theological redefinition. The prophets had suggested clearly enough that obedience to God would lead to prosperity, and disobedience would lead to hard times, and in a general sense the course of Israel's history up to the time of the Babylonian exile could be understood in a way that seemed to confirm this perspective. But in the days following the collapse of the Persian empire, things were quite different. With the arrival of an aggressive Hellenism under Antiochus IV, new questions began to present themselves, and the longer people agonized over the emerging situation the more obvious it seemed that the way to

prosperity must lie more in collaboration with people like Antiochus than in continued faithfulness to the old values of the Jewish faith. Those who tried to keep the traditional practices alive found themselves more and more in a minority, and those who prospered often did so not

The influence of Greek civilization throughout the eastern Mediterranean was enormous. Tadmor was a thriving city as early as the nineteenth century BC. However, its most dominant features today are remains of the endless rows of colonnades dating from Greek and Roman times.

probably in Hebrew though the only traces of it in that language are all fragmentary. The theme is a familiar one from this period, showing how the people could live in faithfulness to God's Law even in a hostile cultural context. Concern for the activities of angels and demons only emerged with the development of apocalyptic literature, and in later writings the book of Tobit became an important source for a Christian theology of angels. Tobit himself is presented as an example of holy living, faithfully observing the Law, then suffering in patience as a direct result of misfortunes stemming from his

---

The book of Daniel and the Maccabean crisis *continued*

by keeping the faith, but by ignoring it, or even abandoning it altogether. There were urgent questions to be answered: Why did faithfulness not lead to prosperity? Why were the righteous suffering? Why did God not put an end to the power of evil forces? And to add more weight to such questions, there seemed little sign of God's activity on the political and military front. God may well have raised up Cyrus in a previous generation, but in the period between Alexander the Great and Antiochus IV Epiphanes, Jerusalem had been captured at least ten times, while scores of major battles had been fought all over the country – and God was apparently nowhere to be seen. In facing up to facts like these, the apocalyptists asserted that all the present difficulties were only relative. They needed to be set in the broader context of God's overall control of the world and its destiny, and in that timescale, the righteous would eventually triumph and the oppressive domination of evil would soon be relaxed.

● There is an increasing body of opinion today that would regard apocalyptic not as an alien intrusion into the religion of the Old Testament, but as a legitimate – indeed, inevitable – development of the work of the great prophets themselves. Even in the earliest of the literary prophets (Amos) we find the expectation of a great day of crisis, 'the day of Yahweh', when God would step into history and inaugurate a new age of justice for the people (Amos 5:18–20). The same idea was developed by others, and passages in both Isaiah (e.g. 2:1–4; 9:1–7; 11:1–9) and Micah (e.g. 4:1–5) are couched in

such idealistic terms that they almost demand the apocalyptic perspective to give them some meaning. With the passage of time, these themes took on a greater importance, and when viewed from the perspective of Jewish experience during the exile and later it is not difficult to see how these earlier expectations were transformed into an altogether grander and more all-embracing vision. Some scholars have tried to link apocalyptic with the wisdom books of the Old Testament, through their common use of encyclopaedic lists, and interest in astronomy and chronology. If this could be sustained, it would again anchor it firmly in the centre of Old Testament thinking. But it is unlikely that its roots lie there, and it is more significant that the messages of Daniel are presented as in some sense a reinterpretation and new application of the messages of the earlier prophets (Daniel 9:1–2).

● From a Christian perspective, it is relevant to note that some of the most distinctive Christian beliefs seem to have originated among people who thought like this. It is unlikely that Jesus himself had too much sympathy for the apocalyptists of his day, but there can be no denying that the Christian understanding of life as a struggle against evil forces, together with the hope of future resurrection – not to mention the belief that history is moving towards a definite and meaningful goal – are clear developments of ideas that were first articulated in the writings of Jewish apocalyptists.

faithfulness, and engaging in traditional acts of piety such as alms-giving and prayer.

The end of the story

From the time of the Maccabees through to the Christian era, Jewish history was dominated by the issues that emerged in the course of these early struggles with Hellenism. The twin issues of politics and religion were to become inextricably interwoven as the Jewish people tried to reconcile their aspirations for a society in which God would be all-important with the plain fact that their world was dominated by rulers with a different world-view and spirituality. Within Jewish society itself, one political intrigue followed hard on the heels of another, until eventually the Romans stepped in and destroyed the Temple at Jerusalem in AD 70, and by the early part of the second century AD, Jerusalem itself had become a city just like any other in the Roman empire. A more comprehensive treatment of the social and religious history of this period is presented in the companion volume to this one, *Introducing the New Testament.*

It is clear that in the midst of this constant turmoil many ordinary people no doubt wondered what had happened to the ideals of the Old Testament stories. At the beginning of their shared history stood their ancestors Abraham and Sarah, a couple in whose lives God was a living reality, portrayed in personal terms as a friend to be known and loved, as well as a God to be worshipped. The same themes of God's love and the people's response had been repeated in the messages delivered by the great prophets, and was reflected in the compilation of Israel's historical narratives by both deuteronomic historians and the Chronicler, not to mention the codification of the Torah. But now, by common consent, the time of direct communication between God and the people seemed to have ended. In the closing decades of the first century BC, many groups in Jewish society were desperately searching for the word from God that would speak to them again in their own situation. Some sought for meaning in the solitary silence of the desert. Others looked in vain to the lurid speculations of the apocalyptists. And yet others concluded that their ancestral faith had lost its relevance, and sought fulfilment in political opportunism.

At the end of the Old Testament story we have a striking picture of God's people in turmoil, alongside a memorable reminder of God's continuing love even for people like this, for out of their failure of nerve the author of the book of Daniel fashioned a picture of a kingdom in which God alone would be the supreme sovereign. For Christian readers, of course, the whole of the Old Testament story needs to be viewed in the light of Jesus of Nazareth. The earliest Christians certainly viewed his life, death and resurrection as the climax without which this ancient story would be incomplete. They saw him as the one person in whose life God was most truly sovereign, describing him as the ideal descendant of David, the Messiah, of whom some of the prophets had dimly spoken. They identified him with 'the Son of man' to whom the authority of God's kingdom had been given in the visions of Daniel, and also as the true descendant of Abraham and Sarah. Not every reader of the Old Testament will wish to understand it from the perspective of Christian faith, and it is important to remember that this collection of literature also – and primarily – constitutes the scriptures of the Jewish faith. Either way, in addition to the Old Testament's value for its insights into the life of ancient Israel, it also highlights significant theological beliefs that go well beyond the times of which it speaks. In order to understand its message more fully, we need to give more detailed attention to this, and these are the themes which will occupy the remaining chapters of this book.

The books of the Maccabees

The books of 1–2 Maccabees are of special importance for understanding the history of the period immediately following the accession of Antiochus IV Epiphanes. The narrative of 1 Maccabees begins in the year of his coronation (175 BC) and ends with the death of Simon Maccabee in 135 BC, and 2 Maccabees documents events in the period from 176 to 161 BC.

1 Maccabees

While the various statistics and indications of dating contained in 1 Maccabees are not easy to integrate into a coherent picture, it is generally agreed that 1 Maccabees is closer to being a historical narrative than 2 Maccabees. It is a translation of a work that was almost certainly originally written in either Hebrew or Aramaic, and stylistically it bears some resemblance to the work of the Chronicler, incorporating official lists, genealogies and formal documents, along with carefully crafted speeches and prayers which are included at crucial points of the narrative, and which frequently serve as a means of highlighting the important lessons to be drawn from this painful period of Jewish history. The author is nowhere named, though must certainly have been a Palestinian Jew in view of his ability to write in a Semitic language, and must have been writing before the capture of Jerusalem by the Roman general Pompey in 63 BC. Most scholars date the work to the final decades of the second century BC, perhaps during the reign of John Hyrcanus (134–104 BC). Whoever wrote it clearly held a view not unlike that promulgated in Ezra and Nehemiah, in which ethnicity and spirituality were combined as hallmarks of true Jewishness. However, while the Maccabees are praised as the deliverers of their people, their mistakes are not overlooked, and what emerges has the feel of an authentic portrayal of this family.

2 Maccabees

Apart from the fact that they cover roughly the same events, the book known as 2 Maccabees has no obvious intrinsic connection with 1 Maccabees, and is so called merely because the two appear alongside one another in the various ancient manuscripts through which they are known. Indeed, whereas 1 Maccabees is clearly of Palestinian origin, 2 Maccabees itself claims to be some kind of summary of what were originally five volumes written by Jason of Cyrene, who is otherwise unknown. Since the book is introduced by two letters written to the Jewish community of Alexandria it is natural to assume this was the context in which it was written, quite probably at about the same time as 1 Maccabees, though there is no evidence that Jason had seen that book. Both the summary in 2 Maccabees, and the original sources from which it was taken, were originally written in Greek. The narratives contained in 2 Maccabees focus on the Temple in Jerusalem, its violation and rededication, interspersed with involved explanations of various aspects of Jewish law, which suggests that its readers were not as well informed about such things as they might have been. There is extensive praise for the martyrs of the Maccabean period, and in the New Testament 2 Maccabees 7:1–42 is referred to in this connection in Hebrews 11:35. Moreover, it also has a number of distinctive theological features, including an extensive angelology (e.g. 3:24–28; 5:2–4; 11:8), a clear belief in resurrection (7:11; 14:46), God's creation of the world from nothing (7:28), and a concept of eternal life and death (7:9, 14) which includes the notion of the living praying to God on behalf of the dead (12:43). The term 'Judaism', a designation for Jewish lifestyle and culture definition in opposition to 'Hellenism', appears here for the first time (8:1; 14:38).

3 Maccabees

This book has no connection at all with the Maccabees. Though it is found in the Greek Bible, it has never been included in the official lists of deuterocanonical books, and in literary style it is a similar work to Judith or Tobit, showing faithful Jews risking their lives for the sake of their beliefs, and being rewarded by God. It was probably written in Greek sometime during the first century BC.

4 Maccabees

This is a different kind of book again, and appears in an appendix to the Greek Bible. Its only possible connection to the Maccabees lies in the fact that events of that period are used as illustrations in some passages. It is essentially a philosophical reflection on certain aspects of Israel's history, which shows considerable signs of the influence of Stoic thought, especially in its insistence that the exercise of reason can control passion and help with resisting temptation. Since its allusions to events of the Maccabean period appear to be drawn from 2 Maccabees, it cannot have been written earlier than the first century BC, and possibly even later.

9 The Living God

Who is God?

The question, 'Who is God?' is as old as the human race itself. Philosophers and theologians, as well as countless multitudes of ordinary people down through the ages, have debated and discussed all the possible answers. To some, God is a kind of invisible 'force' who keeps things ticking over smoothly, maybe even to be identified with something comparable to 'the laws of nature'. To others, God is more specifically associated with the various features of the natural world, such as the sun or moon, trees or rocks, while yet others suggest that since the most significant aspect of existence is the human personality itself, then whoever or whatever 'God' might be will primarily be found in the depths of human experience. Surprisingly, perhaps, all these possibilities are actively pursued in contemporary Western culture. In spite of all the self-confident claims of philosophers during the past two or three centuries, inviting scepticism about the very possibility of religious belief, relatively small numbers of people would call themselves atheists. One of the more surprising facts about changing world-views in the twentieth century was that the number of atheists remained fairly constant at under 5 per cent of the population, while the popularity of spiritual world-views of all kinds increased exponentially, especially in the period from the 1970s onwards. At the start of the third millennium there is a great explosion of interest not only in traditional faiths such as Judaism and Christianity, or the great world faiths of other cultures, but also in the construction of 'designer spiritualities' which will be tailor-made to meet the personal needs of today's people.

Today's spiritual pilgrims tend to be orientated towards philosophical and theological abstractions as being the way to understand the complexities of the world and its workings. That is part of the legacy we have inherited from the time of the European Enlightenment, particularly the assumption that rationality is the only thing that matters. Because of this, any faith or world-view wanting to be taken seriously has been forced to express itself in analytical categories. This is not, however, where the Old Testament begins, and in order to comprehend its message it is important to try to understand the frame of reference within which its writers were operating. Of course, all readers will then want to go on to form value judgments on what it is saying. But in order for our opinions to be as well informed as possible, it is important to try to hear it first from within its own context. Far from arguing about God's existence, the Hebrew Bible simply takes it for granted, and we will look in vain to find any real discussion of the kind of case that might be put forward by the secular atheist. That is not to say that the Old Testament never expresses any searching questions about God's reality and activity; it contains at least one book which (in its original Hebrew form) never mentions the name of God at all (Esther), and another that puts a serious question mark against the idea that God really has a concern for the world and its inhabitants (Ecclesiastes). But even these books assume that God is there, and their questionings and probing are carried out in the context of a community which was well aware of the reality of the God whom it worshipped.

The actual statements made about God vary from one Old Testament book to another. New opportunities and fresh experiences of life pose new questions about many aspects of God's being and activity. 'The Song of Moses', an ancient poem celebrating God's greatness and goodness to the people of Israel, asks this rhetorical question: 'who among the gods is like you? Who is like you, wonderful in holiness? Who can work miracles and mighty acts like yours?' (Exodus 15:11). The implied answer, of course, is, 'No one,' and the poem ends with a commitment that 'You... will be king for ever and ever' (Exodus 15:18). Even at this early period in Israel's experience, they were certain that their God was more powerful than any other, and so must be given their undivided allegiance. They did not stop to ask whether other so-called 'gods' really existed. That was hardly necessary, for they knew in their own lives the reality and power of their own God.

The changing fortunes of the nation over the next 700 years, however, brought that question into clearer focus. In the face of great national disaster, some wanted to suggest that Israel's exclusive worship of just one God had been a major reason for their decline, and if they had paid more attention to the deities of other nations things might not have turned out as they did. But, taking their inspiration from the great prophets who had preceded them, the editors of the deuteronomic history, and also the Chronicler, were convinced that this was quite wrong. Far from allowing the events of Israel's history to turn them away from the exclusive worship of their own God, they felt even more confidence in trusting Yahweh, and went on to deny categorically that any other gods really could exist. The God of Israel was not one God among others – not even the most powerful of them – but, in the words of a later Old Testament prophet, could be described and celebrated as 'the first, the last, the only God; there is no other god but me' (Isaiah 44:6).

Given the immense timescale covered by the Old Testament books, it is to be expected that there will be evidence of how beliefs about God were redrawn from time to time. Nonetheless, the overall picture is consistent and quite clear in its main outlines: the God of whom it speaks is an all-powerful God, whose concern extends not only to the world of creation, but also to the events of history and to the lives of individual people. The changing contours of Israelite belief could be traced in a number of ways, but a good starting point will be to notice those things that particularly distinguish Old Testament beliefs about God from other ideas current in the world of its day.

God is invisible

Every nation with which Israel came into contact depicted its gods and goddesses in the shape of visible representations, such as statues. Animals were a favourite way to portray deities: the Egyptians used many such images drawn from the natural world, while the Canaanite culture represented at Ugarit used the image of a young bull, the symbol of life and sexual power, to portray Baal. There was nothing exceptional about this, and no matter where the origins of Israel as a nation can be placed, the cultural expectation would be that gods should have some form of tangible existence like this. It is not surprising that Israel should have taken it for granted that the same would be true of Yahweh also, and much of the Old Testament narrative history is concerned with the perceived tension between the cultural norms and the faith of Israel. While Moses was on Mount Sinai receiving the Law, his people were down below melting their gold jewellery to make a calf which could represent God, and become a focus for devotion (Exodus 32:1–35; Deuteronomy 9:7–21), but that was a relatively trivial matter when compared with the way this issue presented itself after the once-proud empire of David and Solomon had disintegrated to become the two states of Israel and Judah. At that time, the creation of two national shrines became a political as well as a religious necessity. King Jeroboam of Israel gave religious backing to his political stance by having golden bulls installed at the northern sanctuaries of Bethel and Dan (1 Kings 12:28–33). Both politically and theologically it is not difficult to appreciate his reasons for doing so. The population of his kingdom was ethnically disparate and religiously diverse, with some of his subjects looking to the stories of the exodus and the Sinai covenant as the inspiration for their faith, while others were giving their allegiance to the traditional deities of Canaanite culture. So what better way could there be of gaining the support of the more self-consciously Canaanite elements of the people than by making religious images that could be understood to represent their favourite god, Baal, while at the same time providing a substitute for the ark of the covenant which was now no longer accessible to worshippers in the northern kingdom, since it was still kept in the Temple at Jerusalem? Moreover, the ark itself had often been thought of as an empty throne that could give some visible form to the invisible presence of God – so could these bulls not now be regarded in the same way, as a mount for the invisible Yahweh to ride upon? Whatever Jeroboam's reasoning, and despite its obvious sophistication, he received the unreserved condemnation of the Old Testament history writers for his actions. Whether he had intended it or not, many people honoured these bulls as if they were themselves God, rather than symbols or icons, and as a result Jeroboam went down in history as the king who had 'led the people of Israel into sin' (1 Kings 14:16). It was a serious mistake to create any kind of statue that could be reverenced as divine. The belief that God is invisible is firmly embedded in every strand of the Old Testament. Visual representations are prohibited in the second of the ten commandments (Exodus 20:4–5; Deuteronomy 5:8–9), and the book of Isaiah contains one of the most sophisticated condemnations of idolatry to be found in any literature anywhere (Isaiah 44:9–20).

Canaanite religion centred on worship of Baal, god of fertility, sometimes portrayed as a young bull.

God and the forces of nature

Most of the religions in the world of ancient Israel were means of understanding and coming to terms with the power of nature as it affected the lives of men and women. In Egypt, the annual flooding of the River Nile was essential to the well-being of its people, and much Egyptian religion was therefore concerned with ensuring this would continue. Elsewhere in the region, the fertility of fields and flocks was bound up with the appearance of the rains at the right time of year. This was the case in Canaan, the land in which the people of Israel emerged as an independent nation during the Late Bronze and Early Iron Ages. Though many features of the sagas of traditional Canaanite gods and goddesses – El, Anat, Baal and others – are unclear, it is obvious that the activities of the gods personify the cycle of the seasons. For instance, the story of how Baal dies and is then restored to life by the sexual attentions of his lover, Anat, has close connections with the apparent death and rebirth of the life of nature that took place year by year as one season succeeded another. The historical narratives of the Old Testament show how there was continual tension between the way the people of Israel actually worshipped – using rituals and practices taken from the worship of Baal – and the kind of worship that was understood to be an authentic reflection of the nature of their own God, Yahweh. In the view of the prophets and the history writers, doing this was an indication that they were misunderstanding the character of God in some quite fundamental ways. For Yahweh was above nature, and not a part of it – and though God can on occasion be described in imagery derived from natural phenomena such as light or fire, it is never

acceptable to identify God with the forces of the natural world
(Exodus 19:18; Deuteronomy 4:33, 36; Psalm 104:2; Ezekiel 1:27–28).

God and the philosophers

The Old Testament never tries to define God. In one sense this is hardly
surprising, for in order to be greater than the sum of human intelligence
God must be beyond description. But that has not generally prevented
people from making the effort, and in the early centuries of the
Christian era readers of the Bible spent much time and energy trying to
decide how to describe God. The process still occasionally continues in
books of systematic theology, which can appear to be trying to define
God's being in abstract terms – almost as if there is some chemical or
mathematical formula that, if only it can be uncovered, will provide
access to the innermost depths of God's existence. This approach has a
long and venerable history, and owes a good deal to the work of the
great Greek philosophers who generally attempted to explain their idea
of 'God' in an abstract, or metaphysical, way. To answer the question,
'Who is God?' it therefore became necessary to ask a further question,
such as, 'What is God made of?' The ready acceptance of the validity of
such questions has had far-reaching repercussions for the ways in
which Christians in particular have articulated their beliefs. But this is
not the way in which the Old Testament thinks about God. Its writers
do not try to analyse God like a specimen under a microscope; indeed
the whole world of abstract ideas is generally quite foreign to their way
of thinking. Instead of defining belief metaphysically, by asking
what God is made of, they take a much more functional approach,
by exploring God's relevance to human life and experience.

A simple example will perhaps help to explain the difference
between these two approaches. If someone asked me to describe
my lover I could give two rather different answers. I might, for example,
describe her appearance – height, weight, colour of hair, colour of eyes
and so on. This would certainly answer the question, and it would allow
the questioner to form a mental picture of her appearance. But it would
also leave many things unanswered, and if the questioner really wanted
to get to know and understand my partner, it would be an altogether
unsatisfactory sort of answer. A more useful answer would include some
description of the kind of person that she is, illustrated with personal
anecdotes to show how she has reacted to life in particular circumstances. To give that sort of answer I need never mention things like the
colour of her hair, and I might well refer to vague and undefinable
notions such as 'love' as the key to her personality. I would certainly tell
stories rather than talking in abstract propositions, and for that very
reason this rather emotive description of my partner would quite likely
be more useful to most people than a more dispassionate one. From the
perspective of today's culture in the West, the storytelling approach
would correspond to what is generally called a 'postmodern' way of

Greek philosophers,
such as Plato,
speculated about
God's being. The
Hebrews were
interested in how
to relate to God.

dealing with life, whereas the more analytical one would be dependent on the philosophical assumptions of the European Enlightenment, many of which have now been seriously questioned, if not rejected altogether. In that sense, the Old Testament's way of addressing matters of truth is probably more accessible to today's spiritual searchers, for it takes what is, in effect, a 'postmodern' approach which answers the question, 'Who is God?' by laying all the emphasis on the way in which God relates to the world and its people, rather than attempting to analyse God's being in an abstract, 'scientific' kind of way.

What is God like?

In one sense, the entire Old Testament is the answer to this question. As we read its books we can see how they are all concerned to describe the different ways in which God has been made known through the experiences of the nation of Israel. At the very beginning of Genesis there is a series of ancient stories that tell how God relates to the world of creation. These are then followed by the long and complex accounts of God's dealings with the people from the time of Abraham and Sarah in the Middle Bronze Age (2000–1500 BC) right through to the time of the Persian empire and beyond, just a century or two before the start of the Christian era. Then, in addition to God's revelation through nature and history, the Old Testament contains many books showing how God relates to the more mundane circumstances of everyday life, either the corporate life of society or the personal spiritual experience of individuals. With such variety in its literature the Old Testament contains many different perspectives on the involvement of God in people's lives. But some themes are so common that they are obviously fundamental to the total picture of God that is presented here.

An active God

The Old Testament is distinguished from most other religious books by its great emphasis on historical stories. The messages of the prophets, as well as the history books themselves, all declare that God is most characteristically to be encountered in the varied events of Israel's national life. Other nations in the world of ancient Israel sometimes thought of their gods as being involved in political life, but what distinguishes the Old Testament is that God's activity is seen not in isolated incidents, but throughout the whole story. Indeed, it is only because God is at work there that the history has a coherent meaning at all.

Scholars of a previous generation often saw this as the main key to understanding the Old Testament, and laid all the emphasis on the notion of a 'God who acts'. This is perhaps too simplistic a way of describing the Old Testament faith, for some of its books scarcely mention God's actions in Israel's history at all. But there can be no doubt that this is one of its more distinctive features. Life is not just a meaningless cycle of empty existence, but has a beginning and an end, and events happen not in a haphazard sequence, but as part of a great design that in turn is based on the personal character of God. Moreover, this God is encountered by people in the ordinary events of everyday life, and not through tortuous intellectual debate. This confident assertion dominates the entire story, and from the early accounts of the call of Abraham and Sarah, right through to the apocalyptic visions of the book of Daniel, God is the one who is in control of history. In bad times as well as good, all that happens is dependent on God. Because of this overriding conviction, the way the Old Testament writers tell the story of their people is quite different from the approach of the modern historian. A modern reader may look for historical explanations of a particular event, assuming that if history makes sense at all it is a sense that comes from within itself rather than depending on the external influence of God. It is, of course, possible to read the Old Testament in this way, and to some extent this is what we have been doing in the chapters up to this point. But if we restrict our thinking to historical cause and effect we will miss an important dimension of what the Old Testament writers were saying.

GOD CHOOSES PEOPLE

The story of the people of Israel begins with Abraham, a typical merchant of the day who leaves his homeland in Mesopotamia and heads west and south to make a new life for himself and his family. Abraham's journey was, in fact, typical of many such journeys that were being made in the Middle Bronze Age (2000–1500 BC). People were moving in all directions through the Fertile Crescent, and Abraham was certainly not alone in making the journey from east to west in search of a new way of life. But this was not important to those who preserved the stories. For them, Abraham's migration was not just a symptom of demographic changes: it was an integral part of God's plan for his life. Not only was he to have a new lifestyle: he and his wife Sarah were to become the founders of a great nation. Through them God would 'bless all the nations' (Genesis 12:3). The driving force in Abraham's life – as in that of his successors – was the intention of a caring and all-powerful God whose love was to be shared with the whole world and its people.

This belief found its classical expression in the story of how a group of Abraham's descendants were released from slavery in Egypt (the exodus). Just as this story came to be the foundational epic from which the people took their national identity, so it is also at the very heart of Old Testament spirituality. For centuries afterwards, the people of

Israel looked back to this event to remind them of God's goodness and their responsibilities. Here again, it may well be that various details of the exodus story can be explained by reference to features of the geography or natural history of the area. But for Israel, it was more than just a story. The dramatic escape from slavery and their establishment as a nation in the land of Canaan was due not to social or geographical factors, but was the outcome of the personal action of God. Without that, the exodus could never have taken place, and Israel would never have become a nation. This is why, when later generations wanted to remind themselves of the character of their God, they turned especially to the exodus story. This event was celebrated in poetry and in song, and reported in family groups at every opportunity. It became the central focus of their faith, for not only did it remind them that God was active in history, it also gave a unique insight into the nature of that activity – and therefore into the innermost character of God.

GOD'S LOVE

This is a major theme running through the whole story. The slaves were powerless and weak. Even their leaders were uncertain of the future, and had the nation depended for its survival on human ingenuity and courage, then it would have failed. When later generations celebrated this great event, God's generous actions towards the people ('grace') were always in the centre of their thoughts. An ancient creed, recited as the first-fruits of later harvests were offered, put it like this: 'we cried out for help to Yahweh, the God of our ancestors, who heard us and saw our suffering, hardship and misery. By God's great power and strength we were rescued from Egypt' (Deuteronomy 26:7–8). The prophets took this story and put a powerful spin on it, to remind the people that God had shown a particular care for those who were victims of unjust oppression. For them, the exodus was not just a demonstration of God's powerful

Soldiers from Abraham's original homeland as depicted on the Royal Standard of Ur.

actions in history: it was also an experience of God's love, which found its truest fulfilment when it centred on those who were past helping themselves.

GOD'S POWER

God's power over the whole of life is another dominant theme in the exodus story. God acts in the lives of the people to bring about their salvation, and is also able to control the powers of nature itself. Yahweh meets Moses in the burning bush (Exodus 3:1–10), sends plagues on the Egyptians (Exodus 7:14 – 11:9) and parts the Sea of Reeds – and subsequently the River Jordan – to allow the escaping slaves to cross on dry land (Exodus 14:1–31; Joshua 3:1–17). Later again, God provides food and water in the course of the long desert journey, even sending flocks of birds to feed those who were hungry (Exodus 15:22 – 17:7). Nations are also under divine control, and God's purposes can be accomplished through both Egyptians and Canaanites. On some occasions they become instruments of judgment, at other times, of blessing – but always as part of God's loving purpose for the people.

GOD'S JUSTICE

At the heart of the exodus story is embedded the Old Testament Law, the *Torah*. It is significant that this is an integral part of the story of God's actions on behalf of the people. The Old Testament repeatedly emphasizes that God acts in accordance with clearly defined standards of justice, and never in an arbitrary or unpredictable fashion. The core of God's relationship with humankind is morality, and when a person encounters God it is always in the context of moral challenge. When Isaiah had a vision of God in the Temple, it was not the otherworldly, mystical or supernatural aspects of the experience that impressed him most. They undoubtedly played a part – that should not be under-estimated – but his first response was to confess his own inadequacy in the face of the great moral purity of God (Isaiah 6:1–5). When people encounter God, whether in temple or in exodus, they must first face up to the demands of God's justice.

Finding God in later history

It was in the process of trying to relate God's love, power and justice to the events of their national history that the prophets hammered out some of the most distinctive elements of the Old Testament faith. As time went on, it became increasingly clear that Israel's fortunes were closely connected to the international power politics of the day. Israel and Judah were just pawns in the strategic manoeuvres of the two superpowers based in Egypt and Mesopotamia who constantly vied with each other for domination of the Fertile Crescent. It often seemed as if these powers were in control of things, not God. What, then, was the value of God's promises – not only the promise to Abraham and Sarah, and the great deliverance of the exodus, but also the bold assurance to David that 'I will make you as famous as the greatest leaders in the world... You will always have descendants, and I will make your kingdom last for ever. Your dynasty will never end' (2 Samuel 7:9, 16)?

Viewed in this light, the facts of history raised many awkward questions. If Israel had been chosen by God, should they not be triumphant in all their battles? And if God was in control of things, how was it that other nations were so easily able to get the upper hand? The prophets had a clear answer to these questions. The fact that God had been personally revealed to Israel, demonstrating love and care in so many ways, imposed great responsibilities. As Israel were faithful to their calling, so they would prosper. But when they were unfaithful, then they would need to return and ask God's forgiveness. The misfortunes they suffered were all highlighted as evidence of that. This is how the editors of the book of Judges assessed Israel's early history, and it was a lesson that the prophets repeated in many a crisis of the nation's later life.

The people often misunderstood the nature of God's involvement in their history, and imagined this was a sign that they were God's favourites. But the prophets knew that God's purposes were never so restricted, and had always been motivated by a wider intention: the salvation of all peoples, as promised to Abraham. Though Israel had been the special recipient of God's love, and had witnessed such great acts of power, both love and power could only operate within the framework of God's justice. This conviction often brought the prophets into direct conflict with the politicians of their day. In political terms, they did not always take the same side. Isaiah, for example, could advise the king in Jerusalem that God would protect the city and all would be well in the face of an Assyrian invasion (Isaiah 31:4–5). But a few generations later, Jeremiah said exactly the opposite (Jeremiah 7:1–15). What united them was the knowledge that history was in God's control, and that things were being ordered in accordance with God's own absolute standards. Those who arrogantly set themselves up in opposition – whether Assyrians or Judahites – would be judged. And when the Babylonians took the king of Judah off into exile and later destroyed the city of Jerusalem, that was as much the work of God as the exodus itself had been (Jeremiah 24).

Many people found that kind of thing hard to understand. After all, their entire history seemed to suggest that God was on their side – and if so, how could a catastrophe such as the exile possibly befall them? It was at this time that Israel's historians compiled the story of their nation as we now have it in the Old Testament. The deuteronomic history, stretching from Deuteronomy to 2 Kings, retold the familiar stories in an effort to explain why God had apparently deserted these special people. Following the lead given by the prophets, it declares that Israel had been disobedient. They had failed in their God-given responsibilities, and had suffered the inevitable consequences. Others compiled the story of

Israel's earlier experiences, from creation to the exodus, and they too had a message for their people: disobedience had been a part of human life from the very beginning, but it was always balanced by God's grace and forgiveness. God's justice and God's love could not be separated. However, while the deuteronomic history had a sad and depressing tale to tell, the message from Genesis to Numbers was more encouraging, assuring those in exile that God's love would ultimately triumph.

But what about God's power? Had not the final days of Judah been, in effect, a battle not between two armies but between two sets of deities – and had not the gods of Babylon won? Where did the God of Israel stand in relation to the apparent power of other gods? This question had been faced in a practical way right from the earliest days, when the tribes had decided to worship only one God (Joshua 24:1–28). But they had not denied that other gods might exist – indeed, the enthusiasm with which they continued the worship of Baal suggests that some of them were not at all convinced that their own God really was all-powerful. Some of the earlier psalms (e.g. Psalm 47), as well as prophetic messages such as those found in Amos 1:3 – 2:5, had hinted that God was in control of the lives of people everywhere, and not only of Israel's destiny. But with the exile the question had become even more urgent, and it was given a very clear answer in some of the most remarkable passages anywhere in the Hebrew scriptures. In a series of prophetic messages, the God of Israel is declared to be the God of the whole world. Yahweh is all-powerful, and those who worship other gods are misguided as well as stupid (Isaiah 44:1–20). Far from being a sign of God's defeat, the exile had itself been God's punishment for the people. The Babylonians had indeed been used to accomplish God's purposes, but they in turn had been punished for their excessive violence (Isaiah 47:1–15). God's power was in no way diminished, and there was every expectation that a new deliverer would be raised up for the dispossessed people – this time, not a Moses from among their own ranks, but Cyrus, the emperor of Persia (Isaiah 45:1–4). The future would be even greater than the past had been, as God would move in a new way to fulfil the original intention of the promise given to Abraham and Sarah. God's servant, through whom this would be accomplished, would bring blessing to Israel, but would also be 'a light to the nations – so that all the world may be saved' (Isaiah 49:6).

A personal God

The fact that there is so much emphasis here on God's character being revealed in the great events of history may lead us to wonder if Israel's deity was not perhaps just a personification of 'fate', or even of 'history' itself. Many gods and goddesses of the ancient world were personifications of various aspects of the world of nature; could it be that the God of the Old Testament was just an embodiment of Israel's history? The question is not quite as simple as that, however. In traditional

Canaanite culture, for example, the world of nature seemed to go its own way regardless of human interest, and there was very little that anyone could do to change things. The best one could hope for was to escape the most vindictive aspects of nature by avoiding too much personal involvement with the deities who were in control of it. The Old Testament accepts that God is to be given due respect and honour, and recognizes that God's ways are often beyond human understanding – but it also emphasizes that relationships between people and God do not operate in a purely mechanical way. Indeed, it often goes out of its way to claim quite the opposite, affirming that God is intimately interested in both the world and its inhabitants, and is not at all remote from people and their needs. All the great events of the Old Testament stress that God does not act in a capricious, unpredictable way, but is only concerned for people and their good. Even more striking is the way in which God's love is expressed, for it is not the patronizing care of a moralist who knows what is best, and is prepared to ride roughshod over human need in order to achieve their own ends. Some of the most striking, and unexpected, stories in the Old Testament depict God entering into discussion with people, and even having a change of mind as a result (Genesis 18:16–33; Amos 7:1–6). All this may be a little difficult for people today to understand, with our emphasis on justice as an abstract quality operating in predictable ways. But it explains why morality and justice are so fundamental to the Old Testament view of God, for it is in the context of personal relationships that such qualities are most important.

The Hebrews saw God as one who acted out of love and justice, and never in a capricious or vindictive manner. This would have contrasted with the beliefs of other ancient peoples who spent much time appeasing potentially violent deities. Here the god Ningirsu is seen smiting with a club victims who are caught in his net.

How then does God relate to people? There is no doubt that the Old Testament lays much emphasis on the corporate experience of Israel as a nation. Although it was only Moses who went up the mountain to receive God's Laws, making it a personal experience in that sense, what happened there was not something private and individual, but a represen-tative experience in which all the people were included. The idea that one person could represent a whole nation in this way was widely held in the ancient world, where rulers were regularly regarded as the very embodiment of their nation. The term 'corporate personality' is sometimes used to describe this sense of national solidarity, though it is not a phrase found in the Bible itself and its importance has often been exaggerated. But it does draw attention to an aspect of Old Testament thinking that is sometimes difficult for modern Western people to grasp. The heritage of the Enlightenment has ensured that most of us are accustomed to thinking in terms of the work of an individual, and 'society' is often taken to be just the sum total of individuals living in a particular time and place. This kind of introverted individualism would have been a totally alien idea for the writers of the Old Testament, just as it has been to all cultures throughout the world, apart from the Europeans who first thought of it. The family, the village, the tribe and the nation were all of crucial importance in Israel, and a person could expect to find fulfilment in life only when she or he was in a proper relationship with others. Both happiness and misery were shared with other people, and a sense of social solidarity runs deep in the Old Testament, as it still does in many traditional cultures today. We find this most strikingly in the story of Achan, whose entire tribe was implicated in the wrongdoing of just one person (Joshua 7:1–26). There were clearly risks involved in being closely identified with others, but compared to the fear of being alone, such risks were very small. To have no friends, and to be an outcast, was the final indignity that an Israelite could suffer, for life only found its fullest meaning when a person was part of a broader community (Jeremiah 15:17; Psalm 102:6–7).

At the same time, it would be an exaggeration to suppose that people of the Old Testament period could see no meaning or purpose in life except in relation to their position as part of a large social unit. That

would be to press the idea of corporate personality to a logical conclusion that is never drawn in the Old Testament itself. The book of Psalms, for instance, contains many examples of prayers and hymns which show just how much worshippers in ancient Israel felt that God was personally interested in the details of their own everyday life, and the prophets also stressed the importance of individual commitment to the God who

Modern Western thinking tends to emphasize the individual over the needs of the community as a whole. Such an attitude is alien to the Old Testament, where a sense of social solidarity is deeply ingrained.

was revealed through the events of their national heritage. We would be quite mistaken to imagine that God only deals with people in large numbers. The same theme of God's personal care and concern is prominent in many of the Old Testament's best-known stories, for Abraham and Sarah and their children in a hostile land (Genesis 12:10–20), or for Joseph as he is sold into slavery (Genesis 37:12–36). Moreover, this kind of personal interest in people extends even to those who might be considered of no consequence, such as the boy Ishmael who, with his mother Hagar, was expelled from Abraham's family circle (Genesis 21:9–21). This sort of principle was enshrined in the legislation of the Torah, and in Jonah 4:11 God's pity includes not only the innocent children of the great city of Nineveh, but even the suffering animals in it.

Words for describing God

The importance of recognizing God as a person comes out clearly in much of the imagery used in the Hebrew Bible. The messages of the prophet Hosea apply the terminology of personal relationships to God and people in a particularly sensitive way. God is a loving mother to the people of Israel, who protected them and directed their footsteps from the very beginning of their national history, not only guiding them, but also caring for them: 'I drew them to me with affection and love. I picked them up and held them to my cheek; I bent down to them and fed them' (Hosea 11:4). According to Exodus 4:22–23, this was the message that Moses had given to the pharaoh of Egypt when he reminded him that Israel was God's 'firstborn son. I told you to let my son go, so that he might worship me.' And centuries later, Isaiah depicted God as a broken-hearted father whose children had rejected his guidance (Isaiah 1:2).

At other times God can be depicted as the husband of the people (Jeremiah 31:32; Hosea 2:14–23). After the fall of Jerusalem, God became for Ezekiel a generous stepfather who had rescued the city and its people from certain death (Ezekiel 16:1–7). The application of imagery drawn from family relationships to describe God came naturally to people who experienced God as an essentially personal being, encountered primarily in everyday relationships. It is fashionable in some circles to dismiss the Bible's metaphors for God as hopelessly patriarchal and masculine, but this is far from an accurate appraisal of the facts. God could be described as a father not because God was supposed to be male, but because the divine–human relationship can be as close and life-giving as the best of human family ties. The fact that God can also be described as a mother merely serves to underline the reality that the Bible does not present God in a gender-specific way. What is more, this can be traced throughout all periods of the evolution of the Old Testament as we now have it. 'The Song of Moses', for instance, is widely acknowledged to have originated in a very early historical period, and it contains this statement: 'You deserted the Rock who fathered you; you forgot the God who gave you birth' (Deuteronomy 32:18). God is here represented as the divine parent, both male and female. Elsewhere, God cries out 'like a woman in labour' (Isaiah 42:14), and showers the people with the affection of a mother (Isaiah 49:15; 66:13) – while Psalm 131:2 compares God's love with quiet rest in the arms of a divine mother. When you remember that all this was written in an ancient male-dominated culture, and that the major challenge to Israel's faith came from a traditional Canaanite religion which gave a high profile to sexual worship of the female form, then the acceptance of female imagery with which to describe God is all the more striking. The same inclusive quality of God's being even features on the very first page of the Hebrew Bible, where both women and men are described as made 'in the image of God', a statement that would most naturally imply that there is some aspect of God's own being that corresponds to both femininity and masculinity as those characteristics can be identified within human experience (Genesis 1:27–28).

The Old Testament has often been unfairly criticized for offering a very narrow understanding of the nature of God. The reality, however, is quite different, and the sheer variety of images invoked to explain God's person and purposes shows all the signs of a creative and imaginative people, no doubt struggling as they tried to explain the inexplicable, but certainly not falling back on safe and predictable language. It is this buoyant and lively imagery that has ensured the message of the Hebrew scriptures still speaks relevantly to people of many later times and places.

This is not to say that the Old Testament does not also include more strident imagery to describe God from time to time. God does indeed appear as ruler and sovereign of the people, sometimes in a very literal way. In some early narratives, God is depicted leading the people into battle as their army commander ('Yahweh, God of hosts'), something that was apparently symbolized by the ark of the covenant (1 Samuel 4:1–4; Psalm 24), and though from the time of Saul onwards a human king played a leading role in the affairs of the people, there was still a considerable emphasis on the fact that in reality God was Israel's only true king. Indeed, the Old Testament historians pass their verdict on the various kings of Israel and Judah mainly in relation to whether they have been prepared to recognize that greater kingship of God. This was clearly an important concept, for even when the idea of kingship is not explicitly mentioned, much of the imagery used in speaking of God comes from such a background. The well-known Psalm 23 refers to God as the people's 'shepherd', imagery which to us may suggest a different background altogether, but in the ancient world kings were often referred to as the 'shepherds' of their people, and this is almost certainly what the psalmist had in mind.

It is easy to see why the kingship imagery should have seemed appropriate for describing God, for the rescue of the slaves from Egypt was exactly the kind of thing that any good king would have done for his people. An earlier chapter has already drawn attention to some striking similarities between the covenant formulations of the Old Testament and the way in which a subject nation might define its relationship to a greater power that had delivered it from an enemy. Israel's allegiance to God as king was the grateful obedience of those who had been set free, not the fear of those who had been defeated. This is the context in which statements enjoining the people to 'serve' or even to 'fear' God are to be understood (Psalms 113:1; 123:2). Sometimes the expression 'the fear of Yahweh' is just a term to describe religious worship (Psalm 19:9), but more often it indicates an attitude of mind which recognizes the appropriate differences between God and people. In terms of contemporary usage, words like 'reverence' or 'honour' capture more of the original meaning than 'fear', and this is how many modern versions of the Old Testament translate it. To fear God in this sense has little connection with popular pictures of an angry God before whom men and women can only cower in insignificance. It is rather a matter of giving God an appropriate place in the scheme of things, and the importance of recognizing that God is so much greater than humankind is a common Old Testament theme. Even the prophets, who

God's name

The fact that God is to be understood in personal terms is highlighted by the emphasis the Old Testament places on God's name. In the ancient world a person's name was much more than just a label:

● A person's name established a person's identity, and revealed their character. So, for example, in the early stories of the book of Genesis, Eve (3:20), Cain (4:1) and Noah (5:29) are all given names that indicate something about their personalities. Later, all twelve ancestors of the Israelite tribes have names that reflect either the nature of the recipients or the experiences of their parents (Genesis 29:31 – 30:24).

● Knowing a person's name, or giving a name to someone, was often a way of gaining authority over that person. As the creator, God gives the stars their names (Psalm 147:4), and in naming Israel God asserts some sense of ownership of the nation (Isaiah 43:1). Similarly, when Jacob wrestles with an unknown deity, he first wants to discover that god's name so that he may establish a proper relation- ship with whoever or whatever it is (Genesis 32:29–30). To know the name of a god could therefore be very important, for a god's name gave the worshipper access to power. By invoking a god's name, the presence of that particular deity could be assured. Calling on God's name in this semi-magical way is expressly forbidden in the ten commandments (Exodus 20:7). For the Old Testament writers, God's name was not to be discovered and manipulated by mortals, but was something only God could reveal in the context of a loving relationship with the people.

What is God's name?

Because of this, there is an extraordinary reverence for God's personal name throughout the Old Testament. The reticence to mention the name of God is so widespread that we do not even know for certain how it was pronounced. Hebrew has no vowels, and this name was written down as YHWH. Vowel sounds are needed to pronounce it, of course, but we do not know precisely which sounds were used. By the time the Hebrew Bible emerged in its final form, Jewish religious teachers regarded the personal name of God as too sacred to say and whenever they came across it in reading the scriptures they would substitute the Hebrew word 'Adonai', which means 'my lord'. In this way, the vowels of 'Adonai' came to be pronounced with the consonants of God's name YHWH, to produce something like the English term 'Jehovah'. Nowadays it is customary to write this name as 'Yahweh', and this is the form we have used here.

It is often supposed that this avoidance of God's personal name was a relatively late development within Judaism, though traces of the same reticence can be found throughout the Old Testament. For example, in the stories of Joseph, God's name Yahweh is never found on the lips of non-Israelites (Genesis 37–50), and there is a whole section of the book of Psalms which avoids using it (Psalms 4–83). Other parts of the Old Testament use the expression 'the Name', instead of speaking directly of God (for example Psalms 5:11; 7:17; 9:2, 10; 18:49), and in Deuteronomy it is God's 'Name' that is bestowed on the Temple in Jerusalem to signify God's presence and blessing there (Deuteronomy 12:11; 14:23, and so on). By saying that it was 'the

regularly claimed to have access to God's innermost secrets and to be on close personal terms with God, nevertheless display a strong sense of awe and reverence as they describe how they have been in God's presence and heard the messages they were to deliver.

It is essential to realize that all these images are attempts to describe a phenomenon that is essentially indescribable. They help to portray

---

God's name
continued

Name' and not Yahweh in person that was dwelling in the Temple, the Old Testament was able to avoid the notion that God was restricted to just one locality, and yet still assure the people that the worship in the Temple had special power to put them in touch with the reality of God's presence.

What does Yahweh mean?

From a purely linguistic point of view, a number of suggestions can be made. The word Yahweh could, for example, be related to an Arabic word meaning 'blow'. Some scholars have argued from this that Yahweh was therefore originally the name of a storm god. Others have suggested that the clue to its meaning is to be found in a shortened form of the name Ya'u, which is known in Babylon and other parts of the ancient world. Or perhaps it was originally just a shout of excitement used in the context of religious worship which was subsequently taken and used as a proper name. Of course, explaining where a name comes from is not the same thing as understanding what it means, and the Old Testament gives a quite distinctive meaning to it. When Moses asks on whose authority he is to go and demand the release of the slaves from Egypt, he is told: 'I am who I am. This is what you must say to them: "The one who is called I AM has sent me to you"' (Exodus 3:14). Even this explanation is not without ambiguity. Several centuries later, when the Old Testament was translated into Greek (Septuagint), this phrase was taken as an indication of God's eternal existence, along the lines of Greek philosophical speculation of that period. But in the original context of Moses' encounter at the burning bush it is obvious that, although the name

Yahweh is related to the Hebrew verb 'to be', the emphasis is not on God's existence as such, but on God's activity. It is, like the rest of the Old Testament story, a declaration that God is characterized by actions, the name is intrinsically connected with the nature of the one who bears it, and knowledge of the name provided the assurance to the slaves in Egypt that God was active on their behalf. This God was the one who controlled time itself, and could be trusted for the future because of what had taken place in the past, and was going on in the present.

Other names for God

According to Exodus 6:3, Abraham and the others of that generation did not know God by the personal name Yahweh, but instead worshipped a God called 'El Shaddai' (Genesis 17:1). However, the name Yahweh is actually used in the narratives right from the beginning of the story, and is expressly said to have been given to Abraham and Sarah as the name of the God who led them out of Meso-potamia (Genesis 15:7). In addition, Israel's early ancestors are often said to have worshipped a deity who is simply called 'the God of the ancestors'.

These differences can be explained by reference to the theory that the first five books of the Old Testament were compiled from a number of different sources, one of which used the name Yahweh from the very beginning and another not introducing it until the time of Moses. But others have suggested that the matter is not quite as straightforward. They draw attention to four features in particular:

● The research of Albrecht Alt has shown that the worship of gods identified as 'the

some of God's characteristics insofar as they can be illustrated by reference to what we know and experience in human relationships. Emphasizing some aspects of the picture at the expense of others will inevitably lead to grotesque distortions. By concentrating on any one of them to the exclusion of the others, it is easily possible to misrepresent what is being said here. The sense of reverence and wonder expressed

---

god of the ancestors' was widespread among many tribes in the ancient world.
● We also know that the name 'El' was widely used as a name for local gods. The Ugaritic texts depict El as the father of the gods and head of the pantheon, though there were many local manifestations of this same deity.
● Moses apparently knew nothing of the worship of Yahweh until his meeting with Jethro in the desert of Midian. It was certainly in that area that Moses had his experience at the burning bush (Exodus 3:1–6), and it is notable that after the exodus from Egypt, Jethro reappears in the story and offers a sacrifice to Yahweh (Exodus 18:10–12).
● When Joshua and his people enter into a solemn agreement to worship only Yahweh, it is stated that both in Mesopotamia and in Egypt their ancestors had worshipped other gods (Joshua 24:14–15).

These apparently diverse facts can be explained in a variety of ways. Some have proposed that the worship of El and worship of Yahweh were originally quite distinct and separate. El was identified by the patriarchs with the high god of Canaan, of whom we know from other sources, and Yahweh was originally the mountain god of the Kenites, whose worship was adopted and reformed by Moses on the basis of the exodus experience. Then, eventually, either in the days of the judges or during the later monarchy, the worship of Yahweh became dominant and took over its more primitive predecessor. Others, however, take a different line, arguing that all these names (and others) used for God by the patriarchs referred to the one deity who was later

called Yahweh. To speak of 'the god of the ancestors' would then be just another way of referring to 'El', and 'Yahweh' was the way to address this one God in the context of worship.

This second view has more to commend it, not only because it is closer to the overall theological stance of the Old Testament itself, but also because it recognizes the reality of the fact that early Israel emerged from a religious context that was essentially diverse and syncretistic. There is plenty of evidence to show that the Old Testament was never averse to taking over both imagery and ideas from other religious contexts, just as long as it could be useful in giving authentic expression to Yahweh's known personality and behaviour. In suggesting that the earliest ancestors used traditional ideas from their cultural environment when thinking and speaking about their own experiences of God, the Old Testament's editors were not meaning to diminish Yahweh's power, but to enhance it, by demonstrating that Yahweh was able to do all that the Canaanite El was supposed to do, and much more besides. Whether the people knew it or not, it was none other than the God of the exodus – Yahweh – who had been the guiding force in the life of their nation from the very beginning.

by people in the presence of God will always seem to be in tension with passages that describe God in terms of intimate family relationships. But it is a creative tension, because the gap between God's perfect being and the imperfect world of humanity, which it apparently implies, is bridged by God's loving actions in saving and blessing. In order to make sense of that, it is essential to understand God not as an unseen force or an abstract will, but in personal terms, with all the ambiguities that that involves.

When God is absent

The Old Testament is dominated by the conviction that God's character is revealed most fully in dealings with people, both in history and in personal experience. It is in the common round of everyday life that people meet God. The fact that God is related to the world in which we all live, rather than being relegated to some esoteric, 'heavenly' world, is one of the great strengths of the Old Testament faith, though it can also look like one of its greatest weaknesses. For the plain fact is that we do not normally see events such as the exodus taking place all around us – nor do many of us have experiences similar to that of Isaiah when he stood in awe before God's glory in the Temple (Isaiah 6:1–7). So how realistic and relevant is the Old Testament's picture of God?

As with other aspects of its message, the Old Testament is more subtle and sophisticated than it can be made to seem. The triumphalist view of God's activity in history and personal experience is by no means the only element in its picture of God. God's hiddenness was no less a problem to people in the Old Testament world than it can be today. At the very time when they needed God's assistance to make sense of life, people often found it most difficult to find any traces of divine activity. The facts of history did not always portray the inevitable progress of an all-powerful God, nor did the facts of everyday life always give Israel the assurance that a living and personal God stood alongside them. There were times when life seemed to be quite the opposite, with evil and suffering as the dominating influences of human existence. How then did God relate to this darker side of life? Was Yahweh a God for bad days as well as for good?

The Old Testament takes full account of the fact that there are times when it seems that God, far from being powerful and active, is lost in the depths of human pessimism and despair. This honest recognition of God's apparent absence from the scene is most striking in the book of Psalms, which provide a series of fascinating glimpses into the life of a nation at prayer. Many psalms are great celebrations of joy and optimism, telling the people of God's mighty works and great love for them, and these psalms would no doubt be the ones that were used with enthusiasm at the great religious festivals, as Israel looked back on the major events of their history and traced God's goodness in them. But for every jubilant psalm there are two or three others in which the worshippers express not joy, but sorrow and dismay. Even those with a quiet confidence in God often recognize that spiritual meaning has to be sought in times of 'deepest darkness' (Psalm 23:4), while others complain that life's realities seem inconsistent with the reports of God's mighty deeds in the past (Psalm 44).

Hermann Gunkel's classification of the psalms into five main types has already been highlighted in a previous chapter, and it is significant that only two of these five categories celebrate the triumphs of God in an unreserved way. The other three are all concerned to varying degrees with the fact that God's activity and presence were not always obvious. Indeed, when the psalms are categorized using Gunkel's system, there turn out to be far more of the individual songs of lament than of any other type. Other poems included in this collection express the feelings of the whole nation, as it tried to come to terms with the difference between the great promises that God had made and the less thrilling realities of ordinary life. There is a strong thread of moral and religious realism running through the whole fabric of the Old Testament; God's apparent absence from the world and from human experience is one of its major themes.

When disaster struck, did it indicate that God was impotent or not interested in intervening?

Personal alienation

This is prominent even in the most striking Old Testament stories. Although Abraham, for example, is indeed depicted as someone of great faith who 'put his trust in the Lord' (Genesis 15:6), he also found God's intentions so puzzling and so difficult to reconcile with what he believed about God's character that he was even found arguing with God about it all (Genesis 18:16–33). Moses' experience is quite similar. He is described as having a closer and more direct experience of God than any other Old Testament character, for 'Yahweh used to speak with Moses face to face, as one speaks to a friend' (Exodus 33:11) – but at the same time, Moses' life was full of questions and complaints, as he tried to reconcile God's promises with what he saw going on around him (Exodus 5:22–23).

Nor are the prophets exempt from feelings of doubt and uncertainty about God's intentions. Elijah, for example, won a great and famous victory in the name of God, as the prophets of Baal were put to flight and their specious beliefs were repudiated (1 Kings 18:1–40). But almost immediately after that, it seemed as if God had deserted him, and Elijah suffered an extraordinary attack of uncertainty and doubt about the reality of God's power (1 Kings 19:1–18). For Jeremiah, doubt and uncertainty were a major influence in his life. On the one hand, God had explicitly told him, 'I chose you before I gave you life, and before you were born I selected you to be a prophet to the nations' (Jeremiah 1:4), and he had on many occasions been assured of God's continuing love and protection. Yet, on the other hand, God seemed singularly reluctant to back him up, and a quarter of a century after Jeremiah had first announced the doom of Jerusalem, nothing had happened except that a new mood of national optimism and self-confidence had swept over the city. In the light of that, Jeremiah had to question God's ways: 'Why are wicked people so prosperous? Why do those who are dishonest succeed?' (Jeremiah 12:1). At another time he even wondered why God allowed him to be born at all: 'Was it only to have trouble and sorrow, to end my life in disgrace?' (Jeremiah 20:18). Of course, the prophet knew that God had indeed spoken to him, but that did not make it any easier to come to terms with God's apparent remoteness. The passages in which Jeremiah addresses his complaints to God (the 'confessions', Jeremiah 11:18–23; 12:1–6; 15:10–21; 17:14–18; 18:18–23; 20:7–18) are remarkable for their frankness, and show the depths of despair and questioning to which even those with a personal knowledge of God in their lives can be driven.

National despair

It was not only individuals who often had to look hard to find God at work in their lives. The whole Jewish nation found itself in a similar crisis after the fall of Jerusalem to the Babylonian king Nebuchadnezzar in 586 BC. A once-proud nation had been brought to its knees by events that shattered all their expectations of God. Looking to the past, they could recall God's gracious actions through previous leaders of their nation, as they reminded themselves of God's unfailing promises to earlier generations. But what value could be placed on such a glorious past in the light of the harsh realities of exile in a strange land? The promises had apparently failed, and evidence of God's involvement with the people was now hard to find.

Much of the Old Testament story was hammered into shape on the anvil of this experience. Its pages often reflect the deeply felt anguish of those who survived this great tragedy, as they asked the inevitable question, Why should this have happened in a world controlled by God? In response to that the deuteronomic history asserted quite plainly that national disgrace was the outcome of national wrongdoing. But in looking to the past it did not give a simplistic explanation of the present. For although it emphasized God's great goodness in events such as the exodus, or the establishment of David's throne in Jerusalem, it also reminded them that there had been many a crisis in the past too. The exodus itself had been God's answer to a critical situation faced by the enslaved tribes in Egypt. God can hardly have seemed very real to them in Egypt – but one of the lessons of history was that God's mighty power had often burst in to change the lives of those who were least expecting it.

There could be no doubt that the exiles were suffering as a result of their nation's disobedience. A God whose character was defined in terms of justice and moral standards could not easily turn a blind eye to the rotten state of Jewish society. But though it might seem as if the stringency of

God's justice was greater than the power of God's love, nevertheless the promises could still be trusted and in the end would bring blessing upon the people. This was the view that finally triumphed and transformed the dead husks of exile into the seed corn of new life. Just as in the experience of the prophets and of people such as Job, so here there is no real effort to explain why God seemed to be hidden from the people at their time of dire need. But there is a clear practical message for those who found it difficult to see God at work in their lives. As men and women contemplated the suffering and injustice of their present existence, they were forced to confess that God really is different from humankind, dealing in apparently inscrutable ways. Yet alongside this they could place the evidence of God's

Wrestling with a hidden God

The apparent hiddenness of God is a major theme of one of the great masterpieces of the Old Testament: the book of Job. The book itself begins with an idyllic description of the life of its hero who was a successful man in every respect, surrounded by the material trappings of prosperity, as well as by an affectionate family group. He was also exceedingly upright and religious, and his lifestyle and disposition both show him as a paradigm of virtue. But then things change. God, depicted here as the president of a heavenly court, receives a formal request from the prosecutor (Satan) who suggests that Job is righteous only because he finds that it pays handsome dividends. So the prosecutor is given permission to put him to the test in order to ascertain the value of his faith. One calamity after another comes upon Job and his family, until he is reduced to misery and poverty – the exact opposite of his circumstances at the beginning (Job 1:1 – 2:10).

This ancient story serves the purpose of setting the scene for what is the main theme of the book, namely an extended discussion among Job and his friends about the nature of evil. The book of Job belongs to the wisdom literature of the Old Testament, and its main concern was to answer the questions that were raised by the story: If God rules the world, why do good people suffer so much? Wisdom teachers from Babylon to Egypt and

beyond had wrestled with this problem long before the author of Job, but two things gave it special urgency in Israel: Israel believed that God was active in controlling the life of this world, and Israel also believed that God acted in accordance with strict concepts of morality. The standard answer to the problem was easy, and is in fact represented in some other wisdom books, notably Proverbs: those who were prosperous must be good, and those who suffered must be evil. But it is often difficult to reconcile that with the facts, especially in the case of a person like Job. Of course, his friends were incapable of understanding that, and though they sympathized with Job in his suffering they were quite sure that – regardless of what he thought – he must have sinned against God and brought his suffering on himself. Job knew that he had not done so, and was convinced that the simplistic theology of his friends was quite misguided, even though that in itself did not make it any easier for him to see God at work in his own life: 'I have searched in the east, but God is not there, nor have I found any trace when I searched in the west' (23:8). But he never abandoned his certainty that, though it may be hard to discern, 'God has been at work in the north and the south' (23:9). Indeed, it was worse than just being blind to God's purpose, for it was God's very hiddenness that concerned Job most of all: 'It is God, not the dark, that makes me afraid' (23:17).

The meaningless cycle of Job's

mighty acts in history and in personal experience, both of which gave the assurance that though God may be hidden by the gloom of present experience, that did not mean the world had been abandoned to its fate, for to those who kept the faith the future would offer something even more glorious than what had been lost.

How can God be known?

Finally, we must turn briefly to consider some of the assumptions behind the Old Testament's view of God's relationship to people. Two themes are especially important here.

Wrestling with a hidden God
continued

existence is eventually broken when, after more conventional wisdom from his friends, God personally confronts the sufferer in a great storm (38:1 – 40:2; 40:6 – 41:34), something which reminds Job of God's greatness and might by drawing his attention to the complexity of the world and its workings. In the face of this, Job can place his own questions in their proper perspective: 'I know… that you are all-powerful; that you can do everything you want' (42:2). But what is the answer to the main question? Certainly there is no intellectual discussion here of the presence and power of evil in the world. But it is typical of the Old Testament that even a topic such as this should not be dealt with in an abstract, philosophical way. God is known to humankind not in flights of fancy, but in the reality of divine encounter. Job had appealed to God to answer him, and that is what happened – not in a way that he might have expected, but in a way that ultimately reminded him that, however difficult it might be to understand life's bitterest experiences, and however hard it might be to perceive God at work, nevertheless God was there, and to those who were prepared to seek diligently (unlike the friends who looked for easy answers) God would ultimately be revealed.

Another Old Testament book which tackles similar questions is Ecclesiastes, though its answer is very different from Job's. Indeed, it lays so much emphasis on God's apparent absence from the world

that the Jewish rabbis were reluctant to accept it as a part of scripture. Like Job, this book contains no mention of the great events of Israel's history in which God's hand had so clearly been seen. But unlike Job, it has no clear conviction that God's workings can be seen anywhere in the world at all. Job never actually loses sight of God, even if only in the negative sense that he blames God for his misfortune. The writer of Ecclesiastes does not actually deny that God exists (2:24–26; 3:13; 8:15), though the whole book seems to suppose that God's existence is fundamentally irrelevant, for the author is unable to see much evidence of it in the practical issues of everyday living. For Ecclesiastes, life is essentially meaningless in itself, and the most anyone can do is to try to enjoy what they have while they are here to enjoy it. This might seem a very negative attitude to take towards God. But it is more faithful to human experience than the fanciful and unsatisfying theology of Job's friends. The fact is that human life cannot be reduced to simple formulas – nor can faith in God. Not only Ecclesiastes, but also the whole of the Old Testament, bears witness to the fact that a faith which comes too easily has a certain lack of reality. The experience of honest and searching doubt is often the prelude not to a loss of faith, but to a deeper and more satisfying understanding of God's ways.

God's grace

It was not unusual in the ancient world for the gods to be portrayed almost as if they were a race of superhumans. It is of course inevitable that when people talk about God they should use human analogies to do so, and the Old Testament is no exception. It describes God in very bold figures of speech, describing God's hands or eyes, and imagining God crying and laughing, and sharing in other emotions that can be compared to human feelings. But for all that, there is a clear consciousness that in terms of essential being God is quite different from people, and the way God behaves is not simply to be deduced through a rationalization of the way men and women behave. Moreover, God cannot be bullied and cajoled by magic, or blackmailed in any way, and if God becomes known in the lives of men and women it is not because of discoveries made by people, but through initiatives taken by God.

This affirmation is central to the Old Testament faith: all relationships with God are based on God's own actions in grace and love. It is God's intention to be committed to the whole human race, and it is as a means to that end that Abraham and Sarah are chosen (Genesis 12:1–3). In behaving this way, God acts freely, with the only motive being to shower love on the people who live in this world. At every significant point of the story thereafter, the Old Testament emphasizes that God's own gracious actions are the starting point for any kind of meaningful spirituality. The exodus itself happens because God sees the plight of the slaves and takes pity on them – not because the enslaved tribes ask for it – and individuals can enjoy renewed relationships with God simply as a result of God's own love for them and not because of any inherent claim they might have on God. No one can work up a sense of God's presence for themselves.

Many ancient peoples portrayed their gods as having human characteristics, as if they were a race of super-humans. By contrast, the God of the Old Testament is presented as quite different from human beings. Representations of God were not approved of.

God's word

How then does God communicate? A simple answer would be: through the kinds of mighty acts demonstrated in the history of Israel. There is much truth in this, and the Old Testament often claims that God has been revealed through these things. Indeed, much of the Old Testament's moral law is based on the assumption that the way God acts displays important aspects of God's character. But this answer is not entirely satisfactory by itself. For the escaping slaves, and later generations who shared their perspective, the exodus was the greatest revelation of God's character and will, the crucial event in which God was made known. But what did it mean to the Egyptians? We do not know, of course, for Egyptian annals nowhere mention such an event. But it is quite certain that the exodus was not for them a means of divine encounter in which the God Yahweh met them and changed their national history. Something else was needed to transform the bare happenings of history into a message from God. This is always the way, of course. The 'bare facts' of history only gain significance when they are placed in an appropriate context. A historian does not simply record isolated incidents from the past, but tries to explain them in relation to other incidents, in order to make sense out of what has taken place. The Old Testament does the same, and what makes its story so distinctive is the interpretation that is given to the events it describes. As historians and prophets looked back to the nation's past they did not view it as just a historical chain of cause and effect, but saw in it the evidence that God had been at work in person.

If that was the end of the story, we might conclude that the Old Testament faith was little more than a historian's theory – a neat way of giving coherence and meaning to a rather amorphous collection of events that had happened at different times and places over many generations. But there is more to it than that. For the prophets did not interpret the history of their people in retrospect: they claimed to announce it before it took place. When Amos issued his scathing denunciations of Samarian society, and declared that it would soon come to an end, there was no sign of such an end. Indeed, the nation was enjoying a period of prosperity unparalleled at any other time in its history, either before or after. When Jeremiah announced the doom of Jerusalem, the mood of self-satisfaction that was sweeping the city led people to regard him as a madman. But they – and the other prophets – persisted with their message because they were convinced that what they were saying was the word of God to their people. The earlier story of the exodus was no different, for Moses himself is portrayed as a prophet – indeed, the greatest of all prophets according to Deuteronomy 34:10–12 – announcing the exodus while the people were yet in slavery. It is difficult for today's people to grasp this, and still more difficult to understand it, but it is an essential part of the Old Testament's picture of God. The Old Testament never claims to be able to fathom all the depths of God's personality, and there are many aspects of God's work that can never be fully understood. But this one conviction runs throughout all its writings: that the living God is not a static being, remote and irrelevant to the lives of ordinary people, but a God who acts and a God who speaks in order that men and women might have a full and meaningful relationship with God's own person and also with one another.

10 God and the World

Discovering God in nature and history

In the last chapter, we saw that God's most characteristic method of communication in the Old Testament was through the events of history: the exodus from Egypt, the establishment of David's royal city in Jerusalem – even the exile. When correctly understood and explained, all these things told the people of ancient Israel what God was really like. It would be misleading, however, to think that the spirituality of the Hebrew Bible is concerned exclusively with the events of Israel's history. While the heart of its message is certainly to be found in the stories that begin with the nation's forebears, Abraham and Sarah, and end with Judah's exile in Babylon, this by no means exhausts all that it has to say. The stories contained in the first eleven chapters of the book of Genesis, most of the psalms and all the wisdom books are only loosely related to the great themes of Israel's salvation history. Far from being narrowly concerned only with the experiences of Israel, these books in particular deal with the universal experience of men and women everywhere as they try to come to grips with the world in which they live. Moreover, these particular parts of the Old Testament have many close connections with the religious literature of other nations of the time. Their central concern is not with the unique and unrepeatable experience of Israel. Instead, they place God's activities in an international perspective, and suggest that Israel's spirituality is of such a character that Yahweh's claim over people's lives extends well beyond any single ethnic or racial grouping. Significant evidence of the God of whom the Bible speaks can be discerned in the very stuff of which the world is made, which means that the call to faith issued by the prophets and others is of correspondingly universal application.

It has often been supposed that an interest in this kind of creation-centred spirituality developed only at a relatively late date in the evolution of the Hebrew scriptures. It is certainly true that many aspects of Old Testament faith were worked out in their final detail only during the years following the Babylonian exile (which began in 597 BC). The majestic poetry of Isaiah 40–55 certainly reflects that period, and one of its most striking features is of course the imagery with which it celebrates God's power over the world of nature. Some of this language, together with that found in the creation story of Genesis 1:1 – 2:4, seems to have connections with traditional Mesopotamian stories of how the world was made, and for that reason scholars have suggested that during this period the originally narrow basis of Israel's faith was expanded, and the emphasis moved away from God's acts in history at a time when God seemed to be doing very little for this particular people. This view has been widely accepted and frequently repeated, but it is far too simplistic. Without doubting that some of the Old Testament's most sophisticated thinking about God and creation may well have been more fully articulated during the exile, there are a number of factors which clearly suggest that an understanding of God's relationship to the natural world was an important part of Israel's life long before that:

The Israelites began to discover the character of God in their time as nomads in the wilderness. But the discovery continued as they settled in the fertile land of Canaan and began to live an agricultural life.

■ Most of the psalms reflect the worship and liturgy of pre-exilic Israel. They show quite clearly that Yahweh was worshipped as the creator of the world long before Israel had any first-hand dealings with Babylon. There is no creation story as such in the psalms, but creation imagery (often drawn from the common literary heritage of Canaan and Mesopotamia) is used so often that belief in God as creator was obviously a fundamental theme of worship in the Temple at Jerusalem.
■ We also know that the role of deities in relation to the natural world was a recurring theme throughout the spiritual environment in which

Israel emerged as a nation. The texts from Ugarit may not contain a fully developed Canaanite creation story comparable with those found in ancient Babylon, but all the activities of the Canaanite gods and goddesses were related to the workings of the natural world. One of the key questions debated throughout the history of both Israel and Judah was whether Baal or Yahweh was in control of the natural world. It is inconceivable that those who were responsible for formulating Israel's world-view should have waited for half a millennium before giving an answer to that question. As the Old Testament story unfolds, one of its major concerns is to understand how Yahweh, the God of the exodus, could relate to the demands of life in a settled agricultural community. The prevailing popular view was that the world of nature and the world of the gods were one and the same, which is why the actions of gods such as El or Baal could be understood as a way of giving meaning to the mysterious workings of the world of nature in which Palestinian farmers had to eke out a precarious living. Was Yahweh only a God of history – and did that mean the natural world was controlled by deities such as Baal and Anat? The story of Elijah shows that this was a pressing issue as early as the ninth century BC (1 Kings 17:1 – 19:18). A hundred years later the prophet Amos denounced the behaviour of non-Israelite people in a way that would only have made sense on the basis of a coherent set of beliefs about God's relationship as creator to the whole of the natural world (Amos 1:3 – 2:3).

■ Similar questions must also have presented themselves on a personal level. After all, only one relatively small group of people had witnessed the amazing events of the exodus and the conquest of the land. Not many had any direct contact with the great promises made to David. And, mercifully, few had been left in Jerusalem to witness its final humiliation at the hands of Nebuchadnezzar. If these were the key events in which God was most clearly revealed to the people, then what chance was there that others might hear God's voice? Though the great events of the past could be celebrated in regular religious festivals, the fact was that the everyday experience of ordinary people was more closely tied to the world of nature than to the world of great and unrepeatable historical events. That in itself must have required the development of some coherent belief about the relationship between Israel's God and the natural world.

■ From as far back as the call of Abraham and Sarah, the Old Testament suggests that God's intervention in Israel's history was to be a means to the salvation of all nations (Genesis 12:1–3). This insight was clearly central to Hebrew faith, and is underlined by all the great prophets. It was frequently misunderstood, of course, and the easygoing national optimism that often dominated popular thinking in both Israel and Judah all too readily led people to conclude that other nations were of no concern at all to God. But to overcome such misunderstanding, it must have been necessary to know precisely how Israel was related to other nations. The stories of creation are the only parts of the Old Testament to answer that question.

■ Significant parts of the Genesis stories were certainly composed long before the exile in Babylon, for their imagery, and the assumptions made about the countryside and the moods of the weather, clearly point to a Palestinian background (Genesis 2:4–25).

In the light of all these considerations, it makes sense to conclude that belief in God as the creator was a significant and integral part of Israelite faith from relatively early times. Like other aspects of that faith, it developed and matured as time passed. But one of its underlying assumptions was that 'The world and all that is in it belong to Yahweh' (Psalm 24:1). Its importance is further emphasized by the fact that this subject is introduced in the opening page of Genesis, the first book of the Hebrew scriptures. It is reasonable to suppose that the writers and editors of the Old Testament would begin by outlining some of the most fundamental aspects of their faith.

Thinking about the world

The first eleven chapters of the book of Genesis in fact comprise one of the most important sections of the entire Old Testament. In the stories of creation, the fall, Cain and Abel, the flood and the tower of Babel, we have a concise summary of the underlying infrastructure of biblical spirituality. Such basic themes as the character of God, the nature of the world and the meaning of human existence are presented here with an imaginative subtlety that has given these chapters a place among the great classics of world literature. Yet we need be neither theologians nor literary critics to grasp their message, for like the parables of Jesus, these stories have a universal appeal to people in all times and places. They speak to the deepest needs of men and women, and give an honest answer to questions that have perplexed the world's greatest thinkers.

Understanding the Genesis stories

It is all the more surprising, then, that these early chapters of Genesis should have become a subject of such great controversy. Yet it can hardly be denied that in the last 200 years or so they have been the focus of so many complex debates that ordinary Bible readers are often at a loss to know what to do with them. Extensive studies have been written in the effort to find an appropriate way to understand them, and anything that we can say here must inevitably be brief and incomplete. But two things may be taken as basic for a satisfactory understanding:

■ Ever since Charles Darwin published his *Origin of Species* in 1859, the Genesis creation story has been used by the protagonists in many debates about science and religion. Scientists imbued with a materialistic world-view have sometimes claimed that these chapters demonstrate the naïvety of religious belief, while fervent believers have just as often replied that the creation stories prove the inadequacy of modern scientific endeavour. In some Christian circles, it has been taken for granted that Christian doctrine requires these chapters to be understood as a scientific account of the origins of the universe. This position in turn inevitably sets the Old Testament at variance with the findings of science, and identifies a biblical faith with what most people would regard as an outmoded view of how the world works. In dealing with this, it is important to realize that all this is a fairly recent development, and earlier generations of Bible scholars were much less inclined to try to force the book of Genesis into the straitjacket of a scientific textbook. Even to scientists as long ago as the sixteenth century, it seemed unlikely that there could be waters above the sky in the way that seemed to be implied by a literal understanding of the statement that the dome of the sky ('firmament') was separating 'the water under it from the water above it' (Genesis 1:6–7). John Calvin was no liberal, but in his *Commentary on Genesis* he agreed with this opinion, describing such a notion as 'opposed to common sense, and quite incredible', and going on to dismiss the idea that the Genesis story was supposed to be any kind of scientific account: 'to my mind, this is a certain principle, that nothing is here treated of but the visible form of the world. He who would learn astronomy, and other recondite arts, let him go elsewhere.' Calvin was quite clear that reading the Old Testament as if it was a book of science could only confuse and distort its essential message. The Old Testament writers, he argued, simply took for granted the sort of world-view that was widely held in their day. This assumed that the world was like a flat disc, set upon pillars below, with the sky arching over it like a dome. They never discussed whether this was scientifically correct or not: it was unnecessary for them to do so, for that was not why they were writing. Calvin described details such as this as only props on the main stage – background detail to reinforce the fact that the Old Testament's message was relevant to the world in which ordinary people lived.

■ The message, here as elsewhere in the Old Testament, is about God. We have already seen this same phenomenon in considering the meaning of the great events of Israel's history. The story of the exodus, for instance, was recorded not primarily because it happened, but because it demonstrated God's active and loving concern for the people of Israel. Even in the history books, the main emphasis is on theological explanation rather than historical analysis, and the deuteronomic history certainly explains and applies the lessons that were to be drawn from what it records, as do the books of the Chronicler. Genesis itself was a part of this enterprise. Moreover, the Old Testament uses a variety of literary genres to convey its essential message. Historical story is only one of them. The hymns and prayers of the psalms, the sermons of the prophets and the writings of Israel's wisdom teachers all explain important aspects of God's dealings with the world and its people. As the prophets loved to point out, the message ('the word of Yahweh') was the really important thing, not the medium through which it was communicated. Of course, those who do not share the prophets' faith could read the Old Testament histories and see nothing more than a diffuse account of a small and second-rate ancient Palestinian state. It is possible to do the same with the creation stories, and see nothing but an apparently factual account of the doings of two people in a garden full of plants and animals. At a more sophisticated level, we might join those scholars who have thought of these stories as a collection of folk tales designed to answer such everyday questions as why snakes have no legs, why weeds grow in fields, or why in ancient Israel it was better to be a shepherd than a farmer. But if these are the only things we see as we read the book of Genesis, then we have missed the most crucial points that its authors and editors were intending to make. For they were not concerned with the needs of ancient farmers, nor even with

Genesis in its context

The Assyrian emperor Ashurbanipal is shown on this relief hunting lions. The library that he created at Nineveh is one of our major sources of information about the ancient world.

Towards the end of the nineteenth century, archaeologists uncovered the library of the seventh-century BC Assyrian emperor Ashurbanipal. Politically, he was a failure, but his library survived and is one of our major sources of knowledge of the world in which Israel and Judah struggled for survival. It was written on cuneiform tablets, which are virtually indestructible: flat bricks of river mud inscribed with a wedge-shaped stick

while still soft, and then baked hard in the heat of the sun. The contents of these stories were ancient even in Ashurbanipal's day, and go back almost to the dawn of civilization.

As these tablets were deciphered, it soon became apparent that stories of creation and a great flood had circulated in ancient Babylon long before the Old Testament was written. In a wave of enthusiasm for new discoveries, the scholars who first studied these texts concluded that the Old Testament stories were derived from them, and were therefore of relatively little independent value. Things have changed a lot since then, and modern experts are now far less confident that a direct line of descent can be traced from the Babylonian documents to the stories in Genesis. One of the main reasons for this has been the more recent discovery of other religious texts from the Canaanite stronghold of Ugarit, which tell the stories of Baal and other Canaanite deities, and have shown that in many crucial respects Canaanite religion was rather different from its Babylonian counterpart. Though the precise connection between Ugarit and Israel is itself uncertain, it stands to reason that the religious context in which the Hebrew Bible developed must have had more in

some kind of primitive sociology, but with God. Just as Jesus often explained important aspects of his message by using the familiar experiences of everyday life, so the book of Genesis starts from the common experiences of human life, and goes on to show how God can relate to both the joys and the miseries of the world and its people.

The stories as literature

The Old Testament is a library of many different kinds of literature. In its pages we find not only history, but also law, drama, poetry, sermons, political tracts and much more. They are all held together by their common conviction that God is at the centre of all human life and activity. But before the significance of any particular passage can be fully appreciated, we must obviously decide what sort of literature we are dealing with. We would not read a political tract in the same way as we might read legal documents, while the kind of analytical judgment

---

common with such Canaanite beliefs than with the developed religious traditions of ancient Babylon. As a result, scholars now find it far more productive to compare the Old Testament with what we know of the religion of Ugarit.

Imagery from other religions

Many ordinary readers of the Bible may feel uneasy with the idea that it contains materials connected with the documents of other religions, but in fact this kind of religious borrowing is found not only in the stories of creation and the flood, but in many other parts of the Old Testament as well. The wisdom books contain teachings that are often very similar to ideas found in the wisdom literature of Egypt and elsewhere, and much of Israel's case law resembles the precepts of other nations. Parallels like that are perhaps to be expected, for they concern matters of morality and social organization that are common to people all over the world. It is perhaps more surprising to discover that the Old Testament's religious imagery is also quite similar to the language used of other deities. The Old Testament's language of sacrifice was essentially the same as that used in Ugarit, while the psalms in particular utilized many concepts that were by no means exclusive to Israel:

● For instance the statement that the temple hill in Jerusalem is 'in the far north' (Psalm 48:2) has puzzled many people, for Jerusalem was not in the north, but right in the middle of the country. But the Hebrew word for 'north' is virtually identical to the Ugaritic word 'Zaphon', and in the stories of Baal Mount Zaphon is frequently mentioned as the traditional home of the gods. So, when the psalmist penned these words, it is almost certain the intention was not that this should be understood as a (false) geographical statement about the location of the Temple, but rather as a claim that whatever was supposed to happen at Mount Zaphon was actually taking place on Mount Zion. There are other references to this home of the gods in Isaiah 14:13, and perhaps also in Psalm 89:12.
● Psalm 46:4 speaks of 'a river that brings joy to the city of God'. Again, there is no actual river in Jerusalem, but this statement makes perfectly good sense in light of the fact that the same imagery was used throughout the ancient world to illustrate the life-giving powers of divine beings. In a scene from the palace at Mari, for example, the king is shown being invested by a god, and in one corner two figures stand holding a vase containing the tree of life, from which

required to understand history would be quite out of place in the more aesthetic world of poetry and drama. So how can we classify these early stories in Genesis?

GENRE

Many books on the Old Testament refer to these passages as 'myths'. Though it has a long and venerable heritage in literary criticism, the way in which this term is used in ordinary speech today means that it is not a particularly helpful word to apply in this context. Most people think of a myth as something that is untrue. Literary scholars, of course, do not normally use it in this sense, but even they have no agreed definition of it and it is commonly used to mean at least three different things:

■ A myth can be simply a story about gods and goddesses and their doings, described as if they were human beings. There are many examples of this in Greek and Hindu mythology.

Genesis in its context continued

comes a stream, dividing into smaller streams, and so dispensing the blessing of the gods among the people. The same theme is taken up and developed further in Ezekiel 47:1–12, where the stream that flows from the Temple in Jerusalem transforms the life of everything that comes in contact with it.

● In many passages celebrating God's triumphant power, Yahweh is depicted as winning battles over the sea and various monsters which lived in it. Some of these passages depict unruly waters which are threatening to bring chaos into the world that God has made (Psalms 18:15; 29:3–4, 10–11; 77:16–18; 93:3–4; Habakkuk 3:8), while others speak of monsters emerging from the unruly depths to challenge God's power (Job 7:12; Psalms 74:12–14; 89:10; Isaiah 27:1). These are obviously allusions to incidents that must have been well known to the people of ancient Israel, though the Old Testament nowhere contains a simple descriptive account of them. For that we need to look elsewhere, for these references to a battle between God and the powers of the sea are drawn from the general religious ideas of the time, rather than belonging uniquely to the Old Testament faith. Some of the closest parallels can be

found in the texts from Ugarit. For example, when Isaiah speaks of Yahweh using a 'powerful and deadly sword to punish Leviathan, that wriggling, twisting dragon, and to kill the monster that lives in the sea' (Isaiah 27:1), the wording is virtually identical to a text that speaks of Baal: 'You have killed Lotan the primeval dragon, you have seen off that twisting snake, the powerful one with the seven heads.' Other Old Testament passages attest the belief that such monsters had multiple heads (Psalm 74:13–14), and that they could be called Rahab as well as Leviathan (Psalm 89:10; Isaiah 51:9).

After the outspoken prophetic condemnation of Canaanite religion, it might seem surprising that the Old Testament itself would use such language. Some have taken this to imply that Israelite spirituality was nothing like as distinctive as the prophets wanted to make it, and that this imagery is actually evidence that ancient Israel had a highly developed nature mythology in which Yahweh played much the same role as the Canaanite Baal. There is, however, no real evidence for that, either historical or religious, and the way these materials have been adapted for Israelite use is actually far more subtle. In

■ Myth can also be a technical term for what takes place during a religious rite. In ancient Babylon, for instance, the annual New Year Festival was the most important religious event of the year. Here, the Babylonian story of creation would be recited, while the king acted out the story as it was told. The recitation was a 'myth', to accompany the 'ritual' carried out by the king.

■ Yet others use the term 'myth' to describe a story which expresses a truth about human life that cannot adequately be described in terms of science or history. In this sense, myth is as valid and respectable a way of thinking about life's deepest meaning as science, art, or philosophy. This is the type of 'myth' scholars usually have in mind when they use this term in relation to the Genesis creation narratives.

The trouble is that, with so many possible meanings, 'myth' has become a very slippery term, and for that reason alone is unlikely to be of much

ancient thinking, the waters of chaos were essentially personifications of the natural forces that seemed to bring productive life to a standstill at the end of each season, though in the Hebrew scriptures this imagery is either set very clearly in the context of God's firm control over the powers of nature (Psalms 74:12–17; 95:5; 135:5–7; Isaiah 51:15–16), or else is given a completely different reference altogether by being used to describe and celebrate the great events of Israel's history. In particular, the waters of chaos are often transformed into the waters of the Reed Sea, controlled by Yahweh to allow the people to escape from Egypt (Psalm 77:16–20; Isaiah 51:9–11), and the monsters become symbols of the more tangible enemies with whom Israel had to deal throughout their troubled existence (as in Isaiah 27:1). In other words, the imagery seems to have been separated altogether from its original context, and in its new setting is given a fresh emphasis which is then used to highlight some of the most distinctive aspects of the Old Testament faith.

A 'Babylonian Genesis'?

The same thing has happened in the early chapters of Genesis, with the stories of creation and the flood. It is natural that here the Old Testament should have many

Kings in ancient times were often portrayed as being anointed by gods or other mythical beings, and so given a special status. Here, a magical figure, possibly a priest dressed in the head and wings of an eagle, is seen anointing the Assyrian king Ashurnasirpal II.

elements in common with other texts of its day, for though the events of history were the unique possession of just one nation, stories of creation were part of the common heritage of all humankind. When the Old Testament describes the world, it does so in conventional terms, but in the process it reinterprets these traditional ideas in such a way that they become a means of articulating its own distinctive beliefs about God.

● **The creation story** (Genesis 1:1 – 2:4) This has often been compared with an old Akkadian tale called *Enuma Elish*. This was recited in the temple at Babylon on the occasion of the annual New Year Festival, and was a hymn in praise of the

help to us here. In addition, not all the stories in the early chapters of Genesis can easily be accommodated even within these three commonly used definitions of 'myth'. For although many people would be happy to think of the stories of creation and the fall as a kind of 'theology in pictures', the stories of the flood and the tower of Babel seem to have some connection with historical events. Archaeologists have found mud deposits from a number of great floods which swept over the ancient world from 4000 BC onwards, and the description of the tower of Babel recalls towers (ziggurats) that have been unearthed in the same areas of Mesopotamia.

HOW MANY STORIES?

The conventional way of explaining these stories has been to suggest that Genesis is actually a composite document, and what we now have has been put together out of a number of sources. Scholars have

---

Genesis in its context
continued

This Babylonian account of creation tells of a time when nothing existed except the gods and the great Deep. Then a movement took place in the waters and the god Marduk formed first the earth and then the living world.

god Marduk. It tells how at the beginning nothing existed except the dark waters of primeval chaos, personified as Apsu and Tiamat. In their turn they produced a series of other deities representing the various elements of the universe. Later, a revolt against these forces of chaos led by the younger and more active gods brought into existence the ordered world. Apsu was killed by magic, and Tiamat was cut in two, and Marduk used one half of her body to make the solid sky (firmament), and the other to make the flat earth. The gods were then divided between heaven and earth, and people were made to perform menial tasks for the gods. It is unlikely that there was any direct connection between this and the Old Testament account, though there are some superficial similarities. In both, light emerges from a watery chaos, followed by the sky, dry land, sun, moon and stars, and finally people, and after all this the creator or creators rested. There are, of course, many differences, but one of the most significant features is that, even at those points where there is the closest

resemblance, the Genesis account reads as if it is a deliberate undermining of the assumptions of the Babylonian story.

Scholars of an earlier generation often linked the 'raging ocean' of Genesis 1:2 (Hebrew *tehom*) with the Babylonian goddess Tiamat. This is linguistically unlikely, and in addition the Old Testament idea of the raging sea is quite different, with not the least suggestion of a conflict between God and the watery chaos. Instead, 'the power of God' was 'moving over the water' from the very beginning, and the 'great sea monsters' are explicitly said to have been only a part of what God created. The Hebrew word used to describe their creation is carefully chosen, to indicate that God's control over these creatures was quite effortless and in no way the outcome of some cosmic battle. Underlying the Babylonian story is the expectation that this 'raging ocean' would somehow again get the upper hand and plunge things back into chaos. The way to ensure this did not happen, or that order was soon restored, was through the ritual of the Babylonian New Year Festival, acted out annually by king and people. In Genesis, people are empowered to share in God's ongoing creativity, but the Bible story makes it clear that creation itself

often claimed to be able to distinguish not one, but two (or even more) accounts of creation and the flood. The reasons for this have already been fully explored in our earlier discussion about the writing and editing of the Pentateuch. But even supposing that this understanding is correct, it is difficult to see how it can help us to understand what Genesis is trying to say. To explain where an author's materials came from is not the same as explaining the message which the final narrative intends to convey. Unless we read these stories as they are, we are unlikely to make much headway in discovering their meaning.

WHAT KINDS OF STORIES?

If we take the stories of creation and the fall, it is easy to see that the beginning of the story (Genesis 1:1 – 2:4) is quite different in character from its sequel (Genesis 2:4 – 3:24). This is not because they are variant

---

happened once and for all, and the days of creation themselves could not be repeated.

Other aspects of the Babylonian world-view are also questioned here. Astrologers have always believed that the sun, moon and stars have power over people, but that idea is quite specifically undermined in this story by the description of the heavenly bodies as nothing more than 'lights' (Genesis 1:14–18) – and certainly not gods themselves. The understanding of people is also quite different. In many ancient stories, they were created as an afterthought to serve the deities, so that gods would not have to gather their own food. But in the Old Testament women and men are not only central to God's purposes: they are the pinnacle of the whole of creation. Far from being made for God's selfish benefit, God provides other things for theirs – and so the plants and grains are available for food (Genesis 1:29). As in the rest of the Old Testament, the destiny of people is in the hands of a loving and powerful personal God, and not in the control of either nature or superstition.

● **The flood story** (Genesis 6:9 – 9:17) This displays essentially the same characteristics. Neither Egyptian nor Ugaritic literature contains an account of a

great flood, but again several such stories have been found in Babylon. The most complete of these is in a poem known as *The Epic of Gilgamesh*. This tells how Gilgamesh, king of Uruk (Erech in Genesis 10:10), shattered by the death of his friend Enkidu, realizes that he himself must soon die and decides to try to find the secret of eternal life. He seeks out his own ancestor Ut-napishtim, who had himself gained immortality, and asks him about it. He is told that first he must get a plant from the bottom of the ocean which will renew his youth. But at this point in the story, the dialogue is interrupted as Ut-napishtim goes on to tell Gilgamesh how he himself had escaped from a great flood. He had been warned by Ea, the god of magic wisdom, that the other gods, especially Enlil, had decided to send the flood. Ut-napishtim was advised to build a boat, which he did. This 'boat' was in fact a large cube, and in important respects was therefore rather different from Noah's 'ark'. After coating this cube inside and out with bitumen, he stocked it with food and brought all his family and belongings into it, together with animals and skilled craftworkers. The storm raged for seven days, at the end of which nothing but water was visible. Twelve days later, Ut-napishtim's 'boat' ran

accounts of the same thing (as some think), but because they are different literary forms. The first section has many close similarities to lyrical expressions that are also found in the psalms, and in certain passages in the book of Isaiah. It is written in an obviously poetic style, with a repetitive refrain, and from a literary standpoint it is a hymn in praise of creation, celebrating God's goodness and concern for every living thing. It takes the observable features of the world, and asserts that God is in control of them all. It is the sort of confession of faith that may well have been formulated and used in the context of worship in ancient Israel, and when we come to consider its message these are the terms in which we need to try to understand it.

What follows is quite different, and the dramatic action takes place in a different setting altogether. No longer is it reported in the measured language of lofty poetry, but with the directness of an expert storyteller. In a straightforward account, we read of how the man and

The Babylonian myths had a story of a Great Flood, parallel in some ways to the story of Noah. It forms part of the Epic of Gilgamesh, and tells of a man whom the gods instructed to make a boat and survive the flood.

woman who enjoyed a perfect relationship with God rejected that relationship, and chose instead to be the controllers of their own destiny. Their choice was simple, but its consequences incalculable, for as the story unfolds the reader soon becomes aware that this is no ordinary story. The garden, the trees and the creatures are all described in superlatives, as befits the momentous implications that stem from the action. For the effects of the human behaviour described here were not restricted to the earliest age of human existence, but were to have repercussions for people at all times and in all places. It is no coincidence that the author names the central actors Adam (meaning 'humankind') and Eve (meaning something like 'humanity'), for the experience of all subsequent generations was enshrined in their act of disobedience. This is why in the first chapter of this book I suggested that these stories could most usefully be categorized as 'faith stories', for they represent theological writing at its

---

aground on a mountain, whereupon he sent out a dove and a swallow in turn, both of which came back. Then he sent out a raven, which did not return as the waters had subsided. When he left the 'boat', he made a sacrifice to the gods, who crowded round like flies to smell it and promised that never again would they send a flood. They then bestowed immortality upon Ut-napishtim and his wife.

Here again, there is no compelling evidence to suggest that the Genesis story is in any way based on the Babylonian account, though once more there are sufficient resemblances to make it likely that both depend on the same general stock of ideas. Where they differ, they do so because the Hebrew story is based on a different understanding of the nature of God. In the Gilgamesh story, no explanation is given for the flood, though in another Akkadian source (the *Atrahasis Epic*), the gods decide to destroy men and women because they are making too much noise! In Genesis, however, God sends the flood as a judgment on human disobedience. Throughout this story the recurring theme is that there is only one God, who (unlike the Babylonian deities) is not afraid of the flood but is in complete control of it. Nor are people

dealt with in an arbitrary way, for the deliverance of Noah is the outcome of his own good behaviour just as the destruction of everyone else is traced to their own misbehaviour. In the Genesis story, morality is at the heart of the character of God, whose dealings with men and women therefore depend solely on verifiable standards of justice and love, rather than on capricious and unpredictable self-interest.

Genesis in its context
continued

best and most imaginative, simple yet profound. No reader with even a glimmer of aesthetic appreciation can fail to grasp the message that the author is meaning to convey here.

The message of the stories

What then is the message of these chapters? We shall return to some specific aspects later, but the overall theme is well summed up in the refrain repeated throughout the creation hymn: 'God was pleased.' It is not surprising that the composer of the hymn should have repeated this statement so many times, for its implications seem to cut across some of the intuitive spiritual instincts of conventionally religious people. The idea that any kind of embodied existence is incompatible with spiritual enlightenment is a basic assumption of most eastern world-views, and has often been a dominant theme in Christian thinking as well, encouraging people to opt out of the world in the hope that by so doing they would somehow get closer to God. Within the Christian tradition, this understanding owes more to the influence of Greek philosophy than to the teachings of the Bible. Unlike the Greeks, who could regard the body as only a temporary 'prison' for the immortal soul, the Israelites thought of the body, and the whole physical world, as the most natural home for people, and took it for granted that God would most truly be found not beyond the created world, but in it. One of the basic affirmations of the Hebrew scriptures is encapsulated in the opening words of Psalm 24, with its confident declaration that 'The world and all that is in it belong to Yahweh; the earth and all who live on it are God's.' Moreover, the creation stories emphasize that God is directly involved with the life of this world. There is, of course, a tension here, for God is the all-powerful creator whose word alone is sufficient to bring order out of chaos (Genesis 1:3, 6, 9, 11, 14, 20, 24). But in describing the place of men and women within this wonderful creation, God's own personal involvement is always emphasized. God is like a potter, who takes soil from the ground and lovingly forms a human being out of it (Genesis 2:7). Yahweh can never be identified with nature, but is beyond it and above it – yet, at the same time, God is directly involved in the work of creation, thus demonstrating a close concern not only for Israel, but also for people and animals in general, and even for the very stuff out of which the universe is made.

Men, women and God

'What are human beings that you are mindful of them, mortals that you care for them?' (Psalm 8:4). As people compare their own meagre existence with the greatness of the natural world around them, this question often seems to sum up the basic problem of human existence. Why are we here? Some parts of the Old Testament emphasize the apparent insignificance of men and women, referring to life as 'a puff of wind... a passing shadow' (Psalm 144:4), or 'like grass. We grow and flourish like a wild flower; then the wind blows on it, and it is gone' (Psalm 103:15–16). Others reflect a more positive mood, declaring that people are only a little lower than God, 'crowned... with glory and honour' (Psalm 8:5). Yet all would agree that the life of men and women finds its true fulfilment when they are living in personal openness with God. This is why we were made, and no matter how insignificant or powerless a person may feel, they can be sure that God is still interested in their life and experience: 'for those who honour Yahweh, God's love lasts for ever, and God's goodness endures for all generations' (Psalm 103:17). In the Babylonian creation stories people were made last of all, almost as an afterthought on the part of the gods, and always for menial duties. But the Old Testament will have none of this: women and men are the pinnacle and crowning glory of the world and all its affairs. The heart of the Genesis creation stories is to be found in the simple statement that human beings were made 'in the image of God' (Genesis 1:27). When we recall that the Hebrew Bible consistently and expressly forbids making images of God, this may come as a rather unexpected sentiment. But we have previously noticed that the imagery of the Old Testament is always specific and positive, never abstract and philosophical. God's character and personality are described in relation to what God does, and not by reference to some metaphysical speculation about what God might be made of. This is precisely the emphasis that is intended here, and when men and women are described as being 'in God's image' that does not mean that they look like God, or that they are made of the same stuff. It is, rather, a way of saying they are intended to be extensions of God's own personality, and to play a central role in God's own ongoing activity in the world. They are God's representatives. In this claim at least three important ideas are put forward about the relationship between people, the world and God.

In relation to the earth

Men and women are given God's blessing and told: 'Have many children, so that your descendants will live all over the earth and bring it under their control. I am putting you in charge of the fish, the birds, and all the wild animals' (Genesis 1:28). This statement has often been misunderstood, especially by modern Christians who have taken it as a licence to exploit the natural world in any way that is to their benefit. Older Bible translations may have encouraged this, by articulating God's instructions in terms of 'subduing' the earth, and 'having dominion' over its creatures. But the Genesis story implies nothing of this kind – indeed, quite the opposite. The whole point of the story is that God has made a world of order and balance out of a state of chaos, and people are here called upon to maintain and preserve the world as God intends it to be. God has not wound the world up like a mechanical toy, but continues to be actively involved in its workings, changing night to day (Isaiah 45:12; Amos 4:13; 5:8), controlling the sun, moon and stars, the rivers, and giving life to crops and animals (Isaiah 40:26; 48:13). Any human activity which disrupts the life of nature is contrary to the will of God, for God intended there to be a mutual respect and service between people and the world in which they live (Psalm 104:10, 14–15, 27–30). This is strikingly emphasized when Genesis depicts God as a divine potter forming a person out of the ground. There is a subtle play on words here, for the Hebrew word for humankind (*adam*) is very similar to that for ground (*adamah*), and this similarity is used to emphasize that people are a fundamental part of the natural ecosystem in which they live. Men and women are not above nature: they are a part of it, and are responsible to God for the way they care for their world and the other creatures with whom they share it.

In relation to God

Men and women are distinctive because God can and does speak to them. Though they are intrinsically connected to the world in which they live, that is not the only dimension in which life finds meaning. Indeed, a materialist view which tries to make sense of human existence by only analysing the world of our senses and reason is, in biblical terms, meaningless. Being made 'in God's image' means that people are incomplete without God. They are intended to be in partnership with God, and it is this which gives meaning and direction to life. Communication with God is of vital importance to human satisfaction. It is important to notice that by partnership, the Old

Humanity has been given a responsibility by God to maintain and preserve the order of creation and not merely to exploit it. This detail from the Royal Standard of Ur, made about 2500 BC shows farmers and fishing people.

Testament does not mean a kind of conventional religiosity. One of the
most striking features of these early stories in Genesis is the way God
comes and talks with people, arriving in the evening to discuss with
Adam and Eve the affairs of the day (Genesis 3:8). This statement is
not to be regarded with embarrassment as either hyperbole or
exaggerated anthropomorphism. It is a moving affirmation of the fact
that communication between God and people was intended to be
delightful and personal, not formal and rigid. In ancient Israel, 'the
word of Yahweh' would come to people through many different
channels: the priest would interpret the Law (Torah); the wisdom
teachers would give advice on everyday affairs; and the prophets
characteristically brought either a spoken or acted message from God
as a comment on particular situations in the nation's life. But
underlying all these modes of communication was the conviction that
God and the people related to each other on a personal level. Like the
characters in the Garden of Eden, each individual has been made for
direct and personal encounter with God.

In relation to each other

There are important lessons here about human relationships to the
world and to God, but some of the most striking points of these stories
concern relationships between human beings themselves at different
levels:

■ *Social relationships* The fact that all human beings are made 'in God's
image' implies that all are of equal value and importance. The Bible solves
the problems of ethnicity and race by declaring that we all belong to the
same race. Israel often found it difficult to grasp that, but the prophets

were adamant that no one race was better than another, and no one group in society was of more importance than another. As far as God is concerned, all men and women are equal. Even though Israel was specially privileged to receive God's Law (Torah), this did not mean that others had

no access to God's will: however imperfectly they might have perceived it, every person knew the difference between basic issues of right and wrong, simply because they were made 'in God's image'.

■ *Sexual relationships* The Old Testament takes a pragmatic view here. There is no hint of the narrow asceticism that has often characterized Christian attitudes to sex. The idea that sexual knowledge only emerged in the context of broken relationships after the fall is clearly contradicted in Genesis.

The life of the market place was never intended to be distinct from the life of worship. Repeatedly the prophets condemned a religiosity which made no difference to everyday behaviour.

Human sexuality is an essential part of God's design for humankind right from the beginning. It is also worth noting that procreation is not the only reason given for this, for while men and women are encouraged to 'Have many children' (Genesis 1:28), considerable emphasis is also laid on the fact that an appropriate sexual partner is also to be 'a suitable companion' (Genesis 2:18). Nor is there any suggestion here that in such a relationship one partner is intrinsically more important than the other: a man is incomplete without a woman, and it is only the two of them together who can work out the full potential of human existence. Sex is a part of God's gift to men and women, something to be enjoyed and developed for its own sake – a point that is made most forcibly by the inclusion in the Old Testament of a book of erotic love poems, the Song of Solomon.

■ *Family relationships* Here, there is again an emphasis on the mutual sharing of one person with another. In the Old Testament world, the patriarchal family was the norm, and in that context men as well as women were often seen as chattels to be disposed of to suit the head of the family. The historical narratives themselves provide many examples of family heads doing just that, but it is striking that in this fundamental exposition of God's intentions for humankind there should be a rather different emphasis. There is nothing here that would give grounds for the exploitation of one sex by the other. On the contrary, there is a very strong emphasis on the mutual commitment of men and women to each other in the context of a committed sexual relationship. Moreover, this relationship takes precedence over all other traditional family commitments, and the book of Genesis issues a stronger challenge to traditional patriarchy than we realize, with its injunction that 'a man leaves his father and mother and is united with his wife, and they become one' (Genesis 2:24).

Broken relationships and new beginnings

The book of Genesis paints an idyllic picture of life in this world, with nature, people and God all working together in perfect harmony and mutual understanding and support. But, of course, life is not like that. Though most people have on occasion glimpsed the idealistic possibilities that are reflected here, human experience is more often marred by exploitation, disharmony and suspicion. The real world is a place of dysfunctional relationships.

The root of the problem

So what has gone wrong? Two stories here answer that question: the story of the fall (Genesis 3:1–24) and the story of the tower of Babel (Genesis 11:1–9). Both of them declare that the reason for human misery is that the delicate balance between people, nature and God has been disturbed. Instead of being content to accept God's values, men and women have tried to set themselves up as controllers of their own destiny. They are not content to accept even the benign guidance of a power greater than themselves. Instead, their chief concern has been to 'make a name for ourselves' (Genesis 11:4) or, as the story of the fall puts it, to 'be like God' (Genesis 3:5). One story expresses this as seeking after the fruit of 'the tree that gives knowledge of what is good and what is bad' (Genesis 2:17; 3:5). The fact that God bans the human pair from

The story of humanity's fall into sin speaks of a breakdown of relationships at every level. There is evidence of this breakdown throughout history, particularly in the cruelty and waste of wars.

eating this fruit has suggested to some that there was all along a built-in unfairness in God's original design. After all, why should God want people to be kept in ignorance like this? But a comment like that misses the point, for elsewhere in the Old Testament, knowing the difference between right and wrong is a phrase that is used with a distinctive connotation. It indicates that a person is yet a child, depending for guidance and direction on their parents (Deuteronomy 1:39; Isaiah 7:14–15). The picture of a child and a parent is often used as an appropriate way of depicting the relationship between people and God. Like a good parent, God has laid down limits within which life can prosper, and when human selfishness tries to overstep these limits, disaster will soon follow. One of the most moving aspects of these stories is the contrast between the world as God intended it to be and the world of broken relationships so familiar to us all. The Bible's understanding of the nature of sin at this point is, of course, quite different from the view taken by many people today. It has often been imagined that the history of the human race is one long story of continuous improvement, as people moved from primitive and savage beginnings to the so-called sophistication of our own day. Probably fewer people today believe that than would have been the case 100 years ago, for the experience of the twentieth century seems to have shown fairly conclusively that people are certainly not improving, and may even be getting worse. Genesis explains it by saying that human life has moved from a position of partnership with God to a position of rebellion – and it traces it all back to the disobedience of the man and woman in Eden who knew God so well.

The results of their disobedience and selfishness are simple.

DISHARMONY IN NATURE
Mutual service and interdependence between people and the natural world is replaced by hostility and mutual distrust (Genesis 3:14–21).

ALIENATION FROM GOD
Instead of meeting God in a close personal relationship, the man and woman do all they can to get out of God's way, and are ultimately sent out of the garden (Genesis 3:8–10, 22–24).

BROKEN SOCIETY
With broken relationships between people, the world and God, even family members can become enemies – and so Cain goes out and kills his brother Abel (Genesis 4:1–16).

Searching for the answer
The people of Israel knew well enough what all this meant in the ordinary details of everyday life, for by the time these stories were finally written down, they were already looking back on a long history which amply illustrated the tragedy of human disobedience. But they had also learned

that even when God's judgment was well deserved, God's love could never leave people to languish in the results of their own wrongdoing. These early stories contain a vivid portrayal of broken relationships, but they also have an underlying emphasis on the ever-present possibility of a new beginning. Wrongdoing and disobedience are a tragedy, judgment is inevitable – and well deserved – but God's love and forgiveness for the world and its people will never be defeated. Even in the earliest stories there are hints that God cannot just abandon people. When Adam and Eve feel the need for clothing, God provides it for them (Genesis 3:21). When Cain kills his brother Abel, God condemns him – but then forgives him and takes steps to keep him

Looking to the future

The Old Testament clearly asserts that human existence finds its true fulfilment only in a close personal relationship with God. But where are the boundaries of that relationship to be drawn? Does it end with death – or does it extend further, into an afterlife? To people today this is a natural question to ask. For one thing, we tend to think of people as individuals rather than as a part of some much larger group, and the fate of each person is therefore of considerable importance to us. In addition, we have been nurtured in an environment where popular ideas about death often incorporate the ancient Greek view that a person is composed of two parts: a body, which is mortal and comes to an end, and a soul (or spirit) which is immortal and can last for ever quite independently of the body. Much contemporary New Age spirituality operates on the assumption that the essence of the human personality survives death in some transformed dimension on another plane of existence.

None of these ideas would have meant very much in the Old Testament context. Although we should not overemphasize the corporate aspect of ancient Hebrew thinking, it is certainly true that Israel generally thought far less in terms of the individual than we do. At the same time, the Old Testament contains not a trace of the bipartite view of human nature that leads to the conclusion that people are souls imprisoned in bodies. For the Old Testament writers, all aspects of human

existence were just different facets of the same reality. Though it might be possible to speak of a person's 'heart', or even their 'spirit', terms of this sort did not refer to independent entities, but were only a graphic way of describing a person's emotions and general motivation. A person's bodily existence could in no way be distinguished from other aspects of the human experience. Within this kind of world-view, death was taken for granted as part of the whole business of human life. It may be regrettable, but was still a perfectly natural thing (2 Samuel 14:14), and there was nothing that anyone either could or should do about it (Job 7:9; Psalm 89:48). Two of the great heroes of the Old Testament story – Joshua and David – express this general view in their final speeches: 'I am about to go the way of all the earth' (Joshua 23:14; 1 Kings 2:2). The author of Psalm 90 defines the human lifespan as 'seventy years… eighty, if we are strong' (Psalm 90:10), while with characteristic coolness the author of Ecclesiastes states that 'For everything there is a season, and a time for every matter under heaven: a time to be born, and a time to die' (3:1–2). When the time comes, 'No one can keep from dying or put off the day of their death. That is a battle we cannot escape' (Ecclesiastes 8:8). Even if we try to understand it, 'no one can tell us what will happen after we die'

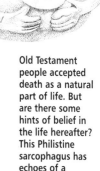

Old Testament people accepted death as a natural part of life. But are there some hints of belief in the life hereafter? This Philistine sarcophagus has echoes of a Mycenean death mask.

safe from the vengeance of others (Genesis 4:15). This theme comes to full expression in the story of the great flood. At a time when men and women were so determined to go their own way and disturb the delicate balance of relationships between God and this world, judgment was the only possible answer (Genesis 6:5–8). Yet, even here, God's purpose is not ultimately destructive, and Noah is saved, spared because of God's love, grace and forgiveness – all of which are encapsulated in the promise freely given by God to all humanity and symbolized by the rainbow, which is presented as a sign of God's continuing love even through the worst excesses of human wrongdoing (Genesis 9:8–17).

Looking to the future
continued

The Egyptians certainly believed in life after death. In this papyrus a man's heart is being weighed against a feather, as he prepares for his final journey.

(Ecclesiastes 10:14; 3:22). Of course, Ecclesiastes has its own cynical viewpoint, and we need to make allowances for that in reading these passages. But when they are compared to the rest of the Old Testament, comments of this sort are not altogether unrepresentative. For although many passages seem to allude to the continued survival of dead people, there is no consistent picture. We can trace a number of different emphases in the Old Testament:

● At a popular level, it seems likely that most people just shared much of the superstition of their cultural context in the ancient world. Egyptians and Babylonians, as well as the people of Ugarit in Canaan, all believed that there was another life after death. The Egyptians made the most elaborate preparations for the comfort of the deceased in this new environment, and it was widely believed that the dead should be given sufficient provisions to ensure a comfortable existence in the hereafter. Just as the pyramids often contained supplies to be used in the afterlife, so tombs discovered at Ugarit were equipped with channels through which living worshippers could continue to pour food and drink to their dead ancestors. Such offerings were often motivated by the view that the dead could influence the lives of the living, and if they were kept well fed then their influence

It is little wonder then that these stories came to form the opening pages of the Hebrew Bible, and thence the Christian Old Testament. In them we have a profound and picturesque summary of all the essential features of the Old Testament faith. Here we meet a God who is both totally different from men and women, and yet deeply involved with them. We are given a glimpse of a world in which people and nature can relate meaningfully to each other, because both of them relate to God. And we see the tragic results that follow when that relationship breaks down. The tragedy is familiar enough to everyone. But the Old Testament has its own diagnosis of the problem. The world is out of

would be good rather than evil. There is evidence of much the same thing in Israel, as for example in Saul's belief that the dead Samuel could somehow affect the course of his own life (1 Samuel 28:3–19). Saul was roundly criticized for this – and other passages also condemn similar reverence for the dead as alien to the true Old Testament faith – though the fact that the prophets needed to keep returning to this theme only serves to emphasize how widespread such a belief must have been (Deuteronomy 26:14; Isaiah 8:19–20; 65:1–5; Ezekiel 43:7–9).

● A more orthodox view suggested that a person could in some way survive through the continuation of their family line. This assumption seems to lie behind the story of the book of Ruth, and is hinted at in many passages which suggest that a person who dies without children to preserve the family name is at a particular disadvantage.

● The most common description of the dead is that they live a shadowy indeterminate existence in a place called Sheol. Sheol is not to be confused with later Christian ideas of heaven and hell, but was a morally neutral term. What actually went on in Sheol was never spelled out in any detail. Sometimes, existence there could be spoken of as an imprisonment, where people would be isolated from God and completely unaware of anything (Job 14:20–22; Psalms 30:9; 88:10–12; 115:17; Ecclesiastes 9:5–6). At other times, God's power might be said to extend even to Sheol (Psalm 139:8; Amos 9:2) – though sentiments of that sort were essentially poetic and rhetorical, more intended to encourage the living to keep trusting God than to make definitive statements about the state of the dead.

● Yet other Old Testament passages have been taken to refer to the idea of resurrection from the dead. The Hebrew Bible contains only one absolutely clear statement of belief in a resurrection, and that is Daniel 12:2. Because of this it is often supposed that the idea of resurrection was a relative latecomer in the Old Testament faith, articulated at a time when the deaths of good people were especially hard to accept – as they were at the time Daniel was written. But this is difficult to

joint because men and women are in revolt against their creator. Human wrongdoing affects both human life and the life of nature; disobedience is a tragedy and wilful neglect of God's values will inevitably lead to judgment. The course of human history has demonstrated all this often enough, but the Old Testament does not leave it there. For it also affirms that God wishes to bring order out of this chaos, to replace alienation with healing, and to ensure that forgiveness and love are always available to those who in childlike simplicity acknowledge their dependence on the creator.

**Looking to the future
*continued***

sustain, and it is more likely that the idea of resurrection emerged naturally from a much earlier period. Some of the oldest poetry in the Old Testament seems to imply resurrection (Deuteronomy 32:39; 1 Samuel 2:6), and there are three stories of resurrections from the dead told in the deuteronomic history (1 Kings 17:17–24; 2 Kings 4:18–37; 13:20–21). Though these stories present other questions, the way they are told suggests that their readers would be familiar with the possibility of resurrection from the dead. The same can also be said about other passages, for instance, Job 19:25–27; Isaiah 53:12; Ezekiel 37:1–14 and Hosea 6:1–3. Some scholars have also argued that the references to Sheol could at least imply resurrection, for existence there is characterized as a sleep in silence and darkness – and in Daniel, resurrection is referred to as an awakening from the sleep of death.

It certainly seems likely that this later articulation of a resurrection belief emerged from the earlier faith of Israel, rather than coming in from some other source, as was once believed. We know that it was the subject of continual argument for a very long time. The deuterocanonical books provide plenty of evidence for an increasing interest in the topic of life after death during the centuries immediately preceding the Christian era, though much later the Sadducees still could not bring themselves to accept that resurrection of the dead was an authentic part of the Old Testament faith, while the Pharisees, and

probably most ordinary people, took a different view. There can be no doubt that the period at the very end of the process of compilation of the Old Testament saw a massive increase in speculation about the subject, mostly connected with the issue of rewards and punishments and no doubt motivated by the knowledge that, following the purge of Antiochus IV, many upright people had suffered in horrendous ways and had apparently not been vindicated. If they had not received the rewards for their faithfulness in this life, then obviously they must be expected to find them somewhere else, presumably therefore in a life to come after the grave. In this context, where resurrection is mentioned it is essentially understood as involving the reversal of physical death, and typically consists of the restoration of the life in this world that was there before, most dramatically illustrated by the story of Razis who, as he was dying, took his entrails in his own hands and dramatically flung them down 'calling upon the Lord of life and spirit to give them back to him again' (2 Maccabees 14:46). This is all quite different from later Christian belief that resurrection life would have a distinctive and different quality from this life, or that resurrection in some way signified the defeat of death, both of which only arose out of the conviction of the earliest Christians that Jesus himself had risen from the dead.

11 Living as God's People

The world-view reflected in the pages of the Old Testament emerged from the corporate history of Israel's people, and this fact alone ensures that the kind of social morality it promotes has a different feel from more speculative systems of spirituality. Though Israel's theologians were constantly questioning and refining their understanding of God, their faith was never merely an intellectual process focused on abstractions about belief and behaviour. At the centre of it all was a strong sense that the people were in relationship with God, and that faith and lifestyle could not, therefore, be separated. Faith was something that could be tested in the affairs of everyday life, and was always expected to make sense in that context. So it is especially important that we reflect on how, in practical terms, Israel was expected to live as God's people.

Belief and behaviour

In traditional societies all over the world, organized religion has provided an almost universal language for people to express their deepest convictions about life. Ancient Israel was no exception to this, and the Hebrew scriptures provide plenty of evidence for carefully structured worship which took place at both local and national sanctuaries and included a wide variety of activities such as prayer, praise and sacrifice. When Israelite people met for organized worship, they were celebrating all that God had done for them not only corporately, but also individually. What the people actually did on such occasions is considered in some detail in the next chapter. But in order to understand the place of ritual in Old Testament spirituality, we need first to paint a much wider picture, for the leading religious activists in both Israel and Judah were constantly emphasizing that what went on in the shrine must never be separated from the way people lived day by day in the market place, on the farm or at home. Indeed some, such as the prophet Micah, could be outspoken in their condemnation of the empty performance of religious rituals, and emphasized instead that true worship of God was quite different and far more demanding: 'Yahweh has told us what is good. What God requires of us is this: to do what is just, to show constant love, and to live in humble fellowship with our God' (Micah 6:8). Most of the prophets made similar statements. So, too, did the history writers, as well as the poets and the wisdom teachers (1 Samuel 15:22; Psalm 51:16–17; Proverbs 21:3). Just as God's actions in history and nature had shown a love and concern that extended to every area of human life, so too every aspect of Israel's experience was to be affected by their commitment to God's values as highlighted and articulated in the covenant. The relationship between God and humankind was to have a moral, as well as a cultic basis. For Israel, that meant the nation's response to God must be shown in the way they behaved, and not just in what they believed.

This conviction runs deeply throughout the Old Testament, and even those books which relate to the formalities of organized worship lay considerable emphasis on moral and spiritual values. At the heart of the book of Deuteronomy is the instruction to 'Love the Lord your God with all your heart, with all your soul, and with all your strength' (Deuteronomy 6:5). Love for neighbours is also advocated in another section of Old Testament Law (Leviticus 19:18), while it is notable that the ten commandments sum up Israel's duty to God predominantly in terms of social and personal morality (Exodus 20:1–17; Deuteronomy 5:6–22). At one time, scholars imagined that this emphasis on behaviour was a late development within the faith of Israel. Many nineteenth-century thinkers believed that the sort of biological evolution popularized by Charles Darwin had been paralleled by moral and spiritual evolution, as human attitudes had developed and matured. Theories such as this encouraged people to take it for granted that Israel's religious experience must have begun as a simple nature worship, which only evolved into high moral standards under the influence of great thinkers such as the prophets, who tried to persuade their people to move from superstition to a more sophisticated understanding of God's person and ways. Although this sort of view continues to be promoted in some popular books on the Old Testament, it is simplistic and superficial:

■ The whole concept of evolutionary philosophy has been completely discredited. The idea that people began in primitive savagery and are getting better all the time simply does not square with the facts. The violence and brutality of our own generation makes it perfectly obvious that people are not improving, and the ferocity of the ethnic cleansing that marred the final years of the twentieth century suggested to many people that things might even be getting worse.

■ Throughout the twentieth century, there was a continual expansion of knowledge of the ancient world in general, and of Israel's cultural context in particular. Because earlier generations of scholars did not have the benefit of these insights, it was correspondingly difficult for them to understand the Old Testament in its own true life setting. We now know that some aspects of Israelite morality were familiar to people throughout the ancient world.

Much of Israel's civil law, in particular, bears a close resemblance to concepts of justice going back at least as far as the law code of King Hammurabi of Babylon (c. 1700 BC).

■ Literary analysis of the Old Testament stories has shown that a concern for good behaviour is central to many of the oldest traditions. The story of the destruction of Sodom and Gomorrah is certainly much older than the time of the prophets, and yet it condemns unacceptable behaviour in no uncertain terms (Genesis 18:16–33). The stories about Moses also go back to ancient sources, and show his anger at moral injustices as they affected both himself and his people (Exodus 2:11–13).

■ The Old Testament law codes themselves contain instructions about the conduct of religious ceremonies alongside clear guidelines for maintaining a just society. Such references were once dismissed as later additions to bring the laws into line with the message of the prophets, but further study has shown that even the very earliest strands of the Old Testament's legal material emphasize the importance of everyday behaviour as a way of serving God (Exodus 23:1–9; Leviticus 19:15–18; Deuteronomy 16:18–20).

The law-code of King Hammurabi of Babylon is inscribed on this column (or *stele*). This ancient code bears a considerable likeness to some Old Testament laws.

Religious people are always faced with the temptation of reducing faith to the perfunctory performance of familiar rituals, and Israel was no different. When the great prophets reminded them that faith in God should affect the whole of life, this was no new revelation: it was the recalling of the people back to the ideals of their ancient covenant faith. There are two main sections of Old Testament literature where these ideals are spelled out and their relevance to everyday life is explained: the wisdom books and the books of Law (Genesis to Deuteronomy), supplemented by the messages of the prophets. The literary and historical contexts of these various writings have already been dealt with extensively in previous chapters, and the discussion here will therefore focus more narrowly on their message as it related to the discovery of God's will, and the doing of it.

Discovering God's will through wisdom

When the Jewish historian Josephus (first century AD) described the wisdom books as 'precepts for the conduct of human life' (*Against Apion* 1.8), he was probably thinking especially of the book of Proverbs, which contains many easily memorized observations on how people should behave in order to enjoy a satisfying life. Here we find advice of the sort that parents throughout the world might give to their children, and for that reason many of the

instructions of the book of Proverbs would not have been out of place in quite different cultural contexts. Indeed, Proverbs 22:17 – 23:11 is at many points identical to an Egyptian document of about the twelfth century BC, the *Teaching of Amenemope*.

Understanding 'wisdom'

In the ancient world, the pursuit of 'wisdom' seems to have involved many different skills. Sometimes a 'wise' person was a good diplomat; at other times, a person with specialist knowledge about the world and its workings – perhaps a botanist or zoologist (1 Kings 4:33). When Solomon prayed for 'wisdom', he asked to be given the ability 'to rule... with justice and to know the difference between good and evil' (1 Kings 3:9). But he could also be called 'wise' because of his literary and artistic interests (1 Kings 4:32). 'Wisdom' was obviously a very wide-ranging series of skills. Perhaps it was a term used simply to denote the possession of whatever abilities were necessary for a particular individual to be successful in their own sphere of life. For some, that meant technical training in the art of international relations, and Israel no doubt had schools attached to the royal courts where this kind of formal education would be given. For others, it meant the study of science and philosophy, the ancient equivalent of a 'liberal arts' education. But for most, it meant the cultivation of those personal qualities that would result in happy and meaningful relationships in the everyday life of home and workplace.

Nowadays, most people would expect to learn these social skills in school, and there is some evidence that the Canaanite city states had a formal education system. But in Israel, the family was always the main influence in the life of a growing child: young people would learn most of what they needed to know from their parents, grandparents and the village elders. The practice recommended in the book of Deuteronomy almost certainly continued through most of the Old Testament period: 'Never forget these commands that I am giving you today. Teach them to your children. Repeat them when you are at home and when you are away, when you are resting and when you are working' (Deuteronomy 6:6–7).

Wisdom in practice

The Old Testament wisdom books contain examples of all these different kinds of 'wisdom'. Job and Ecclesiastes

The Jewish historian Josephus described the wisdom books as 'precepts for the conduct of human life'.

are the product of a well-developed intellectual approach to the great imponderables of human existence: the problem of evil, and the apparent meaninglessness of so much of life. As such, they have little to say about everyday behaviour in ancient Israel, though they do, of course, take certain moral standards for granted. The book of Proverbs lays much greater emphasis on 'practical wisdom', yet even here there seems to be a good deal of interest in scientific study, for moral lessons are often reinforced and illustrated by reference to the life of the animals and the phenomena of the natural world.

The book of Proverbs is itself an anthology of materials emanating from various wisdom teachers, though its contents are remarkably consistent, and deal with personal relationships in a number of different contexts.

THE FAMILY

It is not surprising that this should be a basic concern in Proverbs, since many of its precepts almost certainly originated in the context of advice handed on from one generation to another. As elsewhere in the Old Testament, a stable sexual relationship between husband and wife is seen as the key to family stability. Adultery is singled out as a particularly destructive evil whose repercussions affect more than the two individuals involved: 'A man can hire a prostitute for the price of a loaf of bread, but adultery will cost him all he has' (Proverbs 6:26). As we might expect in view of what we have already seen in the Old Testament creation stories, wisdom teachers in Israel spoke frankly and freely about both the attractions and perils of sexual unfaithfulness: 'The lips of another man's wife may be as sweet as honey and her kisses

There were 'wisdom' traditions in some of Israel's neighbouring cultures. The *Teaching of Amenemope*, an Egyptian document, is quoted almost verbatim in a section of Proverbs.

as smooth as olive oil, but when it is all over, she leaves you nothing but bitterness and pain' (Proverbs 5:3–4). The advice is always clear, but never narrow-minded or prudish. The love poems in the Song of Solomon have a number of connections with the wisdom books, and the frankness with which they depict a developing sexual relationship has often alarmed Christian readers. But the same open and joyful acknowledgment of human sexuality as part of God's creation is found also in the everyday advice of the book of Proverbs. For at the same time as its readers are warned against the dangers of adultery, they are also encouraged to develop and renew relationships within the marriage context: 'be happy with your wife and find your joy with the woman you married... Let her charms keep you happy; let her surround you with her love' (5:18–19).

Within a happy home there will be space for happy children to flourish, and the responsibility for bringing them up is one that should be shared between husband and wife (Proverbs 1:8–9; 6:20–23). Indeed, the provision of guidance to growing children is one of the major themes of Proverbs. Such instruction should be positive, by both example and precept: 'Train children in the right way, and when old, they will not stray' (Proverbs 22:6). Even when parents need to correct their children, that should always be done from a concern to promote moral maturity in the family: 'Those who never chastise their children do them no favours, but those who love them will be diligent to discipline them' (13:24). If the right course is followed in all these matters, then the whole family will be able to share in the mutual joy of a developing relationship in which 'Grandchildren are the crown of the aged, and the glory of children is their parents' (17:6).

FRIENDS

Next to a good family, a person needs good friends and neighbours. In practice, a friend can often be more valuable than members of the family: 'Do not forget your friends or your parents' friends. If you are in trouble, don't travel to go and ask your relatives for help; a neighbour near by can help you more than a family member who is far away' (27:10). Of course, in order to acquire friends we need to show ourselves to be friendly: 'Never tell your neighbours to wait until tomorrow if you can help them now' (3:28). We also need tact: 'Don't visit your neighbours too often; they may get tired of you and come to hate you' (25:17). Above all, a relationship between friends needs to be based on honesty: 'A hypocrite hides hatred behind flattering words... Like a maniac who shoots deadly firebrands and arrows, so is one who deceives a neighbour and says, "I am only joking!"' (26:24, 18–19). Gossip, then as now, was one of the commonest threats to wholesome friendship (18:8; 26:22). Indeed, the way people speak to each other is one of the major themes of the wisdom literature. A slogan in one of the early chapters of Proverbs sums up 'seven things that Yahweh hates' and most of them are related to the way people speak: 'a proud look, a lying tongue, hands that kill innocent people, a mind that thinks up wicked plans, feet that hurry off to do evil, a witness who tells one lie after another, and someone who stirs up trouble among friends' (6:16–19).

Those who behave like this are the opposite of 'wise': they are fools, and there is only one way to deal with them: 'Give a silly answer to a silly question, and the one who asked it will realize that they're not as clever as they think' (26:5). The wise person, on the other hand, is characterized by prudent thought and speech: 'Be careful how you think; your life is shaped by your thoughts. Never say anything that isn't true' (4:23–24).

SOCIETY

Wisdom teachers were not only concerned with the behaviour of people in small groups: they also gave much teaching on how society as a whole should operate. At the very beginning of the book of Proverbs, we learn that its advice 'can teach you how to live intelligently and how to be honest, just, and fair' (1:3). Honesty, justice and fairness in society were among the key themes in the preaching of the prophets – and they are just as important here. We may find this somewhat surprising, for most scholars are agreed that the wisdom books must have originated in fairly well-to-do circles. The fact that the wisdom teachers of Israel had international connections supports that assumption, for wealth is required to make and sustain worldwide contacts of this kind. We certainly know that later Jewish wisdom teachers must have been quite rich. Writing about 180 BC, Ben Sira tells of his wide travels (Wisdom of Ben Sira 34:9–12), and gives advice on such things as behaviour at banquets (31:12 – 32:13) and how to treat slaves (33:24–31). He also mentions the school that he operated in Jerusalem, and invites others to join him there so that they too might 'acquire wisdom for yourselves without money' (51:23–28). In the Hebrew Bible, the description of Job certainly suggests that the authors of that book moved in high-class circles (Job 1:1–3), and even in Proverbs, some pieces of advice suggest a context of relative affluence (e.g. Proverbs 21:14). In the light of all this, it is surprising to find here a morality which recognizes the limitations of wealth. 'Wisdom' itself is more important than riches (Proverbs 3:13–15), and so is 'peace of mind' (17:1) and 'a good reputation' (22:1) – all of which suggests that it is 'Better to be poor and fear the Lord than to be rich and in trouble. Better to eat vegetables with people you love than to eat the finest meat where there is hate' (15:16–17). The other Old Testament wisdom books make exactly the same points, and even the pessimistic author of Ecclesiastes declares that amassing money is pointless: 'It was like chasing the wind – of no use at all' (Ecclesiastes 2:11). The book of Job asserts quite bluntly that trust in money is incompatible with a living

relationship to God: 'I have never trusted in riches or taken pride in my wealth... Such a sin should be punished by death; it denies Almighty God' (Job 31:24–25, 28).

The imagery of the wisdom books may be less picturesque and dramatic than the words of the prophets, but their social perspectives are remarkably similar. Many of the abuses condemned by the wisdom teachers were the same as those that caused so much concern to the prophets: unjust business practices (Proverbs 11:1), bribery (15:27) and taking advantage of people by charging interest on loans (28:8). All of this could be summed up in the slogan that it is 'Better to be poor and honest than rich and dishonest' (28:6). On a positive note, the wisdom literature is full of injunctions to those who are rich to share what they have with the poor – whether it be allowing access to their land and crops (Proverbs 13:23), or giving them clothes (Job 31:19–20), or just general exhortations to be generous to others (Proverbs 14:21, 31). As elsewhere in the Old Testament, this generosity is to apply especially to those with no other visible means of support – which in ancient Israel meant especially widows and orphans (Job 31:16–18; Proverbs 23:10–11). Animals could also be specifically singled out as needing to be treated with due concern for their welfare (Proverbs 14:4). Alongside charity, the wisdom books also advocate justice. It is one thing to give freely to those who are poor, but social justice is a more fundamental human need. The wisdom writers are conscious that it is usually rich people who create divisions within society (Proverbs 30:13–14), and so they advocate taking positive steps to correct social injustices: 'Speak up for people who cannot speak for themselves. Protect the rights of all who are helpless. Speak for them and be a righteous judge. Protect the rights of the poor and needy' (Proverbs 31:8–9)

Here, in the wisdom books, we have much clear guidance on how God's people should behave. Morality, like charity, was to begin at home, but its effects went wider than the individual person: they were as broad as society itself.

Discovering God's will in the Law

The wisdom books reflect the standards of decent behaviour that most people might take for granted. But in any organized society, this kind of moral consensus needs to be clearly defined, and this is what we find in the Old Testament law books. The first five books of the Old Testament, from Genesis to Deuteronomy, were often referred to simply as 'the Law', though much of the material in these books is not at all like the kind of law most people would be familiar with today. Genesis in particular is a collection of stories, which at first sight we might expect to be regarded as some sort of history. But the Old Testament notion of 'law' was much more comprehensive and wide-ranging than ours. When we talk of 'the law' we generally have in mind sets of rules that can be interpreted by lawyers with special professional training, and applied in a court of justice by a judge. It would certainly be unusual for a modern person to agree with one of the Old Testament poets who wrote, 'I take pleasure in your law' (Psalm 119:77). But the Hebrew word for law (*Torah*) meant far more than just rules and regulations, and included everything that God had revealed to the people, especially the 'guidance' or 'instruction' that would enable them to live life to the full. The Torah was the place to discover what people should believe about God, and what might be required of them in return. This explains why the Torah was always closely bound up with the stories of Israel's early history, for knowing and obeying God was not just a matter of blind obedience to religious and moral rules, but a matter of experiencing God's concern and love in a personal and social context. God's undeserved love to the people – shown in events such as the exodus –

Wisdom and faith

People have often thought that the wisdom books present a different message from the prophets or the Old Testament laws. The main strands of Old Testament theology emphasize God's actions in the life of the people, whereas the wisdom books are said to be more 'secular', based not on God's personal revelation, but on human reason. In addition, it is often asserted that whereas the prophets and lawgivers of ancient Israel were concerned with the shape of society, the wisdom books are concerned more with personal morality. We can certainly agree that some features of these books seem to justify such observations:

● They are part of an international way of thinking, and as such have a number of similarities with literature from both Babylon and Egypt. They are not, therefore, unique to Israel, and in that sense cannot be said to be exclusively based on the distinctive characteristics of Israelite spirituality.

● They rarely, if ever, refer directly to the great events of the Old Testament story. Instead, their teaching tends to be based on common sense and on observation of the world of nature.

Some scholars have thought of the wisdom books and their moral teaching as a secular, humanistic intrusion into the Old Testament faith. They regard them as the religious side of those social and political changes that accompanied the institutionalization of the monarchy in ancient Israel, and the adoption of a lifestyle suited to the world of international politics. But this is too simple an analysis.

Is wisdom secular?

To say that the wisdom books are 'secular' is to impose a modern way of thinking on the ancient world. Certainly, the wisdom writers take their starting point from human experience of life, but in the ancient world in general this was never 'humanistic' in the narrow sense of being purely secular and non-religious. Throughout the ancient world, 'wisdom' was always based on an understanding of how the world works – but it was everywhere taken for granted that the world only worked at all because of the intentions of the deities or, in the case of the Hebrew Bible, of one all-powerful God. To refuse to take account of this was something that only a 'fool' would do. A really wise person would never forget that the ordinary world of everyday experience was directly sustained by God. Even a pessimist like the author of Ecclesiastes, who frankly confesses that he sometimes finds it hard to discover God at work in the

is basic to the Old Testament laws. Israel did not keep the Law in order to become God's people, but because they were already living in a close personal relationship to God.

The German scholar Albrecht Alt believed that some of the Old Testament's most distinctive laws emerged in this way out of Israel's experience of God. Many Old Testament laws are similar to the legislation of other ancient societies, for they concern the everyday happenings of rural life. Alt designated these 'casuistic' or case laws – laws in which very specific situations were envisaged, and guidance given as to how disputes may be resolved. A typical law of this kind might deal with violent assault (e.g. Exodus 21:20), or with the processes of responsible farming (e.g. Exodus 22:6). But there are also other, more absolute regulations, such as the ten commandments, in which worship of other deities, murder, adultery, theft and lying are all prohibited

---

**Wisdom and faith
continued**

world, nevertheless takes God's existence for granted as a fundamental part of his view of life. Other writers were more positive: 'To be wise you must first obey the Lord. If you know the Holy One, you have understanding' (Proverbs 9:10).

Wisdom and natural law

In view of the importance the Old Testament attaches to the relationship of God with this world, it is not surprising that contemplation of the way the world is should lead to personal encounter with God. If, as the writer of the first few chapters of Genesis suggests, God can be found in the realities of the natural world, then it is hardly surprising that the discerning moralist can discover there traces of God's way of doing things. This kind of 'natural law' is a widespread phenomenon, and in some respects is the basis for the modern definition of human rights, understood as being inalienable expectations based on some notion of 'natural justice' rather than on standards handed down from God or anyone else. The Old Testament wisdom books often appeal to precisely this sort of argument. Job, for example, asks for justice for himself because he has been just to his servants, and 'The same God who created me created my servants also' (Job 31:15). Moreover, this sort of appeal to 'natural

justice' is by no means restricted to the wisdom books, but can be found throughout the Old Testament. When the prophet Amos denounced the war crimes of the nations of his day, he did so on the basis of natural justice (Amos 1:1 – 2:3), and when the writer of Genesis condemned murder, it was because people were made 'in God's image' (Genesis 9:6). Likewise, when Isaiah complained about the disobedience of his people, he concluded that their behaviour was unnatural and irrational because it was so different from the way that things work in the world of nature (Isaiah 1:2–3). Apart from specific examples such as these, much of the imagery of the messages of the Old Testament prophets is also drawn from the world of nature, just as is the imagery in books like Proverbs. It is not necessary to speculate as to whether the prophets 'borrowed' such ideas from the wisdom teachers, for it is much more likely that both of them were independently basing their teaching on the kind of creation-centred spirituality that is a central element within the Old Testament faith.

Wisdom and social ethics

It has also been claimed that a 'wisdom' morality is inconsistent with an emphasis on social justice. It is certainly true that teaching on the shape of society is

The Israelites were instructed to teach each generation the laws God had given.

presented more forcibly by the prophets and lawgivers in relation to the great themes of Israel's salvation history, but we do an injustice to wisdom teachers in ancient Israel to suppose that they were interested only in themselves. Indeed, in the wider wisdom literature of the ancient world social justice was a major concern. Protecting the poor and disadvantaged members of society was a major theme in Babylonian and Egyptian literature as well as in the texts from Ugarit which tell of Canaanite kings showing the same sort of consideration. At the very beginning of Proverbs, the book's aims are summed up as teaching people 'how to live intelligently and how to be honest, just, and fair' (1:3), while the hero of the book of Job provides a perfect example of a person who always did the right thing by those less fortunate than himself (Job 31:13–23). No doubt the wisdom books generally offer different reasons for promoting equality and justice than did the prophets and history writers, but their ethical stance is none the less 'religious' for that.

Wisdom and the covenant

In point of fact, the actual ethical advice of the wisdom writers is often identical to the lessons drawn from Israel's past by the writers of the deuteronomic history. Caring for the poor, consideration for animals, justice in society and concern for orphans as well as the prohibition of false witness, adultery, bribery and vengeance – all these things are as common in the wisdom literature as they are in the Old Testament laws. Indeed, the wisdom writers often express these ideas more concretely by showing how they relate to specific situations in the life of the family or the community. Time and time again, the wisdom writers apply the same lessons as the prophets and others who stood in the 'covenant' tradition, for they were all consciously serving the same God, whose will could be made known to the people in both the created world and the great unrepeatable events of history.

without any further qualification or explanation (Exodus 20:1–17; Deuteronomy 5:6–22). Moreover, such prohibitions seem to be based on a simple statement about God's nature as Israel had experienced this in the course of their history. In a previous chapter, we have reviewed the evidence suggesting that in giving the commandments this precise form, the Old Testament writers may have had in mind the kind of covenant treaties that small struggling nations often made with more powerful states, in exchange for protection and security. Such covenant agreements would be reaffirmed at regular intervals, and Alt believed that 'apodictic' laws of this kind formed the centre of Israel's renewal of their faith in God every seven years at the festival of shelters, or Tabernacles (Deuteronomy 31:9–13). It was this form of absolute law that was most characteristic of the Old Testament, for it was nothing less than an explanation of the everyday ramifications of Israel's covenant faith. Insofar as it underlines the most distinctive aspects of the Torah, this understanding has certain attractions, though there are also a number of difficulties with it:

■ Casuistic law is a specific literary form, but this so-called 'apodictic' law is not strictly a literary form at all and these absolute laws are expressed in a variety of literary formulations. The two categories are not, therefore, directly comparable to one another.

■ Alt believed that these absolute rules were unique to Israel, though subsequent discoveries have shown that similar terminology could also be used in legal contexts elsewhere, especially among the Hittites, but also in Egypt and Babylon. It was not always the same actions that were prohibited there, of course, but the form itself was certainly found outside the confines of the Old Testament.

■ There is no real evidence that these 'apodictic' laws either originated in, or were regularly repeated at, the great religious festivals in Israel.

■ These statements are not really 'law' in the technical sense at all. They are more a general listing of accepted standards of behaviour, and in this respect the 'apodictic' law is not all that different from the teaching of the wisdom books. It is at least arguable that they could be based on Israel's understanding of the 'natural law' revealed in the work of creation, and not on the covenant at Mount Sinai.

The books of the Torah, like all modern collections of law (and many other parts of the Old Testament), are an anthology of laws relating to different situations and different periods during the whole span of the history of ancient Israel. They are not meant to be read from start to finish as a consistent account of Israel's legal system, and it is obvious that within the books of the Law there are at least four quite separate collections of material: the ten commandments, the book of the covenant, Deuteronomy and a number of priestly laws. The precise way in which these separate law codes might be related to one another will be determined by the view that is taken on the compilation of the first five books of the Old Testament, and the discussion of them here takes account of what has already been said on that subject in a previous chapter.

The ten commandments

Most people who know anything at all about the Bible will recognize this collection of moral rules (Exodus 20:1–17) as a basic part of the Old Testament's view of human behaviour. Its principles have been enshrined in many national law codes since Old Testament days, and in some respects form a charter of fundamental human rights. It was obviously intended to be learned by heart, and often repeated. The fact that there are ten commandments is certainly not accidental, but is a learning device so that they could be counted off on the fingers of both hands as they were repeated. This was a popular way of remembering things.

There are other groups of laws which may originally have been organized in the same way, though they are mostly concerned with the conduct of organized worship (Exodus 34:12–26; Leviticus 20:2–5; 18:6–18). The book of Psalms also contains at least one such list of ten things that summarize good behaviour (Psalm 15:2–5). This is the main subject of the ten commandments themselves. In that sense, they are not technically laws at all, for they contain no mention of penalties for those who break them. Rather, they are a kind of policy statement – a bill of rights – showing how relationships between God and humankind were to be viewed within the Old Testament faith community. It is widely agreed by scholars that this list must have originated at a very early period in Israel's history, and some claim it can be traced back to Moses himself.

The book of the covenant

Many parts of the book of the covenant (Exodus 20:22 – 23:33) are similar to other ancient law codes, especially the codes of Ur-Nammu of Ur (2050 BC) and of Hammurabi, king of Babylon (1700 BC). Though there are many differences of detail between the book of the covenant and these other laws, their general outlook is the same and simply reflects widespread customs in the ancient world. So this is much more like a code of law in the modern sense. It is, however, widely believed to be very ancient, going back to the time of Israel's earliest leaders, Moses and Joshua. The essential concern of these laws is with the life of the community, and they are mostly a 'casuistic' type of legislation, though some sections also deal with the conduct of organized worship.

Deuteronomy

The word 'Deuteronomy' means 'a second law', and here we find an amplification and interpretation of earlier law codes, showing how they could apply to the changing circumstances of Israel's national life. As such, this book is obviously based on ancient materials, and some believe that it found its present form as a liturgy for a covenant renewal

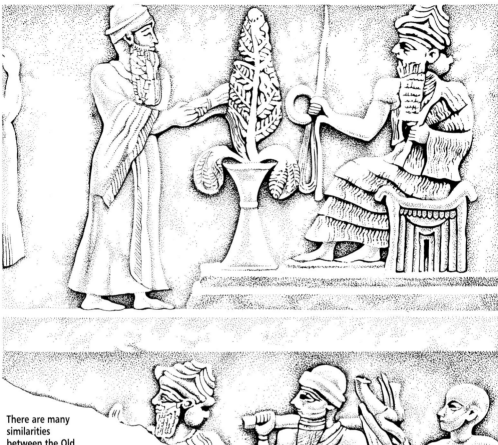

There are many similarities between the Old Testament covenant and the law code of King Ur-Nammu of Ur. In this relief, the king is seen on the left pouring out a libation in front of a seated god.

festival at which the worshippers in ancient Israel would regularly 'relive' the events of their national past, and commit themselves afresh to their God Yahweh. Chapters 5–11 certainly read like sermons, preached as a prelude to the presentation of the actual Law itself in chapters 12–26, and followed by the people's commitment to it in chapters 27–28. The book of Deuteronomy was a major influence in the reform of Temple worship carried out by King Josiah of Judah, though its actual origins were certainly earlier than his day (2 Kings 22:3–20).

Priestly laws

These are found in Exodus, Leviticus and Numbers and, in effect, include all the rest of the Old Testament laws, among which are large sections dealing with the tabernacle and its contents (Exodus 25–30), and various regulations related to priests and sacrificial worship (Exodus 35–40; Leviticus 1–10). There are also detailed regulations governing the preparation and eating of food as well as matters of domestic and personal hygiene (Leviticus 11–16). It was once believed that these rules concerning worship were relatively late developments in the story of Israel, partly because the message of the sixth-century prophet Ezekiel (Ezekiel 40–48) contains some similar notions, but closer investigation has shown that many of the practices referred to here are very similar to practices known elsewhere in the ancient world at a much earlier date. One section of the book of Leviticus (chapters 17–26) is generally regarded as another separate law code, the 'holiness code'. There are several reasons for this:

■ These chapters begin with rules about organized worship, but then make no reference at all to the very full legislation on the matter found in the preceding chapters.

■ The statement that 'All these are the laws and commands that Yahweh gave to Moses on Mount Sinai for the people of Israel' (Leviticus 26:46) seems to be a formal ending, which does not relate to what follows in the next chapter.

■ The theme of 'holiness' runs everywhere through these chapters, but is not a prominent theme at all in the rest of Leviticus.

From theory to practice

Life in the ancient world was significantly different from life today, and most readers now find all these laws dull and tedious. But they can still provide a number of insights into important aspects of the Old Testament faith. There seem to be so many collections of laws that it comes as a bit of a surprise to discover that they are far from comprehensive, and many situations are not mentioned at all. Other ancient law codes were the same, perhaps because the laws that were written down were only intended as samples of how justice should be administered. Or it could be that the written laws were to give guidance in cases of particular difficulty, and alongside them other more straightforward procedures were simply taken for granted. There are many ways of classifying these laws. One area of life controlled by the Torah was what we today would call religion, and those that fall into this category, describing how worship is to be conducted, are considered more fully in the next chapter. Of course, it is important to remember that religion and everyday behaviour cannot easily be separated in the Old Testament, and therefore this division is certainly artificial, if not arbitrary. But in addition to those dealing specifically with ritual matters, four other types of law may be traced within the Old Testament codes: criminal law, civil law, family law and social law.

Criminal law

Whereas civil law deals with arguments between individuals, about which there can be room for different judgments in different circumstances, criminal law concerns principles of right and wrong that are taken as self-evident. Every society has certain actions that are so thoroughly and universally disapproved of that the community itself feels it necessary to punish those who do them. This does not mean that the criminal law of one nation will always be the same as the criminal law of another. Indeed, there are often striking differences, and activities that are branded as criminal in one state may well be regarded as fundamental human rights in another. So by examining those actions which a particular state regards as criminal, we can soon understand the basic attitudes and fundamental values of its people. As far as we can see, the only penalty imposed by the state itself in ancient Israel was the death penalty. Fines were unknown, and though a person could be put under arrest while a case was decided, imprisonment as such was not introduced until after the exile in Babylon. Monetary sanctions could be imposed, but they were regarded as restitution by the wrongdoer to the victim, and therefore came within the jurisdiction of the civil law. Even crimes such as personal assault or theft were dealt with in this way. It is probably significant that every crime punishable by death was related in some way or another to the ten command-ments, which is why these commandments have often been described as ancient Israel's criminal law. Of course, the ten commandments are not strictly 'law' at all in the technical sense, but this way of looking at them is still useful, for all those actions punishable by the community as a whole were closely related to Israel's understanding of their position as the people of God. In that context to commit a crime was, quite simply, to deny the reality of the covenant faith. Such crimes included the following.

OFFENCES AGAINST GOD
Examples of these offences would be the worship of other deities (Exodus 22:20; Leviticus 20:1–5), blasphemy (Leviticus 24:10–16) and magic (Deuteronomy 13:1–18; Exodus 22:18; Leviticus 20:27), all of which in one way or another deny the very basis of the relationship between God and the community. Other offences, such as a priest's daughter working as a prostitute (Leviticus 21:9) or not keeping the sabbath day (Exodus 31:14–15) might seem less serious to us, though the Torah views them in the same light because both priesthood and sabbath are 'a sign of the covenant' (Exodus 31:16).

OFFENCES AGAINST HUMAN LIFE
Intentional murder was a particularly serious crime, though accidental killing was subject to other penalties (Exodus 21:12; Leviticus 24:17; Numbers 35:16–21, 22–29). Kidnapping was an equally serious offence (Exodus 21:16; Deuteronomy 24:7). In Israel, human liberty as well as human life was of great value, and many scholars believe that the eighth commandment refers not to stealing in general, but to

kidnapping more specifically (Exodus 20:15; Deuteronomy 5:19). The theme of personal freedom is certainly important in other sections of Old Testament law.

OFFENCES AGAINST THE FAMILY

If the unnatural termination of life was a criminal offence, so was interference with the natural context in which life is created, namely the sexual relationship between husband and wife. Other kinds of sexual activity, whether incest, buggery or even adultery, were all regarded as serious criminal offences (Leviticus 20:10–21), along with disdain for parents (Exodus 21:15; Deuteronomy 21:18–21).

Civil law

Old Testament civil law has many similarities to other laws found in the ancient world. It deals with everyday matters such as the treatment of employees, violence of various sorts and the duties of owners to protect third parties from injury caused by either animals or property. The book of the covenant consists entirely of this sort of law, and it may be significant that in this law code God is usually referred to as 'Elohim', meaning 'God' in general, rather than by the personal name 'Yahweh'. This may be an indication that Israel simply took over this legal form from the general stock of commonly accepted norms without making too many detailed changes or additions to it.

Punishment under this category was generally understood as compensation for the wrong done, and many penalties are similar to those prescribed in other codes such as the laws of Hammurabi. But there are some differences. Bodily mutilation, for example, was quite a common punishment in the ancient world, but there is only one specific example of it in the Old Testament (Deuteronomy 25:11–12). There is certainly provision for punishments to be exacted 'life for life, eye for eye, tooth for tooth, hand for hand, foot for foot, burn for burn, wound for wound, bruise for bruise' (Exodus 21:23–24; Leviticus 24:19–20; Deuteronomy 19:21), though this seems to be almost a symbolic statement, emphasizing that the punishment should always be in proportion to the wrong that has been suffered. In the ancient world, however, even this apparently ruthless retribution could be a means of limiting what might otherwise be excessive vengeance. In the light of Lamech's boast that 'I have killed a young man because he struck me' (Genesis 4:23), even a basic law of equal retribution could be regarded as an improvement. In the event, though the principle is stated in the book of the covenant, it is both preceded and followed there by laws which show that, in general, forms other than physical punishment could and should be preferred: generally, financial compensation. The payment of compensation to the victim in place of physical punishment was probably quite a widespread practice.

Family law

The whole of Israelite society was family and clan based, and the importance of the family unit is reflected in many Old Testament laws. Relationships between family members had a far-reaching effect on the overall shape of Israelite society. A stable relationship between husband and wife was basic to the Old Testament view of family life. Marriage itself was generally of one man to one woman (monogamy), though kings and other leading figures often seem to have had more than one wife (polygamy), and this practice is never actually prohibited anywhere. Marriages were generally arranged by parents, though love marriages are not altogether unknown (e.g. 1 Samuel 18:20). But alongside a legal wife, a man could also have any number of 'concubines'. They were slave wives, and had a correspondingly lower status than the main wife. Divorce was taken for granted, though in practice it could often leave a woman destitute and was probably not very frequent for that reason. But all these matters were entirely a family affair in which the Law as such would not be involved at all, except that the civil law contains a number of guidelines relating to circumstances that might arise with a breakdown of normal relationships, and the criminal law of course forbids adultery. Detailed regulations are given for the proper treatment of concubines (Exodus 21:7–11; Deuteronomy 21:10–14) and guidance is also given on what should happen after a divorce (Deuteronomy 24:1–4).

Wilful disregard for parents was in certain circumstances dealt with by the criminal law, but usually the authority of the father or patriarch of the family was absolute, and in the earliest period a father could even condemn members of his own family to death (Genesis 38:24). Later legislation provided for such cases to be referred to the village elders (Deuteronomy 21:18–21) and some passages suggest there was an ultimate right of appeal to the king (2 Samuel 14:4–11).

On the positive side, members of a family also had obligations to each other. If family members were forced to sell themselves into slavery to pay off a debt, then it was the duty of their close relatives to buy them back (Leviticus 25:47–49), circumstances which are well illustrated in the story of Ruth. Family life in Old Testament times was generally tough for all but the patriarchal leader of a clan, and though there was a measure of security on offer, that was accompanied by the demand of awesome responsibilities.

Social law

The Canaanite city states among which Israel emerged as a nation were essentially feudal societies, with a powerful and wealthy ruling class. This was in strong contrast to the tribal structure that is always held up as the ideal in the Old Testament. At its best, this emphasis was to ensure that Israelite society would not be dominated by a powerful hierarchy, but was a self-consciously egalitarian society in which all citizens enjoyed the same fundamental rights and privileges.

The conflict between these two models of society runs deep in the Old Testament. In the earliest Israelite settlements, local elders were the leaders of their own communities, but the need for a king was obvious and irresistible. That does not mean there was no opposition, and even once Israel had become a state the power of the king was stringently regulated by the Law (Deuteronomy 17:14–20). When the great kingdom split in two after Solomon's death, it was largely as the result of tensions between the Canaanite, bureaucratic ideal and the Israelite ideal in which every individual was equal, their freedom restricted only by the mutual obligations imposed by the family group.

In practical terms, the central issue was the possession of land. In the Canaanite city states all land was ultimately owned by the king (1 Samuel 8:11–17), whereas in Israel all land was regarded as belonging to God. It was given in trust to the family group as something that could be neither bought nor sold, but must be handed on from one generation to the next (Leviticus 25:23). In this way Israel hoped to avoid the emergence of a land-owning class, and to preserve the relative equality of all the people. Those who tried to amass land for themselves were tirelessly condemned by the prophets (Isaiah 5:8; Micah 2:1–2), and even the king was not exempt from such criticism (1 Kings 21). This emphasis explains why apparently tedious lists of people and land play such an important part in the Old Testament (Numbers 26; 34; Joshua 13–19). Many laws set out to preserve the freedom of the individual to live unmolested on the land which God had given to the family. The Law banned actions such as moving boundary stones (Deuteronomy 19:14), and many other prohibitions relating to loans and debts also find their real significance in this context (Exodus 22:25; Leviticus 25:35–38). Charging interest on loans was forbidden (Deuteronomy 23:19–20), though what often happened was that a person would give either clothes or property as security for a loan. Then, if the loan could not be repaid, the borrower would soon become virtually a slave of the lender, and while technically living on their own family land, would be reduced to a state of destitution. This is why the Law tried to regulate what could be used as security for loans (Exodus 22:26–27; Deuteronomy 24:6). It also provided for debts to be written off every seven years

Boundary stones marked the limits of a person's land; this one comes from Babylon in the time of Nebuchadnezzar I. Some Old Testament laws were aimed at preventing the absorption of smallholdings into great estates.

(the sabbatical year, Deuteronomy 15:1–11), or every fifty years (the Jubilee, Leviticus 25:8–17).

The Old Testament social ethic displays great concern for many disadvantaged groups – foreigners, the poor, the oppressed, widows, orphans and even personal enemies (Exodus 22:21–27; 23:1–9). This emphasis has been a significant reason why some scholars have argued that early Israel originated as a proletarian protest movement against the elitist structures of traditional Canaanite power. As has been pointed out in a previous chapter, there is a good deal to be said in favour of this view, though it is important not to exaggerate its uniqueness. Concern for despised people was not exclusively Israelite, and in the laws of Ur-

These slaves in Assyria at the time of Sennacherib were far worse off than slaves in Israel, where the laws protected them at many points.

Nammu, for example, the following list is given of the king's achievements:

> *The orphan was not delivered up to the rich man, the widow was not delivered up to the mighty man, the man of one shekel was not delivered up to the man of one mina.*

The Old Testament is most distinctive in its treatment of slaves, who were clearly regarded as persons in their own right. Not only could they expect to be set free (Exodus 21:1–6), but they also had rights even if they ran away from their master (Deuteronomy 23:15–16). The master must give slaves a regular day off, and must recognize that there are limits to the power that can reasonably be wielded over another person's life (Exodus 23:12; Deuteronomy 5:12–15). The master who injured a slave could be forced to compensate by allowing the slave to go free (Exodus 21:26–27). If an owner killed a slave, that was regarded as a particularly serious offence, and was to be avenged by the community acting on behalf of the slave, presumably because slaves had no family of their own to defend them (Exodus 21:20). Some scholars believe that the death penalty was prescribed for this, and if they are right such concern for the welfare of slaves would have been absolutely without parallel in the ancient world. It would also suggest that the killing of a slave represented a spiritual as well as a social challenge to the community. The religious background to the slavery laws is certainly made clear in at least one law code, where special treatment of slaves is justified by the statement, 'you were slaves in Egypt and Yahweh your God set you free; that is why I am now giving you this command' (Deuteronomy 15:15). The distinctive nature of Israelite society emerged not out of purely humanitarian motives: it was part and parcel of Israel's experience of their God in the formative events of the nation's history.

Explaining God's will

The impact of Israel's history on the sort of society envisaged by the Old Testament can be seen quite clearly. Indeed, in one way or another, all the most distinctive features of Old Testament morality have been determined by Israel's encounter with God on the stage of human history. The great events which helped formulate Israel's understanding of God's character also gave a special insight into what God required of the people. Events such as the escape from Egypt and the entry into the promised land had their effect on God's people and their behaviour. In the Old Testament, correct behaviour, like many other things, was based on history. But how can the facts of history provide instruction in morality? As we read the messages of the great prophets and explore the teaching of the books of Law, the answer to that question soon emerges, for the Old Testament ethic is not only historical: it also has other characteristics that can be identified by an appreciation of God's involvement in the lives of the people of Israel.

The Old Testament ethic is theological

It is 'theological' in the strict meaning of that word, for the Old Testament code of behaviour always refers back to God's own personality. Correct human behaviour is closely related to the kind of God who was revealed in the events of Israel's history. It is, of course, always true that the kind of God people believe in affects the way they behave. The Hebrew Bible stresses that God is a personal and active being who can be known both by individuals and societies in the context of their everyday experience of life. It takes these characteristics of God and applies them directly to the life of ordinary people. Here, human goodness finds its authority, example and inspiration in the person of God, and nowhere is this summed up more eloquently than in Leviticus 19:2: 'Be holy, because I, the Lord your God, am holy.' God's people are to behave the same way as God behaves, something that has been well expressed by Emil Brunner's characterization of Old Testament morality as being 'the science of human conduct as it is determined by divine conduct'.

The Old Testament ethic is dynamic

How is God's own personality expressed? We have already observed that the Old Testament never tries to analyse or define God in an abstract way. God is not described 'metaphysically', but 'functionally', with the major emphasis being on what God does. Obviously, the two are closely related, because the way people are will be reflected in the way that they work. But Yahweh is not so much a 'God who is', but a 'God who acts' – a dynamic God rather than a static one. What then can be learned about human behaviour by looking at the characteristic actions of God? Three terms are often used in the Old Testament to describe God's moral disposition.

JUSTICE

This might seem to be a very abstract idea, for 'justice' is the kind of thing that lawyers and judges argue about in law courts. In the Old Testament, 'justice' includes this concern for fair play, but more characteristically justice is less something to talk about, and more something to be done. The leaders of early Israel were not 'judges' in the modern legal sense: they were leaders of their people who saw something wrong, and took action to put it right. Indeed, the Hebrew word that is normally translated 'justice' in English versions of the Bible really has a

much wider meaning than that, and refers to everything that a ruler might do to ensure that people would enjoy a stable and satisfying way of life. God, therefore, is like a 'just' ruler, and is concerned to improve the quality of life for the people (Deuteronomy 32:4; Isaiah 5:16; 61:8).

MERCY

When this word is used to describe God, it is emphasizing that God deals with people in a loving and personal way. God's justice is not determined by the stringent requirements of some detached legal system, but always operates in a context of personal love and trust. The entire Old Testament story shows how, against all expectations, God has initiated a relationship with people who by nature are weak and often morally and spiritually powerless. God never abandons them, but stands alongside them to help in their weakness, and will never reject them despite all their inadequacy and imperfection. 'How can I give you up, Israel? How can I abandon you?... My heart will not let me do it! My love for you is too strong... For I am God and not a human being. I, the Holy One, am with you. I will not come to you in anger' (Hosea 11:8–9).

TRUTH

This is also something that we tend to think of in abstract terms, but again in Hebrew thinking 'truth' was most often regarded not as a characteristic of propositions, but of people. When the disguised Joseph put his brothers in prison, he did so to find out 'whether there is truth in you' – in other words, whether they could be trusted or not (Genesis 42:16). In the world of the Old Testament the deities were notoriously unreliable. They did whatever they wished, and all too often their human worshippers had to pay the price. But the God of the Old Testament is quite different, and is depicted as being wholly trustworthy. People can therefore trust God without any fear of failure: 'I have complete confidence, O God!... Your constant love reaches above the heavens; your faithfulness touches the skies' (Psalm 108:1, 4).

God is shown as being completely trustworthy, and it is a trait that should be reflected in dealings between people. The inscription on this clay tablet suggests that it was a receipt for a delivery of gold.

The Old Testament ethic is social

In what context is God's will most truly done? Is God concerned with the moral goodness of individuals, or with the shape of society? Inevitably, these two concerns are not mutually exclusive. Individual people are called upon to respond for themselves to the will of God. When Isaiah was confronted with the moral grandeur of God in the Temple, he confessed to his own shortcomings and became intensely aware of his own personal inadequacy to do the work to which God was calling him (Isaiah 6:5).

The story of Abraham pleading for the deliverance of two evil cities makes a similar point: God cares about the behaviour of individuals (Genesis 18:16–33). Yet throughout the Old Testament, there is also a major emphasis on the whole of God's people: God's will is to be shown not just in the lives of committed individuals, but in the structures of national life as well. We have already noticed this strong emphasis on social justice in both wisdom books and law codes, and it was born out of the formative events of Israel's history. On a social level, the exodus had demonstrated God's concern for those who were unjustly oppressed by the forces of imperialism. Yahweh saw that things were bad in Egypt, and stepped in to change the situation. This is why the ideal Old Testament society always had a special place for the dispossessed, the oppressed and the disadvantaged. Moreover, the very fabric of society should reflect this concern. The prophets loved to remind their people that in Israel all men and women must be equal: they had all started out as equals (as slaves) and therefore economic and social exploitation of one class by another was not only deplorable, but was also a fundamental denial of the very heart of the Old Testament faith.

The Old Testament ethic is personal

This brings us to the crux of the whole matter. Behaviour in the Old Testament is always seen in the context of the covenant that Israel had entered into with God. God was deeply involved in every aspect of the life of this world, not at all aloof from the human predicament, and this involvement was expressed in the notion of the covenant. For as Israel looked back to the foundation events of their national life, they saw the exodus and what followed as the culmination of God's purpose for this people. In the memory of that momentous event, Israel found the meaning of their national life. As the freed slaves had stood before Mount Sinai they had been reminded of God's great and loving actions on their behalf. In return, they were called upon to fulfil God's commands. Israelite society was based on this mutual relationship of love and responsibility, and as the people came together for celebration and worship in the annual cycle of religious festivals, each generation was able to commit itself afresh to this personal relationship between God and the people. That was where life found its deepest meaning. God had called them in love when they were neither expecting nor deserving it, and succeeding generations would respond to that love by following the example set by God in person.

When the Old Testament demands justice, mercy and truth in human relationships, it does not appeal to some abstract notion of morality. Instead, it goes back to the roots of the covenant faith in the justice, mercy and truth of God. When the prophets call for righteousness in society, they look back to the actions of God in caring for outcasts and strangers. It is no surprise, therefore, that one of the most eloquent expressions of God's values and ways of doing things – the ten commandments – begins not with a command, but with a statement: 'I am Yahweh your God who brought you out of Egypt, where you were slaves' (Exodus 20:2). Right behaviour should stem naturally from the response of a grateful people to what God has done for them. Morality and theology are inextricably interwoven with each other, for it is within the context of a personal relationship between God and people that the ethical principles of the Old Testament can most fully be understood.

The administration of justice

We have examined the content of the Old Testament law codes in some detail. But how were these laws put into practice? What sort of legal structures existed in ancient Israel? There is no single answer to that question, for Israelite society underwent a number of profound changes in the course of the events documented in the Old Testament. The life of the tribes in the days of the judges was socially and politically quite different from life in the kingdom of David and Solomon. Things changed again after their kingdom divided, and then following the demise of the northern kingdom of Israel. Changing circumstances inevitably led to changes in national institutions, and the admini-stration of law varied from one century to another in the course of the nation's story. But a number of individuals are mentioned in relation to the administration of justice, and consideration of their functions will provide an insight into some aspects of this complex subject.

The elders

Israelite society was always regarded as an extended family group. The head of each family had jurisdiction over his own relatives and household, and the town or village elders were just the leading members of the various families. The deuteronomic code mentions them quite specifically as acting as a regular court where disputes about the Law could be settled (Deuteronomy 19:12; 21:1–9, 18–21; 22:13–21; 25:5–10), and all the evidence suggests that this was the main law court throughout the entire history of Israel. The elders would gather at the gates of the town, which was a regular meeting place for serious discussion of the affairs of the community (Genesis 23:10–18; Job 29:7–10). There was no official prosecutor, and the complainant would present the case against the accused in person. Some passages suggest there would be an official 'defender' of the accused person (Psalm 109:31). Certainly, both prosecution and defence would call witnesses and produce material evidence (Exodus 22:13; Deuteronomy 22:13–17). Accusations and evidence would normally be presented verbally, though written statements could also be accepted (Job 31:35–36). The elders would be seated during the trial, rising to pronounce their verdict. If a penalty was involved, then the elders would impose it and would usually carry it out on the spot (Deuteronomy 22:13–21). The whole of this procedure reflects the view that most cases were essentially civil disputes. The job of the town elders was to adjudicate between the various parties, and thereby

The administration of
justice *continued*

ensure that justice was done. The story of
the book of Ruth provides a good example
of how it worked in practice (Ruth 4:1–12).

The corruption of such local courts
is a major theme in the prophets
(Amos 5:10–15). It was all too easy for
elders to be swayed by their own
prejudices, or even to accede to the wishes
of a king who wanted to act uncon-
stitutionally. The story of Naboth's trial and
subsequent execution is a striking
illustration of how the whole system could
be abused by the powerful for their own
advantage (1 Kings 21:1–16). Though
false witnesses were liable to severe
penalties (Deuteronomy 19:15–20), this
does not seem to have deterred perjury,
and there is plenty of evidence to show
that justice at the city gate was sometimes
rough and ready.

**The Law was held
in great honour
by the people of
Israel, as it has
been by orthodox
Jews throughout
the generations.**

the 'minor judges' (Judges 10:1–5;
12:8–15), suggesting that the law they
administered was the casuistic law
contained in the book of the covenant.
Martin Noth incorporated this insight into
his theory that early Israel was organized
along the lines of a tribal amphictyony, and
these 'minor judges' thereby became the
guardians of the covenant theology which
held the various tribes together. This view
has been considered in detail in an earlier
chapter, and though neither Alt nor Noth
was ever able to produce any really
compelling evidence to support it, it is a
plausible way to imagine ancient Israel
functioning.

Others have argued that professional
judges were a later development, perhaps
originating in the southern kingdom of
Judah with the political and religious
reforms of Jehoshaphat (875–851 BC)
documented in 2 Chronicles 19:4–11. They
believe that the king always had an
important part to play in both establishing
and maintaining the Law, and that when
Jehoshaphat set up a system of
professional judges he was merely
formalizing a state of affairs that had
existed for a long time.

The king

The king certainly had a central role in
the legal affairs of his people. All the
ancient law codes known to us are
associated with kings, though quite
often their function was limited to
classifying customary procedures rather
than actually originating the Law. Since
the laws of a state are a vital part of its
self-understanding, it was necessary for
the king to be involved in this way if his
own position was to be maintained. But
the Old Testament gives no real
indication that the kings of either Israel
or Judah operated in this way. Josiah
perhaps came closest to publishing a law
(2 Kings 23:1–3), though that story
makes it clear that he was acting as an
intermediary in a covenant renewal
ceremony between God and the people

The judges

As well as the courts of elders, the Old
Testament also mentions professional
judges (Deuteronomy 16:18–20;
19:16–18). The laws of Deuteronomy
seem to envisage a system of local judges,
with a final court of appeal in Jerusalem
itself (Deuteronomy 17:8–13). Albrecht Alt
believed that professional judges were
important even in the earliest days of
Israelite society, and he equated them with

in much the same way as Moses (Exodus 24:3–8) and Joshua (Joshua 24:1–28) had done earlier, and as Ezra was to do later (Nehemiah 8:1–12). When the Old Testament explains the function of the king, there is no mention of lawgiving, and he is himself clearly stated to be subject to the Law of the covenant (Deuteronomy 17:14–20; 1 Samuel 8:10–18).

Some scholars suggest that all this reflects the ideals of Old Testament kingship rather than what actually happened in practice, though incidents in which the king overturned the normal course of justice always seem to be regarded as the exception rather than the rule. There is no substantial evidence that the king was in control of the legal process unless we are prepared to set aside almost the whole of the deuteronomic history as worthless and unreliable. This need not mean that kings never issued law codes as part of their duties. Josiah was certainly involved in reestablishing the laws of Deuteronomy, and there is also good reason to think that the book of the covenant may have been collated and issued in the time of David and Solomon almost as a constitution for their kingdom. But this did not make it 'state law', because it ultimately rested on a religious understanding of the life of the nation. It could just as easily be argued that when kings became involved in promoting the Law they were acting in a religious capacity rather than as purely political leaders.

Nevertheless, kings did have a judicial function. The kingship itself apparently originated within the general framework of family and tribal life (1 Samuel 8:4–5), and in that context the king would automatically be one of the 'elders' of the extended family of Israel. As such he would have a part to play in the administration of the Law, probably acting as a final court of appeal (2 Samuel 12:1–6; 14:1–11; 1 Kings 3:16–28; 7:7).

The priests

Deuteronomy makes a close connection between judges and priests when it provides for a court of appeal in Jerusalem staffed by both, apparently operating on a rota basis (Deuteronomy 17:8–12). Priests and judges are mentioned alongside one another elsewhere (Deuteronomy 19:17; 2 Chronicles 19:8–11), and in other ancient states priests often had judicial functions. In Israel, the close connection between Law and the covenant made it inevitable that priests would be involved in interpreting and applying the Law. No doubt this priestly function went back to a very early period of Israelite history. Whatever may be the truth about the nature of the 'minor judges', there can be little doubt that, like the 'major' judges, they had a religious as well as a political and social function. Samuel, who is presented as their successor, was essentially a priest operating from the shrines of Bethel, Gilgal and Mizpah, though his typical activities at these centres of worship clearly had judicial overtones (1 Samuel 7:16).

The precise judicial function of the priest is unclear. Priests would certainly pronounce on religious affairs (Leviticus 10:10; 13:1 – 14:57), and there are also hints that they could operate in a wider legal context (Leviticus 10:10–11; Deuteronomy 21:5; Ezekiel 44:24), though apart from the stories of Samuel there is no evidence of them ever doing so. Their more usual function would be as guardians of the final court of appeal, namely God. For the Law allowed that in cases where a normal court could reach no verdict, God should be called in as the final judge. God's will would then be ascertained either by a procedure of judicial oaths (Exodus 22:7–13) or by drawing lots – something probably associated with the manipulation of urim and thummim (sacred stones or dice) by the priests (Joshua 7:1–19; 1 Samuel 14:41–43).

Individuals and the community

The Old Testament lays great emphasis on groups: the family, the clan, the tribe, and ultimately the nation, are all of fundamental importance both religiously and morally. The covenant itself is a relationship between God and the whole people of Israel, and salvation and judgment are both corporate experiences. The processes of justice also take account of this corporate solidarity. When Achan stole some goods from the Canaanite city of Jericho, his entire family and all their goods shared in his punishment (Joshua 7:1–26), and some passages appear to elevate this to a general principle, that children will always be punished for the wrongs of their parents (Exodus 20:5; Deuteronomy 5:9). As a matter of common experience, it is true that any generation inevitably carries some burden from the past, but the Old Testament makes a very specific connection between past and present, the individual and the community. The prophets also emphasize corporate responsibility, pronouncing judgment on the whole nation because of the wrongs of some of its members (Amos 3:12–15; 5:16–24).

This emphasis was perhaps inevitable in a faith which was anchored to the events of history. If the exodus was to be relevant to later generations, then they had in some way to identify themselves with the experience of their forebears, and when they went along to organized worship at the shrines, they often did precisely that (Deuteronomy 26:5–10). This same connection between the experience of an individual and the state of the community also comes out in some of the psalms, though the best example of it is in the passages referring to the suffering servant. For here, this one person both represents the community and fulfils its true destiny in his or her own spiritual experience (Isaiah 42:1–4; 49:1–6; 50:4–9; 52:13 – 53:12). This way of

thinking has often been described as 'corporate personality', and it has been assumed that the Old Testament has a unique way of looking at people and their relationships. On this view, the idea of personal responsibility only came into the faith of Israel at a relatively late stage, when the group was in danger of disappearing altogether as an identifiable national entity. Jeremiah 31:29–30 and Ezekiel 18:4, 20 certainly emphasize that each person is responsible to God, but their statements do not really contradict the earlier Old Testament position. In their day, the people were blaming all their problems on past generations, and in response to that Jeremiah and Ezekiel both emphasized that it was not quite as simple as that, for each individual must accept some share of responsibility for the state of society as a whole. In any case, there is plenty of evidence that individuals were believed to have moral and spiritual responsibility long before that time:

● Many individuals in the earlier parts of the Old Testament story are praised for their own personal response and commitment to God. Enoch (Genesis 5:21–24), Noah (Genesis 6:9–12) and Hannah (1 Samuel 1:9 – 2:11) – as well as the prophets – are all specifically described in terms of their own personal spiritual experience.

● Individuals are also condemned and judged for their own wrongdoing. When David committed adultery with Bathsheba, he himself suffered the penalty (2 Samuel 12:1–23), and when Jezebel met her death beneath the ramparts of Jezreel, that was considered a fair punishment for her malicious judicial murder of Naboth (2 Kings 9:30–37). Moreover, the law codes are full of instructions about how individuals are to be dealt with in the light of their own behaviour. The case of Achan, whose entire family was punished for his theft, is in fact exceptional, which implies that it was almost certainly considered to be a specifically religious crime, and for that reason was punishable under different rules.

● Amos seems to have condemned the whole nation without regard for personal responsibility, though he may have expected some to repent and avoid judgment (Amos 5:4–7, 14–15). But other prophets clearly distinguished between the majority of the people who had broken the covenant and a small group who had not and who for that reason would escape punishment (Isaiah 10:20–22; Micah 5:7–8; Zephaniah 2:3; 3:11–13).

The idea of corporate solidarity is both less precise and less extensive than has often been thought. But it is also less distinctive than has sometimes been suggested. Many modern states have a parallel in their memorials to an 'unknown warrior', a military person who has been buried in a public place to be a lasting reminder of thousands of others who died in battle and were laid to rest in unmarked graves where they fell. When people pay their respects at such national monuments, they are not primarily honouring the soldier who happens to be interred there. Through that figure, they are honouring the memory of all those whom the monument represents. The analogy is not exact, for people in ancient Israel obviously felt this strong sense of solidarity at many other levels of everyday life. But a person's place in the nation never encompassed everything, and there was always a belief that people were morally and spiritually responsible to God as individuals.

12 Worshipping God

Worshipping a holy God

A term often used in the Old Testament to explain why God should be worshipped is the word 'holy'. In ordinary usage, to describe someone or something as 'holy' can often mean little more than 'religious'. But when the Old Testament describes Yahweh as 'holy' it is saying some very specific things about God's relationship with people.

God is infinite

In the Old Testament story, God is best known to the people of Israel through the events of their history and of their own everyday life. Because of this, there are many graphic, and often intimate, insights into God's nature and personality. But this never meant that ordinary people could know everything about God. For example, when Job was trying to make sense out of his own frustrating life, he was forced to admit that in the last analysis there are hidden depths to God's workings that defy human understanding (Job 42:1–6). Aspects of God's character might well have been revealed clearly in events such as the exodus, but there are still other dimensions of God's being that remain deeply mysterious. Job was not the only one to feel this way, for both poets (Psalm 139:6) and prophets (Isaiah 40:13–14). knew that God was different from people. In earlier chapters we have repeatedly noticed how God's apparent 'hiddenness' was a major part of Israel's experience on both a personal and a national level. This feeling of perplexity and wonder in the face of an awe-inspiring divine presence is, of course, common to religious people the world over. So, also, is the use of the word 'holy' to describe the difference between God and people. The literal meaning of the Hebrew word translated 'holy' is not certain, though many scholars believe it is linguistically related to a word that means 'to divide'. When people describe the gods they worship as 'holy', they often think of the universe being divided into two quite different modes of existence. There is the place where God belongs, and people, things and events connected with that can be called 'holy'. Then there is also the world where human beings operate, and that is 'profane' or 'common'. In this context, the words 'holy' and 'profane' do not indicate moral judgments, nor for that matter is there necessarily a spatial implication, as if God literally exists in some other place than people. These expressions are simply terms used to convey the fact that God and people are not the same. The Old Testament shares this widely held view with other nations of both the ancient and the modern world (Leviticus 10:10).

Within this frame of reference, one aim of worship is to enable these two domains to meet and relate to each other. Even apparently 'common' things can be made 'holy' – places, times, people and objects. But once they have been set apart to God in this way, special care must be taken by 'common' people in dealing with them. 'Holiness' is often spoken of in the Old Testament as if it were a great power or invisible forcefield, emanating from the very person of God. It is not easy for modern people in a technological society to understand this way of thinking. But a parallel might be found in our own respect for the contents of the core of a nuclear reactor. Though most of us do not understand its workings, we all know that at the centre of the process are materials emitting out invisible rays of energy that, if not properly contained and controlled by those competent to deal with them, could be disastrous for us all. The Old Testament often uses similar sorts of imagery to describe God's holy presence. When God's will was revealed to Moses at Mount Sinai, God's communication was accompanied by an awesome sense of divine presence that ordinary people needed to avoid. The place became so saturated with this divine power ('holiness') that only specially equipped people were able to cope with it (Exodus 19:9–25). Ordinary people such as Moses could readily be set aside and made holy themselves, but if they came into contact with such holiness before that the results could be catastrophic. The Philistines later learned this to their cost when they tried to meddle with the ark of the covenant (1 Samuel 5:1 – 6:19). But even Israelites could suffer the same fate when they as 'common' persons came into contact with the 'holiness' of the divine presence (2 Samuel 6:1–8). God's majesty and power must be respected, and to call God 'holy' is one way of emphasizing that. Though there is some considerable emphasis on the fact that God can be known in a direct and personal way by ordinary mortals, God is still different, and to be esteemed and treated with due reverence (Exodus 15:11; Job 11:7–12; Psalm 139:6–12).

God is good

Many religious people think of their gods only in terms of awe-inspiring power. But Israel's covenant faith led to a distinctive and more carefully nuanced understanding of what it means to be holy. In the wider world of religions, the mysterious, numinous, all-powerful kind of holiness has often been advanced as an explanation for the irrational and capricious actions of the gods. But the events of Israel's history had shown that the

God of the Old Testament was faithful and trustworthy, not fickle and unpredictable. In the light of that, God's holiness was a way of behaving, as well as a state of being. To say that God is holy also implies that God is good, and since people do not always manage to live by God's standards, it can imply a confession of human failure (Isaiah 55:8).

These two aspects of God's holiness – the numinous and the ethical – are brought together most clearly in the description of the call of the prophet Isaiah as he went to the Temple to worship (Isaiah 6:1–7). By definition, what went on in the Temple was holy in the numinous sense, for the Temple was a holy place, set apart for God's own use, and only those who were ritually holy themselves were able to cope with it. As the prophet stood there with the other worshippers, he had an awe-inspiring experience of God's greatness and power – but in response to this revelation, he at once recognized that a state of ritual cleanness was not enough by itself to equip him for God's presence. God's majestic holiness and moral goodness could not easily be separated from each other, and Isaiah instantly knew that he was unfit to encounter God because of his own sinfulness. This recognition was one of the greatest insights of the Old Testament prophets. In traditional Canaanite spirituality it was widely assumed that divine holiness had only a cultic, numinous dimension, and that people could be made fit to deal with the gods by means of appropriate rituals. The people of Israel were constantly tempted to think the same way, but the prophets insisted that they were wrong and that God was concerned with everyday behaviour, not just with ritual at the shrine (Amos 5:21–24; Micah 6:6–8). Personal and social wrongdoing were incompatible with true worship.

The prophets were not the only ones who saw wrongdoing as a barrier to acceptance by God. The writers and editors of the law codes made the same connection between morals and worship, and the very words that worshippers used in the Temple itself often reminded them of precisely the same fact: 'Who has the right to go up Yahweh's hill? Who may enter God's holy Temple? Those who are pure in act and in thought' (Psalm 24:3–4).

Some details of Israelite worship echoed the cults of the surrounding peoples, though Israel's monotheism made the central thrust quite different. This Philistine cult stand showing musicians dates from the early tenth century BC.

God is love

For Isaiah, the painful awareness of God's moral holiness was inextricably linked to his own need for forgiveness (Isaiah 6:5). A way had to be found by which the sinful prophet could be made fit for the presence of such a holy God. In numinous terms, a person could be empowered to deal with holiness by undergoing the required ritual procedures. But how could moral reformation be brought about? Like others both before and after him, Isaiah knew only too well that human effort, while not insignificant, was unlikely to be able to achieve this ultimate transformation by itself, and if he was to be morally right with God, this was something that only God would be able to accomplish. So the means of Isaiah's spiritual reconciliation comes from God, carried directly from the altar, and through this symbolic act he is told 'your guilt is gone, and your sins are forgiven' (Isaiah 6:7). The book of Isaiah frequently calls God 'the holy one' precisely because God forgives wrongdoing and brings salvation to the lives of the people. God is almighty and infinite, as well as morally perfect, but God also cares for ordinary, struggling people. To describe God as 'holy' not only defines God's awesome power, but also implies God's perfect love. At the same time as God's holy presence highlights human failure, it provides the means whereby wrongdoing can be forgiven and new life can be born: 'I am the high and holy God, who lives for ever. I live in a high and holy place, but I also live with people who are humble and repentant, so that I can restore their confidence and hope' (Isaiah 57:15).

This is the background against which Old Testament worship needs to be understood. Sincere worship reflects the response of God's people to the revelation of God's nature, and the nature of God's holiness in turn determines the character of the human response. Because God is almighty, true worship must always respect the barriers between the sacred and the secular, the holy and the profane. Because God is good, true worship must honestly face up to the reality of human wrongdoing. But because God is love, the repentant worshipper can always look for God's forgiveness and anticipate the promise of a renewed life. The precise way in which these themes are related to each other varies from one occasion of worship to another. But all worship begins from the recognition that God is holy and people are not. It is a celebration of the many ways in which they can be made fit for God's presence.

Places of worship

A place of worship in the ancient world was not a space for people to gather and hold meetings, but a place set apart for the use of the deities, in which people would celebrate and bring offerings. Later Jewish synagogues and Christian churches were essentially places for people to meet one another, whereas traditional Israelite places of worship were places where people could encounter God. A place of worship could not therefore be constructed just anywhere, to suit the convenience of those who might wish to go there. It needed to be a recognizably 'holy' place, a spot at which God had been revealed in some specific way, and which men and women could, therefore, assume was a place where the holiness of God's presence might safely intersect with the profane life of the world. When Moses encountered the burning bush in the desert, he recognized it as just such a place (Exodus 3:5–6). That particular spot never became a regular place of worship, presumably because of its distance from the main centres of population in later Israel. But later generations had many such places where they could legitimately worship, because God had previously met there with the leaders of their nation. Inevitably, the most popular places of worship changed with the passage of time, and as we read the Old Testament story we can trace a number of significant stages.

The tabernacle or tent of Yahweh's presence

The stories of the earliest days of Israel's history depict the tribes who escaped from Egypt worshipping at a special tent placed in the centre of their camp. A variety of terms are used to describe this tent, though it is most often referred to as the tent of Yahweh's presence or tabernacle. The practice of having such a place for worship is not unusual among nomadic peoples in the Middle East even today. God's presence in this sanctuary ('holiness') was symbolized by the cloud which covered it.

During the Israelites' time as desert nomads, the central place in their camp was given to the 'tent of the Lord's presence' or 'tabernacle', with the ark of the covenant in its holy of holies. The altar for sacrifice stood on open ground outside the tent itself.

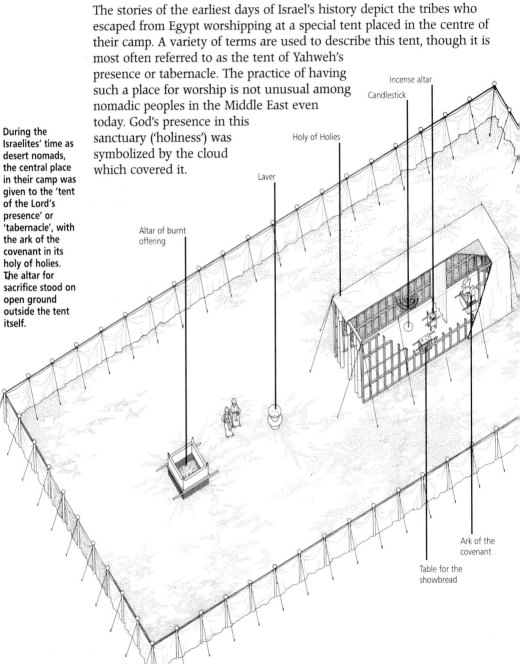

Incense altar

Candlestick

Holy of Holies

Laver

Altar of burnt offering

Ark of the covenant

Table for the showbread

The movement of this cloud provided the signal for the tribes to move on. The Old Testament provides detailed instructions for the construction and use of this portable sanctuary. There is considerable debate among scholars as to the precise origin of these instructions, but the general picture they give is typical of many ancient places of worship. A central enclosure marked the most holy part of the tent (the holy of holies), and this in turn was surrounded by various other enclosures until the boundary of the shrine was reached. Beyond this were the tents of the priests and those of the people. Such an arrangement was found in every place of worship throughout the whole of the Old Testament period. In the words of Ezekiel, it was designed 'to separate what was holy from what was not' (42:20), and to ensure that only those who were properly qualified would come into contact with the awesome holiness of God's presence at the very centre of the sanctuary. The sacred tents of Bedouin tribes would often contain a visual representation of their gods within this most holy place, but Israel never portrayed God in that way. Instead, the holy of holies contained the ark of the covenant. There is a good deal of uncertainty about the precise significance of this ark, but it was certainly identified very closely with God's personal presence in the midst of the people (Numbers 10:35–36; Joshua 4:5–13).

We do not know for sure what happened to either the ark or the tabernacle. The ark features in the Old Testament narratives a number of times after the desert period. It was present at the crossing of the River Jordan (Joshua 3:1 – 5:1). Later it was kept at Bethel (Judges 20:18–28), but was then captured from the sanctuary at Shiloh by the Philistines in the time of Samuel (1 Samuel 4:1 – 7:1), and later again it was taken to Jerusalem by David (2 Samuel 6:1–23), where Solomon finally installed it in the Temple (1 Kings 8:1–13). References in the liturgies of the psalms suggest that it was regularly used in religious festivals at Jerusalem (Psalms 24:7–10; 48:12–14; 132:1–18), and it was probably either destroyed or taken away by the Babylonian king Nebuchadnezzar when he overthrew Jerusalem in 586 BC. In any event, after the exile its place in the Temple was probably occupied by a gold plate, and by New Testament times Josephus says that the holy of holies was completely empty (*Jewish Wars* 5.5.5).

The tent of Yahweh's presence disappears from the narratives even earlier than the ark of the covenant, and there are no clear references to it after the tribes had settled in the land of Canaan. Some passages seem to imply that it was at one stage based in Shiloh (Joshua 18:1; 19:51; 1 Samuel 2:22), but if that was the case it cannot have lasted for long, and by the time Samuel had grown up Shiloh had a permanent building for worship (1 Samuel 1:7, 9; 3:15). 1 Chronicles 16:39 contains a reference to 'the tent of Yahweh' at Gibeon in the time of Solomon, though there is some uncertainty over the precise meaning of that phrase. David placed the ark of the covenant in a tent when he first took it to Jerusalem, but though this was undoubtedly intended to evoke images of the tent of Yahweh's presence, there is no suggestion that the tent he used was anything other than a new construction (2 Samuel 6:17; 7:2; 1 Kings 1:39).

Both ark and tent played an important role in the development of Israel's faith. By their very nature they were a challenge to the widespread view that gods were restricted in power and influence to specific places and peoples. From the earliest period of Israel's emergence as a nation, there was much debate as to whether Yahweh's power was territorial, extending only over the desert, and as a result the people generally included in their worship the traditional Canaanite deities as well, just to be on the safe side. Later on, in the time of Jeremiah, just before the final collapse of the kingdom of Judah, the people of Jerusalem went to the opposite extreme, and concluded that their city could never fall to their enemies because God lived there, in the Temple (Jeremiah 7:1–15). Both attitudes were understandable, but to the spiritual leaders of the nation both were false, and when Isaiah of Babylon declared that Israel's God was in reality the God of the whole world, he was articulating something that had been implicit in the Old Testament faith from a very early period (Isaiah 44:1–8).

Local sanctuaries

People always like to worship where they live, and the local sanctuaries in towns and villages throughout the land had an important part to play for most of the Old Testament period. Almost every settlement must have had its own place of worship, though not all of them would have been buildings. A majority may have been little more than altars in the open air at which regular sacrifices could be offered. A great many such altars have been discovered by archaeologists throughout Palestine, sometimes constructed from heaps of stones, though at other times a natural feature of the landscape or a particularly striking rock would be used for the purpose.

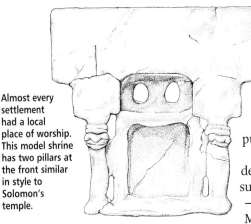

Almost every settlement had a local place of worship. This model shrine has two pillars at the front similar in style to Solomon's temple.

The stories of Israel's earliest ancestors depict them worshipping at a great number of such local sanctuaries right across the country – places like Hebron, Mamre, Beersheba and Mizpah (Genesis 13:18; 18:1–15; 26:23–25; 31:43–55). These places were all traditional Canaanite places of worship, though the final editors of the Genesis stories generally point out that it was really the covenant God Yahweh whom they worshipped there, even if they did not realize it at the time. On other occasions the ancestors are depicted establishing new centres of worship. When Jacob had an unusual dream in the open air, he recognized the place of his dreaming as holy because he met God there (Genesis 28:10–22). As a result, he called it 'Bethel', meaning 'house of God', and later generations of Israelites regarded it as a particularly holy place (Judges 20:18–28; 1 Samuel 7:16; 10:3). After the collapse of Solomon's united kingdom, Bethel became one of the major sanctuaries of the northern kingdom of Israel (1 Kings 12:29 – 13:32; Amos 3:14; 4:4; 5:5–6; 7:10–13).

Local places of worship play an important part in the historical narratives. The stories about Samuel associate him with the sanctuaries at Shiloh, Bethel, Gilgal, Mizpah and Ramah (1 Samuel 1:1 – 3:21; 7:16–17). The shrine at Shiloh was evidently of sufficient importance to be called a temple, though after its destruction by the Philistines in about 1050 BC the centre of attention moved to other places, notably Gilgal (1 Samuel 11:14–15) and Mizpah (1 Samuel 13:8–15), both of which are connected with significant stages in Saul's career as king (1 Samuel 10:17–27). Later, King Solomon was a regular visitor to a sanctuary at Gibeon, and it was there that he had his famous dream in which he was promised the gift of wisdom (1 Kings 3:4–15). In that story, Gibeon is described as the place 'where the most famous altar was', but that was not to last for long, for soon afterwards Solomon built his great Temple in Jerusalem (1 Kings 5:1 – 6:38). After that, the local sanctuaries must have been put in the shade by the splendour of Temple worship. The large staff of priests and other officials there made worship so much more impressive and exciting than what went on in smaller towns and villages, and it was not long before substantial crowds were making regular pilgrimages to Jerusalem. This was what Solomon had wanted, for political as well as religious reasons, but it inevitably meant that smaller shrines had to struggle to survive. Many local places of worship probably fell into disuse at this period, while many more reverted to the traditional Canaanite forms of worship that the prophets denounced as departures from the true covenant faith. Such worship was certainly widespread, for looking back at this period Jeremiah could later comment, 'On every high hill and under every green tree you worshipped fertility gods' (Jeremiah 2:20). This complaint had particular relevance to the sanctuaries of the northern kingdom, but even in Judah every later attempt at religious reform involved the forcible closure of these local sanctuaries which had become centres of alien worship (2 Kings 18:4; 21:2–7; 23:1–20).

The sanctuary at Shiloh was of national importance to Israel until its destruction by the Philistines in about 1050 BC.

The Temple

The Temple in Jerusalem came to occupy a special place in the devotion of the people. Its unique position was celebrated in much of ancient Israel's best-loved poetry. It symbolized all the distinctive features not only of Israel's faith, but also of the self-consciousness of the nation, uniting the political and religious aspirations of the people, centred on the kings who ruled from Jerusalem as the successors of David. Devotion to the Temple could sometimes lead to misplaced nationalism, as it did in the days of Jeremiah when the inhabitants of Jerusalem were certain that nothing could happen to their city because the Temple was there (Jeremiah 7:1–15). The prophets had to remind them that God's holy presence in the Temple could become a sign of judgment as well as salvation, and it was possible to preserve the external appearance of true worship when in reality God's presence was no longer there (Ezekiel 10:1–22).

The Hebrew Bible contains some comprehensive accounts of the building of the Temple by Solomon (1 Kings 6:1–38; 7:12–51; 2 Chronicles 2:17 – 5:1), though the details of the design are never clearly spelled out, and when scholars have tried to construct models of the Temple they have come up with a number of different proposals. It is clear that the general layout was similar to many other temples throughout the ancient world, though no precisely identical temple has been found elsewhere in the region. This similarity is not surprising, as Solomon needed to import workers from Phoenicia to design and build it, presumably because Israel had no previous experience of a large-scale building project (1 Kings 5:1–12; 7:13–14). In general terms, the layout of the Temple was similar to the design of the tent of Yahweh's presence, with a central holy of holies surrounded by other spaces and enclosures. Indeed, most scholars believe that the Old Testament's descriptions of the tent are actually derived from the design of the later Temple. The basic structure consisted of three rooms: an entrance hall, a main room and, at a slightly higher level, the holy of holies. Whereas the entrance hall and main room were rectangular, with the doors on the shorter sides, the holy of holies was a square, and this was where the ark of the covenant was kept, with two large golden cherubim suspended from the ceiling above it.

Most of the worship took place not in the holy of holies, but in the other parts of the Temple building and courtyards. The actual contents of these areas varied from time to time, and the religious symbols and altars used there were often as much an indication of the nation's political alliances as of its spiritual commitment. When Ahaz wanted to seal his alliance with Assyria, he adjusted the Temple contents to prove his good intentions (2 Kings 16:10–18). His successor Hezekiah, on the other hand, wished to reassert Judah's independence, and set about removing such signs of external religious influence (2 Kings 18:4), only to have Manasseh later bring them all back again (2 Kings 21:1–7), until

Josiah eventually inaugurated a thoroughgoing religious reformation, and completely refurbished the Temple as well as closing down local shrines throughout the country (2 Kings 23:1–20). There was obviously a close connection between the kings of Judah and the Temple. Solomon played a major part in building it and in organizing worship there. But he also had his own palace next door, linked to the Temple by a private pathway (2 Kings 16:18). The Temple was more than a national place of worship: it also symbolized the power of the royal family of David. In the ancient world, politics and religion were often two sides of the same coin, and David and Solomon had political reasons for wanting to build a temple in Jerusalem. Various buildings mentioned on the perimeter of the Temple precinct may well have housed the king's personal treasury. Certainly, much of the nation's wealth must have been kept there, for invaders regularly went to the Temple to plunder it (1 Kings 14:25–28; 15:15; 2 Kings 16:7–8; 18:15–16; 24:12–13).

As well as priests, the Temple had a large staff, including administrators (Ezra 2:40–42) and Temple servants who kept the fires burning on the various altars used in worship (Joshua 9:27; Ezra 2:43–54; 8:20). Some of these workers may well have been non-Israelites, for the prophet Ezekiel later complained about the practice of allowing foreigners to be involved in the life of the Temple (Ezekiel 44:6–9). Not everyone, however, was happy with the Temple. There were always radicals who felt that it was a backwards step in Israel's spiritual pilgrimage, and that the covenant faith would be better served by adherence to the less settled ways of worship represented by the tent of Yahweh's presence (2 Samuel 7:5–7; Isaiah 66:1; Jeremiah 35:1–19). But most people were committed to it, and though they knew well enough that God did not literally 'live' in the Temple (1 Kings 8:27–30; Psalm 11:4), this was still the place where they felt most directly in God's presence (Psalms 26:8; 63:1–5; 84:1–4; 122:1). Their anguish was real and deeply felt when it was destroyed by the Babylonians (Psalm 137). After the exile, a replacement was built, of which we know only very little – but it was obviously a much less impressive place than the original had been (Ezra 1:2–4; 3:1 – 6:18).

The synagogue

The exile was in every way a great watershed for the people of Israel, and from that point onwards their worship was never again to be quite the same as it had been in the days of the kingdoms of Israel and Judah. The Temple was rebuilt in Jerusalem, and it continued to occupy a special place in the affection of the Jewish people. But the effective centre of worship shifted to the synagogue. By the start of the Christian era there were synagogues in all the important towns of the Mediterranean world, and Jewish people went there week by week for regular worship. Synagogue worship was quite different from Temple worship. For one thing, it was on a much smaller scale, and in addition, it never included sacrifice. Prayer, and the reading of the Law and Prophets, came to be all-important. Naturally, there was no ark of the covenant or a holy of holies, though later synagogues had their own 'ark of the law' which contained the sacred scrolls of the Hebrew scriptures.

Almost all the evidence for life and worship in the synagogues is later than the Old Testament period, much of it a lot later. It shows that the synagogues were more than places of worship: they were also social and educational centres for the many Jewish communities scattered throughout the world in the early centuries of the Christian era. The synagogues emerged to fill a need which had not existed when Israel was an independent nation with their own land. There is no certainty about how and when the synagogues originated, though several possibilities have been suggested:

■ Some believe they began in Judah itself even before the exile. We know that in the course of his religious reforms, Josiah made a concerted effort to close down the local sanctuaries throughout his kingdom and to centralize all worship in Jerusalem. Of course, that could not eliminate the need for people to worship where they lived and so, the argument goes, they went to Jerusalem only when they needed the sort of sacrificial worship that took place there. At other times they met for more informal local worship, which was the precedent for the emergence of the synagogue. There is, however, no evidence to support this view. Indeed, it is doubtful whether Josiah's reformation was quite as successful as that, for less than twenty years later Jeremiah provides plenty of evidence for worship continuing at traditional sites throughout the country.

■ It seems undeniable that the synagogue must have originated after the Temple at Jerusalem was no longer available for worship. After the destruction of Jerusalem by Nebuchadnezzar, the remnants of the

The Temple belonged to the whole Jewish nation, but the synagogues belonged to each local community. They began to play an important part in regular worship from the time that the Jews returned from Babylon. These remains are of the synagogue at Capernaum in Galilee.

population left in Judah probably worshipped on the Temple site from time to time (Jeremiah 41:4–5), but those who were transported to Babylon had no further access to Jerusalem. Possibly, therefore, synagogues began as places of prayer and contemplation for these exiles in Babylon itself. These people certainly took a close interest in the gathering together of the books of the Law and Prophets. But again there are no real facts to go on, and a certain amount of evidence to the contrary. In Psalm 137, for example, the exiles bemoan their predicament, but no reference at all is made to the possibility of synagogue worship as a way of compensating for the loss of the Temple. Comparatively few remains of synagogue buildings have been unearthed in Babylon, none of them relating to the Old Testament period.

■ It has also been suggested that the synagogue began in Palestine after the return of some of the exiles under Nehemiah and Ezra. There is a good deal of archaeological evidence for the existence of synagogue buildings in Palestine, though again none of it goes back to this period. Perhaps the most we can say is that the need for regular worship, combined with Ezra's strong emphasis on the reading and interpretation of the Law, could have provided suitable conditions for this new form of worship to evolve (Nehemiah 8:1–12).

Wherever the synagogues came from, the simple worship carried on there was an authentic reflection of an important strand in the spirituality of ancient Israel. For though the people rejoiced in the splendid magnificence of the Temple at Jerusalem, it had always been recognized that God's presence could not be restricted to one place. The consciousness that God was with them (symbolized by the ark of the covenant) was more fundamental than the need for a holy place like the Temple. There are many stories which show that God's presence could be enjoyed anywhere: Joseph met God in a prison (Genesis 39:21); Jeremiah at the bottom of a well (Jeremiah 38:1–13). When the Jewish people began to worship in synagogues throughout the world, not only were they coming to terms with the political realities of their national life, they were also exploring new dimensions in the covenant faith itself. Perhaps that is why Jewish writers such as Philo of Alexandria (*Life of Moses* ii:39) and Josephus (*Against Apion* 2.17) insisted that the synagogue began with Moses. Historically, they were certainly wrong, but ideologically they were giving expression to an important aspect of the Old Testament faith.

The character of worship

What was worship like in Old Testament times? Reference has already been made to prayer in the synagogue and sacrifice in the Jerusalem Temple. Other passages mention the use of incense (Jeremiah 6:20) and the giving of monetary offerings (Amos 4:4), though the Hebrew Bible contains no fully detailed account of a complete celebration of worship. The most specific instructions refer to the offering of sacrifices, but worship obviously included a lot more than that (Leviticus 1:1 – 7:38; Numbers 15:1–31; 28:1 – 29:40). What went on in the local sanctuaries and in the Temple was probably so familiar a part of life that it was unnecessary to spell it all out in detail. Of course, it was inevitable that the Old Testament in its final form should ignore some aspects of worship in ancient Israel, for we know from the prophets that the people regularly worshipped their own God Yahweh using the rituals of the local Baal religion – and though this was popular, it was regarded as a denial of the true covenant faith.

In spite of the absence of any comprehensive set of instructions for the conduct of public worship, scholars agree that the Old Testament does contain a good deal of material that was regularly used in that context, especially in the book of Psalms. This has been called 'the hymn book of the Second Temple', and it may well have been compiled at that time, for some psalms clearly refer to the exile and the events that followed it. Not all psalms are hymns in the normal sense. Some of them are more personal and individual expressions of piety, while others refer to the great ceremonial events of

This mosaic from the synagogue at Beth Shan includes pictures of the ark of the covenant, menorah (seven-branched candlestick) and shofar (ram's-horn trumpet).

Understanding the psalms

At one time, scholars tried to understand the psalms either as purely personal poetry, or as poems composed on particular historical occasions in the course of Israel's history. But more recent study has suggested that most of them had their roots in the worship at Solomon's Temple, and quite possibly in the worship at local sanctuaries as well. There are a number of reasons for accepting this:

● At least one Old Testament passage shows psalms being used in the course of worship. When David first brought the ark of the covenant into Jerusalem, its arrival was accompanied by dancing and singing (2 Samuel 6:5). One account of this incident

includes an example of the songs that were sung on the occasion, and this turns out to be surprisingly similar to several of the psalms (1 Chronicles 16:8–36).

● Other Old Testament passages also confirm the important part played in worship by religious songs and poetry of the type found in the book of Psalms (Amos 5:23).

● Much of the imagery used in the psalms is very similar to imagery used in specifically religious poetry and songs elsewhere in the ancient cultures of Palestine. There are particularly close linguistic connections between many of the psalms and the songs used to worship Baal as depicted in the texts from Ugarit. The theological ideas are completely

national life. But whatever their form, the psalms provide an invaluable glimpse into the way God was worshipped in the Temple at Jerusalem in the period before the exile. Sometimes we see individuals at worship. In others, we can catch sight of great national occasions involving the whole community. Some psalms centre on the king and God's promises to the royal family of David. One thing we do not find, however, is worship related to rites of passage such as birth, marriage and death. Most nations celebrate these events in the context of religious worship, but in ancient Israel they were all essentially family matters, and in the time before the exile they had no particular connection with formal worship at all.

When we analyse the psalms and other references to worship, we soon discover that it included many different activities.

Singing and music

This was a vital element in all worship, and it appears throughout the Old Testament as an appropriate way for people to praise God. It was, of course, an important activity in many ancient religions. So, for example, when Elijah confronted the prophets of Baal on Mount Carmel, the Baal worshippers used music to stir themselves up into a frenzy (1 Kings 18:27–29). On occasion, prophets of Yahweh could use it for the same purpose (1 Samuel 10:5, 10–13). Not all religious singing was necessarily pleasing to God (Amos 5:23), but without it, proper praise could not take place. God's holy character found its natural response in this kind of worship (Psalm 22:3), and the awareness of God's presence most naturally led to worshipping with 'glad songs of praise' (Psalm 63:5). Singing became especially important after the exile, and the names of several choirs are mentioned in this connection (1 Chronicles 16:4–7;

different, of course, but a judicious comparison of the psalms with these other texts has led to enormous advances in our understanding of the meaning of many obscure Hebrew words used in the Old Testament.

● The Jerusalem Temple and its worship provide many of the basic themes of the psalms, reflecting the centrality of the Temple as a symbol of God's presence (Psalms 11:4; 46:4–6; 50:2), and the eager longing of the people to share in its worship (Psalms 26:8; 84:1–4; 111:1). Indeed, some of them even seem to refer directly to sacrificial worship (Psalm 36:8) and to the various days over which the great national festivals would be held (Psalm 118:24).

● The structure of some psalms seems to indicate that they were used as comprehensive liturgies for worship on particular occasions (e.g. Psalm 118:1–4). Some depict a number of participants in the worship, asking questions and receiving responses (e.g. Psalm 24). It is quite likely that many of the obscure references in the psalm titles are really instructions about how they were to be used in worship, and the Hebrew word *selah*, which appears in a number of psalms, is almost certainly an instruction to the Temple singers to increase the volume and sing louder.

Music played a central part in worship, and a great variety of instruments were used, just as they were among Israel's neighbours. The leading musician on this relief from Zinjirli is playing a eight-stringed lyre, the second a six-stringed lyre, and the two others are playing on hand drums.

25:1–31; Ezra 2:40–42). Some of the psalms have refrains, which suggests that one part of the song would be sung by the worshippers, and the rest by the choir (Psalms 42:5, 11; 43:5; 46:7, 11). Musical instruments are also mentioned in connection with the praise of God: tambourines, harps, lyres, drums, trumpets, rattles, horns, flutes and cymbals (2 Samuel 6:5; 1 Chronicles 25:1–6; Psalms 43:4; 68:25; 81:1–3; 98:4–6; 150:3–5; Isaiah 30:29). Worship was obviously a joyful business, and the carnival atmosphere of the Temple is captured in one of the psalms which speaks of 'a happy crowd, singing and shouting praise to God' (Psalm 42:4).

Prayer

This was to become one of the characteristic activities of the synagogue, and by the start of the Christian era there were also regular daily times of prayer in the Temple at Jerusalem. It is unclear whether this custom originated in earlier times, though prayer was certainly a vital element in worship right from the start. The belief that ordinary people could have direct access to God was a fundamental part of Israelite spirituality. Not only prophets such as Elijah (1 Kings 18:36–37), or kings such as Solomon (1 Kings 8:22–61), but ordinary people such as Hannah (1 Samuel 2:1–10) could bring their everyday concerns to God. The Torah contains prayers to be said on special occasions (e.g. Deuteronomy 26:5–10), and the book of Psalms contains many examples of prayers that were no doubt used by individuals, as well as by groups of worshippers, to give thanks and to express their trust and confidence in God. Physical movement was always an important part of prayer, emphasizing the essentially embodied nature of Old Testament spirituality. Sometimes the worshipper would kneel to pray (1 Kings 8:54), or bow low to the ground (Psalm 5:7). At other times prayers might be said in a standing position (1 Samuel 1:26), occasionally with hands raised up above the head (1 Kings 8:22, 54; Psalm 63:4; Isaiah 1:15). But while posture was important, it needed to be accompanied by 'a humble and repentant heart' (Psalm 51:17).

Dance and drama

Given the importance attached to singing and music in biblical worship, and the emphasis on the use of the body in prayer, it is no surprise to discover that dancing was also regularly used in the praise of God. Some of the psalms seem to presuppose it (e.g. 26:6), and others specifically encourage it (e.g. 149:3; 150:4). On one occasion even King David himself took part in public dancing as the ark of the covenant was brought into the city of Jerusalem. Indeed, he danced so vigorously that his wife thought his behaviour was indecent, and rebuked him for making a fool of himself (2 Samuel 6:1–22).

There is also evidence for the use of drama in worship, with many indications of occasions on which worshippers would process in and out of the Temple and around the city of Jerusalem (Psalms 26:6; 42:4; 48:12–14; 118:19, 26–27). Sometimes, God is depicted accompanying the worshippers as they go, perhaps in the form of the ark of the covenant, carried at the head of the procession (Psalms 68:24–27; 132:7–9). Other passages suggest that God's mighty acts in the past could be re-enacted in the course of worship, to bring home their lessons to new generations (Psalms 46:8–10; 48:8; 66:5). At the annual Passover festival – celebrated in the home rather than at a public event – drama also played an important part, for at the most solemn moment the worshippers ate a meal together dressed ready to go on a journey, just as the slaves in Egypt had done at the time of the exodus (Exodus 12:21–28). Symbolic actions could also play an important part in more ordinary acts of worship (Psalm 26:6). Drama has always been a powerful medium through which people can express their deepest convictions, and when the worshippers of ancient Israel reminded themselves of God's goodness to their nation they did so in action as well as in word.

Sacrifice

To many people, this is the most characteristic activity of Old Testament worship. Certainly, it was a daily ritual in the Temple, but it was only one element among many. Modern Western people tend to give so much attention to it simply because it is generally remote from their own experience. To us, the gratuitous death of animals in the course of religious worship is something repugnant, and our understanding is not helped here by the fact that the Hebrew Bible never explains exactly why this form of worship was used. As with so many other things, it simply takes it for granted that everyone would know why sacrifice was an appropriate way to worship.

Sacrifice is a worldwide phenomenon, and is not restricted either to the Old Testament or the Middle East. Anthropologists have tried hard to understand the need for sacrifice in different cultural contexts around the world, and the general consensus is that to appreciate the importance of it, we need to return to the observations about 'holiness' with which we began this chapter. Wherever it is practised, sacrifice is always understood as a means of relating the visible, tangible world in which people exist to the invisible, intangible (and often uncontrollable) world in which God or the gods exist. It is a means whereby people can encounter the powerful 'holiness'

that radiates out from the presence of God, without suffering the horrific consequences that would normally be expected to follow such an encounter. This is why animals (particularly domestic animals) were appropriate as sacrifices, for they are themselves living, have a close relationship to people, and could therefore serve as a suitable symbol of the worshippers.

Different faiths will have different understandings of the nature of sacrifice. For example, in many contexts it is thought of as a way of feeding the deities, though this is a view that the Old Testament rejects. The Israelite understanding of sacrifice was dominated by their perception of the meaning of holiness, which meant that an important function of sacrifice was concerned with securing ritual purity (Leviticus 11:1 – 15:33). At the same time, the moral dimensions of God's character were never far from view, and as time went on and the events of history made the need for forgiveness of wrongdoing more obvious, this came to be the predominant meaning that was attached to sacrifice (Ezekiel 45:18–25). This does not mean

that sacrifice and the forgiveness of wrongdoing were linked only at a late date, for at an earlier period, even sacrifices that were not identified as 'sin offerings' could be accompanied by great repentance (Judges 20:26; 21:1–4; 1 Samuel 7:2–9; Job 1:5). The prophets and others often reminded the people of the need for true confession and repentance to accompany sacrificial worship (Psalm 51:16–19; Amos 5:21–24; Micah 6:6–8). As in so many other things, the actual practice of ancient Israel varied according to time and place, and there is no shortage of evidence indicating that traditional Canaanite styles of worship continued, even though they were opposed by the prophets as being alien to Israel's true faith (Jeremiah 44:24–25; Amos 5:25–27).

The Old Testament mentions many different types of sacrifice. In some ways, they defy comprehensive analysis, though anthropologists have identified three major types of sacrifice in more general use, and it will be helpful to use these divisions in our discussion here.

The Israelites and their neighbours sacrificed animals as part of their worship. The small group of Samaritans who remain today still practise the sacrifice of animals.

GIFT SACRIFICES

Sacrifices would often be given to God as a way of returning thanks for some particular benefit that the worshipper had received. The very first sacrifices mentioned in the Hebrew Bible were of this type (Genesis 4:3–4), as also was the sacrifice of Noah after the great flood had subsided

Understanding sacrifice

So far, we have looked at the ways in which sacrifices were used in the worship of God in the Old Testament. But what is sacrifice all about? Just what did the worshippers think they were doing when they engaged in this sort of activity? At one time, it was thought that sacrifice was based on superstition and ignorance, and that it was only relatively late in Israel's history that it came to have any theological significance attached to it, as it came to be understood as a way of making amends for wrongdoing. But the anthropological study of sacrifice in many different cultures has shown that, whatever else it is, sacrificial worship certainly is not unsophisticated.

Wherever it is practised, sacrifice is a means of reaffirming the structures of organized life: it declares that God and people are united in a relationship of mutual interdependence, and, by means of the meal which often follows a sacrifice, it affirms the importance of good social relationships as the basis for a contented life. In the context of Israelite faith, those affirmations are central. Peace and harmony with God are fundamental requirements for a good life, and these things can be found only in a living relationship with God. Sacrifice, therefore, needed to be offered at those points in a person's life when they were out of tune with the 'holiness' that characterized God's own being.

Sacrifice was practised in many ancient cultures, and was a way of reaffirming the structures of organized life. This drawing, inscribed on shell, is of a worshipper carrying a kid. It comes from Mari, and dates from the middle of the third millennium BC.

Sacrifice and holiness

Just as God's holiness was defined in a number of ways, so sacrifices could be offered for a number of purposes:

● In relation to the mysterious, numinous holiness that radiated out from the divine presence, sacrifice was the means by which a person who was 'unclean' could be made 'clean' and fit to encounter God's holy power. In this context, the notion of 'unclean' was not related to morality or behaviour: things such as illness, touching a dead body, giving birth, menstruation – even having mildew in houses or clothing – all rendered a person 'unclean' in this ritual sense (Leviticus 11–15). This might well appear to be an odd collection of things, but what unites them seems to be the fact that they are all things that happen occasionally, and are not a part of everyday life. In this context, those things that are 'clean' are perhaps what we might call 'normal' – and any unusual occurrence renders a person 'unclean'. The precise reasons for this are no doubt lost in the mists of antiquity, but before a person could approach the holy presence of God in the sanctuary, such uncleanness had to be dealt with by the offering of appropriate sacrifices.

● There was also a moral side to the way God's holiness was understood in Israelite society. Wrongdoing was another thing that made people 'unclean', and therefore unfit to deal with God. An inadequate understanding of this led to many problems in the history of ancient Israel. The people were naturally inclined to think that worship was concerned only with the ritual aspects of holiness, and the prophets were continually reminding them that ritual worship and everyday behaviour could not be separated. There can be no doubt that the nation as a whole took a long time to

(Genesis 8:20). At the other end of the story we find the exiles who returned from Babylon offering the same sort of sacrifices (Ezra 6:16–18), while they are also mentioned in many of the psalms (e.g. 54:6–7; 56:12–13). On other occasions, gift sacrifices might be offered in order to secure God's guidance for the future (1 Samuel 7:9), though quite often a gift sacrifice would be

---

learn this lesson, which probably explains why offerings for sin came to assume more importance as time went on. For sacrifice was also the way that sin could be forgiven, and people could be restored to fellowship with God.

Making a sacrifice

The worshipper who made a sacrifice in ancient Israel did so out of a consciousness of being alienated from God, for whatever reason. Reconciliation with God had to be achieved in order for life to proceed as God intended it to. This sense of alienation is familiar enough to modern people, as also is the usefulness of some visible, tactile, symbolic way of dealing with it. Protestant Christianity has tended to place all the emphasis on internal spiritual change as the means of addressing personal dysfunction, but in the Old Testament (as in other Christian traditions) this change of internal disposition was always displayed externally. Here, sacrifice became a visible symbol of change in a person's life, and the actual act of sacrifice was designed to correspond with the stages whereby such change could be brought about.

First of all, the worshipper would approach the altar of God with their sacrifice, and would then lay their hand on the animal's head, to indicate that they wished to be identified with the animal. This was most important, for it meant that from this point onwards the animal was to be symbolic of the worshipper: whatever happened physically and outwardly to the animal was to happen to the worshipper spiritually and inwardly. Four things then took place:

● The animal was killed. In this action, the worshipper was reminded of the consequence of uncleanness: death, and separation from fellowship with God. The worshipper would perform this action personally, thereby declaring that he or she was ready to undergo some radical change.

● The priest then took the blood of the sacrifice (which now represented the worshipper's life offered up to God) to the altar. Depending on the identity of the person, different altars would be used. For an ordinary person, it was the altar of burnt offerings in the Temple courtyard; for a priest, the altar of incense in the Temple itself; and for the whole nation (on the day of atonement), the lid of the ark in the holy of holies. This action constituted the moment when the worshipper's uncleanness was removed (Leviticus 17:11) – the moment of reconciliation, or 'atonement' as it is sometimes called. God and people had been reunited in fellowship.

● After this, the animal's body was placed on the altar in the Temple, as a sign that the worshipper was now offering their whole life to God. In the case of a gift offering, the entire sacrifice would be burned there.

● Finally, depending on the nature of the sacrifice, some of the meat still left was eaten in a meal. Not only were things right between God and the individual worshipper: true fellowship with other people had also been restored.

We can see from all this that sacrifice was a very important part of worship. It both represented basic aspects of the Old Testament faith (people made for fellowship with God and with one another), and also externalized the faith in such a way that no one would be left in any doubt about what it meant to address Yahweh as a 'holy' God.

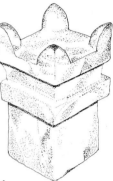

A horned altar found at Megiddo. It may have been used for burnt offerings, or as an incense altar, with the four corner projections supporting a bowl of incense.

given as a simple expression of joy on the part of the worshipper
(1 Samuel 6:14; 2 Samuel 6:17; Psalm 96:8). Such offerings would usually
be given in their entirety to God, by being burned on the altar of the
sanctuary – hence the alternative term that could be used to describe
them, 'whole burnt offerings' (Leviticus 1:1–17). Offerings of grain could
also serve the same purpose (Leviticus 2:1–16), while the annual offerings
of the first-fruits of the crops were, in effect, gift sacrifices given to
celebrate a successful harvest (Leviticus 23:1–25).

FELLOWSHIP OFFERINGS

Not all sacrifices were presented completely to God as whole burnt
offerings. Often, only a part of the animal was burned on the altar, and
the rest was eaten in a fellowship meal at the sanctuary, shared by
worshippers and priests (Leviticus 3:1–17). A shared meal is a symbol of
friendship throughout the world, but in this instance the worshippers of
ancient Israel were doing more than simply expressing their mutual
affection. For the most important event of their history, the covenant
ceremony at Mount Sinai, had been accompanied by a fellowship offering
like this (Exodus 24:1–8), and whenever this event was celebrated, a
fellowship offering was usually at the centre of things (Joshua 8:30–35;
2 Samuel 6:17; 1 Kings 8:63–64). No doubt the same themes would be in
the worshippers' minds whenever fellowship offerings were made. In
these meals the people were constantly reminded of the keynote of their
covenant faith: that they and God enjoyed a personal relationship, whose
repercussions influenced the whole of life.

FORGIVENESS OF SINS

The Old Testament mentions two sacrifices that were designed to
remove the barrier of wrongdoing that made fellowship between people
and God impossible: the sin offering (Leviticus 4:1 – 5:13) and the guilt
offering (Leviticus 5:14 – 6:7; Numbers 5:5–8). The precise difference
between these two classes of sacrifice is not very clear, but in view of
the way that God's holiness was equated with moral perfection, it is not
surprising that sacrifice and forgiveness should have been related to
each other in this way. Human wrongdoing broke the covenant
relationship between God and people, but fellowship could be restored
by the offering of an appropriate sacrifice.

An awareness of the seriousness of wrongdoing seems to have
developed most fully in the later stages of Israel's history. The earlier
prophets had found it difficult to convince the people that worship and
behaviour belonged together, but then when the awful events of the exile
had proved them right, everyone could see that disobedience to God was a
real problem that needed to be dealt with. The Hebrew Bible never
specifically discusses how a sacrifice was believed to deal with sin, but it
seems to have been assumed that those who did wrong deserved to die
(Ezekiel 18:20), and that a sacrifice could in some way substitute for the

condemned sinner. Certainly, the blood of these sacrifices (representing the life of the animal) played an important part (Leviticus 17:11) and it was as this was daubed on the altar that the worshipper was pronounced to have been forgiven. Depending on the identity of the sinner, different altars would be used. There was one occasion when the whole nation was united in seeking forgiveness: the annual day of atonement (Leviticus 16:1–34; 23:26–32; Numbers 29:7–11). On this day, the blood of the sacrifices would be taken into the holy of holies itself, and applied to the top of the ark of the covenant. This was why the lid of the ark came to be known as 'the mercy seat'. After the exile it was replaced by a gold plate which served the same purpose. When the main sacrifices had been offered, a second ritual took place. This involved the selection of two goats, one to be

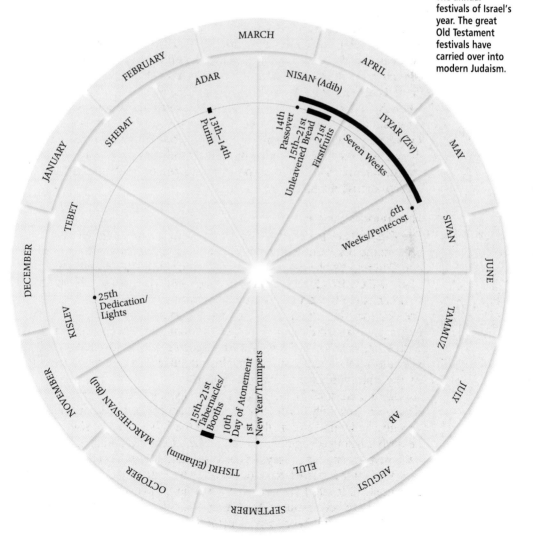

The annual festivals of Israel's year. The great Old Testament festivals have carried over into modern Judaism.

sacrificed in the Temple and the other to be sent away into the desert beyond the boundaries of the inhabited land. The priest's hands were laid on the head of the goat which was to be sent out, and at the same time the sins of the nation would be confessed. These two procedures were quite different, but they both emphasized the same underlying conviction: that wrongdoing is a serious business as it disrupts fellowship between God and people. They were also a dramatic declaration that wrongdoing could be forgiven and obliterated from the lives of God's people just as surely as the goat was driven out into the desert, never to be seen again.

Times for worship

We have already seen that worship involved a whole style of life, including daily behaviour as well as what went on at the sanctuaries. It was, therefore, a continuous activity. One of the major themes of the Old Testament faith is that God is available to people at every time and in every place. Formal worship was one way of expressing this, and the sanctuaries would be open every day. But there were also special times when the great national festivals would interrupt the normal run of things and the people would join together to celebrate God's goodness to them corporately, usually in relation to some particular event in the nation's history. The significance of the different festivals changed with the passage of time, but we can trace a number of important occasions that would be celebrated in this way.

The sabbath day

Many nations in the ancient world had a regular day of rest, and the celebration of the sabbath every seventh day was an important part of Israelite life from a very early date. There is no one single passage which describes what a sabbath should be like, but it probably began as a day of rest, so that every member of the population (including slaves and foreigners) could renew themselves for their daily work (Exodus 23:12; 34:21). Worship was a part of this renewal process, and no doubt it was an occasion when crowds would throng to the various sanctuaries throughout the land (Leviticus 19:30; Numbers 28:9–10), though what they did there was not always approved of (Isaiah 1:13). On the sabbath, no regular work would be undertaken (Jeremiah 17:21–22; Amos 8:5), though it would not necessarily be a day of complete rest for everyone (2 Kings 11:5–8).

The main emphasis was on the sabbath as a day when people could look back to their nation's roots, celebrate God's goodness and greatness, and renew their commitment to the covenant faith. This is no doubt why its observance is required in the ten commandments (Exodus 20:8–11). The whole day was specially dedicated to God ('holy', Exodus 31:12–17), because it was a reminder of God's greatness both in creation and history

(Exodus 20:11; Deuteronomy 5:15). It was also a reminder that belief in God implied concern for other people (Deuteronomy 5:13–14). In the period after the Babylonian exile, the sabbath became very important in the synagogues, though eventually it turned out to be a day that was rigidly controlled by many prohibitions. But in the Old Testament period it was a day for joyful celebration (Isaiah 58:13–14).

The Passover

The greatest event of all to which the people looked back was God's deliverance of the slaves from Egypt (the exodus). This was marked in an annual festival at which an animal was sacrificed and a meal was shared. In this respect, the Passover was just a special form of fellowship offering, celebrating the relationship inaugurated between God and people in the exodus events. These events themselves had a profound impact on the way the festival was celebrated, as the people dressed up in the same way as their ancestors had done: 'with your sandals on your feet and your stick in your hand', as if ready for a long journey (Exodus 12:11).

According to the story of the exodus, the people prepared to leave Egypt in their family groups and this is how the Passover was celebrated in the earlier part of the Old Testament period. A lamb was sacrificed in the home, with none of the splendour of worship found in the sanctuaries, and the animal's blood was then daubed not on an altar, but on the doorposts of the house. At this time, the animal was always a lamb roasted for the fellowship meal, a custom perhaps going

This Jewish family are celebrating Passover, recalling their ancestors' deliverance from slavery in Egypt.

back to the origin of the festival in the days when Israel had been a nomadic sheep-rearing people. Later, it became a national occasion, centred on the Temple in Jerusalem, with all the impressive pageantry associated with worship there (Deuteronomy 16:1–8; 2 Kings 23:21–22; 2 Chronicles 30:1–22; 35:1–19). The ritual naturally changed to suit the different circumstances. Both sheep and cattle could be used in the celebrations, boiled rather than roasted. There was also a provision whereby anyone who missed the Passover because they were ritually unclean could celebrate it a month later than the proper date (Numbers 9:1–14; 2 Chronicles 30:23–27). It has been suggested that the worshippers in the Temple may have recited the story of the first Passover and exodus, perhaps acting out the events and culminating with the singing of the 'song of Moses' (Exodus 15:1–18). By the start of the Christian era, both the family and the national elements of the occasion were united, with the sacrifices being killed in the Temple, but the fellowship meals then being eaten in a family home.

The harvest festivals

The Old Testament mentions three major religious festivals that relate to the agricultural year (Exodus 23:14–17; 34:18–23). These celebrations had probably always been a part of the traditional cycle of Canaanite life, but the Old Testament links each of them to the great and unrepeatable events of Israel's history, and not to the cycle of the seasons and the inevitable concern of farmers for the continuing fertility of their land.

THE FESTIVAL OF UNLEAVENED BREAD

This was apparently related to the barley harvest and the offering of the first-fruits (Leviticus 23:9–14; Numbers 28:17–23), but was celebrated at the same time of year as Passover, which, together with the fact that unleavened bread features in the Passover story, meant that the two festivals came to be closely connected, and together served to commemorate the escape from Egypt.

This limestone tablet, dating from about the time of King Solomon, has written on it a kind of children's rhyme that describes the farmer's year.

THE CORN HARVEST (OR FEAST OF WEEKS)

This celebrated the end of the wheat harvest. Special offerings would be made in the sanctuaries, though the central action was the ceremonial presentation of the first sheaf that had been cut (Numbers 28:26–31). Following this, individual worshippers could bring offerings from their own crops (Leviticus 23:15–21). The events of the exodus were also in the minds of the worshippers on this occasion (Deuteronomy 16:12), though after the exile the harvest festival came to be used as a time for celebrating the giving of the Law at Mount Sinai.

THE FESTIVAL OF SHELTERS (OR TABERNACLES)

This came at the very end of the growing season, and was a celebration of the fruit harvest from vineyards and orchards (Leviticus 23:33–43; Deuteronomy 16:13–17). This was a particularly joyful festival, and took its character from the practice of the farmers who would stay out all night to guard their crops, with only flimsy huts to protect them. For the seven days of the festival, the worshippers lived in similar structures. The main feature of this occasion was the simple expression of joy at the safe gathering of the harvest. But there also seems to be a close connection between the festival of shelters and the renewal of the covenant faith, for Leviticus 23:33–43 identifies the temporary shelters with the tents in which Israel lived in the desert. Some have suggested that this association only came in later, when the shelters traditionally used at this time of year no longer had any practical relevance to the essentially non-agricultural life of the exiles. But many more are of the opinion that the covenant theme was always an important part of this festival, even from the earliest days of Israel's emergence as a nation in the land of Canaan. Allegiance to the covenant certainly seems to have been the bond that united the various tribes in the days of the judges. It is likely that they renewed their commitment to God and to one another in annual ceremonies which would include the reading of the covenant law (Exodus 24:7; Deuteronomy 27:9–10; Joshua 24:1–28). There are also indications that this covenant law could be read out as a part of the festival of shelters (Deuteronomy 31:9–13; Nehemiah 8:13–18), and many scholars therefore believe that this would have been followed by a solemn moment when the people committed themselves once again to the demands of God's covenant and Law.

The Festival of Shelters is in direct continuity with the Jews of Ezra's day. As well as celebrating the fruit and vine harvest, it reminds participants of the Israelites' wilderness days and the beginning of their covenant faith.

Old Testament worship was clearly a varied experience, though one thing not found in it was preaching. The Torah was regularly expounded during organized worship after the exile (Nehemiah 8:7–9), but in the earlier period the main emphasis was always on praise and celebration. Like daily behaviour, worship was a response to God's revelation through the events of Israel's history and in the everyday experience of ordinary people. As the joyful worshippers went to the sanctuaries, they were reminded of God's past goodness, and given fresh inspiration for their own lives. But they were also challenged by God's holiness, as they faced the central need for repentance and forgiveness, and offered sacrifices in order to secure it. As time went on, it was this repetitive nature of much traditional worship that led prophets and others to question its lasting effectiveness, and to see it as but one stage on the road to a closer relationship with God. Could God not forgive sin in a more comprehensive way, they asked, so that humankind really could celebrate as those who were 'pure in act and in thought' (Psalm 24:4)?

The Old Testament never really gives an answer to that question, though some of its writers looked forward to a time when the covenant

would be renewed in such a way that the past would be forgiven, and the future could hold out the hope of real victory over the power of evil in all its many forms (Jeremiah 31:31–34). They never spelled out the meaning of that in detail, but they were sure that God could be trusted to work for the benefit of the whole world, which was both God's creation and the object of God's continuing love. Whenever people commit themselves to God in humble trust, whether it be in great corporate acts of worship or in the private recesses of their own lives, they will always learn more about the true meaning of life and faith:

> *Don't you know? Haven't you heard?*
> *Yahweh is the everlasting God,*
> *who created all the world*
> *and never grows tired or weary.*
> *No one understands God's thoughts,*
> *but this is the One who strengthens those who are weak and tired.*
> *Even those who are young grow weak;*
> *young people can fall exhausted.*
> *But those who trust in Yahweh for help*
> *will find their strength renewed.*
> *They will rise on wings like eagles;*
> *they will run and not get weary;*
> *they will walk and not grow weak (Isaiah 40:28–31).*

Kings, priests and prophets in worship

The existence of a regular system for public worship inevitably requires full-time officials to look after the places of worship, and to supervise what goes on there. In the Old Testament a number of figures appear to be important in this connection. As we would expect in a patriarchal society, the vast majority of them were men, though there are references to 'the women who served at the entrance to the tent of meeting' in Exodus 38:8 and 1 Samuel 2:22. Unfortunately, next to nothing is said about their function, though some have assumed it to have been sexual, in view of the fact that Eli's sons are said to have had intercourse with them. The narrative, however, makes it clear that this kind of behaviour was an abuse of their priestly office, and it is just as likely that they carried out some kind of recognized role in worship at the shrines. It may be relevant that this narrative is set in the earliest period of Israel's life as a nation, at a time of considerable upheaval and social disruption. It is a well-attested fact that women and other marginalized members of society are more likely to hold public office in such circumstances than in times of peace and stability, and several of them feature in the stories of the book of Judges. Generally speaking, though, religion – like the rest of life – was dominated by men throughout the Old Testament period.

The kings

Kings everywhere had a special role in religious affairs, though their precise function varied from place to place. In Egypt, for example, the pharaoh was often thought to be himself a divine being, while in Babylon the king was more likely to be regarded as a messenger of the gods, a special intermediary though not himself divine. Although some have argued otherwise, it is unlikely that the kings of either Israel or Judah were ever thought of as being divine. Indeed, when the Syrian general Naaman assumed that one of them was, he was quick to disclaim it (2 Kings 5:7). The psalms contain ample evidence to show that the people prayed not to the king, but to God on his behalf (Psalms 20; 72:1–19). From the earliest days of Israel's arrival in the land of Canaan, God had always been regarded as the nation's true ruler. The tension between this belief and the political need for a militant leader was recognized in the stories of Saul's appointment (1 Samuel 8:1–22; 10:17–27), and occasionally features in the messages of the prophets (Hosea 8:4). But even when the idea of the monarchy was accepted, God was still regarded as the supreme sovereign of the people, and the king was God's servant (Deuteronomy 17:14–20).

The special nature of the king's position was symbolized in the fact that he was anointed. This ritual signified his close relationship with God, and declared that he was, in effect, a 'holy' person. David recognized this quality even in Saul (1 Samuel 24:5–7), and when he was killed in the heat of battle his murderer had to be punished for killing 'the one whom Yahweh chose to be king' (2 Samuel 1:14–16). This special relationship between God and the king was expressed in the idea of a 'covenant' existing between God, the royal family of David and the people of Judah (2 Samuel 7:8–16), and the king could on occasion even be called God's 'son' (Psalm 2:7).

The king could also be called a priest (Psalm 110:4). Kings in general often had an important part to play in organized worship, and the kings of both Israel and Judah are shown engaging in such activities. David established centres of worship (2 Samuel 6:17; 24:25), and Solomon, of course, built the Temple itself (1 Kings 5:1 – 6:14). The first king of the northern kingdom of Israel also set up sanctuaries in his own land, and decreed

Kings everywhere had a special role in religious affairs. In Egypt, the king (via the priesthood) provided for the gods, and in return the gods showed favour to the king. In this painted limestone relief, Pharoah Seti I makes an offering to the god Thoth.

Kings, priests and prophets in worship *continued*

the sort of worship that should be carried out there (1 Kings 12:26–33). As a result, these shrines were thought of as 'the king's place of worship, the national temple' (Amos 7:13). But the same was true of the Temple in Jerusalem, for the kings of Judah controlled the worship there too, and the priests were effectively members of the royal household, under the control of the king (2 Samuel 8:17; 20:25; 1 Kings 2:26–35; 4:4; 2 Kings 12:4–16).

The responsibility of priests in any ancient culture was to offer libation to the gods. This plaque from Babylon shows at the top a priest before a god, and on the lower half, men driving animals, possibly for sacrifice.

The kings also took charge of religious policy-making. Asa (1 Kings 15:11–15), Joash (2 Kings 12:1–18), Ahaz (2 Kings 16:1–18), Hezekiah (2 Kings 18:1–7), Manasseh (2 Kings 21:1–9) and Josiah (2 Kings 22:3 – 23:23) are all specifically credited with having reorganized Temple worship in one way or another. As well as being responsible for the general tenor of organized worship, the kings could also on occasion lead the people in their worship. Saul (1 Samuel 13:8–10; 14:34–35), David (2 Samuel 6:13; 24:25), Solomon (1 Kings 3:3–4; 8:62–63), Jeroboam I (1 Kings 12:32 – 13:1) and Ahaz (2 Kings 16:1–16) all offered sacrifices regularly. Kings could also pray on behalf of the nation, and issue blessings in God's

name (1 Kings 8:14–66; 2 Kings 19:14–19). On one occasion, David offered sacrifice and gave a blessing while clothed in the apparel of a priest (2 Samuel 6:12–19).

The kings obviously had an important role in the religious life of their people. Since they were believed to be appointed by God, this is not surprising, for they had the power to encourage their people to maintain the covenant faith – and, on occasion, to corrupt it. There have been many arguments as to the precise nature of the kingship, in view of the many 'priestly' functions that kings could carry out. But a number of factors suggest that we need to be cautious in claiming that the king's main function was religious rather than political:

● Religion and politics were always closely related in the ancient world. In particular, the various superpowers of the day often expected defeated nations to adopt their own religious practices, as a means of demonstrating appropriate subservience. This fact alone explains why the kings of Judah were so often involved in changing the furniture and equipment used in the Temple. Restoration of the covenant faith meant reasserting Judah's independence.

● The exclusive functions of the priests were not as well defined during the time of the monarchy as they were later to become after the exile. As we shall see below, any head of the family could offer sacrifices or establish a new place of worship – and when the kings engaged in such activities they could well have been acting mainly in that capacity.

● It is perhaps significant that the only occasions from which we have specific reports of kings conducting worship were specially important times in the life of the nation. No doubt, in general, the day-to-day conduct of worship in ancient Israel would be left in the hands of other religious officials, appointed by the king for the job.

Priests

We have already seen that during the period of the monarchy the priests often had a close relationship with the king himself. Some experts have suggested that the priesthood only emerged at this period, but it is more likely that its existence and functions go back much further than that. It is certainly true that the Old Testament shows a lot of flexibility in worship at an earlier time. A number of stories show the heads of families offering sacrifices (Genesis 22:13; 31:54; 46:1; Judges 6:19–27; 13:19–23; 1 Samuel 1:3; 2:12–13; 9:12–13), though this is not of itself evidence that there were no priests, for even much later the actual act of sacrifice was always performed by the individual worshipper and not by the priest. More surprising, perhaps, is the way that in this early period it was apparently possible for clans and other groups to appoint and dismiss their own priests at will (Judges 17:1 – 18:31). Again, however, incidents of this kind might well have been exceptions, for it would have been odd for Israel to have had no organized priesthood at this time. Other nations certainly had well-developed priesthoods, and the Old Testament mentions some of them: the Canaanite priest Melchizedek (Genesis 14:17–24), the Egyptian priest Potiphera (Genesis 41:45–46), the Midianite Jethro (Exodus 18:1) and the Philistine priests of Dagon (1 Samuel 5:5). In the context of the religious ideas of the time, the existence of the ark of the covenant and the tent of the Lord's presence would almost certainly have necessitated the existence of professional priests to take care of them.

So what did priests do, and how did they operate? The answer to that question naturally changed over time. After the exile, with the disappearance of the kings, the priests came to occupy an important political place. But in the earlier period, they must have operated in a more restricted religious capacity, at least in the great national sanctuaries that were closely controlled by the kings. Some aspects of their work are unclear, especially the

relationship between priests and Levites, though information is given about several of their functions:

● Priests cared for the sanctuaries throughout the land (Judges 17:1–13; 1 Samuel 1:1 – 3:21; Amos 7:10–13). They would get their living from the gifts of worshippers and, of course, they also had their share of the meat from the sacrifices (Numbers 18:8–32; 1 Samuel 2:12–17). They could also have their own lands and property (1 Kings 2:26; Amos 7:17).

● People would also consult the priests in order to get advice for particular situations. One story tells how Saul first met Samuel while he was searching for some lost donkeys (1 Samuel 9:3–26). The account does not say precisely how Saul expected Samuel to know where they were, but other passages seem to imply that the priest would use a set of special dice (Urim and Thummim) to give the answer to such questions (Exodus 28:30; Deuteronomy 33:8; 1 Samuel 14:41–42). It is not known how this procedure operated, but it seems to have died out quite early in any case. After the time of David, it was the prophets who gave direct advice and instruction of this kind (1 Kings 20:13–14; 22:6; 2 Kings 3:11–19).

● More generally, the priests would give instructions (Torah) on questions relating to worship. They were able to pronounce on whether things, places or people were clean or unclean, holy or profane, and so give guidance to the worshippers (Leviticus 10:8–11; 13:1–58; Ezekiel 22:26; 44:23; Haggai 2:11–14). Some scholars believe that moral law such as the ten commandments may also have been 'preached' in this way by the priests. After the exile, the Levites had the job of teaching, but their 'Torah' was different from the earlier priestly teaching, since it now consisted of exposition of parts of the written books of the Hebrew Bible (Nehemiah 8:7–9). Priests could also have certain judicial functions, as we saw in a previous chapter.

● Priests were involved in the offering of sacrifices. It would be the worshipper who

**Kings, priests and
prophets in worship**
continued

actually killed the animal, but the priest
gave advice about the appropriate form of
sacrifice to be offered on different
occasions, and it was always the priest (as
a specially 'holy' person) who took the
blood to the altar. In this context, the priest
served as a mediator, representing God to
the people, and the people to God.

● The priest could also mediate between
God and people in giving answers in God's
name to the prayers of the worshippers
(1 Samuel 1:17), or pronouncing a blessing
upon them (Numbers 6:22–26). It was this
function as mediator which was most
characteristic of the priest's work. A priest
was specially consecrated to God, and as
such was able to deal with the awesome
holiness of a place of worship. Through the
presence of the priest, God and people could
be brought together in a tangible way.

Prophets

When the people of Jerusalem were
planning to get rid of Jeremiah, they
commented that even if they disposed of
him, 'There will always be priests to
instruct us, the wise to give us counsel,
and prophets to proclaim God's message'
(Jeremiah 18:18). At one time, scholars
were surprised to see prophets and priests
mentioned in the same breath, as if they
were complementary to each other.
Indeed, by the end of the nineteenth
century it was an 'assured result' of Old
Testament study that priests and prophets
were implacably opposed to each other.
They were believed to represent different
kinds of religion: priests being concerned
with the arid and mechanical performance
of pointless ritual, and prophets with the
communication of a vital and life-giving
message from God. It was widely
supposed that the great Old Testament
prophets were moral preachers, with no
interest in organized religion at all, and
that it had only been after the exile that a
lesser breed of prophets emerged, who
then became involved in formal worship
because the fire of the original prophetic
message had been all but extinguished.

It is certainly true that some of the
prophets were outspoken in their criticism
of empty formality (Isaiah 1:10–17;
Hosea 6:6; Amos 5:21–24; Micah 6:6–8),
but we can now see that it was wrong to
dissociate them altogether from the
organized worship. Closer study has
shown that the prophets as a group often
were closely linked with the shrines. A
number of factors have led to this
conclusion:

● As we have seen throughout this book,
formal worship and everyday behaviour
were closely linked in Israelite spirituality.
Both of them were part of the people's
response to God's goodness. The prophets
could not have denied outright the
importance of organized worship without
also denying the very foundations of the
covenant faith.

● The general picture often shows priests
and prophets working alongside each
other. Samuel and Elijah are the only
prophets whom we know to have carried
out priestly functions (1 Samuel 7:9;
11:15; 1 Kings 18:36–39), but other
passages connect them quite clearly
(Jeremiah 5:31; 23:11; 26:7, 16; 29:26;
Lamentations 2:20; Zechariah 7:1–3), and
there is mention of at least one prophet
who had his own room in the Temple at
Jerusalem (Jeremiah 35:3–4).

● The prophets often delivered their
messages in the context of organized
worship, and the themes of their teaching
were related to the great festivals. For
example, when Amos spoke of the coming
'day of Yahweh', he was probably taking
up the popular expectations in the minds of
the worshippers as they approached the
climax of one of the regular festivals –
though Amos then proceeded to turn their
expectations upside down (Amos 5:18–24).
When the priest Amaziah challenged Amos,
he suggested that he should go and
proclaim his message somewhere else,
because he could not expect to be
employed in Bethel, thereby implying that
prophets would on occasion be employed
there (Amos 7:10–13). Then we also need

to take account of the fact that both Jeremiah (Jeremiah 1:1) and Ezekiel (Ezekiel 1:1) were themselves members of priestly families. Observations of this kind have been taken to indicate that Jeremiah, Ezekiel and others were actually on the staff at various places of worship, though that is going beyond the evidence, which shows them going to the Temple only to speak and to attend worship. It made good sense for them to take their message to where the people were, and to use familiar motifs to present a message. In any case, the prophets never restricted their preaching to ritual occasions, but went into the market place, the fields and anywhere else that people would listen.

● Certain psalms seem to imply that someone spoke in the name of God during the liturgy of worship. A number of psalms that begin as lamentations end in thanksgiving – implying that at some point during the prayer the worshipper has been reassured of God's continuing presence (Psalms 20; 22; 86). Others contain messages of reassurance said to have come directly from God (Psalms 12:5; 85:9–13; 91:14–16). One psalm clearly says that such messages were delivered by 'an unknown voice' in the course of Temple worship (Psalm 81:5–16). Since worship often included drama, and since other parts of the Old Testament show the prophets to be not only speakers on God's behalf, but also dramatists and mime artists, who better than a 'cultic prophet' of this kind to play such a part in worship? There is some evidence for this in the work of the Chronicler, who in one passage gives the title 'Levites' to people who were designated 'prophets' in the earlier account of Kings (compare 2 Chronicles 34:30 with 2 Kings 23:2). In other passages, these same 'Levites' are expressly given prophetic functions, including the deliverance of messages on God's behalf during worship (1 Chronicles 25:1–6; 2 Chronicles 20:13–19). Scholars have naturally speculated on the exact tasks performed by such prophets who played a

regular part in the Temple worship, but apart from these rather vague references in Chronicles, and the implications of certain psalms, there is unfortunately no specific information that could help to define their role more exactly.

Several prophets compared themselves to lookouts in their watchtowers, set to give warning when the people left God's ways. The prophets hated empty, formalized worship with no moral content.

13 From Hebrew Bible to Old Testament

The Hebrew scriptures have always been of the highest importance for Christians, and are quoted on nearly every page of the New Testament. Yet the Hebrew Bible (in the form of the Christian Old Testament) has also presented them with a problem, and even in the very earliest days of the church its meaning and relevance were among the most hotly debated subjects, sparking off endless controversy that lasted over generations. The death and resurrection of Jesus was the one issue that, in the years immediately following it, caused most friction and dissension in the emerging churches. Jesus himself had claimed that his own life was in some way a 'fulfilment' of the Hebrew scriptures (Matthew 5:17), yet many of his actions seemed to set aside its most distinctive teachings, not only on subjects such as sabbath-keeping (Mark 2:23–28) and the food laws (Mark 7:14–23), but also some of its moral teaching (Matthew 5:21–48).

In the very first chapter of this book I emphasized that it has been written from a self-consciously Christian perspective, and it is therefore appropriate that we should conclude by taking a look at some matters related to the kind of authority that the Old Testament is supposed to have in the context of Christian faith. This question is, in turn, related to even more extensive matters of understanding and interpretation, many of which are of significance no matter what the presuppositions of those who enquire about them. For the Old Testament has not only played an important part in the evolution of the Christian tradition, it has also been an influential text in the development of recent Western civilization, and its stories have often been quoted as the inspiration and justification for many aspects of the expansion of Western values throughout the world during the last two or three centuries.

Questions of belief

The very first generation of Christians were also Jews, and for them there was no particular sense of discontinuity between the Hebrew scriptures and their own belief in Jesus. For the most part they continued to observe the way of life in which they had been brought up, based on the Greek Septuagint as it was understood in first-century Judaism. But once it became clear that the Christian message was for non-Jewish people, and that Romans and Greeks could also become followers of Jesus Christ, the question of the authority of the traditional scriptures presented itself in an altogether more pressing form. Was it necessary for a Gentile person to become a Jew in order to be a Christian? Paul and other New Testament writers answered that question with a firm, 'No,' though they still valued the Hebrew scriptures, and often used these ancient books as a basis for their own exposition of the Christian faith. Therein lies the problem, for if certain parts of the Old Testament can be set aside as being no longer relevant to Christian faith and action, how can we tell which those bits are, and what should we do with the rest of it?

Searching for solutions

The question of the relationship between Old Testament and New was expressed in an outspoken way by a second-century Christian called Marcion. Not only did he see the ambiguities in the position evidently taken by the apostles, but he also noted other problems that the Old Testament posed for Christian belief. Jesus had spoken of a God of love who was concerned for the well-being of all men and women. However, as Marcion read the Old Testament he often saw there a rather different picture of God, one which seemed to be associated with extreme savagery and cruelty, appearing to imply that, far from seeking the salvation of people, God was more often connected with their annihilation. Of course, Marcion presented an oversimplified picture, underestimating the extent to which stern judgment was an important part of Jesus' teaching, and playing down the fact that God's love was never absent from Israelite spirituality. Nevertheless, the contradiction to which he drew attention is definitely there, and most modern readers would probably feel much the same as Marcion did. Even the most ingenious interpreter would find it exceedingly difficult to reconcile the sentiments of Psalm 137:8–9 with the statements about loving enemies in Jesus' Sermon on the Mount (Matthew 5:43–48), and in addition to that kind of issue there are topics like sacrifice which (at least to Western people) seem primitive and cruel, if not completely incomprehensible.

Marcion's solution to all this was simple: tear up the Old Testament and discard it altogether as an unworthy part of the Christian scriptures. But his view found no widespread support in the early church, not least because Marcion wanted to dispose of much of the New Testament as well, and that seemed to put a serious question mark against the reality of his Christian faith. Nevertheless, the leaders of the early church could understand well enough the point that Marcion was making. There was a real question about the Old Testament. For if (as they believed) the coming of Jesus was God's new and decisive action in the life of the world, then what relevance could the history of an ancient people have for faith in him? The usual answer was that when the Old Testament was correctly understood it could be seen to be saying exactly the same thing as the New Testament. But in order to demonstrate this, it was necessary to interpret the Old Testament in such a way as to show that its real meaning was somehow hidden from the casual reader.

By coincidence, Jewish scholars had already faced this question in a different context. A century and more earlier, Philo (c. 20 BC–AD 45), a member of the Jewish community in the Egyptian city of Alexandria, had taken up the challenge of reconciling the teaching of the Hebrew scriptures with the thinking of the great Greek philosophers. There were few obvious connections between them, but by applying a mystical allegorical interpretation to the Old Testament, Philo had succeeded in demonstrating (at least to his own satisfaction) that Moses and other Old Testament writers had actually declared the same ideas as Greek philosophy, only they had done it several centuries before the Greeks thought of them. Some of the early Christian leaders, especially those based in Alexandria, adopted this approach with enthusiasm, and in a very short time were using the same techniques to demonstrate that the Old Testament books also contained everything that was in the New Testament, for those with the eyes to see it. Even apparently insignificant details in its historical narratives could be understood as symbols of the

A Roman schoolmaster with his pupils. Paul writes in Galatians of the law as 'our tutor to bring us to Christ'.

FROM HEBREW BIBLE TO OLD TESTAMENT

Christian gospel. Anything red, for example, might be interpreted as a reference to the death of Jesus on the cross (for example, the red heifer of Numbers 19, or Rahab's red cord in Joshua 2:18). References to water soon became pictures of Christian baptism, and the story of the exodus, with its combination of blood (on the doorposts at Passover) and water (in the crossing of the Sea of Reeds), engendered many complex explanations of the relationship between the cross and Christian salvation, as well as the two Christian sacraments of baptism and the Lord's supper.

Hilary, bishop of Poitiers in France (AD 315–68), explained this way of reading the Old Testament in the following terms:

> *Every work contained in the sacred volume announces by word, explains by facts, and corroborates by examples the coming of our Lord Jesus Christ... From the beginning of the world Christ, by authentic and absolute prefigurations in the person of the patriarchs, gives birth to the church, washes it clean, sanctifies it, chooses it, places it apart and redeems it: by the sleep of Adam, by the deluge in the days of Noah, by the blessing of Melchizedek, by Abraham's justification, by the birth of Isaac, by the captivity of Jacob... The purpose of this work is to show that in each personage in every age, and in every act, the image of his coming, of his teaching, of his resurrection, and of our church is reflected as in a mirror (Introduction to* The Treatise of Mysteries*).*

Not all church leaders, even in those early centuries, were happy with this approach to the Old Testament, especially those connected with the other great Christian centre at Antioch in Syria. But it was generally taken for granted that the Old Testament was basically a Christian book, and in one way or another its contents had to be related to the fundamental beliefs of Christian theology.

During the Protestant Reformation the whole subject was once again opened for fresh examination. Martin Luther (1483–1546) and John Calvin (1509–64) both emphasized the need to understand the Old Testament in its historical and social context, and in that respect their approach was not dissimilar from that of many modern scholars. But

Martin Luther

Luther wanted to distinguish the value of Old and New Testaments by seeing the Old as 'Law' and the New as 'Gospel'. This gave him a neat tool with which to separate out the wheat of the pure gospel (which for him was found in Paul's New Testament letters) from what he regarded as the chaff of a superseded legalism (identified with the Old Testament, and Jewish Christianity more generally). This thinking has had a profound influence on biblical scholarship right up to our own day, often further fuelled by the inclination of Protestant (especially Lutheran) scholars to see what they regarded as Jewish legalism as a foreshadowing of medieval Catholicism, and even, in the early twentieth century, by the kind of anti-Semitism that flourished under the Nazis. But it is misguided in at least two fundamental ways:

■ It ignores the fact that 'law' is not actually the basis of the Old Testament faith – nor for that matter is it entirely absent from the New Testament either. In both of them, law is placed in the context of a covenant understanding in which God's love is the foundation principle.

■ Luther quite misleadingly identified Judaism with a moralistic legalism. This was unfair even to the Pharisaic viewpoint which the Christian Paul so clearly rejected, and there is no question that Luther allowed his own negative experiences of Roman Catholic Christianity to colour his view of Old Testament spirituality.

Calvin recognized some of these deficiencies, and instead he emphasized the importance of the covenant theme in both parts of the Christian Bible. By a careful comparison of God's relationships with people in ancient Israel and the Christian church, he was able to claim that the two testaments hang together as a 'progressive revelation' in which the ancient promises made to Israel in the Old Testament found their culmination in the ongoing life of the Christian church. This view is not without its own problems, but it does at least try to take the faith of Israel seriously, and Calvin's position is still widely held today by many conservative Christians.

After the Reformation, the question of whether the Old Testament is a Christian book was effectively shelved until our own generation. The European Enlightenment, with its emphasis on understanding the Old Testament as a collection of ancient books in the context of its own times, directed scholarly endeavours elsewhere, but the theological question could not be banished for long, not only because of its relevance to the events of the early twentieth century in Nazi Germany, but also because of the way in which the Old Testament seems to have been used as a justification for anti-Palestinian sentiments in the Middle East and movements of ethnic cleansing in places as far separated as South Africa and the Balkans.

John Calvin

Christians adopt various attitudes to the value of the Old Testament:

■ Some insist on giving the Old Testament an equal value and authority to the New, on the grounds that every word of each is the direct utterance of God. But considerable caution needs to be exercised before accepting this outlook, for there are whole sections of the teaching of Jesus himself where he makes it clear that his message involved either a rejection or a very radical revision of some fundamental aspects of Old Testament teaching.

■ Others argue that the Old Testament is completely replaced by the New, and so can be discarded. Here again, we need to preserve the kind of careful balance we find in the teaching of Jesus himself, for he also described his ministry as in some sense a 'fulfilment' of the Old Testament. There can be legitimate argument about what that means – but it must certainly involve the assumption that the Old Testament has something to say to Christians, and therefore has a place in a Christian Bible.

■ Some try to distinguish between various parts of the Old Testament, perhaps by separating out things such as laws about priests, sacrifices and purity (which Christians no longer observe) from other parts such as the ten commandments and the moral teachings of the prophets (which are still considered relevant). Calvin made a similar division to this, but it is a good deal easier to make such distinctions than it is to justify them. By removing such apparently irrelevant elements, we are in fact displacing some of the most basic aspects of Old Testament spirituality. In addition, it is precisely in such concepts as sacrifice that the New Testament itself most often finds some intrinsic connection between the Old Testament faith and Christian beliefs about Jesus.

■ It is also common for Christians to speak of a 'progressive revelation' of God's will and character running through both testaments. On this view, God's will is revealed in a number of stages, roughly corresponding with the growing spiritual capacity of people to understand. This allows some of the more difficult parts of the Old Testament to be explained as being appropriate to a primitive age, but subsequently replaced by other more sophisticated notions, culminating in Jesus' teaching about a God of love. This also raises more questions than it solves. Not only is it based on an outmoded evolutionary idea of an inevitable moral progress in human affairs, but it also confuses statements about how God really is with statements about how people think of God. In addition, it contains the dubious implication that modern people invariably know more about God's will, and are more obedient to it, than were the prophets and other leading figures in the Old Testament story.

Making connections

There are obvious difficulties involved in interpreting the Old Testament within the context of the Christian scriptures. We need to recognize that it is in many ways a strange and alien book, to Christians as well as to others. Whatever assessment we may make of Israelite spirituality, it is not the same thing as Christian faith, and in practice when Christians read the Hebrew scriptures they often find them hard to understand because they belong to a completely different world from their own faith experience. Much of this strangeness can be dispelled once the Old Testament is placed in its proper historical and social context, which is why so much attention has been given to doing that in this book. At the end of it all, we may not find things such as sacrifice any more appealing, but at least we can begin to appreciate their significance when they are viewed in the total context of Israel's faith.

In practice, however, the relationships between Judaism and Christianity are more complex than that, and it is impossible to articulate an adequate Christian faith without reference to the Old Testament. At the most fundamental level, it is a simple fact that we will not get far in making sense out of the New Testament itself if we are ignorant of the Old. Jesus and his disciples were practising Jews, who were thoroughly immersed in Old Testament ways of thinking about God and the world. For them the Old Testament faith was a living and vital part of their total existence. Of course, in many respects they grew out of Judaism, as they found it necessary to discard or develop some things in the light of the exciting newness of God's actions in Christ. But for all that, they continued to think of their new Christian experience very much in terms of the faith with which they had been brought up. The earliest Christian churches used the Old Testament in its Greek translation as their Bible, and the language of the New Testament itself has a good deal more in common with that than it does with the secular literature of Greek and Roman culture. Inevitably, that language influenced the way the first Christians articulated their understanding of their own faith. Indeed, Old Testament language still permeates Christian thinking today, and those who have never seen an animal sacrifice (and would be horrified if they did) still talk about the 'sacrifice' of Jesus on the cross and continue to call a part of their church building an 'altar', even though no blood has ever been shed there. In the broader scheme of things, it is arguable that all this kind of imagery needs to be translated into different concepts in order for it to be effectively contextualized within today's culture, but to do that successfully it needs to be properly understood first, otherwise there is a constant danger that some significant aspect of Christian belief will be thrown out along with the language of sacrifice, altar and atonement. The place to find a proper understanding of all these notions is certainly the Old Testament.

But the Old Testament provides more than just a linguistic and cultural background to the thinking of the New Testament writers. It also contains important statements about God's relationships with humankind and the world that are as valid now as they were then. Each of the key concepts which we have used in this book to explore Israelite spirituality and beliefs forms an indispensable theological foundation for the Christian faith as it is presented in the pages of the New Testament. There is such a close interconnection between both testaments at this point that it is no exaggeration to claim that the Christian faith itself would make imperfect sense if we were to remove the basic affirmations of the Old Testament faith from the Christian Bible.

THE LIVING GOD
Nowhere is this more strikingly obvious than in the case of beliefs about God:

■ The belief that there is only one God, who is both all-powerful and yet personally interested in the welfare of ordinary people, is fundamental to both testaments. Nowadays, theologians often talk of these two aspects of God's character in terms of 'transcendence' and 'immanence'. We can be quite sure that this language would have meant little to the people of Old Testament times. Indeed, it is unlikely that these facets of God's character would have been perceived with equal clarity by all sections of the people of Israel at all periods of their history. But they were certainly implicit in the very earliest creedal confessions which exhort the people to worship only one God (Exodus 15:11–18), even if it was several centuries later that God's sole control of the world and its affairs was systematically asserted by one of the great prophets (Isaiah 40:12–31; 41:21–29; 44:1–20).

■ Bound up with the fact that God is unique is the belief that God's demands on people are primarily moral rather than being connected to religious services or ritual taboos. We have already noticed the distinctiveness of this idea in a world where religions were generally more interested in sacrifices and ritual than in morality. Yet the whole Old Testament understanding of worship makes no sense at all if these two aspects are separated – and again, the combination of these two is fundamental to the New Testament.

A popular image of God in the Bible is that of a shepherd.

■ Then there is the notion of God's grace, the fact that God gives undeserved gifts to people. The entire Old Testament story is given coherence by the knowledge that God had done great things for the people of Israel, and on that basis could challenge them to loyalty and obedience. Every stage of the narrative shows God's active concern to work for the salvation of the people, and this covenant principle is still basic to any Christian understanding of God's ways. The Old Testament, just as much as the New Testament, depicts God working in love for the good of humankind, and though the focus in the New Testament shifts from events such as the exodus or the exile to centre on Jesus, there is still an underlying assumption that God is an active and loving God, whose workings can be seen by ordinary people in the course of their everyday lives.

■ We have observed more than once that the Hebrew scriptures do not describe God 'metaphysically', by asking about the stuff of which God is made, but 'functionally', by reflecting on the ways in which God behaves. The New Testament shares this approach, when it says, in effect, 'Look at Jesus: this is what God is like.'

GOD AND THE WORLD

It is not too difficult to show that important aspects of God's character are common to both testaments. But without the Old Testament, the Christian faith would also be seriously lacking a perspective on the way God relates to the natural world.

■ In the world of the earliest Christians, it was commonplace to believe that the natural, physical world in which we live was intrinsically evil, and any sort of meaningful salvation would therefore need to involve an escape from this world to some other, more 'spiritual' and therefore more perfect world. This was part and parcel of the Greek outlook, and as the Christian church moved out from Palestine into the wider Roman empire it was always a temptation for Christians to incorporate it into their own thinking. Though there were fierce arguments on this very point, Christians never did accept the view that physical existence in this world is second best. But they were able to assert the basic goodness of life only because of the strong Old Testament conviction that informed their thinking. As a consequence, instead of regarding salvation in terms of escape from this world, the Christian writers of the New Testament declared that the world itself had its own part in God's plan of salvation: the coming of Jesus' meant vitality and renewal for the very stuff out of which the world is made (Romans 8:18–25; Colossians 1:15–20; Revelation 21–22). In incorporating the physical world into their expectations of salvation, the New Testament writers were quite firmly grounded in the Old Testament faith that had gone before them, which saw the whole creation as blessed by God. Christians have not always taken this as seriously as they ought, but without this they would have little theological foundation for saying anything at all on major issues such as care for the environment and the use of the world's natural resources.

■ When the New Testament sets out to explain how Jesus Christ relates to people, it again does so on the basis of the Old Testament view of people and their relationship to God. It takes for granted the basic theological concepts that we have located in the creation stories, and sees human fallenness as a barrier between God and people that needs to be dealt with if open relationships between people and God are to be restored. This whole structure of thought is so crucial for Christian theology that without the Old Testament insight it is doubtful whether the apostolic faith could have developed at all in the way it did.

LIVING AS GOD'S PEOPLE

New Testament ethics also owe a good deal to the Old Testament:

■ The notion of natural law and a creation-centred spirituality, as we have discussed it in relation to the Old Testament, is a fundamental prerequisite of the Christian faith, and Paul takes it up as a key element in his explanation of how the life, death and resurrection of Jesus applies to all men and women, whatever their social or ethnic origins (Romans 1:18 – 2:16).

■ Equally central to the New Testament is the covenantal framework within which much Old Testament morality operates. The coming of Jesus was viewed as a further great act of God's love, comparable with the exodus and calling for a similar response of obedience and commitment. But the whole pattern of the Christian ethic is also based on the fundamental Old Testament assertion that people should behave in the same way as God (Matthew 5:48). The only difference is that the divine pattern is made even more explicit because of the model provided by Jesus himself, and which Christians are called on to follow (2 Corinthians 8:8–9; Philippians 2:5–11).

■ There is also the whole question of a Christian social ethic, which depends so much on the Old Testament heritage. For a variety of reasons, the New Testament has very little to say about how God deals with nations, and without the Old Testament the Christian faith would undoubtedly be considerably impoverished at this point. For the Old Testament provides the foundations for a Christian philosophy of history. No doubt the Old Testament position requires modification here and there in the light of the teaching of Jesus himself, but it is no coincidence that when modern Christians make pronouncements on social and political affairs, they often depend on the insights of the prophets and lawgivers of ancient Israel.

WORSHIPPING GOD

Here, too, the New Testament faith owes more to its Old Testament antecedents than is sometimes appreciated:

■ The style of worship of the early church grew out of the patterns of praise and joyful celebration that we have seen in the pages of the Old Testament.

■ Even more striking is the correlation between the understanding of what worship means in both testaments. For  the undergirding principle of both Old Testament and Christian worship is that though God can be described as 'holy' – in every sense of that word – God is also open and accessible, and the reality of that can be represented in the events of worship in the presence of God's people.

■ We can hardly ignore the vast importance that the theme of sacrifice has come to assume in Christian thinking. The New Testament writers asserted that in Jesus' life, death and resurrection, all that was promised by the sacrificial worship of the Old Testament had been brought to fulfilment. It was impossible to speak of what Jesus could do in the lives of his people without some reference to the hopes and aspirations of the wor-shipper in ancient Israel. Indeed, the whole concept of sacrifice is so significant in the Christian tradition that at least one large section of the church thinks of it not only as a series of theological metaphors and images, but also as a continuing symbolic part of the ongoing liturgy of the worshipping Christian community.

Questions of behaviour

Reference has already been made to the question of the way in which the Hebrew scriptures not only report, but also seem actively to approve and promote repeated brutality and ethnic cleansing. Once we move away from aspects of theological belief, this is one of the major issues that contemporary readers of the Old Testament need to deal with. The question comes to a focus most clearly in relation to the stories in the early parts of the deuteronomic history, concerning the settlement of Israel in the land of Canaan. The books of Numbers and Deuteronomy – and, to a lesser extent, Joshua and Judges – express an intense hatred for the indigenous people of the land, insisting that they are so worthless that virtually any kind of barbarity against them can be justified. Ethnic cleansing and genocide are not merely reported, but apparently seem to be applauded as being God's will. Moreover, this is not just a historical issue that can be dismissed as belonging to a world far removed from our own, for throughout much of the last 1,000 years of Western history, these stories of how Israel attempted to annihilate

One of the great formative experiences of Israel's history was their entry into the promised land, seen here from across the north end of the Dead Sea. The people were called to remember that their land was held in trust from God.

the Canaanites have provided the ideological underpinning for imperialist adventures including the Crusades, the European invasion of the Americas and of Australasia, as well as being a major inspiration for the development of the Afrikaner mythology that led to apartheid in South Africa, and the emergence of a militant Zionism in the Middle East. Viewed in this light, the Bible appears not only to tolerate, but also to actively promote practices which, if they happened today, would be regarded as war crimes. Those who are familiar with the Bible, and read it regularly, often fail to appreciate the extent to which the presence of such elements leads others to question the value of its message, if not to disregard it entirely. In order to have integrity, these moral issues need to be addressed.

Possession of land as a sign of God's favour is mentioned more than 1,700 times in the Hebrew Bible, and the idea that 'success' is to be defined in terms of possession of land has been the driving force behind all colonial Western oppression of indigenous peoples. Christians read the accounts with the eyes of liberated slaves finding new land for themselves, but the liberating God of the exodus story can be made to

The Hebrew scriptures report, and appear to approve of, the destruction of entire communities in the process of settling the promised land. The thriving Canaanite city of Hazor lay in an important strategic position, and was taken by Joshua's army. The population was slaughtered and the city burnt to the ground.

look considerably more menacing when viewed from the perspective of those who are conquered. Nor is any of this just a matter of interpretation, for the oppression seems to be in the text, and racism and genocide are not only taken for granted, but are morally accepted as well. By comparison even with other religious literature, where deities are violent but unpredictable, there is something especially abhorrent to modern readers about the carefully planned massacres of ancient Canaanites, where some parts of the narrative portray Yahweh as not just allowing it, but actually requiring it. There is a serious moral and spiritual question here, for what kind of a God will recommend behaviour that falls well short of regular secular values? If it was not for the religious provenance of the Bible, Christians themselves might easily be campaigning to have passages like these banned as racist propaganda.

So much for the question, which has been deliberately spelled out here somewhat starkly in order to emphasize its importance. How can it be dealt with, from the perspective of the Christian reader of the Old Testament? Several points can be made.

Revisiting history

In previous chapters, a good deal of space was allocated to exploring what exactly it was that happened at the time when Israel was in the process of emerging as a recognizable nation in the land of Canaan. From all the evidence that has been surveyed there, two things seem absolutely certain, namely that there was no single cause that led to, or explanation for, the establishment of an Israelite state, and that the relationship between Israelite culture and traditional Canaanite ways was a good deal more complex than the presentation of the deuteronomic history seems to imply. In terms of cultural change, all the

available evidence indicates that the values identified with the notion of 'Israel' existed alongside and in competition with the traditional values of the Canaanite city states for a very long period of time, centuries rather than decades. The relevant archaeological data shows this, as does the evidence of the Old Testament itself, with its constant references to the way in which Canaanite practices never really disappeared from the culture of either Israel or Judah. While there is no reason to doubt that some elements within the people of Israel looked back to the exodus as an actual event experienced by their own forebears, there is also evidence that some other elements of the nation were attracted to the new state by its egalitarian ideology. We can discount the idea that a peasants' revolt would have been sufficient by itself to account for the emergence of Israel, but the biblical story provides evidence indicating that this happened in some cases, and that these people, therefore, far from being ethnically different from others in the land, were in effect converted Canaanites.

Earlier chapters have highlighted the fact that the narrative histories of the Old Testament are edited versions of traditional stories, and while this again does not necessarily undermine or question their usefulness, that does mean it is important to be aware of the editorial spin that has been placed on them. In the case of the stories of the conquest, it is not the accounts of individual episodes that contain the incitements to genocide, but the connecting tissue of editorial comment. The stories themselves describe a number of smallish military skirmishes, at the end of which the Canaanites are still a major force to be reckoned with, which is why Israelite settlements are then described as emerging predominantly in the poorer hill country. The editorial stance, however, taking in the whole subsequent history of Israel and Judah, right through to the effects of the Babylonian exile and beyond, traces the disastrous events of the exile back to the perceived failure of these earlier generations to annihilate the Canaanites. In other words, the kind of wholesale genocide which can seem to be such a pressing moral problem did not actually happen at all, but was the product of the kind of thinking about racial purity that had its origins in later history, particularly after the exile.

Moral tensions

Interestingly, the kind of moral dilemma that modern readers can identify in these stories is also to be found in the Hebrew Bible itself. Taken as a whole, and understood in relation to its theological and moral consequences, the Old Testament adopts a position that is the exact opposite of the one just highlighted. At the very beginning of the story, in the promise to Abraham and Sarah, God tells them that they were being chosen 'so that you will be a blessing... and in you all the families of the earth shall be blessed' (Genesis 12:2–3). The same theme had featured already at the beginning of the book of Genesis, with the insistence that all people – with no mention of race – were made 'in the image of God' (1:26–27), and the subsequent lists of people groups depict them as all being related to one another and, by implication, suggests that race is an artificial construct.

There is no doubt that in the post-exilic age, xenophobia was rife, as was observed in our discussion of the work of Ezra, who refused to have any dealings with the people of Samaria even to the point of insisting that Judahites who had married outside their own families and clans should divorce their partners. But even in that context, there were dissenting voices. It is hard to miss, for instance, the contrast between the universal message of God's love in Isaiah 40–55 and the more narrow-minded jingoism of Ezra. Moreover, the books of Jonah and Ruth, both of them probably written at roughly the same time, also stand in stark contrast to some strands of thought within the post-exilic community, with their overt insistence not only that people of different races would be accepted by God, but also that they could play a significant part in the purposes of God. The spirituality and commitment of the people of Nineveh turned out to present a radical – and divinely inspired – challenge to Jonah's more restricted vision of things, while the non-Israelite Ruth became one of the ancestors of King David, the most powerful icon of national identity for the kingdom of Judah and its successors.

The same uneasiness about the violation of human rights also surfaces elsewhere in the prophetic books, in at least one case taking the form of an outright challenge to the spin placed on a story by the deuteronomic editors. This is the case of Jehu, whose merciless massacre of Jezebel and the royal household of Israel (itself largely inspired by racial considerations) is singled out as a praiseworthy venture in 2 Kings 9:17–37, but was, according to Hosea, so contrary to standards of covenant-inspired decency that God would personally deal with it: 'in a little while I will punish the house of Jehu for the blood of Jezreel, and I will put an end to the kingdom of the house of Israel' (Hosea 1:4). Amos's condemnation of the systematic abuse of human rights is very similar (Amos 1:3 – 2:8).

Texts and readers

This entire debate highlights some underlying matters related to the way in which we read texts, for in considering the way in which the narratives about early Israel have been understood and applied within a more recent colonialist culture, it is obvious that the context of their interpreters has been at least as important as the contents of the text itself, for it appears to have blinded readers to the more subtle nuances that can be found in the Old Testament when viewed from a more holistic perspective. Looking at the history of Western imperialist expansion over the last 1,000 years and more, it is obvious that the main driving force has not been texts from the Bible. While it would be impossible to deny that these narratives have sometimes played a part in the formulation of expansionist policies, they have only done so in a context whose essential characteristics were formed through other influences. The main forces within that context were drawn from quite different sources, not least the increasing secularization of Western culture as a result of the Enlightenment, and selected aspects of the Hebrew scriptures were used more as the ideological icing on the cake than as any of its essential ingredients.

From the point of view of the victims of genocide, the most dangerous context is not that of the Hebrew Bible, but of those who would interpret and apply it in this kind of way. This is one reason why it will be worth spending a little more time reflecting on the relationship between texts and their readers. For the last two centuries or there-abouts, study of the Bible has been dominated by what was called the 'historical-critical method', in which all the emphasis was on getting back to ancient writers and their texts, trying to understand them in their own contexts, and assuming that if we can somehow imagine ourselves into their skins, we will be better placed to get to grips with what they have written. There is no question that the conclusions which have emerged from this way of studying the Bible have provided many valuable insights into the Bible and its world, and much of this book has been taken up with such matters, if for no other reason than that the world of professional biblical study still regards them as very important. However, reading and understanding the Bible is a far more subtle business than that, for it is not a one-way process in which we hear today what the ancient text and its author were saying in their world – it is, rather, a two-way process in which we are speaking to the text as well as listening to it. It is a fallacy to imagine that there is some truly 'objective' way of comprehending the Hebrew Bible (or indeed the Christian New Testament) which relies on self-validating 'scientific' procedures. There is no such thing, for we all bring our own presuppositions, our personal baggage and filters, to bear on everything we read. It is a pointless exercise to try to deny that, and those who do so lack credibility as well as integrity. Interpretation is a dynamic process, in which we bring something to these books, at the same time as we expect to receive something from them.

Questions related to biblical interpretation have a full chapter to themselves in the companion volume to this one, *Introducing the New Testament*, and readers who wish to understand all this more fully are recommended to consult that, for the same principles of reading and interpretation apply equally to both sections of the Christian Bible. But the point to be made in this context is that, if the stories of the Hebrew Bible are used to justify violence and genocide (as they have been), that is hardly something intrinsic to the text, but arises out of the social and cultural preferences and prejudices of readers of the text. The reality of this can easily be illustrated by reference to those millions of Jewish and Christian people in all times and all places (and notably, among today's Christians, in the non-Western world) who have read its stories and, far from being inspired to indulge in ethnic cleansing and racism, have been moved in exactly the opposite direction, to oppose those colonialists who, often, were the very ones who claimed the Old Testament as the justification for their own actions. A classic example would be the struggle against apartheid in South Africa during the second half of the twentieth century, for both the proponents of that political theory, and those who campaigned for its downfall, were motivated by their reading of the Bible. In its origins, apartheid was essentially a disagreement among Christians about the meaning of the Old Testament, which was then transformed into a racial policy. If there is any case to answer, it is not the Bible *per se* that stands in the dock, but those advocates of the historical-critical method who have insisted that understanding the Bible is a neutral project, and who have therefore tended to ignore altogether the moral and spiritual consequences of certain ways of using it. What is now needed is, on the one hand, a recognition that the Hebrew scriptures originated in a patriarchal society, and reflect all that goes on in such a context – and that could include horrific brutality in the ancient world, just as it often does in today's world. On the other hand, we need to be honest about the need for incorporating matters of faith and morality into our understanding, and recognizing that what we as readers bring to the text is at least as likely to determine our conclusions as what the text itself appears to say in abstraction. These texts are not meant to be models for human behaviour, so much as a sort of two-way mirror, through which we can come face to face with ourselves as well as catching a glimpse of the world as it is, and the world as God intends it to be. What we then do with those images is a matter of our own moral choice.

Glimpses of a different future

In the opening chapter, it was made clear that this is a Christian book about the Old Testament, and at various subsequent points the same emphasis has been repeated. If the contribution brought by the reader to the text is to be taken seriously, it is important – indeed, essential – that we all come clean about our starting points. The starting point here has been motivated by the conviction that the books of the Hebrew · Bible, and its Greek translation, have an authentic place within the Christian scriptures, and that when viewed from this perspective the two testaments of the Christian Bible are coherent one with another, and have an inner integrity in their message. So how can we define what that integrity and coherence might be?

The early sections of this chapter have already drawn attention to some significant points of continuity between a Christian world-view and the Old Testament, and while few would wish to dispute the reality of the various connections traced here between the two, it is legitimate to ask whether some of this is not just wishful thinking from the Christian's point of view. After all, it is easy enough to look at the Old Testament with the benefit of hindsight and convince oneself that this or that element of Old Testament spirituality is somehow related to Christian thinking. Are we perhaps in danger of falling into the same kind of subjectivism as those more ancient expositors who looked at things such as Rahab's scarlet cord and saw in them a clear reference to the blood of Jesus on the cross? We are certainly not in the same predicament as the medieval scholars, for we have restricted our discussion here to features in the Old Testament which were an integral part of its historical development, and which were clearly perceived by the Old Testament writers themselves. But we still need to explain how we can be so sure that the Christian interpretation we want to place on these facts is not an alien intrusion into the Old Testament's essential message. In the final analysis, the truth is that it is only our Christian conviction that Jesus is God's final word to humankind that enables us to see both Old and New Testaments as parts of the same story. But we could certainly qualify that by drawing attention to the obvious fact that the Old Testament writers themselves seem to have regarded their faith as incomplete in itself, and therefore requiring some kind of future 'fulfilment'.

In many important respects, the Old Testament faith was anchored in the past. Some of its most distinctive insights emerged out of reflection on the great events of Israel's history, as they were reported by traditional tribal storytellers and then eventually incorporated into the historical narratives of the Hebrew Bible. When men and women wanted to know what God was like, they turned for an answer to events such as the exodus or the exile, as explained and interpreted by the prophets and others. But they never thought that God was locked up in the past. Quite the opposite, for one of the Old Testament's fundamental convictions is that God can be known by ordinary people in the everyday events of their present life. The prophets extended this conviction to its logical conclusion, observing that if Yahweh was the God of the past, who is also still active in the present, then this same God must also be working to create a new future. The Old Testament historians express this view right at the beginning of their long story, with their reference to the fact that the covenant made with Abraham and Sarah and their family was to be a blessing for all the nations (Genesis 12:3). At the time the final touches were being put to the Hebrew scriptures, this blessing of the nations was certainly not a reality, but represented a future hope that had yet to be accomplished, and as the Old Testament story proceeds, this hope is expanded and combined with other themes until a coherent future expectation emerges. There is a sense of growing anticipation that Israelite spirituality will be completed, which is expressed in at least three fundamental concepts.

This 'Good Shepherd' is from a painting by Christians in the catacombs of Rome. The idea of God as a shepherd is taken straight from the Old Testament.

A new covenant

A notable articulation of this hope is to be found in the expectation that there would need to be a 'new covenant', which would take up and fulfil all the unfulfilled commitments of the original Sinai covenant, and at the same time herald the beginning of a new era of relationships between God and humanity. This hope first emerged about the time of the exile, when it was clear that the original covenant had been a failure because of the disobedience and disloyalty of the people. For all its God-given potential, they had been unable to keep its terms, and as a result leading thinkers began to see that a complete change would be needed in the lives of God's people if ever they were to do God's will. This change would be based on forgiveness for what was past, but its most striking feature would be a radical transformation of the human will in such a way that God would empower people actually to keep the covenant: 'The new covenant that I will make with the people of Israel will be this: I will put my law within them and write it on their hearts' (Jeremiah 31:33). The key to success is found in the new initiative personally undertaken by God to enable people to live according to new values: 'I will give them a new heart and a new mind. I will take away their stubborn heart of stone and will give them an obedient heart... I will put my spirit in you' (Ezekiel 11:19; 36:27).

A messiah

The Hebrew word *mashiach*, like its Greek equivalent (*christos*), means 'an anointed person'. In the ancient world kings and priests were both anointed with oil, and attention has already been drawn to the significant part played by the king, especially in the southern kingdom of Judah. As the representative of God to the people, the king could be referred to as 'God's anointed', even as 'God's son' (Psalm 2:7), and this close relationship between God and the king in Jerusalem was cemented in the covenant made with the royal family of David (2 Samuel 7:1–17). Because of that, the king was in a very real sense the focus of the people's hopes as they looked for God's will to be done in their midst.

In the ancient world, priests and kings were anointed with oil. This mural, from Dura-Europus, shows Samuel anointing David as king.

If Israel's social relationships were to reflect the character of God's own person, then it was through the king that this would be put into practical effect. At least, that was the theory, though the reality was often different, as one king after another showed himself to be quite unfit, both morally and spiritually, to lead the people in ways that would reflect God's values and standards. The prophets generally hoped that the next king would be better, which is one reason why so many of them (at least in the early period) became involved in plots to overthrow even their own rulers. But from about the time of Isaiah onwards they were to become increasingly disillusioned with David's family. Though the prophets greeted each new king with optimism, their hopes for the future came to be expressed in more idealistic terms that show their expectations moving away from the actual kings in Jerusalem and towards an ideal king who would be commissioned directly by God to lead their people (Psalms 89:1–4; 132:10–12; Isaiah 9:6–7; 11:1–5; Jeremiah 23:5–6; Micah 5:2–5). It was out of this frustration that the hope of a messiah was eventually born, and by the end of the Old Testament period it was widely believed that God would once more intervene in history, and send a new king who would perfectly fulfil the hopes and aspirations of a genuine Israelite spirituality.

A new world

The Old Testament also looks forward to a time of physical renewal for the world itself. Since failure in the lives of people had often been linked to corruption in the world of nature (Genesis 3:17–19; Amos 4:6–12), it is not surprising that future personal and social renewal should also include plans for a revitalized world. This, too, became an important part of the Old Testament's view of the future, and many passages depict the material world sharing in the rejuvenation of the human world (Isaiah 11:6–9; 25:6–9; 51:3; 62:1–5; Ezekiel 47:1–12; Amos 9:13–15; Micah 4:1–4). The Old Testament faith is not a closed system, but a dynamic living spirituality that always expects God to do new things. This message was given its most comprehensive expression by Isaiah of Babylon who, in encouraging the exiles, exhorted them to direct their attention away from sentimental assessments of the past, and to look for God to do new things in their midst (Isaiah 43:18–19). He knew they could trust God not only because of all that God had done in the past on their behalf, but also because their trust was in 'the first, the last, the only God', one who could claim that 'there is no other god but me' (Isaiah 44:6). He also identified God's action on behalf of humankind with the work of a figure he called 'the servant of Yahweh'.

It has become customary in Old Testament studies to refer to four 'servant songs' which describe the work of this person (Isaiah 42:1–4; 49:1–6; 50:4–9; 52:13 – 53:12). Though there has been much discussion about the literary character of these songs, there is no doubt that 'the servant' had an important place in the prophet's message, for this person is portrayed as one who fulfils in his or her own life and experience all those aspects of God's will that Israel as a nation had been unable to accomplish. This figure has never been identified with the Messiah in Jewish readings of the scriptures. One of the distinctive features of these poems is that the servant undergoes great suffering, something that seemed incompatible with a messianic expectation of an all-powerful conquering king. But it was this very feature of the servant's work that led the early Christians to see here an expectation which they believed had been fulfilled in Jesus himself. In the final servant passage in particular, there are two themes that correlate very closely with the facts of Jesus' own life: the servant, though innocent, suffers for the wrongdoing of other people (53:4–9); and following that, God will vindicate the servant in such a way that the great and powerful will be astonished while those for whom the servant suffers will realize that this suffering was in their place (53:10–12). The correlation between the image of the servant here and the experience of Jesus is remarkably striking, and for Christians is perhaps the one theme above all others that helps to define the continuity between Old and New Testaments. Many efforts have been made to identify the consistency of the Christian Bible, with terms such as the covenant, or the idea of 'salvation

Nowhere in the Bible is the believer thought to have arrived at moral perfection. Paul, in his letter to the Philippians, takes an image from the chariot races and writes of 'pressing on' to reach that goal.

history' being put forward as the glue which binds together such apparently discordant literature into one coherent block. But the only real continuity in the midst of such diversity and discontinuity is God, whose personality and values appear throughout all the books, ultimately finding their very specific focus in the person of Jesus, who is presented as the definitive image of God. God constantly occupies the centre of the stage, searching for people, making new relationships with them, motivated only by undeserved and generous love. God is ultimately the unifying factor in the message of the Bible, engaged from beginning to end in the establishment of order out of the chaos which so easily engulfs the life of society and of the physical world, as well as the personal experience of individuals. For Christians, that process culminated in the life, death and resurrection of Jesus, and the gift of the Holy Spirit at Pentecost, though those stories themselves contain an insistent looking forward, and the belief that God will continue to work to empower future generations to reach their full potential as human beings, as they rediscover the nature of true faith in God. The New Testament itself is no more a closed book than the Old Testament, and it is this flexible quality of its spiritual understanding, expecting God to continue working in the world, and therefore allowing itself to be endlessly reinterpreted to address new situations and concerns, that has ensured not only its survival, but also its continuing appeal to those of all times and places who search diligently for the truth.

Other Books on the Old Testament

There are many series of books on the Old Testament which, in different ways, will provide a good introduction to the current state of play on any given topic among the scholars. The following are particularly recommended as being easily accessible to beginners in this field, and most of them have separate volumes on different Bible books:

Guides to Apocrypha and Pseudepigrapha, Sheffield: Sheffield Academic Press.

IBR Bibliographies, Grand Rapids: Baker.

Old Testament Guides, Sheffield: Sheffield Academic Press.

The Old Testament Library, London: SCM Press.

Old Testament Readers, Sheffield: Sheffield Academic Press.

Word Biblical Commentaries, Dallas: Word Publishing.

General

Brotzman, Ellis R., *Old Testament Textual Criticism*, Grand Rapids: Baker, 1994.

Coggins, R.J., *Introducing the Old Testament*, Oxford: Oxford University Press, 1990.

Friedman, Richard E., *Who Wrote the Bible?*, New York: Summit, 1987.

Gottwald, Norman, *The Hebrew Bible in its Social World and Ours*, Atlanta: Scholars Press, 1993.

Knight, D.A. and Tucker, G.M., eds, *The Hebrew Bible and its Modern Interpreters* , Chico: Scholars Press, 1985.

Moorey, P.R.S., *A Century of Biblical Archaeology*, Guildford: Lutterworth Press, 1991.

Rogerson, J., ed., *Beginning OT Study*, London: SPCK, 1983.

Rogerson, J., *Old Testament Criticism in the Nineteenth Century*, London: SPCK, 1984.

The History of Israel

Miller, J. Maxwell and Hayes, John H., *A History of Ancient Israel and Judah*, London: SCM Press, 1999, revised edition.

Pixley, J., *Biblical Israel: A People's History*, Minneapolis: Fortress Press, 1992.

Soggin, J. Alberto, *An Introduction to the History of Israel and Judah*, London: SCM Press, 1999, 3rd edition.

Historical and Cultural Background

Beyerlin, W., ed., *Near Eastern Religious Texts Relating to the Old Testament*, London: SCM Press, 1978.

Coogan, Michael D., ed., *Stories from Ancient Canaan*, Philadelphia: Westminster Press, 1978.

Dothan, Trude and Dothan, Moshe, *People of the Sea: The Search for the Philistines*, New York: Macmillan, 1992.

Fritz, V., *An Introduction to Biblical Archaeology*, Sheffield: JSOT Press, 1993.

Mazar, Amihai, *Archaeology of the Land of the Bible 10,000–586 BCE*, New York: Doubleday, 1990.

Moran, William, ed., *The Amarna Letters*, Baltimore: Johns Hopkins University Press, 1992.

Pritchard, J.B., *Ancient Near Eastern Texts Relating to the Old Testament*, Princeton: Princeton University Press, 1969, 3rd edition.

Redford, Donald B., *Egypt, Canaan and Israel in Ancient Times*, Princeton: Princeton University Press, 1992.

Sandars, N.K., *The Sea Peoples: Warriors of the Ancient Mediterranean 1250–1150 BC*, London: Thames and Hudson, 1985, 2nd edition.

The Emergence of the Nation

Coote, Robert, *Early Israel: A New Horizon*, Minneapolis: Fortress Press, 1990.

Gottwald, N.K., *The Tribes of Yahweh*, Sheffield: Sheffield Academic Press, 1999, 2nd edition.

Harrelson, Walter J., *The Ten Commandments and Human Rights*, Macon GA: Mercer University Press, 1997.

Hoffmeier, James K., *Israel in Egypt: The Evidence for the Authenticity of the Exodus Tradition*, Oxford: Oxford University Press, 1997.

Hopkins, David, *The Highlands of Canaan: Agricultural Life in the Early Iron Age*, Sheffield: JSOT Press, 1985.

Lemche, Niels Peter, *The Canaanites and Their Land*, Sheffield: JSOT Press, 1991.

Shanks, H., ed., *The Rise of Ancient Israel*, Washington: Biblical Archaeology Society, 1992.

Stiebing, William H., *Out of the Desert? Archaeology and the Exodus/Conquest Narratives*, Buffalo NY: Prometheus, 1989.

Thomson, T.L., *Early History of the Israelite People*, Leiden: Brill, 1992.

de Vaux, Roland, *The Early History of Israel*, London: Darton, Longman & Todd, 1961.

Kingdom and Nationhood

Alberts, R., *A History of Israelite Religion in the Old Testament Period*, London: SCM Press, 1994, 2 vols.

Brueggeman, W., *A Social Reading of the Old Testament: Prophetic Approaches to Israel's Communal Life*, Minneapolis: Fortress Press, 1994.

Dearman, J.A., *Religion and Culture in Ancient Israel*, Peabody: Hendrickson, 1992.

Frick, Frank S., *The Formation of the State in Ancient Israel*, Sheffield: Almond Press, 1985.

Fritz, Volkmar, *The City in Ancient Israel*, Sheffield: Sheffield Academic Press, 1995.

Gunn, D. and Ferrell, D.N., *Narrative in the Hebrew Bible*, Oxford: Oxford University Press, 1993.

Exile and After

Ackroyd, P.R., *Exile and Restoration*, London: SCM Press, 1968.

Christensen, Duane L., ed., *A Song of Power and the Power of Song: Essays on the Book of Deuteronomy*, Winona Lake: Eisenbrauns, 1993.

Clines, D.J.A., *The Theme of the Pentateuch*, Sheffield: JSOT Press, 1978.

Collins, J.J., *Jewish Wisdom in the Hellenistic Age*, Louisville: Westminster John Knox Press, 1997.

Jellicoe, S., *The Septuagint and Modern Study*, Oxford: Clarendon Press, 1968.

Noth, Martin, *The Deuteronomistic History*, Sheffield: JSOT Press, 1981, 2nd edition.

Porten, B., *Archives from Elephantine*, Berkeley: University of California Press, 1958.

Weinfeld, M., *Deuteronomy and the Deuteronomic School*, Oxford: Oxford University Press, 1972.

Theology

Allen, R.J. and Holbert, J.C., *Holy Roots, Holy Branches: Christian Preaching from the Old Testament*, Nashville: Abingdon Press, 1995.

Brueggeman, W., *Old Testament Theology: Essays on Structure, Theme and Text*, Minneapolis: Fortress Press, 1992.

Brueggeman, W., *The Psalms and the Life of Faith*, Minneapolis: Fortress Press, 1995.

Childs, B.S., *Biblical Theology of the Old and New Testaments*, Minneapolis: Fortress Press, 1993.

Clements, R.E., *Wisdom in Theology*, Carlisle: Paternoster Press, 1992.

Craigie, C.P., *The Problem of War in the Old Testament*, Grand Rapids: Eerdmans, 1978.

Crenshaw, James L., *Old Testament Wisdom*, Louisville: Westminster John Knox Press, 1998, 2nd edition.

Day, J., et al., eds, *Wisdom in Ancient Israel*, Cambridge: Cambridge University Press, 1995.

Eaton, John, *Mysterious Messengers*, London: SCM Press, 1997.

Gowan, Donald E., *Theology of the Prophetic Books*, Louisville: Westminster John Knox Press, 1998.

Hasel, G.F., *Old Testament Theology: Basic Issues in the Current Debate*, Grand Rapids: Eerdmans 1991, 4th edition.

Hubbard, R.L., et al., eds, *Studies in Old Testament Theology*, Dallas: Word, 1992.

Knierim, R.P., *The Task of Old Testament Theology*, Grand Rapids: Eerdmans, 1995.

Koch, K., *The Prophets*, London: SCM Press, 1982/83, 2 vols.

Mays, J.L., *The Lord Reigns: A Theological Handbook to the Psalms*, Louisville: Westminster John Knox Press, 1994.

Murphy, R.E., *The Tree of Life: An Exploration of Biblical Wisdom Literature*, Grand Rapids: Eerdmans, 1996, 2nd edition.

Ollenburger, B.C., et al., eds, *The Flowering of Old Testament Theology*, Winona Lake: Eisenbrauns, 1992.

Perdue, L.G., *Wisdom and Creation: The Theology of Wisdom Literature*, Nashville: Abingdon, 1994.

Preuss, H.D., *Old Testament Theology*, Louisville: Westminster John Knox Press, 1995, 2 vols.

Simkins, R.A., *Creator and Creation: Nature in the Worldview of Ancient Israel*, Peabody: Hendrickson, 1994.

Terrien, S., *Till the Heart Sings: A Biblical Theology of Manhood and Womanhood*, Philadelphia: Fortress Press, 1985.

Wolff, H.W., *Anthropology of the Old Testament*, Mifflintown: Sigler Press, 1996.

Wright, C.J.H., *God's People in God's Land*, Grand Rapids: Eerdmans, 1990.

Methods and Interpretation

Alter, R., *The Art of Biblical Poetry*, New York: Basic Books, 1985.

Barton, J., *Reading the Old Testament*, Louisville: Westminster John Knox Press, 1997.

Charlesworth, J.H. and Weaver, W.P., eds, *The Old and New Testaments*, Valley Forge: Trinity Press, International, 1993.

Clines, David J.A., *The Bible and the Modern World*, Sheffield: Sheffield Academic Press, 1997.

Duggan, M., *The Consuming Fire: A Christian Introduction to the Old Testament*, San Francisco: Ignatius, 1991.

Exum, J.C. and Clines, D.J.A., eds, *The New Literary Criticism and the Hebrew Bible*, Sheffield: JSOT Press, 1993.

Goldingay, J., *Theological Diversity and the Authority of the Old Testament*, Grand Rapids: Eerdmans, 1987.

Goldingay, J., *How to Read the Bible*, London: SPCK, 1997, 2nd edition.

Grabbe, L., ed., *Can a 'History of Israel' be Written?*, Sheffield: Sheffield Academic Press, 1997.

Long, V.P., *The Art of Biblical History*, Leicester: Apollos, 1994.

Niditch, S., *Folklore and the Hebrew Bible*, Minneapolis: Fortress, 1993.

Perdue, L., *The Collapse of History: Reconstructing Old Testament Theology*, Minneapolis: Fortress Press, 1994.

Petersen, D.L. and Richards, K.H., *Interpreting Hebrew Poetry*, Minneapolis: Fortress Press, 1992.

Steck, O.H., *Old Testament Exegesis: A Guide to Methodology*, Atlanta: Scholars Press, 1995.

Index of Subjects

Index of Maps, Charts and Diagrams

Index of Quotations from Ancient Authors

Index of Secondary Sources